LAW ENFORCEMENT
An Introduction

LAW ENFORCEMENT
An Introduction

RICHARD N. HOLDEN, PH.D.

Professor & Chair
Department of Criminal Justice
Central Missouri State University

Prentice Hall, Englewood Cliffs, New Jersey 07632

Library of Congress Cataloging-in-Publication Data

Holden, Richard N., 1946-
    Law enforcement : an introduction / Richard N. Holden.
      p.   cm.
    Includes bibliographical references and index.
    ISBN 0-13-524687-3
    1. Law enforcement—United States.   2. Police—United States.
I. Title.
    HV8138.H57   1992
    363.2'3'0973—dc20   91-19753
                                                CIP

Editorial/production supervision and
   interior design: Eileen M. O'Sullivan
Acquisitions Editor: Robin Baliszewski
Editor-in-Chief: Barbara Christenberry
Marketing Manager: Mark Hartman
Prepress Buyer: Mary McCartney
Manufacturing Buyer: Ed O'Dougherty
Cover design: Wanda Lubelska

 © 1992 by Prentice-Hall, Inc.
A Simon & Schuster Company
Englewood Cliffs, New Jersey 07632

Printed in the United States of America

10 9 8 7 6 5 4 3 2 1

ISBN   0-13-524687-3

PRENTICE-HALL INTERNATIONAL (UK) LIMITED, *London*
PRENTICE-HALL OF AUSTRALIA PTY. LIMITED, *Sydney*
PRENTICE-HALL CANADA INC., *Toronto*
PRENTICE-HALL HISPANOAMERICANA, S.A., *Mexico*
PRENTICE-HALL OF INDIA PRIVATE LIMITED, *New Delhi*
PRENTICE-HALL OF JAPAN, INC., *Tokyo*
SIMON & SCHUSTER ASIA PTE. LTD., *Singapore*
EDITORA PRENTICE-HALL DO BRASIL, LTDA., *Rio de Janeiro*

*To Don Stephens,
a good cop and a lifelong friend*

Contents

CHAPTER 11   POLICE DEVIANCE   *276*

Preface

Law enforcement is the most visible and most critical component of the criminal justice system. While the courts serve a vital role in the administration of justice, they deal with but a small percentage of the cases handled by the police. Justice, for the majority of the public, is a law enforcement function.

To understand the administration of justice in the United States one must first understand the police. It is the purpose of this text to introduce students to the institution and occupation we call law enforcement.

While different agencies refer to themselves by different terminology, this text will be somewhat broader in the use of such labels. For ease of understanding, both law enforcement and police will be used generically. These terms will encompass all agencies with enforcement responsibilities, from municipal through state and federal levels.

I wish to emphasize that this is an introductory text. It is not intended to address each and every controversy facing law enforcement in the United States. Instead it is written to provide a foundation from which further study can commence. For that reason much of the information presented is descriptive. Moreover, the first segment is intended to provide a somewhat more in-depth historical review than is usually provided in texts of this type. It is my belief that one cannot begin to understand the present without first understanding the past.

The text is not merely a description of American law enforcement with a history attached. It also attempts to look into the future. For this view, this book owes much to Dr. David Carter and Dr. Allen Sapp. The chapter they provided on law enforcement and higher education is based on the most extensive study ever completed on that relationship. Law enforcement is changing in this country; nowhere is that more obvious than in the information provided in this chapter.

Finally, this text is written in the hope that the people who read these pages will acquire an appreciation for the complexity of the law enforcement function. In a dictatorship, it is the police who maintain the power of government, while in a democracy it is the police who guarantee the freedom of the individual. The police of a free people must understand their role and the necessity of legal limitations on their actions. The first step in process of gaining this understanding, is knowledge. This text is written with the hope that the acquisition of such knowledge begins here.

Richard N. Holden

Acknowledgments

No text book is written in a vacuum. There are always those who aid in the creation of such a project without thought of personal gain. I would like to acknowledge the people who helped to make this book better than it would have been without their contributions:

Vic Kappeler, Central Missouri State University, who helped in the historical and futuristic research.

Don Stephens of the Irving, Texas Police Department, who went to great lengths to provide relevant police photographs.

FBI Special Agent Joe Harpold, FBI Academy, for his aid in acquiring photographs.

FBI Special Agent Bill Tafoya, FBI Academy, whose groundbreaking work in futuristic analysis was vital to the production of the final chapter.

David Schleve, for his generosity in providing access to private photographs of major major criminal cases with which he was involved as a criminal investigator.

Jim Huff, and Tom Charrette, Central Missouri State University Department of Public Safety, for their help in acquiring photographs.

Paul Corbin, Missouri Highway Patrol, for his help in acquiring photographs.

Jim Glover and Steve Payne, Missouri Water Patrol, for their help in acquiring photographs.

Richard Sharp, London Metropolitan Police, who went to great lengths to acquire and provide all of the photgraphs seen in the section on the development of the London Police.

Allen Sapp, Central Missouri State University and David Carter, Michigan

State University for providing a chapter based upon their research on police and higher education.

David Carter, additionally, for his support in the acquisition of photographs and material.

Darrel Stephens, Executive Director of PERF, for his help and support.

My wife Denise and our children: Julie, Jeff and Greg, who sometimes wondered if they had been abandoned while this book was being written.

Ruth Doyle, Central Missouri State University, who was kind enough to provide translations for correspondence with the personnel of the Paris Police Museum.

The staff at the Paris Police Museum, for taking a personal interest in this project and for the kindness and support they showed to Mark Blumberg during his visit.

And a special thank you to Mark Blumberg, Central Missouri State University, whose efforts—that included a trip to Paris—went above and beyond the call of either duty or friendship.

Each of the people, in their own way, provided information or other items that enhanced the production of this book. It would have been a lesser product without them. I would like to take this opportunity to express my thanks.

Chapter 1

The Evolution of Law Enforcement

Key Terms:

Kin police
Code of Hammurabi
Lex talionis
Law of Moses
Draco
Solon
Code of the twelve tables
Vulgar law
Justinian's code
Canon law
Nicolas-Gabriel de La Reynie
Lieutenant-general of police

Joseph Fouché
François Eugéne Vidocq
Alphonse Bertillon
Shire-reeve
Thomas De Veil
Henry Fielding
John Fielding
Robert Peel
Charles Rowan
Richard Mayne
Howard Vincent

Chapter Objectives

At the conclusion of this chapter, students should be able to:

1. Identify the contributions to law enforcement of ancient societies.
2. Demonstrate an understanding of the development of the earliest of the modern police agencies, especially that of France.
3. Identify the contributions to policing of Nicholas-Gabriel de la Reynie.
4. Demonstrate an understanding of the development of the British police and the social factors that inhibited its early creation.
5. Identify the contributions of Sir Robert Peel and his police commissioners.

INTRODUCTION

The study of law and its enforcement is necessary to gain an understanding of society. In no other arena is human society's values more thoroughly tested than in the legal process. How we treat those who refuse to live by society's rules, how we protect the individual from the power of the government, and how we protect ourselves from human predators all make a statement as to what kind of people we are.

The focus of this book is on enforcement of the law. Of necessity we also look at the law itself to determine what must be enforced. When we speak of law enforcement it should be remembered that we are speaking generically. When the word *police* is used, for example, we are not necessarily referring to the city police. The county sheriff, state police, and federal agency may all fall under this category, for they all fulfill a police function. When we speak of police powers and roles, therefore, we are speaking of all police.

To understand the police, it is first necessary to know their origins. We begin with a look at the history of the police. I should point out that this is only a cursory look. The history of the police is rich and fascinating. Two chapters will hardly do it justice. It is my hope to at least lay a solid foundation for the remainder of the book. In subsequent chapters we look at the structure of police organizations, police socialization, the police relationship to the courts, police selection and promotion practices, issues and trends in policing, and finally, a look at the future of law enforcement. It is hoped that by the end of the book, the student will have a better understanding of the complex issues facing American law enforcement.

Beginnings

Law enforcement as an institution is relatively new in human history. Early human societies, organized on the basis of tribal custom rather than law, saw no need for an internal police force. Punishment was a simple process; offenses against the tribe resulted in death or banishment—often leading to the same result. Offenses against individuals were dealt with by the victim or the victim's family, a concept known as *kin police*.

The evolution of law enforcement depended on factors that are as valid today as they were in antiquity. Small agrarian societies have less need of law and its enforcers than do large complex urban societies. The smallest units, the family and tribe, have little need of anything beyond mores or customs. Modern high-tech societies require extensive regulation and full-time regulators. It should come as no surprise, therefore, to discover that the evolution of law enforcement paralleled the transformation of societies from primitive to modern.

These developments transpired neither quickly nor evenly. While societies were mostly hunters and gatherers, tribal leadership often fell to the strongest or most skillful. Full-fledged government did not evolve until human beings began grouping around farming communities. As the size and complexity of these communities increased, so did the need for efficient civil administration.

Still, these early governments were more concerned with protecting the government than with protecting the citizens. Armies were developed for the defense of the king; therefore, any legal actions taken by this group were aimed at those opposing the king. Under that system, crime was limited to acts we would today label treason. Courts were mostly limited to the king's court, where the reigning monarch dispensed whatever justice this person was inclined to grant. Law, as we know it, had its foundations in antiquity. From the Egyptians and Sumerians to the Greeks to the Romans, law and its enforcement progressed to the boundaries of modern time.

THE NEAR EAST

Historians have long recognized that there is a remarkable similarity between Biblical law and the code of Hammurabi. The code itself, however, has been found to be a compilation of laws based on a Sumerian prototype. There is good reason to believe that the extraordinary growth and development of legal concepts, practices, precedents, and compilations in the ancient Near East go largely back to the Sumerians and their rather one-sided emphasis on rivalry and superiority.[1]

The Sumerians

Somewhere around 2400 to 2500 B.C., Urukagina, king of the city-state of Shirpurla, drew up a code of laws. He abated the privileges of the priests (sacred animals and possessions were being used for secular purposes; bribery, oppression, and cruelty were rife). He returned the property of the gods to their proper use and then sought to better the conditions of his people. His law was designed to "set right what was wrong and make safe the lives and goods of the peasant classes."[2]

The laws of the Sumerians, such as that of Urukagina, appear to be the rule rather than the exception. Historians knowledgeable of this culture state that by 2400 B.C., laws and legal regulations by Sumerian rulers were a common phenomenon. Given the importance this people attached to education and political stability, it is more than likely that many of the laws and court precedents were put into writing. Unfortunately, no written record of the period between Urukagina and Ur-Nammu, the founder of the third dynasty of Ur (around 2050 B.C.), remains.

The Babylonians

The most famous written code of the Babylonians began with the statement, "Law and justice I establish in the Land and promote the welfare of the people." Both the theory and practice of law took a large step forward in Babylon during the reign of Hammurabi (1947–1905 B.C.), Babylon's greatest ruler. At the beginning of Hammurabi's reign, the territory was a collection of city-states that had their own laws as well as a series of laws adhered to by all local governments. Hammurabi incorporated or conquered all of these independent and quasi-independent communities, thus creating a centralized government structure. Subsequently, he created a law for all the lands and cities he ruled.

The Code of Hammurabi, consisting of 4000 lines of writing, was carved on a pillar of stone located in the Temple of Marduk. Based on existing Sumerian codes, this code established criminal acts and penalties for a variety of offenses, such as personal violence, sex crimes, and even sorcery. The code also attempted to control many aspects of social life; it dictated wages for all categories of worker and laid out the procedure for prosecution.[3]

More important, the law laid the foundation for modern criminal procedure. The code emphasized three important principles of law. First, the law was based on individual responsibility. Second, the Babylonians believed in the sanctity of an oath taken before God. Finally, the law required the submission of written evidence in all matters.[4]

The primary theory of justice under Babylonian law was *lex talionis,* equal injury inflicted for injury suffered: more commonly, an eye for an eye. Much of the enforcement, however, was still in the hands of the people. The government would act on the law, but apprehension and prosecution were still principally the responsibility of the aggrieved party. Nevertheless, the quality of justice during this period reached a level unimagined by earlier societies. The development of law by Hammurabi would lay the foundation for later justice systems.

The Egyptians

The Egyptians were probably the first civilization to develop a true police system. An organization called the *judges commandant of the police* was in place during the first and second dynasties, around 2900 B.C. This organization was responsible for security in each of Egypt's provinces. It is also known that by the same year, the Egyptians had a written legal code that judges were obliged to follow when deciding cases. Nothing is left of this set of laws, but their existence is attested to by the many references made to the law in surviving Egyptian documents.[5]

During the reign of Har-em-hab (or Hur Moheb) around 1340 B.C., a river police was organized to ensure safe navigation on the Nile. This force fought pirates, searched suspect ships, and protected commerce.[6] This was no easy task considering that the Egyptian empire was spread along a 300-mile stretch of the Nile River. During the reign of Har-em-hab, a major reform in the justice system occurred. Much of what is known about the law of ancient Egypt comes to us from this period.[7]

Perhaps the most important early police units were responsible for the security of the tombs. The Egyptians were known for burying their kings among great splendor. The amount of riches buried within the tombs of the kings was sufficient to make people wealthy beyond their dreams. The temptation to loot these tombs was tremendous, proof of which is the relatively small number of intact tombs discovered by modern archaeologists. The officers guarding the tombs were the first to use dogs in the fulfillment of their duties. The police of early Egypt also had judicial powers. These officers tried some cases, passed judgment, and executed the sentences.[8]

Egypt also developed a corps of highly respected judges. The laws of Egypt consisted mostly of a code of laws and jurisprudence, but were also partly compiled from decisions of learned judges in noted cases.[9] In fact, ancient Egypt so valued the position of judge that a careful selection process was used to ensure that only the most capable were admitted to this post.

The Hebrews

The next groups to promulgate a written legal code were the early Hebrew tribes. No precise date has been determined as to when the *law of Moses* was put into writing. Hebrew law was, however, heavily influenced by the early development of Egyptian law. Moreover, it is also quite likely that Hebrew law developed parallel to later refinements of law under the pharaohs of the twentieth dynasty (1200–1090 B.C.). Because of the popularity and longevity of the Hebrew system, we have a much better understanding of that particular code than we do of most other ancient legal systems.

The foundation for the Hebrew law, or law of Moses, was laid in Sumer and later, Babylon. The simplest and most straightforward expression of the Hebrew law can be found in the Ten Commandments.[10] Through these simple statements of propriety, the Hebrews established a basis for their relationships with each other and with God.

A significant aspect of the Hebrew code was the belief that violation of the law was a failure in the sight of God. Criminals were, therefore, not only guilty of harming another person, but were also guilty of inflicting injury on God himself. Through this process the Hebrews refined the notion of honor and morality. People were, through their own conscience, encouraged to punish themselves for transgressions. Sin thus became a major force in the socialization process of the tribes.

The harshness of the code reflected the strength of the religious influence on this society. Wrongful conduct was offensive for two reasons: first, it destroyed the bonds of society and caused dissention among the people of Israel, and second, the wrong of any member of God's chosen people could easily bring divine wrath down upon the entire nation.[11] Law enforcement was still the responsibility of the victim or victim's family. Even the process of judgment and execution of sentence required a significant contribution by family members or witnesses.

The Hebrew law, although developed before the birth of Christ, remains a primary factor in modern justice systems. This is especially true in the Middle

East, where theocratic institutions have had an inordinate amount of input into governmental affairs. Islamic law, for example, is heavily laced with crimes and punishments derived from this ancient text. Thus the law of Moses may be said to be the oldest legal system still being practiced in the world today.

THE GREEKS

The development of Western law and law enforcement began its evolution among the city-states of ancient Greece. The Hellenistic culture provided an environment in which the rule of law could flourish. The progression toward democratic principles did not happen overnight, but took centuries to evolve. Within this progression there were several distinct phases, with Athens assuming an increasingly predominant role with the passing of each.

The Early Greeks

The earliest description of Greek law comes to us from the works of Homer: *The Odyssey* and *The Illiad*. The early legal system was still based on lex talionis and enforced by the victim or victim's family. However, a subtle change in society's attitudes became apparent during this period. The Greeks began to identify certain acts as crimes against society. For example, if a person killed a parent or guest in his home, the citizenry reacted against the criminal. These were the only forms of homicide not dealt with by the victim's family. The concept of summary execution, a major element of criminal law, was thus developed.

Additionally, the concept evolved whereby a victim not wanting to resort to violence could appeal to the king for arbitration.[12] The dispensing of justice during this era was a royal prerogative. This was an early version of tort law. In essence, the victim would file a complaint, similar to today's law suit, against the accused. The king would then decide on the proper payment owed the victim by the criminal. Should the person accused be unable to pay the debt, he was sold into slavery, sometimes with his entire family.

In the seventh century B.C. the idea of *pollution* began to develop. This was the belief that certain crimes led to divine retribution and was the beginning of the concept of outlawry. Person's declared outlaws became social outcasts, subject to execution by any person who encountered them. Such crimes also tainted the criminal's entire family. Pollution meant that the blood line of the criminal was forever tainted; the person's current family and future descendants were deemed contaminated by the culprit's evil.

This period also witnessed the development in Western culture of the idea that certain acts against individuals were also crimes against the state; perversion of justice was seen as such an offense. Arbitration and the use of witnesses continued to develop and by the sixth century B.C., the *reign of law* was society's rallying cry.

The Crises of Athens

In the late seventh century B.C., Athens had become a predominant Greek city-state. The government was constructed around an oligarchy that shared power through a democratic process. The *aeropagus,* a court of the aristocracy, operated with impunity to their own benefit, much to the dissatisfaction of the lower classes.

In 621 B.C., *Draco* ("Dragon") produced Athens' first set of written laws. These were produced at the demand of the lower classes, who wished to have a means of comparing the decisions of the aeropagus with traditional law. The code was heavily biased toward the wishes of the aristocracy. Debt slavery was introduced, meaning that a creditor could sell a debtor into slavery to recover money owed. Capital punishment was established for a wide variety of property crimes, even relatively mild ones. When someone asked Draco why death was prescribed for most offenses, he replied, "Small ones deserve that, and I have no higher for the greater crimes."[13] It was said that Draco's laws were written in blood. For this reason, the term *draconian* has come to symbolize rules that are inhumanly harsh or severe.

The crisis facing Athens later in this period was brought about by a combination of growth in the noncitizen population, accompanied by a declining citizen class. Draco's debt-slavery was a major cause of this situation. Lower-class citizens, the poor, borrowed money from the rich. If the borrower could not repay the debt, he was sold into slavery, often with his entire family. In times of economic depression, large segments of the lower classes were converted to slaves. Thus the Athenian citizen class found itself outnumbered by noncitizens, a situation that threatened to disrupt the social order.

Amplifying the Athenian social problems was a legal crisis. The aeropagus was still responsible for administering this system, which consisted of the aggrieved party taking a claim before a tribal leader. Both accused and accuser stated their cases before the aeropagus, which voted by secret ballot for guilt or acquittal, with a majority of the votes determining the outcome.[14]

The system continued to favor the oligarchy. The Athenian nobility, recognizing the growing discontent of the population, began to recognize that it might be better to make some peaceful concessions rather than face losing everything in a revolution. In 594 B.C., over the objections of a number of citizens who wished the system to remain as it was, sufficient numbers of the aristocratic class were able to elect *Solon* to the office of nomothete. In essence, as archon, he became a one-man legislature, essentially a king.

The Reforms of Solon

Solon set out to immediately rectify the source of Athens' problems. He eliminated debt slavery, but not being completely satisfied with that step, he further prohibited parents from selling their children into slavery, as well as prohibiting boys from selling their sisters.[15] Solon further used tax monies to buy citizens out of slavery and even sent emissaries out of Athens to buy back Athenians who had been sold outside Attica.

The most notable reform of Solon, however, lay in his approach to solving the problems in the court system. He lacked the power to attack the aeropagus; therefore, he found a means to bypass this institution. Solon created magistrates to oversee an appellate process. The magistrates acted in a manner similar to that of circuit courts. Aggrieved citizens presented a case in the traditional manner but were allowed to appeal unfavorable rulings to the circuit court, where, with its jury of peers, there was a much needed infusion of fairness into the legal structure. Solon further repealed all of Draco's death penalties, except for murder. He also invoked a new law that vested the right of action in society. He permitted any Athenian citizen to prosecute for an attack on the rights of a fellow Athenian. He thus began the shift from tort law to criminal law.[16]

Under Solon (whose name has come to be used as a synonym for "lawmaker" and in the United States is frequently used to mean a member of congress or the Senate), Athens began its assent to social and political dominance in the age of antiquity. The reforms began by Solon were carried on by successors (not all of whom were in favor of democracy—some were tyrants), and finally, by the reign of Ephialtes (426 B.C.), Athens had fully developed its judicial system.

THE ROMANS

At the time Athens was developing as a social and political leader in the world, Rome was a little known city in Italy. It was not until the fourth and third centuries B.C. that Rome achieved sufficient size to be called large by modern standards. Legal evolution in Rome paralleled that of the social evolution. Roman jurisprudence therefore experienced four distinct periods of development. These took place in the early republic, late republic, early empire, and late empire.

The Early Republic

In 451 B.C., the Romans published their first written set of laws. The *code of the twelve tables* was a comprehensive codification of the legal system at that time. It was taken mostly from Roman custom and did not deal so much with the duties of government as with the rights and duties of individual citizens. The code was drawn up by a 10-man commission, the *decemviri*. This document was prepared at the behest of the *plebs* (lower classes), who complained that because the law was oral it was not being applied in an equitable manner.

The code of the twelve tables still relied heavily on the right of an injured party to exact vengeance. A number of provisions were included, however, to reduce the devastating effect of blood feuds caused as a result of this procedure. A number of crimes were defined and given a prescribed punishment. For example, a person committing arson was to be burned to death, while a person caught stealing crops was to be hanged at the site of the theft as a sacrifice to the gods.

The Late Republic

As Rome's size and strength escalated, bringing it closer to the position of world power, the legal system began to show signs of severe stress. By the third century B.C., the code of the twelve tables had given way to a more dynamic legislative process. The system that developed, however, lacked sufficient flexibility and efficiency to resolve effectively the rapidly increasing numbers and types of crimes. The justice system had become institutionalized by the late republic, with a number of distinct magistrates and committees responsible for its administration. Highest of the judicial officers were the *praetors,* who possessed general jurisdiction and exercised police justice. They were responsible for actions against criminals. Usually, if the accused was of high social rank and denied guilt, a *praetor* handled the case personally. Otherwise, he might assign a *quaesitor* (investigator) to investigate and prosecute the case. Neither the praetor nor the quaesitor had the power to alter the punishment, but they could allow the convicted person to escape and then declare him an outlaw.

Magistrates of lower rank, the *tresveri capitales,* policed the city, superintended the state prison, and carried out executions. Criminals who confessed or were caught in the act were put to death by the tresveri without trial. In the case of slaves, confessions were induced through torture. If the accused denied the charges, guilt or innocence was decided by the *consilium,* a form of advisory committee.

Criminal procedure during this period was initiated through information *(nominis delatio).* The information was presented to a competent judicial magistrate, who may or may not have accepted the complaint. Sometimes this decision was made by a consilium of judges. If accepted, the person submitting the information obtained the rights and duties of a litigant; it was his duty to prosecute the accused before the court.

Every citizen of good reputation was, in principle, permitted to initiate a prosecution (except in the case of infringement of domestic peace). It was in this process that the special character of the public criminal process differed from the process under the code of the twelve tables, which allowed only a private suit by the victim or victim's kin.

If the judicial magistrate accepted the information, he next ordered the consilium to be formed by lot from the judge list of the *quaesto* concerned. In this process both the accused and the accuser had the right to reject a certain number of judges. The members of the consilium chosen in this way (the number varied in times and in the quaesto concerned, but might be as high as 75) were sworn in before the beginning of the trial. The trial itself was dominated by the accuser's initiative. Guilt or innocence was determined by a secret ballot of the consilium.

The Early Empire

By 265 B.C. Rome had become one of the most powerful states of the time. With the victorious struggle with Carthage, which reached its climax with the Hannibalic War (219–201 B.C.), Rome became mistress of the western Mediterranean. It was only hesitatingly and under the pressure of circumstances that in the second century B.C. the Roman government extended its power to the east. In barely 150 years and without any great external opposition, Rome became ruler of the known world. The Roman Empire and the earth were from the end of the republic onward, regarded as equal.

From a legal point of view, this gigantic empire was a highly complicated structure, a system of relationships of alliance and dependence in the center of which stood the city of Rome. One of the ingredients of the Empire's success was Roman imperial policy, which allowed each conquered province to retain its own system of self-government and law. In matters of religion, Rome was completely tolerant.

The evolution from republic to empire was not without its problems. The popular assemblies lost their significance as soon as the most able members of Roman society became unable to participate. Farmers and inhabitants of the country towns lived too far away from Rome to participate in political affairs. The annual change in magistrates also proved fatal to administration of the provinces. Even more troublesome was the effect of ever-changing magistrates on the military. This led to repeated catastrophes in wars that should have been easy Roman victories. The time was ripe for major change in the philosophy of government and its administration.

Monarchy emerged at first as merely the supremacy of the strongest. Ultimately, Octavius Caesar, the great nephew and adopted son of Julius Caesar, founded the Roman monarchy. He is known to us by the name of honor that the Senate bestowed upon him in the year in which the new order was founded; he is called Augustus. The constitution he created (monarchial in essence if not in outward form) is known as the *principate*.

Under the principate, the legal system underwent a major transformation. Augustus subjected the police system and police justice to a thorough reform by appointing a senator of consular rank to the permanent post of *praefectus urbi* (urban chief of police). He also created a strong force of police *(cohorts vigilum)*, who also acted as firefighters, quartered in barracks. The praefectus urbi and also, though with limited jurisdiction, the commander of the *vigiles (praefectus vigilum)* replaced the tresveri capitales as the organs of police justice.

Outside the city of Rome and its environs, Augustus also took steps to reduce crime. He particularly attacked gangsterism, which had grown greatly in the lax conditions of the late republic and during the civil wars in Italy. He covered the country with military posts, probably mostly garrisoned with men drawn from the *praetorian guard* (the only military unit stationed in Italy and under the command of the *praefecti praetorio*). It is likely that post commanders were given jurisdiction over lower-class criminals while other cases were sent to the praefecti praetorio.

The organization of the police system by Augustus represented not only a decisive advance in the combatting of crime, but also an important improvement in criminal justice. Police jurisdiction no longer lay in the hands of young magistrates of inferior rank who changed each year and thus had little time to gain expertise. It was now exercised by experienced men, some of whom were prominent jurists, whose duration in office made possible a certain stability in the administration of justice.

The Late Empire

The creative period of Roman jurisprudence came to an end during this period. Late in the fourth century, the level of jurisprudence declined rapidly. The cause was due in large measure to the emergence of *vulgar law*, a result of the infusion of barbarian ideas and values into Roman society. As the various barbarian tribes made contact with Roman society, their legal practices, definitions, and interpretations began to obscure the philosophies and practices of Roman institutions. The most famous of these was the Visigothic Roman code of Alaric II, which contained hardly a trace of the spirit of classical law.

The vulgar law had completely lost the procedural foundations of the classical law. Even many of the conceptual distinctions were obscured. For example, the Roman system of contracts all but vanished. The distinction between possession, ownership, and real rights over another's property was confounded. The vulgarized legal thinking overshadowed all else in legal life. The eastern half of the empire saw some attempt to return to classical law with the development of law schools, but even this was difficult due to the growing influence of vulgar law.

Another problem had confused the Roman legal system. The government had always created legal codes but had never repealed any. Thus the system had become seriously confused without the added problem of the vulgar law. Several attempts to codify Roman law *(Codex Theodosians, Codex Gregorianus,* and *Hermogenianus)* merely led to more confusion. On February 13, A.D. 528, the emperor Justinian formed a 10-man commission to draw up a collection of imperial laws. This work was completed on November 16, 534. The *Codex, Digest,* and *Institutes* formed a unified codification. They were not supposed to have contradictions and confusions. The commissions that designed these codes, however, worked independently, which led to a variety of contradictions.

Justinian proclaimed this code the law of Rome—and then did something unheard of; he repealed all other Roman law, thus leaving his code as the sole law of Rome. This law, *Justinian's code,* became the primary document in the teaching of law in the law schools of the era, and later became the foundation for the legal systems of Europe and South America.

THE DARK AGES

With the arrival of the Middle (or Dark) Ages, almost 4000 years of legal development collapsed. The integrity of the Egyptians, wisdom of the Athenians, and progress of the Romans were all but forgotten. In the eastern half of the old Roman Empire, the emperors of Byzantium attempted to retain the spirit of the classical law of Justinian, but this became known as a *scholar's law* and was regarded as too complex for the daily affairs of the people.[17] Instead, a form of vulgar law developed community by community in response to the ever-shifting needs of life in the different settlements.

In the western half of the old Roman Empire, only a vestige of the classical law remained. A few institutions existed to attempt to enunciate the law (Frankish *rachimbourgs,* Scandinavian *laghman,* Icelandic *eosagari,* Irish *brehons,* Anglo-Saxon *withan*), but the reign of law had ceased. Conquered totally by the various Germanic tribes, the area that is now Western Europe took the legal system back to its very roots, maybe even beyond. What existed as law was nothing more than rules created by different people at different locations in an attempt to place some control over social interaction. It would be difficult to classify these rules as law; they were not universally accepted and no authority was capable of enforcing them.

Law and its enforcement returned from criminal law to tort law, with a violent twist. Success in litigation was placed in the hands of God, the oaths of parties, wager of law (compurgation), or trial by battle or ordeal. Proceedings were dominated by appeals to the supernatural and by a system of nonrational proof. The execution of judicial decisions was not assured, for no government leader or institution would act on the court's behalf.[18] Disputes were resolved by the law of force or by the discretion of a tribal leader.

Even the ideal of a society founded on the rights of individuals was largely abandoned. Christianity took some responsibility for this trend, for some reasoned that a Christian society should be founded upon the ideas of brotherly love. Saint Paul (died A.D. 67), in his "First Epistle to the Corinthians," urged the faithful to submit to the arbitration of their spiritual leaders or brothers rather than resort to the tribunals of the pagans. Saint Augustine (A.D. 354–430) defended the same ideas. In Germany as late as the sixteenth century it was said that jurists are bad Christians; law was considered a bad thing.

THE RENAISSANCE

European society's view of law changed with the end of the Middle Ages and coming of the Renaissance. The new society, with its developing cities and commerce, became once more conscious of the need for law to assure order and security. As René David and John E. C. Brierly stated, "the idea of a Christian society was abandoned; the City of God was not to be created on Earth."[19] The

Church itself admitted this by distinguishing more clearly between religious and secular concerns. The Church published its own *canon law,* and during the thirteenth century, religion and morality were no longer confused with civil order and law. Pope Innocent III made it official at the Fourth Lateran Council in November 1215, when he prohibited clerical participation in preparations for trial by ordeal. The effect on this practice was amazingly swift. By 1219, this practice no longer existed in England and had been greatly reduced throughout Western Europe.[20]

The canon law did not emerge overnight. Even before the Renaissance, the Catholic Church had been promulgating rules and procedures for the governance of the Church. As Roman civil law had been the universal law of the temporal empire directly associated with the authority of the emperor, canon law was the universal law of the spiritual domain, directly associated with the authority of the pope.[21]

As a rational legal system became more desirable, law schools were developed, with Italian universities leading the way. The study of law in these institutions recognized the validity of both legal systems. A merging of these codes was inevitable; the degree J.U.D. (*Juris Utriusque Doctor,* or Doctor of Both Laws) was soon bestowed on students who had completed the full course of legal studies. Because the two were studied together, there was a tendency for them to influence each other. Canon law's major influence was in the area of family law and succession, criminal law and procedure. These areas, while addressed by the Roman law, were substantially better developed in the canon law. By the time the ecclesiastical courts of Europe were deprived of their civil jurisdiction, many substantive and procedural principles they had developed had been adopted by the civil courts.[22]

As civilization moved back toward the reign of law, the necessity for law enforcement reemerged. Representative of the evolutionary patterns of the early European police are the countries of France and England, which by taking different paths at different times, nevertheless arrived at similar institutions and philosophies.

THE FRENCH

The Old Order *(Ancien Régime)* is a term applied by the French revolutionary government to describe the centuries of monarchy preceding the French Revolution. During the tumultuous centuries that preceded the downfall of the king, the police of France evolved into a model of effectiveness and efficiency that now seems amazing.

Late in the Middle Ages, the cities, which suffered and languished with the collapse of the Roman Empire, begin to show a resurgence of vitality. Law and its enforcement were in the hands of the feudal lords, who ruled over geographic areas known as *comtés* (counties). Gradually, the kings introduced royal judges (seneschals and baliffs) to feudal courts, slowly bringing some form of royal order and providing a mechanism for enforcing royal laws. French kings, facing continuing obstinacy from these members of the landed nobility, began to recognize the cities as a force that could counter this aristocratic power.

Municipalities were encouraged to develop their independence, on a limited scale. Kings provided charters that enabled the governing officers the right to maintain order within their jurisdictions. The result was a crude form of municipal policing, the forerunner of today's police.[23] During the eighth century, Charlemaigne established his empire in what is now France. In A.D. 785, he published his *Capitularies of Charlemaigne,* a collection of laws and customs. In A.D. 875, the idea of law enforcement took a step forward when marshals were created by the king to maintain security.[24]

By the end of the Middle Ages, the principle of maintaining a standing army under royal command was well established. The provost corps was developed to provide an internal policing mechanism to ensure more orderly administration. Given the unsettled and dangerous conditions of the age, the king extended the scope of the military police to include the protection of his subjects in the rural areas and along the main roads. These soldier-policemen were instrumental in extending the king's protection into the French countryside.

French kings, seeking self-protection and self-enrichment, created a police force in Paris. The position of provost of the city was created in 1032; Stephanus was the first person appointed to this position, which included the duties of governor, judge, and police chief. This office was the forerunner of the prefect of the police of Paris. The provost of merchants, a civic administrator, was also created, with its own police force, although it was less effective.[25]

Since its creation in 1032, the police organization of Paris had grown in both size and responsibility. Policing outside the jurisdiction of Paris also progressed in size and effectiveness. In the early seventeenth century Cardinal Richelieu lay the foundation for the modern French prefects when he stationed a royal supervisor, the intendant of justice, police and finance, in each of the 30 provinces of France.[26]

The court system that was in operation at the beginning of the reign of Louis XIV was a two-stage process adopted by France as a result of the Ordinance of 1539. This process (known as *inquisitional,* as opposed to *adversarial*) called for a hearing before a single judge (examining magistrate) to be followed by a full trial before the entire bench of the court. The accused was severely limited in the means by which a defense might be presented. There was no right to counsel and the defendant was not even permitted to argue the case.[27] Torture was still used, but not as frequently as it had been a century earlier. The new king therefore had a considerable task ahead of him as he attempted to improve the quality of French justice.

Unhappily, at the time Louis XIV was crowned in 1661, the police of Paris were also beset with problems. The provost of Paris was still technically in command, but the position had sunk to the level of mere figurehead. Instead, numerous lieutenants-deputies to the provost actually administered the department, and the police jurisdictions and duties had become hopelessly confused and controversial.

Louis XIV began a series of reforms. A very able minister, Colbert, proposed a series of great ordinances, all sanctioned by the king. These dealt with civil procedure (1667), criminal procedure (1670), commercial law (1673), and maritime law (1681).[28] Prior to these actions, however, he focused his attention on the police.

The Lieutenant of Police

The young king set out to rectify the problems besetting his realm. Ultimately, he realized that one of the key factors in resolving the disorder besetting Paris was reformation of the police. In December 1666 the king created the position of *lieutenant of police*. Louis expected a special kind of man to fill this position. His minister, Colbert, drew up a specific and demanding job description:

> A man of the robe and a man of the sword and, if the doctor's learned ermine must float upon his shoulder, on his foot must ring the strong spur of the knight; he must be unflinching as a magistrate and intrepid as a soldier; he must not pale before the river in flood or plague in the hospitals, any more than before popular uproar or threats of your courtiers, for it must be expected that the court will not be the last to complain of the useful rigor of a police carried on in the interest of the well-being and security of all.[29]

The man selected to fill the position of lieutenant of police was *Nicolas-Gabriel de La Reynie,*. He was appointed in 1671 and filled all of Louis XIV's fondest expectations.[30] The duties of this post were vast in comparison with today's police administrator. La Reynie was given responsibility for and authority over:

1. The security of the city and its environs
2. The illicit bearing of arms by all, including the police (only long swords, weapons easily seen, were allowed on the streets of Paris)
3. The cleaning of streets and public places
4. The provision of necessary orders in time of flood or fire
5. The responsibility for the city's food supply and prices
6. The inspection of markets and fairs, hostelries and lodging houses, gambling houses, and places of ill repute
7. Illicit assemblies, tumults, seditions, and disorders
8. The elections of masters and wardens of the six merchant guilds, surveillance of the commercial regulations, and indentures of apprenticeship
9. Weights and measures
10. Publishing, printing, and bookselling

11. Reviewing reports of surgeons concerning patients who had been wounded (the surgeons were required to report such incidents to this office)
12. Passing judgment on all persons caught in the act of committing a crime
13. The police organization
14. Citizens who were compelled by law to assist in carrying out his orders[31]

La Reynie was ideally suited for this position. Trained as an advocate and a judge at the law school of the University of Toulouse, he participated in the king's conferences on police reform as a crown lawyer. Thus the new lieutenant of police was well versed in both law and in the problems besetting Parisian law enforcement.

La Reynie's accomplishments were nothing short of spectacular. When he took office, Paris was much like any other European city: dirty, dark, and dangerous. By the time he left office in 1697, the city was being cleaned on a continuing basis, and the streets had been thoroughly paved and lighted. La Reynie had required that lanterns be posted throughout the city at 20-yard intervals. Through these actions La Reynie struck at two factors related to crime: dirt and darkness. He also brought order to the city by requiring the alignment of houses. Further-

Photograph 1-1   La Reynie (Photo by Mark Blumberg.)

more, he was responsible for the construction of a bridge over the Seine, alleviating a serious traffic problem.

The police placed under La Reynie's command were substantial in numbers and became a formidable force. The royal watch force, the *guet,* was augmented and a new company of guards was created. La Reynie justified an increase in the number of police officers on the grounds of crime prevention. He argued: "It is easier to preserve the tranquility which Parisians currently enjoy than to restore it once it has been disturbed."[32]

The structure of the Paris police was multifaceted. There was the police force of the "lieutenant of the short robe." The man holding this office was primarily a man of the sword, although he had some judicial authority. This unit was responsible for dealing with violent crime within the city. The provost of the Ile de France maintained and commanded a military force responsible for patrolling the suburbs and the surrounding countryside. There also existed a group of special agents, *exempts,* created by Cardinal Mazarin for special investigations and undercover police work. Finally, there were the *commissaires-enquêteurs au châtelet,* police officials having magistrate status who were locally responsible for law and order in each of the 16 administrative sections of Paris *(quartiers).* All were placed under the control of the lieutenant of police.

Louis XIV, through the office of La Reynie, was also able to reduce drastically the amount of duelling in and around Paris. Although members of the upper class maintained this tradition, La Reynie was fierce in his enforcement of the antiduelling laws and regulations controlling the possession of weapons. He was instrumental in disarming the population, which by law could not carry weapons. Further, Louis XIV is credited with ushering in the age of reason with his decree of 1672, ending legal prosecution on the simple charge of sorcery and bringing an end to the era of witch trials that had plagued all of Europe and Britain since the fifteenth century.[33]

In 1674, La Reynie's title was changed to *lieutenant-general of police.* Through the years that followed, this exceptional man made a tremendous contribution to urban law enforcement. He emphasized the value of preventive patrol and his measures for lighting and hygiene set standards that were copied throughout Europe. He promulgated an edict on the control of prostitution that was in effect until 1946. He attempted to find a solution for the problem of homeless children by building a foundling hospital. All of these actions were taken to make the city of Paris safe. He was so successful that by the end of his 30 years in office, Paris was transformed from a dark, dirty, medieval city into the best administered city in the world.[34]

La Reynie resigned his post in 1697. Even the waspish memorialist of the age, Duc de Saint-Simon, paid homage to this man when he expressed surprise that La Reynie took pains to do as little harm as possible when he might have done so much. Saint-Simon concluded, "a man of honor and a great and upright judge."[35]

The King's Police

Louis XIV attempted to accomplish in all of France what he had done in Paris with La Reynie. Alas, the attempt proved futile. He passed an edict that established the position of lieutenant-general of police for each of France's major cities. These local police chiefs were to enforce both local laws and the king's ordinances. Unfortunately, the prevailing political system was a form of economic patronage. Each office seeker was required to purchase the office from the government, as La Reynie had. Feeling that this new position would be a threat to the well-established principle of local control, many of the positions were bought by local governments. Even the local churches occasionally bought these positions to gain a favorable position with respect to the courts. Despite the failure of this edict, the king did have some power of intervention. The position of intendant of justice, police and finance provided a form of royal intervention in the cities and provinces of France. This officer had the last word on police matters and could requisition civil and military forces in his province.[36]

Policing in the countryside, however, progressed very well. The *maréchaussée,* France's military-police force, had been evolving for several centuries. The name *maréchaussée* was derived from the military police in medieval times, having been under the marshals *(marechaux)* of France. In 1536, King Francis I had given the military the power to handle all criminal matters on the roads. This marks the beginning of the dual military-police status of modern France's *gendarmerie.*

Until 1720, the maréchaussée had been a loosely organized force, operating locally with low status or pay. One company had served as body guard to Joan of Arc and one was under the personal command of Cardinal Mazarin, but the group operated primarily as a cavalry unit used to charge into collective disturbances. This changed with the Ordinance of 1720, when the organization was transformed into a national force. The force was organized into 565 five-man squads (brigades), stationed at 10- or 12-mile intervals along the main roads. Each squad had its own sector to patrol. The companies were organized into inspectorial districts for supervision and command strategies. They were further grouped into territorial companies with a provost in command, a court staff, and legal officers for judicial purposes. The network, thus formed, is the basic network of today's departmental gendarmerie.[37]

Just prior to the revolution, in 1789, the Paris police had grown to include seven bureaus: The *bureau de cabinet* received and answered letters, addresses, complaints, and reports. The *bureau de sûreté* comprised three inspectors who were freely at the disposal of the public to listen to complaints and undertake enquiries and investigations. The *bureau de ravitaillement* for Paris employed six officials. It was responsible not only for the capital's food supplies, but also for refuse collecting and street cleaning and, more generally, for the upkeep of public thoroughfares. The *bureau des prisons et maisons de force* was concerned with all internment centers except the state prisons (the *Bastille* and the *Château de*

Vincennes). It was also responsible for surveillance of the Jewish population and for control of the public lotteries. The *bureau des arts et manufactures,* with a staff of eight, had jurisdiction over trade corporations, manufactures, commerce, the Bourse, foreign exchange, licenses to import and export, and the suppression of smuggling. A special bureau was in charge of wet nurses, a highly important matter at a time when all children of the nobility and bourgeoisie, and even many working-class infants, were put out to nurse (it was reckoned that on the eve of the revolution, not one child in 30 was breast-fed by its mother). Peasant women had to be recruited as wet nurses and arrangements made to bring them to Paris to collect the babies, or else to send the babies out to the country. A seventh bureau was in charge of disputed claims.[38]

At this same time the size of the Paris police had also grown. For a city of about 600,000, there were some 1500 police officers of various types at the disposal of the lieutenant-general of police. There were 48 *commissaires de police,* or *commissaires du Châtelet* (men holding their posts by right of purchase and for life) scattered throughout Paris, 20 inspectors with their assistants, 150 watchmen *(archers du guet),* three companies of Paris guards comprising some 1000 men, and 300 to 400 police officers *(exempts).*[39]

The thirteenth of the Ancien Régime's lieutenant-generals of police, and the last of the great ones, was Pierre Lenoir. In his own right, this man advanced the cause of public safety and hygiene. He was responsible for the numbering of the streets and the improvement of street lighting. He improved the city's hygiene when he closed down cemeteries inside the city limits. Furthermore, to reduce the number of drownings, Lenoir instituted a service of rescue work, with medals for lifesaving. It was also Lenoir who reorganized the Paris fire brigade into a 60-man volunteer force working in conjunction with the police and army.[40] All in all, and despite the instability of the French structure of government, the city of Paris was both safe and orderly under the reign of Louis XVI and this lieutenant-general of police.

From the time of its creation until the French Revolution, there were 14 lieutenant-generals of police, beginning with La Reynie and ending with Thiroux de Crosne. The office was filled by other exceptional men, some—like Lenoir—the equal of La Reynie. At other times, the incumbent was not so successful. What is certain, however, is that by the time the citizens of France rose against the government, Paris was vastly superior to London or Rome in terms of cleanliness, public safety, and public health.

The dark side of French policing, however, had taken its toll. The police had been the king's agents and were expected to suppress religious freedom as well as the expression of ideas. They were required to act as censor and literary critic. They policed the church, the arts, and the schools. At these tasks they were not only destined to fail, but they badly stained the reputation of the police in their attempts at enforcement.

The massive use of informants and internal espionage also stained the reputation of the French police. Long before the revolution, the French were thor-

Photograph 1–2   Pierre Lenoir (Photo by Mark Blumberg.)

oughly aware of the practice of compiling secret dossiers on individuals who had committed no crime but had "come to the notice of the authorities." Lenoir was said to have had a quarter of the maids and lackeys in Paris in his pay. An exasperated Briton, visiting France in the early 1780s, wrote that "they attend to the very meals you eat and the *Lieutenant of Police* is as well informed of the meat you have eaten, as the *Traiteur* who dressed it."[41]

Another bad idea was the "black cabinet," business of opening, reading, and resealing letters in transit. The police also used the Paris brothels as a source of criminal intelligence or as a means by which to coerce customers. The police tolerated brothels for a variety of reasons, but they helped finance their secret funds through gambling houses.

Thus, despite the very real service provided by the police of Paris, they had abused their authority and function. That problem would be addressed quickly and violently.

The Revolution

Prior to the revolution, judicial offices were regarded as property that could be bought, sold, traded, or left to one's heirs. Montesquieu himself inherited such an office and held it for 10 years before placing it up for sale. The judges were an aristocratic group who supported the landed aristocracy against the peasants and the urban middle and lower classes, and against the centralization of power in Paris. When the revolution came, the aristocracy fell, taking with it the aristocracy of the robe.[42]

The control of the judiciary by the aristocracy was not all bad. Even at the height of the monarch's power, the judiciary maintained its independence, thus creating a cohesive court system free of administrative authority and politics. Through litigation on concrete questions, the law was developed and applied by a professional body with a high moral idea of its own functions and of the law. French law was thereby protected from the arbitrariness that prevailed in certain neighboring countries. Thus, prior to the revolution, French law was similar to common law in that both were "judges' law."[43] When their own interests were not at stake, the French courts were reasonably enlightened. The concept of equity, the royal prerogatives of grace and mercy, was blended into the judicial process and did not develop into a separate, competing court system as it did in England. It was the pettiness and venality of the French courts when aristocratic interests were at stake that destroyed their reputation. As with the police, the courts of France were developing rapidly toward a fair and efficient system. The inability of the nobility to exorcise the demons of class bias from the justice system, however, gave it the appearance of being just another weapon of the affluent.

The judicial aristocracy were the targets of the revolution not only because of their tendency to identify with the French nobility, but also because of their failure to distinguish very clearly between applying law and making law. As a result of these failings, efforts by the kings to unify France and to enforce relatively enlightened and progressive legislative reforms had often been frustrated. When their own prerogatives were threatened, the courts refused to apply the new laws, interpreted them contrary to their intent, or hindered the attempts of officials to administer them.

Montesquieu and others developed the theory that the only way to prevent this type of judicial abuse was to separate the courts from the executive and legislative branches of government and to regulate the judiciary carefully to prevent its encroachment on executive and legislative functions.[44] This theory would establish the foundation for the modern French judicial system and make it distinctly different from the court system evolving in England. Whereas the common law continued as judge-made law, from the French Revolution onward, French courts would be forbidden to make law, set legal precedents, or declare any legislative or executive act unlawful.

The Reign of Terror

The police suffered badly under the revolutionary government. The one exception to this was the military-police organization, the maréchaussée or gendarmerie, which was briefly suspended, then returned to its normal duties. The other police units were eliminated. The commissaires-enquêteurs au Châtelet were replaced in May 1790 by a commissaire of police for each of the 48 sections that had replaced the former quartiers. Elected locally for two-year periods, each was supervised by 16 *section commissaires*. In September 1791, the inspectors of police were replaced by 24 *officiers de paix* (peace officers).

The most visible of the revolutionary police forces was the National Guard, initially commanded by the Marquis de La Fayette, hero of the American War for Independence. This unit was created on July 14, 1789 and had a battalion in each of Paris's 48 sections by August 1792.[45]

Despite the existence of these police elements, the law and order, so carefully orchestrated during the Ancien Régime, crumbled. The revolutionary government was able to replace people but could not duplicate the vast intelligence network or experience of the old police system. Crime not only flourished, it was rampant. In all areas of France, policing was ineffective; in Paris, it was atrocious.

The revolutionary government found itself facing both internal and external enemies. Its control threatened in a variety of areas, the French leaders established a new policy, the reign of terror. The idea was to generate unity and control within the nation by an unrelenting policy of ruthless suppression of anti-revolutionary fervor. Between 1793 and 1794, the government tribunals ran amok. The climax in terror occurred when the city of Lyon rebelled and overthrew its revolutionary government. The revolutionary tribunal, in a frenzy of indignation, promptly sentenced 1667 people to die. The guillotine, already overworked, was unable to handle so many executions. The condemned, therefore, were killed by concentrated cannon fire, also destroying 1600 houses in the process.

The terror, once unleashed, eventually devoured its parents. Robespierre, Saint-Just, and 20 other members of the revolutionary government, including the public prosecutor of the terror, Fouquier-Tinville, were convicted in the revolutionary courts and executed as they had ordered the executions of so many others.

At the end of the terror, the police had not much improved. The only notable contribution to the police was the creation of the minister of general police of the directory. Reminiscent of La Reynie, the argument put forward to justify this ministry was that they were convinced that it is easier to maintain public tranquility than to reestablish it once it has been disturbed. Finding a capable minister, however, was much more difficult than creating the position. France went through nine such ministers before settling on *Joseph Fouché*. It was this man who would be responsible for both the mass executions in Lyon and the removal of Robespierre and associates. Fouché reorganized the police and gave them new

Photograph 1-3   Dr. Guillotine (Photo by Mark Blumberg.)

purpose. His first love, however, was politics and political intrigue. He was responsible for major advances in policing, but he himself always focused on the "high police," the police of politics and security of the state.

Other than this, the revolutionary government was devoid of effective law enforcement. It would remain for Napoleon to overhaul that system, as well as the other institutions of justice. Fouché, convinced that Napoleon Bonaparte was

Photograph 1-4   Guillotine Blade (Photo by Mark Blumberg.)

the only man who could save France, happily entered into the general's conspiracies. When Bonaparte seized power from the councils of the legislature, it was Fouché who secured Paris for the general.

Napoleon's Police

The first act of Napoleon concerning the police was taken the day following his appointment as the first of three consuls. He appointed Fouché to the newly created position of minister of police of the consulate.

Napoleon then addressed the structure of the police in all of France. He reinstituted the idea of the old intendant of justice, police and finance in an expanded form. They were to be known as prefects and each was responsible for one of 98 administrative departments created by the revolutionary government (prior to the revolution there had been 34). Over the four or five *arrondissements* of each department, he placed subprefects.

Each community of 5000 inhabitants was given a commissaire of police appointed by the central government and a mayor, appointed the same way. Commissaires-general of police were appointed for cities of 100,000.

The police framework was effectively reinforced by the gendarmerie. Napoleon raised the strength of this organization to around 30,000. He then placed it under General Moncey, soon to be a marshal of France. This organization, also given a military role in Napoleon's campaigns, provided the primary police agents for the prefects. Thus within a short time period, France was effectively overlaid with a unified police network.

In Paris, Napoleon quickly established a police chief. The office of lieutenant-general of police was recreated, without its previous judicial powers, as the prefect of police of Paris. At the top of this police empire sat Joseph Fouché and the Ministry of General Police. This man, remarkable in his own right, established an organization of policing and intelligence gathering unheard of at that time. Napoleon, frequently on military campaigns, depended on Fouché's information to maintain both his control over France and his military effectiveness. Six days a week, every week, Fouché sent secret reports to Napoleon (who made himself emperor in 1804). The information represented an incredible array of topics:

1. Palace gossip
2. Audience reaction to a new play
3. Stockmarket prices
4. Desertions from the army
5. Arrests of foreign agents
6. Results of interrogations
7. News of crime

8. Offenses by soldiers
9. Fires
10. Rebellion against the gendarmerie
11. Intercepted correspondence
12. Visiting personages
13. Public reception of news of victories
14. Shipping news
15. Indiscretions of Fouché's enemies
16. Contractor's tenders
17. Agitation against the draft
18. Suicides
19. Prison epidemics
20. Progress of construction
21. Unemployment figures
22. Extracts from interministerial correspondence
23. Persons detained or under special surveillance[46]

Fouché had a large number of contacts with local and foreign dignitaries. He supplied the Emperor with an impressive amount of intelligence which gave Napoleon the ability to stay ahead of both military and political opponents. These contacts and his control over France's vast police network allowed Fouché to claim that three men could not meet and talk indiscreetly about public affairs without the minister of police being informed about it the following day.

All societies are bound to their history. So it was with France. The abuses of the king's police were revived and amplified by Napoleon's. More secret orders of arrest *(lettres de cachet),* so hated by the people during the Ancien Régime, were executed by Fouché than by all the ministers under Louis XIV and Louis XV combined. The detested informant network was reestablished with a vengeance. Napoleon simply recreated the police system of the Ancien Régime, provided new titles, and increased its power, size, and accountability to himself.

Even so, the reorganized and highly centralized police created under the reign of Emperor Napoleon returned France to the peace and order it had enjoyed under the Old Order. The durability of the system he left behind is attested to by the fact that it is basically the same system in place in France today.

With the fall of Napoleon, France experienced a return to the political upheaval experienced immediately following the revolution. Through the remainder of the nineteenth century, France would flip-flop between monarchy, empire, and republic. The fortunes of the French police would oscillate around the tempestuous conditions of the French government. By the twentieth century, however, the police of France would be stabilized and among the world's finest.

Criminal Investigation

Without a doubt, the finest achievement of the nineteenth century French police was development of the detective branch. By the end of the nineteenth century, Paris was regarded as having the finest detective organization in the world. They had a definite advantage over their London and New York counterparts. The common law nations felt compelled to remove the police from any activity that might appear to be domestic espionage. A high-profile uniformed image was thus preferred by these two organizations, at the expense of investigative capability. The use of criminal intelligence, while recognized as useful, was nevertheless poorly utilized in London and New York. The Paris police not only had an extensive documentation section on the movements and actions of a large number of its citizens, it also had the centuries-old mystique of a police presence and a long tradition of plainclothes officers working with a veritable army of paid informants.[47]

The real history of the Paris detectives begins toward the end of the First Empire (the era of Napoleon) when the head of the criminal division of the prefecture of police, Monsieur Henry, recruited *François Eugène Vidocq*. Henry recognized the potential talents of Vidocq when the latter was in prison. As an informant *(mouton)* inside the prison, Vidocq produced such good results that Henry decided to put him in command of a small detective unit. At that time criminal investigation was conducted by the 24 *officiers de paix,* each with a few men under them. This made investigations a local function rather than a centralized operation. Henry wanted a centralized detective unit that would report directly to him.

Vidocq established his unit by hiring ex-criminals as detectives. These were paid in accordance with their results. Vidocq established a record system and developed techniques of intelligence gathering and investigation that quickly became an established feature of the criminal division, which became known as the *Sûreté,* until 1913, when it became the *Police Judiciaire.*

In 1832, the prefect of Police, Gisuet, felt obliged to reorganize the Sûreté. It had developed a reputation for entrapment (the agents were frequently charged with using the ruse of an *agent-provocateur*). The backgrounds of the detectives themselves were also having a detrimental effect on the outcome of the court cases. Gisuet replaced the ex-offenders with regular police officers and placed it under the command of a commissaire of police, Pierre Allard, who was required to give up his magisterial status and accept the rank of *officier de paix* in order to accept this position. The new organization was placed under the chief of the municipal police and called for four *brigadiers* (sergeants), 21 *inspecteurs* (detectives), and four clerks.

This newly organized investigation division learned very quickly that success depended on sound intelligence. By 1848, with Canler succeeding Allard, the Sûreté established a network of informants among ex-criminals and people knowledgeable about criminal activity. The regulation of prostitution also proved a valuable source of criminal intelligence. The Paris police had been in the prostitution regulation business since the Middle Ages, and in a city known for its earthly delights, this was a full-time task. In 1894, it was reported that 26,000 women were arrested for prostitution; it was estimated that there were 40,000 in the city. The prefect of police registered prostitutes up until 1946. It also maintained a medical dispensary and had a staff of doctors that conducted regular medical examinations.

In 1887, the police organization was reorganized so that Sûreté was allowed to report directly to the cabinet of the prefect of police. This was a badly needed reform since the communication process between the Sûreté and the regular police through bureaucratic channels was frustratingly slow.

Criminalistics

In 1877, *Alphonse Bertillon* was appointed to the prefecture of police as a records clerk. He shortly became disgusted with the way in which records were maintained. Within a year he presented a new scheme for identifying criminals, based on body and head measurements. Using this technique (anthropometric or "man measurement"), he identified his first recidivist in 1883. In 1884, Bertillon identified 241 and was recognized for developing the first scientific method of identifying a criminal to be used by a police force.

This system was soon incorporated into the British and American police systems. Although it would be replaced by fingerprinting in the early twentieth century, the Bertillon system was responsible for bringing precision into a haphazard

Photograph 1-5 Alphonse Bertillon
(Photo by Mark Blumberg.)

process. Prior to this development, criminal identification depended on the memories of witnesses. Criminals were able to commit their crimes and disappear into the streets with the knowledge that the police were unlikely to capture them. The Bertillon system made identification possible without requiring the witness to be present at the arrest. More than just a system of measurements, Bertillon also created the *portrait parlé* (speaking likeness) system, which was a precise method of describing a person's facial and physical characteristics.[48] This portion of Bertillon's system is still used by the majority of the world's police departments, although it has lost much of its exactness, due to the evolution of shortcuts in the process.

The problem that finally led to the discrediting of Bertillon's anthropometric system was the inability to ensure uniformity in measurement. The problem was twofold. First, different officers frequently obtained different measurements on the same person. This was caused by a lack of agreement on how tightly the calipers should fit to obtain the measurement. The second problem was caused by the aging process. As people age, so do many of the bodily characteristics, especially if the original measurements were obtained when the person was not yet an adult.

The system was ultimately discredited as a result of the Will West case in 1903. Will West was mistakenly identified in Leavenworth, Kansas, as a previous convict, William West. The use of fingerprints allowed the police to identify the real William West, who was serving time in another prison. This case marked the end of anthropometric measurements and the beginning of fingerprinting as the principal means of criminal identification.

Bertillon received great criticism as a result of these flaws in the system, and that sometimes obscures his other achievements. It was those other contributions, however, that make this man one of the great pioneers in criminalistics. He was instrumental in introducing the use of photography to police investigations, especially at crime scenes. He introduced handwriting and forgery analysis; ballistics; galvanoplastic preservation of footprints; the dynamometer, used in determining the degree of force used in housebreaking; and the Bertillon Kit, a case containing instruments of evidence collection taken by detectives to a crime scene.

Thus the greatest developments in the introduction of eighteenth-century science to policing took place in France. Along with Bertillon, we also find the French medical doctor, Mathieu Orfila (1787–1853), who first proved in court the presence of arsenic in a murder victim. Finally, in 1884, Jean-Alexander Lacassagne founded the first criminalistics laboratory in Lyon.

THE BRITISH EXPERIENCE

The genesis of effective English law enforcement came not from strong leadership in the central government, as it had in the Rome of Augustus and the Paris of Louis XIV, but from within the inadequate and obsolete system of justice itself.

The early system of justice was created during the Anglo-Saxon era. Society was grouped into families, tens (10 families), hundreds (10 groups of 10 families), and shires (roughly comparable to today's counties). The *shire-reeve* was appointed by the king to act as tax collector and to enforce a variety of royal ordinances. This officer was the the forerunner of the county sheriff.

After the conquest of England by William of Normandy, a more centralized approach to law enforcement was introduced. Eventually, the office of coroner was created to investigate deaths. This system evolved slowly toward the modern era. Eventually, the watch system was created in the city of London. This was the principal means of law enforcement in England through the early eighteenth century. It took a number of men of great foresight to begin the development of a truly professional police force.

Bow Street

In 1740, Thomas De Veil became justice of the peace in a court set in Bow Street, Covent Gardens. At the time De Veil assumed this post, this area was known as an inner-city pleasure district, a little world of theaters, clubs, taverns, gambling houses, and brothels. De Veil was not known as a pillar of virtue. His sexual rapacity was well known, and he was on occasion corrupt. His unflinching and resourceful attacks on crime, however, gave Bow Street its reputation as the leader among London's magistrate's courts, a position it still maintains.[49]

Following De Veil's death in 1746, *Henry Fielding* was appointed to the Bow Street court. A well-known author *(Tom Jones),* he was given this position through the efforts of a few influential friends who wished to provide some relief to a man with financial and health problems. To this end they convinced the government to provide a small salary to Fielding, making him the first paid English magistrate.

Fielding, who already had an interest in law and crime, completely immersed himself in the new position, at times even working in defiance of his doctor's orders. By all accounts Henry Fielding was a true gentleman. Kind, generous, and incorruptible, he was asked by the government to submit a plan to stop the murders and robberies plaguing London. His plan included a modification of the thief-takers (in essence, these were bounty hunters) who were still active in England. He established a group of special thief-takers to bring criminals to justice by working through informants. These thief-takers were not criminals, such as the late Jonathan Wild (so called Thief-Taker General of England and Wales, who was ultimately hanged as a thief), but were honest men who had served as constables in the past. They served voluntarily at Fielding's request. As a result, Henry Fielding established the first British detective force. They would be known in the following century as the Bow Street Runners.[50]

Fielding also wrote what may be the first English criminological treatise in 1751. This work, *Enquiry into the Causes of the Late Increase of Robbers,* provided valuable insights on the social context of crime. Being a man of his times,

Photograph 1–6   Henry Fielding

his theories of criminality focused on the belief in the criminal tendencies of the lower classes. He also attributed much of the problem to an inefficient criminal justice system as well as noting that the legal system alone would never be capable of truly addressing the crime problem. Henry Fielding was in office only six years but accomplished more than he realized. His fair-mindedness as well as his extraordinary writing ability left a legacy that others would build upon.

The man who more fully developed the ideals that Henry Fielding had striven for was Henry's half-brother, John. Blinded in an accident at the age of 19, *John Fielding* nevertheless developed into one of the foremost magistrates in British history. There was obviously a close personal bond between the half-brothers. Henry and John went into business earlier in life, and when Henry became the Bow Street magistrate, he was instrumental in getting John appointed to the position of assistant. When Henry Fielding retired, John, known at Bow Street as the Blind Beak, became the principal magistrate.

Like his half-brother, John Fielding had a keen sense of social responsibility. Finding numerous children brought before him on felonious charges, he sought to alter their life-styles. He believed that poverty and lack of proper parental guidance was the cause of so much delinquency and attacked the problem in that light. He began sending young boys to sea with the Royal Navy as cabin boys. This idea became so popular that it was institutionalized and ultimately developed into the Marine Society. At the same time he attempted to aid young girls through the creation of Magdelan Hospital and Female Orphan Asylum.

Photograph 1-7   John Fielding

Policing was still done primarily through the watch system. Law and order on the street was in the hands of the parish watchmen, called "Charleys" (so-named for Charles II, who created the "watch and ward system"). There were about 2000 of them on the streets of London in the late eighteenth century. John Fielding referred to them as those "poor old decrepit people." Many of them were charity cases who had cast themselves at the mercy of the parish, due to an inability to get other forms of work. From the parish each Charley received a greatcoat with three capes, like a coachman's; a lantern, to light his tottering progress through the alleys; a wooden rattle to summon help; and a staff to defend himself. He would bang the butt of the staff rhythmically against the cobbles as he walked, to give the thieves sufficient warning so that the embarrassment of a meeting between law and crime could be averted. Easily bribed with sixpence or a quart of gin, the deterrent power of the Charleys was slight.[51]

John Fielding pushed hard for an organized police force. He was partially successful for a time. The government authorized 10 mounted patrol officers in 1763, to patrol London's suburban perimeter. Within one year this force more than proved itself as a detective and patrol force. The government cut funding after that period, however, and the force was reduced to two mounted officers.

John Fielding also did a great deal to improve the image of the magistrate's court. He was successful in moving the court out of his private residence, where magistrate's courts traditionally were held, and into a building open to the public. He encouraged citizens to report crime to him and regularly published accounts of various theft and confidence schemes so that the public would be forewarned. John Fielding became the first British proponent of crime prevention and police public relations.

Recognizing the territorial limitations of the magistrates and the advantage this provided criminals, John Fielding communicated regularly with other magistrates. He encouraged the sharing of information and cooperation in enforcement. He further founded two police newspapers, *The Quarterly Pursuit,* and *The Weekly,* or *Extraordinary Pursuit,* to be sent free to justices at large. These papers contained names and descriptions of wanted criminals. From these publications eventually evolved the *Police Gazette,* founded in 1828 and published by New Scotland Yard since 1883.

John Fielding was knighted in 1761, the first of an unbroken string of such honors bestowed on Bow Street magistrates up until the present. His contributions to police development were vast. The first person to use the term *police* in its law enforcement sense, John Fielding confirmed the value of a detective unit, demonstrated the value of patrolling, exploited the crime preventive capacity of the press, and never lost sight of the social context of crime.[52]

The end of an era.   In 1780, as Sir John Fielding lay dying in his home, London experienced the worst riots of its history. The Gordon Riots, named for one of the leaders, Lord George Gordon, resulted from a protest against Parliament's relaxation of repressive legislation against Roman Catholics. To the modern student of law enforcement, it seems that the English surely should have seen that the time was ripe for the development of a modern police force. And such was almost the case. In 1785, the government, under the leadership of William Pitt the Younger, brought a bill to the House of Commons designed to create a system of magistrates along the Bow Street model as well as a police force under three commissioners for London, Westminster, and contiguous areas. The opposition was so strong that the bill had to be withdrawn. All was not a total loss, however; the next year this scheme was put into effect in the capital of Ireland by the Dublin Police Act.[53]

Amazingly, the people who had the most to gain from the establishment of a modern police force fiercely opposed its founding. This was a source of wonder to foreigners, especially the French.

When the Duc de Levis asked his friends in 1814 why there was no maréchaussée—the rural police, with powers of arbitrary pursuit and arrest, that had all but stamped out brigandage in the French provinces—he was firmly told that "such an institution is not compatible with liberty."[54] There lay the major source of the controversy. The English were well acquainted with the French legal institutions, where no Frenchman's home was his castle. One returned traveler wrote: "I would rather half-a-dozen peoples' throats be cut in the Ratcliffe Highway every three to four years, than be subject to the domiciliary visits, spies and the rest of Fouché's contrivances."[55]

It should be noted that those opposed to a police force did so because of a concern for the rights of property rather than concern for the rights of suspects. Still, the common law was developing into the most liberal of legal systems for that era. English suspects had rights unheard of throughout the remainder of Europe. They could not be tortured until they confessed, they were considered innocent until proven guilty, and they could not be held indefinitely without bail or trial. This liberalism astonished European visitors, who noted that while it undoubtedly reduced the chances of convicting the innocent, it increased the likelihood of freeing the guilty.

The English, well aware of this flaw in their system, attempted to counter it by legislating the most brutal set of criminal laws in existence at the time. They reasoned that since the police (such as they were) and the courts could not reasonably be expected to deter crime, it was necessary that the laws themselves provide this function. Between the reign of Charles II in 1660 and George IV in 1819, 187 new capital statutes were passed, nearly all designed to protect property (attempted murder was classified a misdemeanor until 1803).

Such legislation was a by-product of a philosophy of the times, the growth of the *rule of law,* the idea that law was an absolute and immutable process by which society was structured. This idea was transformed into a pseudoreligion, which, as some have argued, began to replace the waning moral power of the Church of England.[56]

In 1792, Pitt returned to the idea of magisterial reform, with more success. He was able to establish seven police courts in addition to Bow Street, at each of which would sit three stipendiary magistrates. This bill also provided for six paid constables at each court with limited powers of arrest on suspicion.

One of the major benefits of this act was the appointment of Patrick Colquhoun, as one of the stipendiary magistrates. A friend of the early criminologist, Jeremy Bentham, Colquhoun adopted wholeheartedly Bentham's philosophy of preventive policing. He opened kitchens to feed the poor and maintained a fund to help workers retrieve the tools of their trade from pawnbrokers.

Like the Fieldings, whom he greatly admired, Colquhoun used the printed word to spread his ideas. Two of his books are police classics: *A Treatise on the Police of the Metropolis* (1795) and *The Commerce and the Police of the River Thames* (1800), which described his successful attempt to create a river police to deal with corruption in the shipping industry.

The late eighteenth and early nineteenth centuries were tumultuous years for Great Britain. Napoleon's France and growing insurrection placed even greater stress on England's inadequate legal structure. The magistrates and constables were frequently utilized for counterespionage. With the public still equating po-

Photograph 1–8 Patrick Colquhoun

licing with tyranny, there was no hope of the government reforming the police. Tragedy was inevitable; it occurred on August 16, 1819, at St. Peter's Fields.

The event that brought about "Peterloo" (a combination of St. Peter and Waterloo) was a public meeting in which the famous radical orator Henry Hunt spoke to the crowd on parliamentary reform. Thinking he was inciting a riot, magistrates at the scene ordered him and the other speakers arrested. The justices, knowing the constables would be unable to penetrate the large crowd to serve the warrants, ordered a contingent of yeomanry cavalry to apprehend the suspects. The cavalry achieved their goal, after first running down a 2-year-old-child—the first victim. Having tasted success, the cavalry then became overly enthusiastic and began to rip down the podium. The justices, thinking the crowd was attacking the soldiers, ordered a troop of newly arrived regular cavalry to break up the gathering. The result was 15 dead and several hundred injured. The name *Peterloo* was coined and the event was generally spoken of as a massacre. The government maintained its hard line and praised the magistrates and soldiers. Hunt and the others were sentenced to long prison terms. However, this incident was instrumental in preparing for the police reforms that would take place 10 years later.

Peel's Reforms

Sir *Robert Peel* (1788–1850) has been called by some the "father of modern policing." Although this label is open to debate, especially in light of the earlier development of the French police, there can be little doubt that Peel is the father of the modern British police. In 1822, Robert Peel became Home Secretary. His first act was to appoint a committee under his own chairmanship. This group, created specifically to study the consolidation of various magistrates and watchmen into a central police force controlled by three magistrates, sat idle for three months unable to overcome the opposition to such an organization before Peel temporarily conceded defeat.[57]

Peel was no stranger to public turbulence. Chief Secretary of Ireland from 1812 to 1818, he had seen a country with wretched peacekeeping machinery ravaged by rioting put down by such troops that could be spared from Britain's war with France. He had been instrumental in the creation of the Peace Preservation Act of 1814, which gave the Lord Lieutenant of Ireland the power to create a police force in any area he proclaimed a state disturbance. The newly created Peace Preservation Force enjoyed early success and Peel came to believe strongly in the idea of a civil police force.[58]

Thwarted in his attempt to create a police force in England, Sir Robert turned his attention to badly needed reforms in the criminal law. When he took office, England was held in the grip of the old "bloody code," which proclaimed capital punishment for a vast array of criminal acts. Challenging the belief that severity of punishment was a greater deterrent to crime than certainty of arrest

Photograph 1-9 Sir Robert Peel

and punishment, Peel began submitting bills to Parliament, replacing death sentences with prison sentences and transportation. Even this process was dreadfully slow. It was not until 1861, well after Peel had left office, that the slow process of legal reform was completed.

Peel's second term in office dawned with more support for his police initiatives. The Duke of Wellington, hero of the Battle of Waterloo, became Prime Minister. In 1823, Wellington had told Lord Liverpool that measures should be taken "to form either a police force in London or a military corps which should be of a different description from the regular military force, or both."[59] Peel, therefore, was to gain the strong support necessary for his police reforms. Sir Robert wasted no time in presenting his ideas to Wellington. He wrote the prime minister that it was his intention to "teach people that liberty does not consist of having your house robbed by a gang of organized thieves."[60]

Scotland Yard.   The battle to create a professional police force was in its own way as arduous as a military campaign. Common people and landed nobility, both pro and con, passionately argued their respective positions. Some feeling for the intensity of the controversy can be gleaned from an article that appeared in the *Times* on April 3, 1829:

> We have received so many letters on the subject of Mr. Peel's Police bill, but they are so voluminous and some of them so intemperate that insertion cannot be given to them.

> A case is reported in Lambeth as having happened yesterday, which proves, if any proof were needed, the absolute want of a central and controlling power in the Metropolitan police. Here were a gang of robbers pursued by one set of watchmen and actually suffered to escape by another set who would not stir a foot beyond their own boundary line to cross and turn the flying villains. It is impossible, without a spirited and cordial cooperation, to afford protection to property or to punish crime.[61]

On May 26, 1829, the Metropolitan Police Bill was passed by the House of Commons. On June 6, the Duke of Wellington moved its adoption in the House of Lords and it became law. The long battle between common sense and false notions of liberty had been won.[62] Concessions were made, however, that eased the passage of the bill. One of the primary stumbling blocks had been the political power within the City of London. Wellington and Peel eliminated that problem by excluding the City of London from the Police Act. As a result, only Metropolitan London would be policed by the new force; the actual City of London was left to handle its own affairs.

Peel's first problem was the appointment of the three men who would help him administer this new organization. He knew that if he selected a prominent man, he would be accused of jobbery (the improper use of patronage). The selection of nonentities incapable of maintaining sufficient discipline would be equally dangerous. This new force would be carefully scrutinized by both the government and the public. Peel knew that there were too many people who wanted the police to fail; he could afford few mistakes.

Peel's first choice was Colonel Rowan, later known as Sir *Charles Rowan,* who fought under Wellington at Waterloo. Rowan had become a police magistrate in Ireland, where Peel had met him and observed his performance. The second commissioner's position was given to *Richard Mayne,* a young barrister on the northern circuit and son of an Irish judge. Both were given equal powers and each had access to the Home Secretary without consulting the other. It is a tribute to their abilities that they worked together amicably for 20 years. The third commissioner position, that of receiver, was filled by John Wray, also an advocate.

Rowan was in charge of the discipline; Mayne established the general guidelines for the organization. While idealistic and noble, these guidelines reflect the minds of men who knew little about the underworld of London: "The primary objective of an efficient police is the prevention of crime; the next that of detection and punishment. The protection of life and property, the preservation of public tranquility, and the absence of crime will alone prove whether those efforts have been successful and whether the objects for which the police were appointed have been attained."[63]

In pushing his bill through Parliament, Peel always stressed the crime prevention function of the police. From his writings and those of his magistrates, it is clear that they believed that crime could be eradicated and that the police alone

Photograph 1-10   Sir Charles Rowan

Photograph 1-11 Richard Mayne

could somehow accomplish this task. The police instructions and arguments posed by Peel in debate read well but are somewhat naive. Nevertheless, organized law enforcement in England was in its infancy; Sir Robert can be forgiven idealistic fervor. It was that fervor that led to the creation of the modern English police force, and Peel truly did not understand the causes of crime. He was a product of his times and believed, as did much of the English intelligentsia, that crime was the product of a criminal class.

The organizational principles upon which this force was based were published in a pamphlet and given to every officer upon acceptance to the force. This in itself was a dramatic change in police management and is of immense historical value. The basic tenets of Peel's instructions were:

1. The police must be stable, efficient, and organized along military lines.
2. The police must be under government control.
3. The absence of crime will best prove the efficiency of the police.
4. The distribution of crime news is essential.
5. The deployment of police strength both by time and area is essential.

6. No quality is more indispensable to a policeman than a perfect command of temper; a quiet, determined manner has more respect than violent action.

7. Good appearance commands respect.

8. The security and training of proper persons is at the root of efficiency.

9. Public security demands that every police officer be given a number.

10. Police headquarters should be centrally located and easily accessible to the people.

11. Policemen should be hired on a probationary basis.

12. Police records are necessary to the correct distribution of police strength.[64]

The police force was not an immediate success. Derisive names such as "Peelers" and "Blue Devils" haunted the steps of the new officers. Some of the hostility was the natural resentment to what many people honestly believed was a new system of government repression. Also, however, the Metropolitan Police Act provided for a new form of tax to support this organization, which meant that the people who had the most to gain from the police, the property owners, were given an equally compelling reason to hate the new force. Peel and his magistrates recognized the immense hostility they faced and took every means possible to neutralize the public's perceptions. Most of the police orders of that era show a determination not to furnish their critics with material for agitation against the new force.[65]

The Metropolitan Police District, with a population of some 2 million, was divided into areas, to which was assigned a division, under a superintendent, with four inspectors, each inspector having four *parties* under him, and each party with a sergeant and nine constables. The area was divided into *beats,* to be patrolled by constables throughout the 24 hours. Each beat was designed to allow the constable to cover it every 15 minutes.

Headquarters was established in a house, Number 4, Whitehall Place, adjacent to a court known as Scotland Yard. From the outset, therefore, the force was associated with this now famous address. (Headquarters have moved twice since then, now to be known as New Scotland Yard.)[66] The selection of personnel was troublesome but moved with surprising speed. Initially, there were thousands of applicants, mostly laborers and ex-soldiers. Peel wanted a force that was representative, but recruitment was hampered by Sir Robert's own biases. Himself born of wealth, Peel had little understanding of what money meant to the working class. The British government was also unwilling to spend any more than was absolutely necessary to fill the rosters. Peel apparently believed that he could hire an entire force of men who were fit, under 35, literate, and of good character, for 3 shillings a day, a wage that was considerably lower than that of an artisan.

Regardless of these problems, by June 1830, the force had recruited 17 superintendents, 68 inspectors, 323 sergeants, and 2906 constables, every one of whom had been interviewed by the commissioners. Peel also believed that divisional superintendents and inspectors should be from the warrant officer and noncommissioned officer ranks of the military. He felt that commissioned officers would find these duties "beneath" them. This organizational decision would have two effects. First, it probably eased the resentment of the middle and upper classes. Second, it gave the police a lower-class stereotype that they have had difficulty overcoming.[67]

Command personnel came from the ranks of military officers. Despite the fact that military titles were rarely used by the metropolitan police, it was designed on rigid military lines. Care was taken not to make the new force appear military. The constables wore uniforms, but of a distinctly nonmilitary style. Each officer wore a blue swallow-tailed coat, a leather stock, and a reinforced tophat. A rattle was carried to give the alarm and summon help (the whistle replaced the rattle in 1846; the helmet replaced the tophat in 1864).

Acceptance and Respect

Resentment against the metropolitan police force did not die away immediately. In fact, the organization faced the greatest crisis in its short history in the early 1830s. The government, of which Peel was a part, left office in 1830. The new government was made up of people partial to the old justices of the peace and hostile to the new police force. First Lord Melbourne and then Viscount Duncannon, successors to the position of Home Secretary, seemingly set out to destroy the new force. Their motive for playing the metropolitan police against the magistrates can only be construed as an attempt to force Rowan and Mayne to quit. Although the frustration must have been almost unbearable, neither resigned.

Their own government's attempt to eliminate them on one front was matched by an equally ardent set of enemies on the street. The constables found themselves confronted by unrelenting opposition: soldiers pitched in to fight these wearers of an alien uniform; firemen fought them for the possession of the scenes of fire; coachmen lashed them in defiance of traffic directions. At night, a more insidious foe awaited in the alleys and streets: the free drink offered to men who were members of a class that had been prone to alcoholism for over a century. The commissioners, with the support of their military-trained midlevel managers, maintained a steady unrelaxed discipline. Between 1830 and 1838 there were 5000 dismissals and 6000 resignations. Drunk on duty caused most of the dismissals; the search for better paying and less onerous jobs caused the majority of resignations.[68]

It took public reaction to a tragedy to generate acceptance of the police. The tragedy occurred on May 13, 1833, on a piece of wasteland called Coldbath Fields, behind the prison in Clerkenwell. A group known as Ultra-Radicals (a radical left-wing group with a small membership) mobilized the National Political Union (a large, moderate, working-class group) with inflammatory notices of police abuse. Some 800 people peacefully gathered to hear speakers, some carrying banners proclaiming "Death or Liberty," others carrying the American flag. The speakers adopted a rhetoric of violence and soon the police were compelled to break up the meeting. The result was a riot in which three officers were stabbed, one killed. It appeared that the police had lost a serious battle of public opinion. The newspapers attacked the police conduct with a vengeance. Moreover, a coroner's jury found the killing justifiable homicide, a perverse decision that was eventually overturned by a higher court.

A government commission appointed to study the event, however, discovered that police discipline had been strictly enforced. There were no civilian deaths and very little evidence of police misuse of force. Furthermore, public sympathy for the slain constable began to build, with money pouring in from all over the nation to support the officer's widow. From that point forward, the police became more and more accepted by the public. Gradually, the derisive names given to the police officers were replaced with a single term of endearment. In honor of their founder, Robert Peel, the British police came to be known as "bobbies."

By the end of the 1830s, the crisis was over. The magistrates had lost their police powers. Even the legendary Bow Street Runners were disbanded. London's public order was firmly in the hands of the metropolitan police.

The detectives. The metropolitan police was designed to be a uniformed force only. The fears that led to the opposition of a police organization were largely the result of the belief that Europeans such as the French and Prussians had forfeited their freedom through the creation of police forces, especially plain-clothed officers acting surreptitiously. Also, the magistrates had their own detective forces, of which the Bow Street Runners were an example. As long as the old detectives survived, Scotland Yard remained a completely uniformed force.

By 1839, the last of the Bow Street Runners had retired. This left the metropolitan police with all of the responsibilities that had been shared between them and the runners. It was clear that a void had been created that badly needed filling. There was one attempt, and that went badly. A constable named Popay was assigned to infiltrate the National Political Union to obtain intelligence information on that movement. Alas, he possessed an excess of zeal. He became one of the leaders of the movement, ostensibly to gather information on the other leaders. When he was discovered, there was a great cry raised about the police spying on the public. Popay was dismissed from the force, but the damage was done. It would be two years before the idea of a detective unit resurfaced.

As with other developments in British law enforcement, it took a dramatic jolt to the conscience of the public before such a unit could be created within the metropolitan police. The necessary impetus for the institution of a detective branch took place in April 1842. It was the murder of an unknown woman. A middle-aged coachman named Daniel Good attempted to shoplift a pair of trousers. Accused by the owner, Good fled the scene with a constable in pursuit. Good ran to the stable where he worked and backed himself against a door, where he refused to move or allow anyone to enter. The policeman told Good that he was under arrest and placed a neighbor to watch over the suspect while he searched the premises. Good suddenly offered to return the stolen items as well as pay for them.

The police officer, while looking through stacks of hay, suddenly exclaimed, "My God! What's this?" Good fled through the barn door and locked the police officer and would-be guard in the barn. Trapped in the barn, the officer decided to continue the search. He returned to the hay stack and uncovered the rest of the item that had caught his attention. It was a human torso, that of a woman about 25 and obviously pregnant. The head and limbs had been removed by a sharp instrument. Following a foul smell to the harness room, the police found the charred remains of the head and limbs, and a bloody ax and saw.

The crime itself created a sensation in London, but the fact that the culprit had escaped appeared to the public to be scandalous. The very people who had clamored for the destruction of the police now protested their inefficiency. Out of the storm rose a cry for a detective branch to deal with such crimes. Eventually, Good was captured, convicted, and executed, but the momentum necessary to develop a detective unit was already picking up speed. Just two days after Good's execution, the government announced the creation of a detective unit. The Criminal Investigation Department would work out of Scotland Yard and consisted of two inspectors and six sergeants.[69]

This small unit remained the sole detective force in London until 1862. In that year it was ordered that some 200 divisional officers would be employed in plainclothes. These were scattered among the various divisions. By 1869, the year Mayne died in office, there were still only 16 detectives assigned at the headquarters, but their reputation was solid and the practice of provincial police asking their assistance in difficult cases had already begun.

Mayne's replacement, Colonel Edmund Henderson, formerly of the Royal Engineers, who had spent the last 13 years administering convicts in Australia, immediately set out to change the detective branch. He assigned 40 detectives to Scotland Yard while allocating 10 detectives to each division. The idea was to have the "yard men" handle the tough cases while the divisional detectives handle routine affairs. The plan was a failure; divisional parochialism proved as pronounced as had been the old jurisdictions of the magistrates.

It was left to an enterprising young barrister named *Howard Vincent* to establish the final organizational structure of the Criminal Investigation Department (CID). A scandal in 1877, in which four detectives from Scotland Yard were involved with race-course swindlers, left the police humiliated and the detective department badly damaged. Vincent, at the time having no connection with the London police, went to Paris on his own to study the French detective system, which was widely regarded as the best in the world. He submitted a meticulous report to the London authorities, who were so impressed that they appointed Vincent as an assistant commissioner with the title Director of Criminal Investigations. His reorganization of Scotland Yard led to a fully centralized unit, strongly resembling that of the French Sûreté.[70]

Photograph 1-12 Howard Vincent

SUMMARY

The development of law enforcement organizations was a slow process that was dependent on the demands of social control by evolving societies. There were a number of distinct stages in this development. The earliest policing was that of kin police. Crime against society did not exist. Because of this, each family member was responsible for both himself and his family. Organized policing developed as societies became sufficiently complex to require protection of government interests. Still, the majority of the crimes were considered to be against individuals rather than society.

With the growth of the early empires in Egypt and Sumeria came both written law and mechanisms of enforcement. These ideas were later refined, first by Athens and later within the Roman Empire. Unfortunately, the coming of the Dark Ages all but obliterated the developments in law and enforcement.

As society embraced the Renaissance, the idea of law once more emerged. Within France, the concept of professional law enforcement developed rapidly. As far back as the Dark Ages, the French had created the prototype of both city and rural policing. It was not until the reign of Louis XIV, however, that policing took a giant leap forward. The appointment of La Reynie as lieutenant of police of Paris marked the largest single advancement in law enforcement at that time. The development of the Paris police from the time of La Reynie through the era of Napoleon and his minister of police, Joseph Fouché, was impressive. These men, and all that came between, elevated the French police to a standard of excellence that is maintained today.

The British experience followed that of the French. The English, always fearful of a standing military force within their country, resisted all attempts at the creation of an organized police force. The first proponents of such a force, DeVeil, the Fieldings, and other magistrates at Bow Street, succeeded in creating small detective forces and managed to lay the foundation for later developments. It was left to Sir Robert Peel, with the prestige of the Duke of Wellington, to create a professional police organization. Although this was the last European nation to create such a force, it was based on such sound principles of management that Scotland Yard eventually became a model for other nations to follow.

DISCUSSION QUESTIONS

1. Describe the contributions of Solon.

2. Discuss the accomplishments of Nicolas-Gabriel de La Reynie.

3. What social conditions were addressed by de La Reynie that helped in the prevention of crime?

4. What aspects of criminal investigation were developed by the French police?

5. Identify the contributions of Alphonse Bertillon.

6. What were the weaknesses in the French police system prior to and immediately following the French Revolution?

7. What impact did the Fourth Lateran Council have on criminal procedure?

8. Identify the men who made Bow Street famous as a seat of justice. Describe the contributions of the Bow Street magistrates to English law.

9. Discuss the police reforms of Sir Robert Peel.

10. Compare the development of the British police with that of French police. What factors can be attributed to the evolutionary differences in both the style and substance of these two organizations?

NOTES/REFERENCES

1. Samuel Noah Kramer, *The Sumerians: Their History, Culture, and Character* (Chicago: The University of Chicago Press, 1963), p. 295.

2. Sir E. A. Wallace Budge, *Babylonian Life and History,* 2nd ed. (London: The Religious Tract Society, 1925), pp. 21-22.

3. Budge, p. 34.

4. Donald O. Schultz and Erik Beckman, *Principles of American Law Enforcement and Criminal Justice,* 2nd (rev.) ed. (Sacramento, Calif.: Custom Publishing Company, 1987), pp. 1-2.

5. James Henry Breasted, *The Conquest of Civilization,* rev. ed. (New York: Harper & Brothers, 1954), p. 67.

6. Carol Trojan, "Egypt: Evolution of a Modern Police State." in *CJ International,* Vol. 2, No. 1, Jan.-Feb. 1986, p. 15.

7. John A. Wilson, *The Culture of Ancient Egypt* (Chicago: The University of Chicago Press, 1951), pp. 237-239.

8. Trojan, p. 15.

9. Sir J. Gardner Wilkinson, *A Popular Account of the Ancient Egyptians* (New York: Harper & Brothers, undated), pp. 201-202.

10. Whether the Ten Commandments were a gift from God or a set of guidelines developed to simplify the learning of the Hebrew law is a debate best left to religious scholars and historians.

11. Herbert A. Johnson, *History of Criminal Justice* (Cincinnati, Ohio: Anderson Publishing Co., 1988), pp. 50-51.

12. Robert Flaceliere, *Daily Life in Greece at the Time of Pericles,* translated by Peter Green (New York: The Macmillan Company, 1965), p. 226.

13. Plutarch, *The Lives of the Noble Grecians and Romans,* The Dryden Translation (Chicago: Encyclopaedia Britannica, Inc., Great Books of the Western World, 1952), p. 70.

14. Wallace K. Ferguson and Geoffrey Bruun, *Ancient Times to 1520,* 4th ed. (Boston: Houghton Mifflin Company, 1969), pp. 28-29.

15. Flaceliere, p. 47.

16. Isaac Asimov, *The Greeks: A Great Adventure* (Boston: Houghton Mifflin Company, 1965), p. 76.

17. René David and John E. C. Brierly, *Major Legal Systems in the World Today,* 2nd ed. (New York: The Free Press, 1978), pp. 34-35.

18. David and Brierly, p. 35.

19. David and Brierly, p. 36.

20. Johnson, pp. 23-24.

21. John Henry Merryman, *The Civil Law Tradition* (Stanford, Calif.: Stanford University Press, 1969), pp. 11-12.

22. Merryman, p. 12.

23. Philip John Stead, *The Police of France* (New York: Macmillan Publishing Company, 1983), p. 13.

24. Schultz and Beckman, p. 5.

25. Merryman, p. 13.

26. Stead, p. 12.

27. Johnson, p. 61.

28. René David, *French Law,* translated by Michael Kindred (Baton Rouge, La.: Louisiana State University Press, 1972), p. 11.

29. Stead, pp. 14–15.

30. David Maland, *Culture and Society in Seventeenth Century France* (New York: Charles Scribner's Sons, 1970), p. 247.

31. Stead, p. 15.

32. Stead, p. 16.

33. Frances Mossiker, *The Affair of the Poisons* (New York: Alfred A. Knopf, 1969), p. 156.

34. Nancy Mitford, *The Sun King* (New York: Harper & Row, Inc., 1966), p. 84.

35. Stead, pp. 19–21.

36. Stead, pp. 21–22.

37. Stead, p. 24.

38. Jacques Godechot, *The Taking of the Bastille: July 14th, 1789,* translated by Jean Stewart (New York: Charles Scribner's Sons, 1970), p. 70.

39. Godechot, pp. 78–79.

40. Godechot, p. 72.

41. Stead, p. 31.

42. Merryman, p. 16.

43. David, p. 8.

44. Merryman, p. 17.

45. Stead, pp. 34–35.

46. Stead, p. 41–48.

47. Stead, p. 60.

48. Henri Souchon, "Bertillon," in *Pioneers in Policing,* Philip John Stead, Ed. (Montclair, N.J.: Patterson Smith Publishing Corp., 1977).

49. Stead, Philip John, *The Police of Britain* (London: Macmillan Publishers Ltd., 1985), p. 20.

50. Stead, 1985, p. 20.

51. Robert Hughes, *The Fatal Shore* (New York: Vintage Books, 1988), p. 26.

52. Stead, 1985, p. 25.

53. Stead, 1985, p. 28

54. Hughes, p. 28.

55. Hughes, p. 28.

56. Hughes, p. 29.

57. Sir Basil Thomson, *The Story of Scotland Yard* (Garden City, N.Y.: Country Life Press, 1936), p. 65.

58. Stead, 1985, p. 34.

59. Stead, 1985, p. 35.

60. Thomson, p. 66.

61. Thomson, p. 69.

62. Thomson, p. 69.

63. Thomson, p. 70.
64. Schultz and Beckman, p. 26.
65. Thomson, p. 77.
66. Stead, 1985, p. 40.
67. Stead, 1985, p. 39.
68. Stead, 1985, p. 44.
69. Thomson, pp. 108–112.
70. Stead, 1983, p. 64.

Chapter 2

The Evolution of Law Enforcement in the United States

Key Terms

Inquisition
Code of eighty laws
Dale's laws
Colonial punishment
Chesapeake sheriff
Rattle watch
Slave patrols
Metropolitan Police Bill
Texas Rangers

Alcalde
IACP
Wickersham Report
August Vollmer
O. W. Wilson
J. Edgar Hoover
Task Force Reports
Law Enforcement Assistance
    Administration

Chapter Objectives

At the conclusion of this chapter, students should be able to:

1. Identify the contributions to American law enforcement by earlier societies.

2. Demonstrate an understanding of the development of policing in the colonial era.

3. Identify the factors leading to the varied development of law enforcement throughout the United States.

4. Demonstrate an understanding of the development of the modern American police.

INTRODUCTION

It is commonly believed that policing in the United States descended directly from the British with little or no input from other cultures. If this were true, it would make understanding American law enforcement much easier. Unfortunately, such is not the case. A number of cultures have made large contributions to the American police tradition.

It is even difficult to identify the first American law enforcement organization, if that is important. Discovery and study of the initial American police agency is meaningful if all other agencies descended from and copied that one organization. Such was not the case. It appears that law enforcement developed in a variety of settings as the need arose, with little influence from existing organizations. Police evolution in the United States, therefore, was a parallel process rather than a systematic one. This means that identifying the first police agency is more a matter of historical trivia than historic significance.

The development of the American police is tied directly to the sociopolitical development of the nation as a whole. There appear to be four nations that provided the major contributions: the Spanish, Dutch, British, and French. Within these nationalities are also found subgroups. For example, the contributions of the Puritans in New England are different from contributions of the Royalist English, the Cavaliers, of the deep south. Law enforcement developed parallel to the needs and desires of the various groups in different parts of the country. In this chapter we undertake the arduous task of tracing these diverse but converging forces of culture, to develop an understanding of why the American police are the way they are.

THE EARLIEST SYSTEMS

Strange as it may seem, the first system of justice was not in North America but in Central America. At the time of the discovery of the West Indies by Columbus, the land we now called Mexico had a justice system the equal of anything in the world. In many respects the Aztec judicial system was vastly superior to many European systems. This was certainly true concerning the nation that conquered this proud people. It can be stated unequivocally that Spain, which probably had the worst legal system in Europe, ruined the Aztec legal system. I might add that this is hardly a controversial statement; the Spanish annihilated the entire Aztec culture.

The Aztecs

In the year 1519, the Spaniards arrived in Mexico. They brought with them one of the most confused and brutal legal systems yet devised. Although at the pinnacle of her glory, Spain was held tightly in the grip of three different legal traditions.

The primary legal influence was that of the Roman code of Justinian. The second tradition was Islamic law. The third legal power was the Roman Catholic Church through its canon law. The almost overwhelming influence of the two religious legal systems served to transform the more moderate Roman law. As a result, the Spanish Church was allowed to run rampant in search of heresy.

The *Inquisition* was not originally a product of the Spanish. Beginning in the thirteenth century, the Roman Catholic Church initiated this process to counter what appeared to be waves of heresy sweeping Europe. The criminal process involved was based on secret testimony and confession, frequently induced by torture. Punishments ranged from fines to life imprisonment to death by fire. To some degree all of Europe was exposed to this process.

In Spain, however, the Inquisition attained power unmatched by any other nation. It reached its peak under King Ferdinand and Queen Isabella, between 1420 and 1498. The Inquisition survived in Spain in some form until well into the nineteenth century. This somewhat dubious legal process was therefore at full power when it was dropped unceremoniously on the unsuspecting people of the Aztec nation.

What the Spanish found on their arrival in Mexico was a highly developed culture. Most of Middle America was under the control of the powerful Mexica tribe, from whom the country was eventually named. In each Aztec town there were judges *(teuctli),* one for each clan, which elected him for a period of one year. These judges ruled on minor civil and criminal matters. For serious crimes, they gave some limited instructions to the higher court. In addition, these judges were responsible for apprehending delinquents and sending them to Tenochtitlan for further trial and sentencing. They also reported periodically to their superior, the *tlacatecatl,* on all cases passing through their courts. The major function of the teuctli was to keep minor cases out of the major courts. They routinely handled each case within one or two days.

Each clan also had its own inspectors *(centectlalixque)* who watched over the family's conduct. They were empowered to detain individuals in order to recite moral speeches to the wrongdoer. The higher court, the *teccali,* met in continuous session in Tenochtitlan (present site of Mexico City) in a room in the palace called the Teccali, from which it took its name. The senators and other learned men lived in this place to hear litigation and petitions placed before them by the populace. The cases were heard, put into writing, and judged. In criminal cases, sentencing was the responsibility of the next highest council, the *tlacxitlan.*[1]

The teccali court had three members: the president *(tlacatecatl)* and two assistant judges (the *cuauhnochtli* and the *tlailotlac).* Each of these judges had a number of assistants to aid them in their duties. These included a sheriff *(achcautli),* a scribe *(amatlacuilco),* a messenger policeman *(topilli),* and criers *(tecpoyotl).* Each principal Aztec city had a teccali court. They could hear original cases or appeals from the lower teuctli court.

The supreme court or court of appeals, called *tlacxitlan,* sat under the presidency of the *cihuacoatl,* who was second only to the emperor. This court heard appeals from the teccali courts and occasionally heard an original case involving affairs of state. There was no appeal from this court, not even to the emperor himself. Occasionally, however, when a case was very difficult or sensitive, this court might refer it directly to the emperor for a decision.

The emperor was the supreme justice, but he did not sit alone to hear cases. He was aided by 13 men of high principles and qualifications. The emperor's court met every 10 to 12 days, where they reviewed lower court decisions and decided cases put before them.

Consistency in the legal process was aided by another procedure, the extraordinary court, called the tribunal of the eighty days *(nauhpohualltlatolli)*. This court met in Tenochtitlan every 80 days and all judges were required to attend. The session lasted 10 to 12 days, during which all cases and decisions were discussed. If there were difficult cases pending, this court heard it and rendered a decision. It is noteworthy that no case took longer than 80 days, unless it was so complex that justice required a longer time period.

Not all cases went through the courts described above. The merchants had their own tribunal (the *pochtecatecuhtin*), which legislated and decided cases concerning commerce and conflicts between merchants. The nobility were judged either in the Tlacxitlan or by a board of nobles *(tecpilcalli)* that oversaw high military functionaries and ruled on all military courts martial.[2]

Some historians say that the rulers of Tenochtitlan submitted the difficult cases to the courts of Texcoco (a city approximately 50 miles northeast of Tenochtitlan), because of their reputation for efficiency and fairness. The great Aztec ruler, Nezahyalcoyotl of Texcoco, was noted for his *code of eighty laws,* and Texcoco judges were known for their wisdom and impartiality.[3]

The judges sat all day, from around 8:00 in the morning, with a little more than an hour for lunch. They sat on special mat-covered seats and listened to evidence. All witnesses took an oath to tell the truth. Evidence had to be rational and honest, offered by confession, documents, testimony by witnesses, and cross-examination. Torture was never used. Perjury was a capital offense, but lying seems not to have been a problem in the Aztec courts. The civil government was intertwined with the Aztec church. A deeply religious people of uncommon discipline, few who went before the court would dream of defying both the civil and religious authorities. They believed that to do so would bring massive retribution from the gods.[4]

Lawyers did not exist in ancient Mexico; only the judge was allowed to mediate between the defendant and his gods. In fact, interference or trickery in a trial was punishable with burning off the hair or public strangulation. An insulting or sarcastic remark in court was thought extremely rude, and the offender would be severely admonished. The judge desired to get at the truth without confusing factors. Oratory for oratory's sake was rarely attempted. A defendant might try evasion, but direct examination by the judge quickly forced him into straightforward testimony.[5]

The principal base of Aztec law was custom. A militant people, many of the laws read like articles of war. The death penalty was frequently given for a wide array of crimes. Religion also played a major part in their legal system. The Aztecs led a spartan life, believing that conspicuous wealth or too much happiness would bring the wrath of a jealous deity. This philosophy led to a fatalistic view of the world. There was no pity for the wrong-doer. Instead, it was believed that the crime and punishment were fore-ordained. The victim of the system did nothing to avoid his fate, believing that he was helpless before the gods.

The concept of lex talionis did not apply in Aztec law. Citizens were not allowed to take the law into their own hands. The severity and certainty of the law made that unnecessary. Punishment was swift and barbarous. Death was sometimes administered by tying the condemned hand and foot, after which his head would be bashed with a large heavy stone until the skull was crushed. Others were strangled with garrotes. Occasionally, they burned a male adulterer alive and hanged the woman. Sometimes the adulterer was stoned to death in the town square. To protect the reputation of the nobility, they would, when capital punishment was required, secretly take the condemned from his home at night and drown him. The features and limbs of traitors were cut off; others were sacrificed or disemboweled, with the cavity stuffed with ashes. Minor punishments included enslavement, removal from office, banishment, destruction of property, amputation of limbs, mutilation of features, confiscation of property, restitution, forced labor, enclosure in a wooden cage, shearing of the hair, and deprivation of employment.

Aztec prisons consisted of small cages for minor offenders and larger, stronger cages for prisoners of war or those awaiting execution. Escapees seemed to have been no serious problem. Spanish observers noted that all that was really necessary to imprison an Aztec was to draw a line around the prisoner and order him to stay there. Such was the strength of the Aztec educational, political, and legal system; such was their discipline.[6]

The Spanish West

The entry of the Spanish into Mexico signaled the doom of the Aztec culture. The primary cause of the decimation of the Aztecs was biological. By the year 1650, six-sevenths of the Indian population was dead. The Spaniards introduced smallpox, typhoid fever, and measles. The introduction of slaves from Africa also brought malaria and yellow fever. The natives, having no natural immunities to these diseases, were subjected to one plague after another. They were simply unable to fight off the onslaught of deadly viruses.

Aztec measures that would have mitigated the degree of devastation caused by the plagues were nullified by the Spanish conquerors. The Spanish insisted that the natives gather in towns and cities, where they would be better subjected to religious and political training, as well as more easily exploited as a work force. This grouping of the natives increased the intensity of the plagues.

The Spanish priests contributed to the final destruction of the natives by placing religious sanctions against bathing. The Spanish, who associated bathing with the pagan rites of the ancient Mediterranean, fought hard to stop this practice among the natives. Thus, cleanliness, one more defense against disease, was eliminated. Finally, the Inquisition, took its toll. Natives that did not accept Christianity were burned at the stake for heresy.[7]

The Spanish contribution to the law was one of brutal self-interest. The new rulers held total control of the industries and cities. They allowed a certain amount of self-government in the smaller outlying communities. The greatest change, however, was in the philosophy of life. The Aztecs lived their religion; everything and everyone had a purpose. The Spanish took that away and made the natives strangers in their own land.

The legal system that eventually emerged in Mexico was a variation of the Napoleonic Code, similar in outward appearance to that of France but lacking the historical foundation that made the French system successful. Dictator law, enforced by military rulers and local warlords and enmeshed in bribery and preferential treatment, became the underpinning for Mexican justice; class and racial conflict, the driving force for social development.

It was this system, French in outward appearance but thoroughly altered to the conditions of New Spain, that made its way into the west and southwestern portion of North America. It was also this system that shaped the future legal structure of this area after the arrival of the Anglo settlers some 300 years later.

Colonial America

Much of the law enforcement in the colonies was accomplished by military elements. In fact, many militia units were created for a dual role. The first was that of protection from organized enemies, such as Indians and hostile military units. The second purpose was law enforcement. Many communities maintained a militia for law enforcement long after police agencies had been created in other communities. Fort Ponchetrain (Detroit), for example, existed under martial law for the first 100 years of its existence. New Orleans left law enforcement in the hands of the military for 85 years before creating an organized police force. In Cincinnati, soldiers from Fort Washington provided such protection for a long period of time. Such was also the case in many other American communities.[8]

The move from martial law to an organized civil police force was not a smooth transition. Using the military as a police force made a great deal of sense to many colonists. The soldiers were there for protection and paying another unit to enforce the law seemed to be a needless and expensive duplication of effort. Change became necessary when communities grew and became too complex to be handled by anything but a full-time police organization.

Jamestown.   The first English settlers on the eastern shore of North America were ill suited for survival. This group of 600 men, women, and children left England for the new colony in 1609. Almost destroyed by a harsh winter, the colonists faced almost certain extinction. They survived by a supreme force of will and by creating a set of laws, necessary for the situation, but incredibly harsh by English standards.

The laws, called *Dale's laws,* were officially titled *Laws Divine, Moral and Martial.* The law was rigid and enforced ruthlessly. In 1612, when several colonists attempted to escape from Virginia in stolen boats, they were shot, hanged, or broken on the wheel, according to their degree of guilt. Rigid though they were, these laws provided two crucial elements for survival. They prevented the subversion of the colony and gave the settlers a government of laws.[9]

Boston.   The Puritans brought the idea of religious law to the colonies. They believed that there was a fundamental law of God that transcended any human-made legal code. Their idea was to create a "Bible commonwealth." Within the confines of this dominion there was no room for "outside" ideas.

Ultimately, Puritanism failed as a government, leaving in its wake a legacy of both political intolerance and high intellectual development.[10] Like it or not, however, the Puritan philosophy is permanently stamped into the American psyche. For many generations after the end of Puritan rule, the rigid moralism that marked this group's philosophy would permeate all aspects of law and its enforcement. An example of Puritan law can be seen in the following examples of punishment in early Boston:

1639:   Edward Palmer, a carpenter, was commissioned to build stocks for the city of Boston. When finished, he presented his bill to city officials, who thought it to be exorbitant and proceeded to fine him 5 pounds and lock him in his own device.

1649:   Margaret Jones was hanged for witchcraft when it was reported that "a little child was seen to run from her."

1650:   The wearing of "great boots" and other such extravagant articles of dress was forbidden unless the wearer was worth 200 pounds.

1650:   Oliver Holmes was whipped for being a Baptist.[11]

Justice was harsh in the colonies. The idea that an accused should be considered innocent until proven guilty had not yet appeared in this part of the world. Accusation was usually tantamount to conviction: if not in court, then certainly in the eyes of the other citizens. Conviction, of course, always meant punishment, and usually in a painful form. In addition, the colonial laws extended well beyond the usual ban on murder, rape, and robbery into other forms of behavior. Offensive conduct such as gossiping, name calling, mockery, and taunting were also subject to criminal sanctions.

Frequently, a person was accused in secret, tried, convicted, and publicly punished in one day. The punishments were deliberately harsh because the colonists believed that this would deter crime. If they did not deter crime, they certainly limited the person's ability to commit many offenses; the likelihood of surviving frequent brushes with colonial justice was low.[12]

A wide variety of *colonial punishments* could be inflicted by judges on those unfortunate enough to appear before the court. A person could be sentenced to the *bilboes,* a device that locked a person's legs to an iron bar in such a manner that he could not move. Two days in the bilboes for swearing was common.

The most ignoble of devices, usually reserved for gossiping housewives and drunken sailors, was the *ducking stool.* Designed much like a large modern teeter-totter, this device was stationed next to a river or lake into which a person strapped into the seat could be submerged as many times as the sentence called for.

In New England, even before the first public building was completed, the *stocks* were built. This device was a low wooden bench with leg holes in which prisoners were secured. It was the duty of each and every person passing by the prisoner to chastise him for his sins.

The *pillory,* or "stretch-neck," was an upright hinged board with a hole in which a person's head was locked. In the early years of its use, the prisoner's ears were nailed to either side of the head hold. The prisoner was thus forced to stand in an upright position for hours. People caught working on the Sabbath could look forward to spending their next workday in the pillory.

The *brank,* sometimes called the "social bridle," was a heavy iron cage that covered the prisoner's entire head. It often had an iron tongue which was placed in the prisoner's mouth to prevent conversation. This device was normally used on paupers, blasphemers, and insubordinate housewives.[13]

Law enforcement in Boston originated on April 12, 1631, when the Boston court ordered that "watches" be established at sunset. This was the creation of the first night watch in America. The original watch consisted of six men and one officer. It was set up much like a military guard.

The position of constable was created in 1634, with William Chesebrough assigned to that post. A minor alteration in the watch took place on February 27, 1636, when it was designated a town watch to be staffed by citizens rather than soldiers. These men were appointed by the town government. The early watches were unpaid and would remain so until 1712. The watch system, however, remained generally unchanged for almost 200 years.

Chesapeake. The Chesapeake Bay area was settled by people who wished to recreate their own England. The old English hundred was designated as the key local unit. Originally, law enforcement was in the hands of a provost-marshal, a military official (the earliest Maryland settlement was considered a military outpost). By 1632, however, this office was replaced by the sheriff, referred to as the Chesapeake sheriff, whose duties were very close to that of the English sheriff. He served warrants, made arrests, and collected taxes, dues, and fees owed the governor. His salary consisted of 10 percent of the moneys he collected. Initially, the sheriff was chosen by the county court from among three men recommended by the governor. Later, in 1645, he was picked from among eight members of the county court, with the post rotating annually to a new member. The position became a financial reward for magistrates, who were otherwise unpaid.

The magistrates worked out of county courts, also patterned after the British. Appointed by the governor, the magistrates were required to travel their districts and dispense justice. The officers of the court were the sheriffs, constables, clerks, and coroners.[14]

New York.   The area now known as New York was originally settled by the Dutch West India Company, who named it New Netherlands. Law enforcement was first put into the hands of a *schout fiscal*, a position encompassing both the duties of sheriff and attorney general. The first such officer was Hendrick Van Dyck. His duties included enforcing all rules and regulations of the governor (called the *states general* in this community). In addition, he acted as a check on the excesses of the other officials.[15]

In 1643, as the population of New Netherlands grew, the Dutch government created the *burgher watch* to assist the schout fiscal enforce the laws. So that people would be encouraged to obey the law, a *gibbit* (whipping post) was installed on the waterfront, on which violators were spread-eagled, beaten, and displayed for all to see.

In 1652, a settlement on Manhattan Island was incorporated and named Nieuw Amsterdam (New York City). That same year the *rattel wacht* (*rattle watch*) was formed. This unit was made up of citizens equipped with rattles for summoning assistance. The watch was a sentinel-type organization with the citizens assigned to fixed posts. In 1658, the first paid law enforcement unit was created when eight paid watchmen took over the responsibilities from the nonpaid citizens.

In 1664, the British took over Nieuw Amsterdam and changed the name to New York. Dutch and British culture blended, resulting in the creation of the position of high constable to take command of the watch. The first high constable of New York City was Obe Hendrick.

Few changes occurred over the following three decades. In 1693, however, the first uniformed officer was appointed. The mayor, Isaac De Reimer, selected a 12-man watch to secure the city. At the time, New York City had 5000 inhabitants. Thirty-eight years later (1731) the first precinct station, called a watch house, was built.[16]

POSTREVOLUTIONARY DEVELOPMENTS

At the close of the American Revolution, the new nation found itself separated from the stability of a mother country. It was also experiencing tremendous growth. The rules and political systems that had sustained the colonies were insufficient for an evolving society with its ever-increasing complexity. Still, the police remained primarily as they had been. Other institutions might change, but the police would see only minor alterations for the next 50 or so years.

The only real divergence would occur between north and south, where social developments would cause the emphasis of the police to focus on different problems. Westward expansion would also bring the Spanish influence into the legal system as American settlers merged with the Spanish culture already developing in the southwest and west.

A look at three cities will provide us with some understanding of the forces at work during this time period. The cities of Charleston, New York, and Houston are reasonably representative of the divergent styles of law enforcement between the Revolutionary War and the Civil War.

Charleston

The city of Charleston, South Carolina, was incorporated in 1783. This date is somewhat misleading, since the colony of Charles Town had been one of the oldest in the nation. In fact, Charleston was one of the foremost harbors and centers for mercantile prior to and during the Revolutionary War. More battles were fought between the colonists and British on South Carolina soil than in any other state. Charleston, considered crucial to both sides, was at the heart of that war.

Despite its age, little is known of the Charleston police prior to 1805. There were undoubtedly constables. We know that much from the old city ordinances that proclaim that such officers were subject to the call of the intendant in case of tumultuous riots.

In 1805, an ordinance was passed arranging for the election of a constable from the different wards. This office was paid no salary but collected a portion of fines and fees resulting from their activities. Both the badge and weapon of office was a stave.

By 1806, the city guard was established. This unit had a captain and two lieutenants as elected officers. In addition, it had an unknown number of sergeants, privates, fifers, and drummers. The guard was uniformed at the expense of the city. Each member wore a short jacket, the sergeants were supplied with swords, and each private had a musket, bayonet, cartouche-box (cartridge case), and rattle. Any citizen called upon to assist a member of the guard was required to do so or face a fine ranging from $25 to $50.

In 1807, the office of city marshall was created. This person was also given the authority to hire deputies. His salary was $250 per year and a portion of the fines he collected. The city guards and city marshal continued to operate more or less as described above until the marshal was abolished in 1846 and the guards were changed to the city police. In 1852, the police was reorganized into a chief, two captains, six lieutenants, four orderly sergeants, four street sergeants, and 150 privates. They were called "Paddy Miles Bull Dogs" in honor of the Charleston mayor, William Porcher Miles.[17]

In addition to the Charleston police, there were also the *slave patrols*. All southern cities had such organizations, which is evidence of the deep fear that white southerners had of slave rebellion. In the year 1830, Charleston was a city of 30,289, of which 17,461 were black. Everything from architecture through law was affected by an increasing paranoia of a slave revolt. Buildings were designed for security from assault. The courts were severe in punishing slaves for behavior considered minor when the culprit was white. The police, more highly developed than in most southern cities, were in place primarily to control the slaves.[18]

New York

Policing postrevolutionary New York was mainly a larger version of colonial New York. Two factors would converge to alter this structure. First, New York was experiencing a large population boom. Second, while the southern part of the nation was locked into a slave-based rural economy, the northeast was rapidly emerging as the industrial center of the nation. This emphasis on industry was one of the reasons for the population growth. The urban life-style also called for a different style of policing, one with an accent on the protection of personal property.

Two other social factors also speeded up renovation of the New York police. The practice of dueling, introduced by French officers, became a frequent event, especially among the prominent members of the upper class. This was looked upon with horror by the other members of New York society, but the legal system had no effective means to address the problem.

The second factor was the frequent riots that plagued New York in the years immediately following the Revolution. Typical of such events was the *doctor's riot,* which took place in 1788. This disorder was directed against physicians using dead bodies for experimental purposes. To bring a return to order required the calling out of the militia. This was not the only such mob action. In 1791, a mob of some 30 foreign sailors attacked the city watch with clubs. In 1793, another mob attacked and destroyed two brothels. A similar incident in 1799 once more required the militia to be called upon.[19]

Additionally, a succession of spectacular murder cases caught the public's attention. Most notable of these was the disappearance and subsequent murder of Juliana Elmore Sands, whose body was found in a well of the Manhattan Company.

It was obvious that a better organizational structure was needed for the police. The concept that emerged during this time period was multiple organizations with specific duties. The position of high sheriff was created, with a number of under-sheriffs assigned to this office. There remained the high constable with his 16 elected constables. There was also the city marshall with his deputy marshals (appointed by and working for the mayor) and, of course, the city watch.

The sheriffs, constables, and marshals were responsible for apprehending offenders during the daylight hours, while the watch was responsible for security at night. The titular head of the city's police force was the high constable, who was responsible for bringing suits on behalf of the city until 1801.[20]

Around the turn of the century, three important steps were taken to strengthen police administration. The first was in 1798, when a state law was passed establishing a police office for New York. Along with this office came the two special police justices, whose duties included the dismissal of the city watch each morning and an examination of the facts surrounding any arrest made the previous evening.

The second step was the adoption in 1800 by the common council of regulations for the "better government of the watch." These regulations created a personnel system and required that captains of the watch keep regular records of watch activities.

The third development occurred in 1801 when the council passed an ordinance for the appointment of a person to take responsibility for law enforcement and regulation in the city. The high constable was appointed to this office, which was virtually that of police commissioner. By this time the watch consisted of 72 men.[21]

Law enforcement in New York City continued in this fashion until 1845, when the watch was disbanded. In its place was created the New York municipal police. While structured along lines that were similar in outward appearance to those of the London metropolitan police, there were significant differences. Initially, the New York officers did not wear uniforms, relying instead on a simple copper badge mounted on a circle of leather. It was from this symbol of authority that the public coined the term "copper" to identify a police officer. The police resisted uniforms because they believed it gave them the appearance of being subservient, a connotation they strenuously opposed.

Additionally, the New York police were subject to the spoils system in American politics. Their London counterparts were well into a form of civil service, with selection based on competence and qualifications. The New York officers were selected through political patronage. This meant that not only were the officers expected to be subservient to the politicians, but when their party lost an election, the police officers were out of a job as well. The new administration brought in its own hand-picked officers. This had some interesting effects on policing. Officers tended to be selected to work their own neighborhoods; thus they were seen as old friends rather than impartial officials. This was expected; since the officers represented the political party in power, it was only natural that they equally represent the party's interests in the neighborhoods. The idea of the political machine was based on grassroots political support, requiring intense contact between all elements of government and the electorate. The police were expected to play a major role in maintaining the political power base. This notion was alien to the theory of the London police.

It should be noted, however, that the results were not all bad. New York politics was based on cultural rather than class lines. The neighborhoods were mostly immigrant or nonimmigrant. Neighborhood policing meant that the Irish wards were policed by Irish police, Germans were policed by Germans, and upper- and middle-class native New Yorkers were policed by native white officers. While the police administration was too obviously under political control to be trusted by the populace, the officers on the beat were very much accepted and trusted. This led to a degree of decentralization in policing radically different from the highly centralized London police.

It also led to attempts to provide for a more professional means of administering, or overseeing the police. Believing, with some justification, that the police were subjected to too much of a corruptive influence by the city governments, states began to experiment with police boards. These organizations, made up of selected businessmen, were designed to review police operations. The intent was to protect the police from the harmful influences of city political machines. They were supposed to be a means by which state government could protect the citizens of the larger urban areas.

The closest an American community has come to having a London-style police force occurred in 1857 when the New York state legislature proclaimed that the city of New York was too corrupt to govern itself. The state, in effect, seized the New York city police. The law accomplishing this was the *Metropolitan Police Bill.* This created a police force answerable to a police board formed by the governor.

The New York mayor, Fernando Wood, promptly formed his own police force, one loyal to him. The result was inevitable. The two forces, the mayor's police and the state-appointed metropolitan police, clashed in what has been called the *police riots.* The Mets, as the state police were called, won the battle and gained control of the city, a control they would hold for 13 years.

The concept of state control spread. By 1866, a number of major cities had adopted one or another version of the New York Plan. Baltimore in 1860, St. Louis and Chicago in 1861, Kansas City, Missouri in 1862, Detroit in 1865, and Cleveland in 1866 all placed their police forces under state control. It was a sign of the times, an experiment in police administration—one that for most cities was short-lived.[22]

Texas

Between the American Revolutionary War and the Civil War, law enforcement also emerged on the frontier. The first experiment in state policing emerged during this time period. Although the force was not American in origin, it was designed by American immigrants to the Mexican state called Texas. This first force was the *Texas Rangers.*

This force was created in 1823 by Stephen F. Austin to protect outlying settlers from marauding bandits and Indians. The name "Rangers" came from their assigned duties. They were to range the frontier and guard against unwelcome intruders. On the eve of the Texas War for Independence, the Rangers formally adopted the title of Texas Rangers. They also grew to a force of 25 men.

When Texas became a state in 1845, the Texas Rangers officially became the first state police organization. This force, which in a short period of time became legendary, frequently disdained the niceties of the court system. Thieves, rapists, and killers might be hanged at the first available tree or sometimes simply shot where they were caught. All in all, however, the Rangers brought a certain amount of law and order to an untamed frontier.

Selection to this force was not as scientific as in modern police organizations. Prospective rangers were asked three questions: Can you shoot? Can you ride? Can you cook? Three affirmative answers all but assured acceptance to the Rangers. It might also be noted that the applicants were usually large, tough, and not afraid of fist fights.[23]

Although not the first frontier settlement to initiate a police force (St. Louis instituted such a force in 1808, further expanding and modifying it in 1818),[24] Houston owed its beginning to the Spanish influence. In 1832, prior to the founding of Houston, John W. Moore, an Anglo settler, was appointed alcalde of the Eastern Province of Texas. This position, part sheriff and part justice of the peace, provided no additional manpower. The settlers were responsible for apprehending criminals in their own settlements. The alcalde and a judge would be called in to handle the trial and decree a punishment

In 1836, the Texas army defeated the Mexican army at San Jacinto. Law enforcement would take on a more Anglo-American flavor. The city of Houston was founded that same year, one of the most successful promotional hoaxes ever conceived. Augustus C. and John K. Allen bought a block of land from a Mrs. Elizabeth E. Parret and thus founded the city, naming it after Texas hero, Sam Houston. With no buildings and only a single tent housing a saloon, the brothers convinced the fledgling legislature to name the town the temporary center of government for the republic of Texas. On that basis they were able to obtain loans and promote the new town in eastern newspapers. Settlers flocked to the new settlement expecting to find a fully developed city. Instead, they found empty land marked by stakes showing where the town should be.

Elections held in the fall of 1836 inserted John W. Moore as the first sheriff of newly constituted Harrisburg County (later renamed Harris County). In 1837, law enforcement began in Houston itself when President Sam Houston appointed a committee of influential citizens to form the citizens into a patrol for procuring order. This citizens patrol had no leader but answered to the sheriff. That same year articles of incorporation were approved for Houston, giving the town the authority to pass laws and collect taxes.

As a frontier community, Houston rivaled the worst of the western towns. The city was beset with flagrant drunkenness, gambling, prostitution, counterfeiting, and violent death. The noted naturalist James Audubon reported witnessing drunken Indians hallooing in the muddy Houston streets.

The conditions called for the construction of a jail. What happened might have been comical were it not for the seriousness of the problem. The jail was completed in March 1838. It was in operation barely for a month when the city of

Houston sued the county commissioners to remove the jail because it was a public nuisance. An example of the problem as well as of frontier legal reasoning can be seen in the case of a gambler named Quick.

The Quick Case

Quick had been convicted and sentenced to a term in jail. His attorneys, after several unsuccessful appeals, argued that their client should be released due to the condition of the jail. They argued, accurately, that the security was so poor that inmates had to be chained to prevent escapes. They also noted that the jail was very cold due to improper heating. All in all, they argued, the jail was an unfit place to hold a prisoner. Judge J. W. Robinson heard these complaints and then listened while Sheriff Moore verified them. This being the fact, Judge Robinson reversed his earlier verdict of imprisonment and, based on the documented poor condition of the jail, ordered Quick to be hanged. Sheriff Moore carried out the execution on the following Friday.[25]

The first paid city police position was established in 1840 when the city created the position of town marshal. Daniel Busley was the first town marshal. He appointed deputies from men he knew and attempted to enforce law in a town very similar to modern television's version of Dodge City. Horse thefts, barbwire cutting, dueling, and gunfights over gambling were common events. The marshal was also responsible for the collection of fees, fines, and taxes. The remarkable aspect of this position was that despite the potential for violence in early Houston, not one of the first three marshals found it necessary to shoot anyone.

As with other parts of the country, this system of law enforcement would remain relatively unchanged until after the Civil War. Law enforcement nationwide would not be the same afterward.

POST–CIVIL WAR REFORMS

The American Civil War had a pronounced impact on the power and structure of the American government. Earlier political debates had centered on states rights and to what degree the national government might be allowed to infringe on the states. States rights ended with the war. The new United States was a nation with a strong central government and greatly weakened, subservient states.

Law enforcement was also drastically altered. The southern states, economically and politically devastated at the end of the war, were placed under martial law. When the army turned the governments back over to civil authorities, the military structure of the police was retained. This was due to the structure imposed by the military and also because the southerners who became police officers were also recently separated from the Confederate army. As ex-military men it seemed only natural that the structure of the police should also be military.

The northern states did not escape this transformation. During the war, police personnel had to deal with an entirely new law enforcement problem. Espionage and antiwar activity in the north forced the police to ally themselves closely with the army (the draft riot that struck New York City in 1863 was the bloodiest riot in the history of the United States. In the three days of the riot, 1200 people were killed and 8000 injured). As a result, the northern cities began the transformation to a strict military style of police before the war was over. The result, for both north and south, was a vastly different police organization than had existed prior to the war.

The end of the war brought yet another transformation, the shift from rural political dominance to the power of the urban areas. Population in the cities boomed. Between 1860 and 1910 America's urban population increased by a multiple of 7. New York City alone jumped from 1 million inhabitants to 3 million. The structure of the institutions controlling this society was subjected to great internal pressures. They had to change, and change they did.

One of the first casualties was state control of the police. The idea behind state control had been to protect the police from political corruption. This had not worked well. Principally, the police had merely traded one form of corruption for another. Most state control of local police ended with the Civil War, although some states would reinstate it sometime later. In 1939, for example, Missouri passed a law returning the cities of St. Louis and Kansas City to state control.[26]

State control also ended because the political machines of the big cities found having a police force they could not control to be a menace. The true death knell for state control was sounded at the Democratic Convention in 1868, when the leaders called for home rule. This was not surprising, as most major urban centers were controlled by Democratic political machines. The precedence for the final end to state control was established in New York City by the prototype for corrupt politicians, Boss Tweed. Under his direction the police were systematically brought under the political manipulation of the Tweed machine, until they, like all other New York City institutions of government, became instruments of power to be wielded against any and all opponents of Tweed and his henchmen.

The Chiefs of Police

Policing became vastly more complex following the Civil War. The growth in the cities and the development of better transportation systems meant that criminals were beginning to become more mobile. The police, lacking modern vehicles or communications systems, recognized that they were fighting a losing battle.

In 1871, a man of vision, St. Louis Police Chief James McDonough, proposed that the police chiefs of the nation should meet and formulate a code of

Photograph 2–1 Boss Tweed

behavior and a plan for coordinating the fight against crime. Later that year, 112 of the nation's police chiefs met for the first time to discuss mutual problems. Although it was obvious that the chiefs needed a permanent organization to meet regularly, they were unable to agree upon a plan of implementation.

Twenty-two years after that historic first convention, the chief of police in Omaha, Nebraska, William S. Seavey, proposed a similar meeting in Chicago. Fifty-one chiefs attended and finally agreed to an organizational structure of a permanent nature. This organization was called the National Chiefs of Police Union. In 1902 this group changed its name to that which it still proudly bears, the *International Association of Chiefs of Police (IACP)*.

An Age of Experimentation

In attempting to find a suitable method for managing the police, law enforcement officials as well as other government leaders searched long and hard for the best approach. This was true not only of law enforcement, however, but of government itself. At no time in our history have so many different forms of government been proposed and tried. With each new attempt at the perfect form of government, new forms of corruption emerged, causing yet another experiment. The experience of the city of Cincinnati offers a prime example of this era:

1859:   Board of four commissioners appointed by the mayor, police judge, and city auditor.

1860:   Board abolished; chief of police appointed by the mayor.

1873:   Board of four commissioners popularly elected.

1874:   Control by mayor reestablished.

1877:   Board of five commissioners appointed by governor.

1880:   Control of mayor reestablished.

1885:   Board of three commissioners appointed by local board of public works.

1886:   Board of four commissioners appointed by governor.

1902:   Board of four commissioners appointed by mayor council.

In the nineteenth and early twentieth centuries, six major methods of controlling the police were undertaken: by popular elections, partisan administrative boards, state control, bipartisan administrative boards, commission-government plans, and single executive control. All but the last method, single executive control, proved largely unsuccessful.[27] Ultimately, it was this form of police administration that emerged as predominant. Such is the case still.

THE EMERGENCE OF THE MODERN POLICE

The first implication of professionalism in policing appeared with the late 1920s and emerged more pronounced in the 1930s. What makes this truly remarkable is the fact that this era was one of the most corrupt in American history. Organized crime achieved strides undreamed of by earlier criminals. The cause was prohibition, that noble experiment that not only failed but seriously jeopardized the political fabric of the nation's cities.

During this time, however, a handful of men, both dedicated and honest, emerged to lead law enforcement in a new direction. The nation owes these men a great debt. Among these were giants such as August Vollmer, O. W. Wilson, and J. Edgar Hoover.

The Wickersham Report

In 1931, the first exhaustive look at the American police was completed by the National Commission on Law Observance and Enforcement, commonly referred to as the Wickersham Commission. This commission published 14 volumes, the *Wickersham Report,* devoted to a complete and intricate examination of the nation's criminal justice system. What they discovered was not pretty to look at. The two reports devoted exclusively to the police provided a panorama of corruption, brutality, and incompetence.

Generally, the police had been found to be using third-degree methods (physical and psychological torture) to extract confessions from suspects, as well as the following:

1. Police corruption was widespread.
2. Police training was almost nonexistent.
3. Police communications were ineffective.
4. Political interference in police operations hampered honest enforcement efforts.
5. Police executives were often ill-suited to handle their jobs.

The Commission cited one example of a major city where the mayor had appointed his tailor to the position of chief of police. His reasoning was that the tailor had been a good tailor for 20 years, therefore, he would quite likely make a good police chief.[28]

Among the authors of this report, and especially notable among those prescribing recommendations for police reform, was *August Vollmer,* the chief of police for Berkeley, California.

August Vollmer

According to August Vollmer:

A policeman should typify the ideal American by his cheerful and kindly disposition; by his habits and industry, thoughtfulness, truthfulness, neatness and cleanliness; by his pride in rendering public service; by his earnest efforts to improve his knowledge; by his courteous treatment and sympathetic knowledge of human beings regardless of their stations in life; by his simple, democratic tastes, healthy interests and strength of character.[29]

August Vollmer, son of German immigrants, may well be the father of American policing. In 1904, at the age of 29, Vollmer was elected to the post of city marshal in Berkeley, California. This position was changed to chief of police in 1909, a post held by Vollmer until 1932.

During his tenure with Berkeley, August Vollmer created a police force that became the model for the rest of the nation. His innovations included radios in patrol cars, a fingerprint and handwriting classification system, a workable system for filing and using M.O. *(modus operandi)* files, the use of both motorcycles and bicycles on patrol, the use of the polygraph for lie detection, a scientific crime investigation laboratory, the selection of college graduates as police recruits, and the creation of a police school at his department in which scientists taught courses in criminalistics. He also encouraged colleges to offer police courses and urged the development of a record bureau in Washington, D.C., a bureau that eventually became the FBI. He firmly believed that police officers should be trained

Photograph 2-2   August Vollmer

professionals, capable of using the most current technology in the investigation of crime. He also believed that police officers were social workers who had a deeper responsibility to the community than just fighting crime. He urged his officers to intervene in the lives of individuals, especially juveniles, before they entered a life of crime.

A scholar as well as a police officer and administrator, Vollmer encouraged other police professionals to publish their observations and theories. Practicing what he preached, Vollmer wrote proliferously. His book, *The Police and Modern Society* (1936), details his vision of the professional police officer and became a classic work in the field of law enforcement.

Upon his retirement from the Berkeley police department, August Vollmer helped to create the first college program in police science at the University of California at Berkeley, where he eventually became professor of police administration. Moreover, until his death he was a consultant to police agencies and governments all over the world.

Perhaps the finest tribute to this man was paid by O. W. Wilson, another giant in the field of American law enforcement, when he wrote: "August Vollmer contributed more to the advancement of police service in this country, and probably in other countries as well, than did any other law enforcement man, including those at the state and federal levels."[30]

The report recommended that the following steps be taken with regard to the police:

1. The corrupting influences of politics should be removed from the police organization.
2. The head of the department should be selected at large for competence and leadership and should preferably be a man of considerable police experience and removable from office only after preferment of charges and a public hearing.
3. Patrolmen should be able to rate a "B" on the Alpha Test, be able-bodied and of good character, weigh 150 pounds [minimum], measure 5'9" tall [also minimum], and be between 21 and 31 years of age. These requirements may be disregarded by the chief for good and sufficient reasons.
4. Salaries should permit decent living standards, housing should be adequate, eight hours of work, one day off weekly, annual vacation, fair sick leave with pay, just accident and death benefits when in performance of duty, reasonable pension provisions on an actuarial basis.
5. Adequate training for recruits, officers, and those already on the roll is imperative.
6. The communication system should also provide for call boxes, telephones, recall system, and Teletype and radio.
7. Records should be complete, adequate, but as simple as possible. They should be used to secure administrative control of investigations and of department units in the interest of efficiency.
8. A crime prevention unit should be established if circumstances warrant this action, and qualified women police should be engaged to handle juvenile delinquents' and women's cases.
9. State police forces should be established in states where rural protection of this character is required.
10. State bureaus of criminal investigation and information should be established in every state.[31]

It is difficult to overestimate the impact of the Wickersham Report. This commission established a model for professional policing that was badly needed. Among the reforms that followed the publication of this report were the creation of numerous merit systems for both selection and promotion, the introduction of two-way radios to patrol cars, and the creation of crime laboratories around the country.

The concept of statewide law enforcement also received a major boost. By 1940, every state but Wisconsin had created some form of state police. In addition, education for police personnel also started to receive serious interest from police administrators as well as academicians. The state police forces had something to do with this. Unlike their municipal and county counterparts, the state police forces created serious training programs, usually of a duration of three months or more. As the state's training requirements increased, it was only natural that the city and county law enforcement agencies should benefit from the state's experiences.

In the realm of colleges and universities, San Jose State College (later changed to University) led the charge. In 1931, they created the first major police program in the nation. The next year San Jose State hired August Vollmer as professor of police administration. Under his guidance, San Jose State provided the model by which future police science, and later criminal justice programs would be designed.

As noted earlier, another giant in the history of the American police was *O.W. Wilson,* who would achieve his greatest accomplishments while chief of police for the city of Chicago. While chief of the Wichita, Kansas police department, however, he created the first police cadet program in 1935. Later that year Michigan State College (later University), created a four-year baccalaureate program in police science. By the time the 1940s arrived, more than 20 colleges and universities were offering courses devoted to law enforcement.[32]

O.W. Wilson

Orlando Winfield Wilson continued the movement toward the professionalization of the police begun by August Vollmer. A protégé of Vollmer (Wilson both studied under Vollmer at the University at Berkeley and worked for Vollmer as a Berkeley police officer), Wilson eventually became chief of police at Fullerton, California, and Wichita, Kansas, and superintendent of police in Chicago, Illinois.

While at Wichita, Wilson introduced many of the innovations he had observed at Berkeley. These included the use of the polygraph, marked police cars, and a crime laboratory. After leaving Wichita, Wilson returned to Berkeley, where he became a professor of police administration at the university.

One of Wilson's great strengths was his firm belief in honest law enforcement. He gained a reputation as a reform chief. It was this reputation that earned him an invitation to bring professional police management to the Chicago police. Wilson believed that corruption was the by-product of poor organization, scant planning, and tangled lines of command.[33]

Wilson was well aware that the police had little control over the root causes of crime, but he developed the concept of preventive patrol. He believed that an aggressive police force could thwart criminal behavior by reducing the opportunity for crime. Like Vollmer before him, he believed in scholarship. His most noted works are *Police Records* (1942), *Police Administration* (1950), and *Police Planning* (1957).

Photograph 2-3   O.W. Wilson (Photograph courtesy of UPI/Bettmann.)

The Federal Bureau of Investigation, under *J. Edgar Hoover,* added to the momentum for increased training and education when it created its National Academy for the training of local police officers in 1935. When Hoover had taken command of the FBI, it had low morale and prestige. He had transformed it into one of the most respected law enforcement agencies in the world. The opening of the National Academy provided a means whereby local law enforcement could draw upon the FBI's resources and improve their own effectiveness.[34]

J. Edgar Hoover

The Federal Bureau of Investigation became the epitome of professionalization under the direction of J. Edgar Hoover. Appointed to the position of director of the FBI by President Calvin Coolidge in 1924, Hoover immediately began to professionalize an agency that was innundated with internal politics and poor morale. Hoover, himself an attorney, believed that agents should be college educated. He instituted a personnel system that would bring many other attorneys into the ranks of the FBI. Believing that training was the key to effective law enforcement, Hoover was also instrumental in the development of extensive

Photograph 2-4   J. Edgar Hoover

training programs, first for the FBI's special agents, then for local and state officers as well.

Under Hoover, the FBI also developed the world's most extensive crime laboratory, a nationwide fingerprinting system, and the National Crime Information Center. Director Hoover was also a master of public relations. Shunning the
quagmire of organized crime (Hoover never publicly admitted there was a mafia),
the FBI was aimed at the more high-profile criminals, such as John Dillinger, the
Ma Barker Gang, Machine Gun Kelly, and Bonny and Clyde. During the 1930s
the FBI gained a reputation as gun-toting G-men, a reputation that made the FBI
the most admired law enforcement agency in the nation, perhaps the world.

Late in his career, J. Edgar Hoover came under increasing attack from civil
rights groups, who accused him of abuses of power. Still, Hoover's contribution
to law enforcement management and training make him one of the giants in the
field of law enforcement.

The Task Force Reports

Thirty-six years would pass before another government commission would look
at policing in this country. Much had happened between 1931 and 1967, when the
President's Commission on Law Enforcement and the Administration of Justice

issued its reports. The commission, formed in 1965 by President Lyndon Johnson, examined every aspect of the criminal justice system. From its findings, experts in the field of justice were able to measure accurately how far the system had come, and more important, how much farther it needed to go.

The impetus for this investigation was the widely held belief that the nation was experiencing a crime wave of a magnitude never before seen. In addition, civil unrest over both the Vietnam War and the growing civil rights movement were creating a strain on the legal system unseen since the days of the Civil War.

Unlike the Civil War riots, which were localized and largely unheard of around the rest of the country, the riots and disturbances of the 1960s were quickly transmitted into every home in the United States via television. The police, whose tactics had remained relatively stable over the centuries, found that those tactics were no longer acceptable. Club-swinging police officers did not play well on live television. The police therefore became the focal point of criticism aimed at the government in general.

Against this backdrop, the President's commission set out in 1965 to closely scrutinize the American legal system. Nicholas Katzenbach was appointed chair of the commission and was aided by an impressive list of advisors, consultants, and witnesses. The result was a marvel of sound research. While the *Task Force Reports* were numerous and lengthy, a general report was released to the public. This book, *The Challenge of Crime in a Free Society,* is still a classic text on the American justice system. The study of most interest to the police, however, was titled *Task Force Report: The Police.* The observations and recommendations of this report included the following:

1. The police were isolated from the communities they had sworn to serve, and from other components in the criminal justice system. Police science and law enforcement programs were adding to this isolation by offering courses so technical and vocational in nature that classes were attended primarily by police officers, to the exclusion of interested students.

2. City officials had all but abdicated their responsibilities for running police agencies by delegating that responsibility to police chiefs.

3. Police chiefs were often appointed because of demonstrated skill as investigators rather than for administrative competence.

4. Police executives had failed to assume their roles as major policymakers.

5. Fresh blood should be infused into police departments by creating new entry-level classifications, and by allowing lateral entry (personnel movements between police departments).

6. Minority recruitment should be emphasized.

7. Minimum training and educational requirements should be established for all levels of officers.

8. Formal community relations and internal investigation units should be created.

9. Fragmented local police services should be pooled or consolidated to eliminate waste and duplication.[35]

With the guidelines of the Task Force Reports, and under incredible pressure, the police set out to modernize. All that was needed to make great strides was money, a lot of money. The federal government responded with the Omnibus Crime Control and Safe Streets Act of 1968. This bill created the *Law Enforcement Assistance Administration* (LEAA). Under the auspices of this agency, massive amounts of money were infused to all aspects of the criminal justice system. The element of the system that benefited most directly, however, was law enforcement.

A number of benefits were derived from this government agency. First, regional criminal justice councils were established in an attempt to better coordinate the fragmented efforts of the legal system. Second, large block grants were made available to the police in order that they upgrade badly outdated equipment. Third, and probably most important, a large sum of money was set aside to provide for educating the police. Under the title of Law Enforcement Education Program (LEEP), police officers were entitled to monetary grants for the purpose of paying for college tuition and textbooks. Preservice students were entitled to loans of a similar nature, although the loans could be worked off by entering the field of law enforcement, or a related field, and remaining there for the required number of years. As a result of LEEP, the number of college-educated police officers multiplied tremendously over a short period of time.

Ultimately, the Law Enforcement Assistance Administration was abandoned. Its impact, however, was long lasting. The regional criminal justice councils provided some benefits, but admittedly, this concept never produced the hoped-for results. The equipment expenditures quite probably were much of the reason for the elimination of this program. While many of the items purchased were badly needed and proved worthwhile, still others were unneeded and excessively costly. Horror stories of police chiefs using this money to equip their departments with army tanks, or plush vehicles for administrators, abounded. Ultimately, LEAA was seen as a boondoggle and suffered the fate of programs thus categorized.

The high point of this program was the educational portion. LEEP alone accomplished what it was meant to accomplish. Under this program many current police administrators received a college education. The belief in the necessity of a college-educated police force did not die with LEAA, but remains. Today, we are very close to the time when all persons seeking a career in law enforcement will be required to possess some college education. If nothing else, the Law Enforcement Assistance Administration accomplished that goal.

SUMMARY

The earliest police organization in North America was provided by the Aztec nation. Unfortunately, the Spanish invasion destroyed all aspects of those institutions. Other early law enforcement was the product of life in the colonies, with the institutions of the homeland serving as the model for each colony. The primary organizational structure was based on some variation of the watch system or was provided by military units.

There were three major eras of change in American law enforcement. The first occurred with the American Revolution. The severing of ties with Great Britain propelled the nation toward the creation of institutions with a uniquely American flavor. At this time, policing style was relatively unchanged, but the focus of law enforcement diverged widely. The major differences appeared between east, west, and south. New England law enforcement was influenced by massive population growth and a shift to heavy industry. The west was wild and untamed, requiring a different form of policing. The south, with its growing paranoia of slave revolts, designed its police with that possibility in mind.

The second era of change came with the Civil War. Following this period, police organizations were structured along military lines. The basic police structure of today, with its emphasis on lines of authority and central administration, can be traced to this period.

The third era of change was a longer and more gradual phase. This was the era of technology and refinement. Beginning early in the twentieth century and continuing through today, the police have undergone constant modification in their use of technology and training. Early in this era men such as Vollmer, Wilson, and Hoover led the way. Much of what the police have become can be attributed to these men and others like them.

TIME-LINE CHART

Date	Location	Event
5000–4000 B.C.	Egypt	Law begins to evolve
2900 B.C.	Egypt	Judges' commandant of police created
2500–2400 B.C.	Shipurla	Urikagina's code
1947–1905 B.C.	Babylon	Hammurabi's code
1340 B.C.	Egypt	Creation of river police, tomb police; first use of canine patrols
1200–1090 B.C.	Palestine	Mosaic law develops
600–700 B.C.	Greece	Legal concept of pollution develops
621 B.C.	Athens	Draco's law
594 B.C.	Athens	Rise of Solon
451 B.C.	Rome	Code of twelve tables
426 B.C.	Athens	Solon's reforms completed by Ephialtes
265 B.C.	Rome	Peak of Republican legal system
27 B.C.	Rome	Founding of the principate
A.D. 200	Rome	Growth of vulgar law
A.D. 528	Rome	Justinian's code

Date	Location	Event
A.D. 785	France	Capitularies of Charlemaigne
A.D. 876	France	Marshals of France created
1032	France	Provost of the city of Paris created
1066	England	Norman invasion—beginning of common law
1215	Rome	Fourth Lateran Council
1215	England	Magna Carta
?–1519	Mexico	Aztec legal system develops
1519	Mexico	Spaniards arrive
1536	France	Maréchaussée given power to police roads; beginning of dual powers of gendarmes
1539	France	Ordinance of 1539
1612	U.S.	Dale's laws created in Jamestown
Mid to late 1600s	U.S.	Religious law developed in New England
1631	Boston	Watch created
1632	U.S.	Creation of Chesapeake sheriff
1634	Boston	Constable appointed
1643	New York	Creation of burgher watch
1652	New York	Creation of rattle watch
1658	New York	First paid watch officers
1664	New York	First high constable
1666	France	First lieutenant of police (Paris)
1672	France	Age of Reason commences; witch trials end
1693	New York	First uniformed constable appointed
1720	France	Maréchaussée becomes national force
1731	New York	First precinct station built
1740	England	Thomas De Veil becomes first magistrate at Bow Street
1746	England	Henry Fielding succeeds De Veil
1746	England	Bow Street Runners created
1752	England	John Fielding succeeds Henry Fielding
1780	England	Gordon riots
1785	Ireland	Irish police created
1788	New York	Doctor's riot
1789	France	French Revolution
1793–1794	France	Reign of Terror
1798	New York	Police office created
1801	New York	High constable given control of city
1804	France	Napoleon becomes emperor
1805	Charleston	Office of elected constable established
1806	Charleston	City guard established
1807	Charleston	City marshal established
Early 1800's	France	Vidocq organizes sûreté
1819	England	Peterloo
1822	England	Robert Peel becomes Home Secretary
1823	Texas	Earliest Texas Ranger units formed
1829	England	Metropolitan London police created

Date	Location	Event
1832	France	Sûreté reorganized by Gisquet
1832	Texas	First alcalde appointed in E. Texas
1836	Houston	First sheriff of Harris County
1840	Houston	First town marshal
1842	England	Detective force created in London
1845	New York	Watch replaced by city police
1845	Texas	Texas Rangers become first state police
1846	Charleston	City police established
1857	New York	Metropolitan Police Bill
1866	U.S.	Peak era of state-controlled police
1877	France	Bertillon begins work in Paris
1877	England	Howard Vincent reorganizes London detective branch
1884	France	First criminalistics lab founded
1893	U.S.	IACP founded
1903	U.S.	Will West case; fingerprinting era begins
1904	Berkley, CA	August Vollmer appointed city marshal
1924	U.S.	J. Edgar Hoover made director of FBI
1931	U.S.	Wickersham Report
1931	San Jose, CA	First police science program created
1935	Wichita, KS	First police cadet program
1935	U.S.	FBI creates national academy
1967	U.S.	Task Force Reports published
1968	U.S.	Omnibus Crime Control and Safe Streets Act passes

DISCUSSION QUESTIONS

1. Discuss the effect of Puritan philosophy on legal thinking.

2. Compare and contrast the law enforcement efforts of early New York, Charleston, and Houston.

3. What impact did the Civil War have on law enforcement?

4. Describe August Vollmer's contribution to professional policing.

5. Compare the reports of the Wickersham Commission with that of the *Task Force Report: The Police*. How far did police progress between those two eras?

NOTES/REFERENCES

1. Frederick A. Peterson, *Ancient Mexico* (New York: G.P. Putnam's Sons, 1959), p. 118.

2. Peterson, p. 119.

3. Peterson, pp. 119–120.

4. Peterson, p. 120.

5. Peterson, pp. 120–121.

6. Peterson, pp. 123–124.

7. Eric R. Wolf, *Sons of the Shaking Earth* (Chicago: The University of Chicago Press, 1959), pp. 194–201.

8. Donald O. Schultz and Erik Beckman, *Principles of American Law Enforcement and Criminal Justice,* 2nd (rev.) ed. (Sacramento, Calif.: Custom Publishing Company, 1987), pp. 12–13.

9. David Hawke, *The Colonial Experience* (New York: The Bobbs-Merrill Company, Inc., 1966), p. 97.

10. From Cotton's letter to Lord Saye in 1630, reprinted in Gerald N. Grob and Robert N. Beck, Eds., *American Ideas,* Vol. I (New York: The Free Press, 1963), pp. 5–6.

11. Schultz and Beckman, p. 14.

12. Schultz and Beckman, pp. 15–16.

13. Alice Morse Earle, *Curious Punishments of Bygone Days* (Montclair, N.J.: Patterson Smith Publishing Corp.; originally published in 1869, reprinted in 1969), as cited in Schultz and Beckman, p. 16.

14. Schultz and Beckman, pp. 11–12.

15. Herbert L. Osgood, *The American Colonies in the Seventeenth Century* (Gloucester, Mass.: Peter Smith, 1957), pp. 105–106.

16. Schultz and Beckman, p. 15.

17. Information provided through the courtesy of the Charleston Police Department, Reuben Greenberg, Chief, 1988.

18. Herbert A. Johnson, *History of Criminal Justice* (Cincinnati, Ohio: Anderson Publishing Co., 1988), pp. 182–184.

19. Sidney I. Pomerantz, *New York: An American City, 1783–1803* (New York: Columbia University Press, 1938), p. 300.

20. Pomerantz, p. 301.

21. Pomerantz, pp. 304–305.

22. Schultz and Beckman, pp. 38–40.

23. Schultz and Beckman, pp. 50–51.

24. Victor Kappeler, notes compiled from archives of St. Louis Police Department.

25. *Houston Police Department Yearbook,* 1985, p. 19

26. Kansas City, Missouri, Police Department, Personnel Policy 110-1: *Department History,* 1986, p. 4.

27. Schultz and Beckman, pp. 60–62.

28. National Commission on Law Observance and Enforcement, *Report on the Police* (Montclair, N.J.: Patterson Smith Publishing Corp.; originally published in 1931, reprinted in 1968), p. 3.

29. Alfred E. Parker, *The Berkeley Police Story* (Springfield, Ill.: Charles C Thomas, Publisher, 1972), p. 23.

30. Parker, p. vii.

31. National Commission on Law Observance and Enforcement, p. 140.

32. Allen Z. Gammage, *Police Training in the United States* (Springfield, Ill.: Charles C Thomas, Publisher, 1963), pp. 64–72.

33. George F. Cole, *The American System of Criminal Justice,* 5th ed. (Pacific Grove, Calif.: Brooks/Cole Publishing Co., 1989), p. 179.

34. Gammage, p. 19.

35. Schultz and Beckman, p. 153.

Chapter 3

American Police Agencies

Key Terms

Municipal police
County sheriff
State police
Highway patrol
State investigation agencies
FBI
ATF

DEA
Marshal's Service
Customs
INS
Coast Guard
INTERPOL
Private security

Chapter Objectives

At the conclusion of this chapter, students should be able to:

1. Identify the different levels of law enforcement within the United States.

2. Differentiate between the functions and responsibilities of the various law enforcement organizations.

3. Identify the problems resulting from the fragmented nature of law enforcement within the United States.

INTRODUCTION

The structure of the American police must appear a hopeless tangle of duplication and proliferation to outside observers. Driven by the conflicting beliefs in both local control of the police and in the effectiveness of big government, we have created a vast array of police agencies to serve every possible constituency. When we speak of the American police, therefore, we must be careful to define which police agency we are discussing. There is no such organization as *the American police.* There are a myriad of police agencies that serve different functions. The most appropriate breakdown for a discussion of the police is to look at each type of agency by the level of government to which it is attached.

In this chapter we look at local law enforcement, state organizations, and federal agencies. Finally, we discuss international police organizations and private security.

LOCAL LAW ENFORCEMENT

By far, the most critical police service is provided by local police agencies. These are the organizations responsible for the day-to-day maintenance of peace and order within the cities and towns of the nation. Local law enforcement is provided by *municipal police* agencies and *county sheriff's departments.* The vast majority of arrests, traffic citations, and investigations take place in these jurisdictions, by these officers.

Evidence of the dominance of local government in providing police service can be easily seen in the statistics. In 1986 there were 11,743 municipal, 79 county, and 1819 township general-purpose police agencies in the United States. Their combined employment was composed of 533,247 full-time personnel. Additionally, there are more than 3000 sheriff's departments in the United States. The percentage of police officers employed in urban areas is approximately 82 percent.[1]

Metropolitan Police Agencies

When one thinks of local law enforcement, the picture of the big city police department comes to mind. Policing the major metropolitan areas is unlike any other law enforcement function. The sheer size of the jurisdiction, both geographically as well as in population, requires a police force that resembles a small army.

Urban police departments do absolutely everything that a police agency can do. These departments provide police service at maximum intensity. They have the greatest workloads and respond to the widest variety of requests. The greatest challenge in policing is faced by the men and women of these departments.

The special problems of the large departments revolve around personnel. Natural attrition and, in some cases, growth require a constant recruiting and

Photograph 3-1   City Police Officer

training process. Also, many potentially excellent applicants shun working in the large cities. Television has done irreparable harm to the image of our cities. We have a generation of young people who think that the large cities are sinkholes of crime, death, and corruption. This is not the case. The large urban departments offer greater benefits and career possibilities than any other law enforcement agency. Television imagery, however, is hard to overcome. Most of the larger agencies always need good people, many of whom are afraid of the large city.

Medium-Sized Departments

The majority of police personnel actually work in medium-sized departments. These agencies, with 100 to 500 officers, provide police service for the suburban areas and for many of the larger cities in the less populous states.

For many who seek a police career, this type of agency offers an ideal compromise between the large urban area and the smaller departments. The salary and benefits are usually satisfactory, although less than those offered in the bigger departments. The ability to get to know each member of the agency, as well as the opportunity to work every part of the jurisdiction, is attractive to many potential applicants.

Generally speaking, another attractive aspect of the medium-sized agency is that it offers roughly the same kinds of challenges as the urban department, save one. The inner city, or urban ghetto, is a problem relegated to the large urban departments. Most medium-sized agencies lack such an area. They may have poor people and may even have large groups of minorities. The urban ghetto, however, is a unique, and to some, frightening place, a place usually found in only the largest urban areas. Because of this fear of bigger cities and the belief that there is a better quality of life in the suburbs, many highly qualified police applicants seek positions with the medium-sized agencies.

Small-Town Agencies

While the majority of the police officers in this country are employed by large or medium-sized agencies, the majority of police departments have fewer than 20 officers. These agencies present a great challenge to professional policing.

There is a direct relationship between resources and the ability of the agency to obtain and train quality personnel. Small towns, for the most part, lack sufficient resources to provide high-quality law enforcement. The result, unfortunately, is that the old adage, "you get what you pay for," is all too true in policing. By far the least trained, least qualified police officers are found in the smaller departments.

The problem is acerbated by the tendency of some states to provide lower standards for selection and training of small-town officers. The state of Missouri, for example, has three different standards. The highway patrol requires, by law, a minimum of 1000 hours of basic training. First-class cities and counties must provide over 600 hours of training, while lower-class cities and counties are mandated 120 hours of training. Town marshals are exempted entirely from the training requirements.

The reasons for these multiple standards relate to economics and politics. Training costs money, and smaller jurisdictions have less money. Politically, there are also far more small town chiefs and small county sheriffs than there are administrators from the larger jurisdictions. Since these administrators have fewer resources and greater access to the political system, by virtue of their numbers, they have been successful in holding training standards to a minimum.

The tragedy of this is that it is the small-town officer who is expected to know all aspects of policing. The larger jurisdictions have specialists for crime scenes, traffic accidents, and a wide variety of other circumstances. The small-town officer has no specialists to call upon and sometimes does not have even a single backup officer. We thus have the situation of providing less training for those officers in need of more training. It is for this reason that I state that these agencies represent the greatest challenge to professional policing—this fact and the depressing realization that the loudest and most powerful spokespersons for nonprofessionalization of the police are the county sheriffs and small-town chiefs, the very people who should be urging higher standards.

The problems of small-town policing are essentially the same as urban policing, with a few differences. First, the pace is slower. The smaller communities are subject to the same types of crime as the larger cities, but the incidents of crime are spread over a much larger time span. All police officers complain about periods of boredom, but small-town police officers go entire months without encountering anything of significance.

The second difference is the contact between officer and citizen. Because the small-town force has so few officers, they are all well known throughout the community. The citizen expectations are therefore different. Police officers in small towns are expected to be less formal and more helpful than urban officers.

Unlike the larger agencies, the small-town police are likely to be beset with nuisance problems unique to the small-town. Animal complaints, related to leash laws, and parking meter enforcement are often within the purview of the small-town officer. These complaints, and similar types, generate tremendous hostility and disrespect for the police. Larger jurisdictions dispose of these problems by creating specialized units such as animal control or "meter maids." The small-town agency does not have this luxury; therefore, they suffer through the dilemma of dealing with no-win situations.

The County Sheriff

The sheriff is considered to be the top law enforcement official in the county. This is due to tradition and to the fact that in most jurisdictions the sheriff is the only law enforcement official elected by popular vote. There are currently more than 3000 counties in the United States, most of which provide for the election of the sheriff. Only Alaska has no counties and therefore no sheriffs. Moreover, there are other variations in Hawaii, and several counties in New York, Florida, and Colorado where the sheriff is appointed. Additionally, there are city sheriffs in Virginia, Baltimore, Maryland, and St. Louis, Missouri. Louisiana has both criminal and civil sheriffs.

The duties of the sheriff have changed somewhat over the years. Once the primary agent of law enforcement, this function has been taken over in many areas by municipal and state police agencies. There are many counties that no longer have any rural areas at all and are totally encompassed by municipal boundaries. Still, there are services that only the sheriff's office provide. Among these are the maintenance and operation of the county jail, serving civil processes, such as eviction notices, providing security and bailiffs for county courts, and collecting some county taxes. The trend in metropolitan areas is toward a lessening of the role of the sheriff. In much of the country, however, the sheriff retains strong political influence.

The problems associated with the office of sheriff are related to the political aspects of the office. In many jurisdictions all employees of the sheriff's department work at the pleasure of the sheriff. Lacking even minimal job protection, a deputy's career hangs on the ability of the sheriff to get reelected. There are still county law enforcement agencies in the United States where the defeat of the sheriff signals the complete changing of personnel within that office. The change can be so dramatic that pending court cases are dismissed as file cabinets are cleaned out to prepare for the arrival of the new regime.

Fortunately, the situation above occurs less frequently than in the past. Unfortunately, the office of the county sheriff, in many jurisdictions, is an example of inefficiency and political wheeling and dealing.

STATE AGENCIES

The first modern *state police* agency was created in Pennsylvania in 1905. This was not, however, the first state police. That distinction belongs to Texas. The Texas Rangers were initiated in 1845 (they were actually created in 1824, but Texas did not become a state until 1845). Following the Texas model, Arizona created the Arizona Rangers in 1901, and New Mexico created the New Mexico Mounted Police in 1905. These three organizations were used primarily to guard the borders and to deal with Indian raids and Mexican bandits.[2] Of these agencies, only the Texas Rangers evolved into a regular state police organization.

The Pennsylvania State Police was a centralized police force using traditional principles of organization. The officers wore uniforms and were selected and promoted through a process designed to reward ability rather than political connections. The officers, called troopers, were housed in barracks and operated along paramilitary lines.

This force was created as a response to growing labor unrest. Local police authorities were unwilling or unable to respond effectively to labor actions. The state police was created to "crush disorders, whether industrial or otherwise, which arose in the foreigner-filled districts of the state."[3] It is the structure of this organization, therefore, that provides its reputation as the first modern police force. Its purpose was very similar to that of the southwestern state police agencies. The Pennsylvania State Police was created to control the violent tendencies of "outsiders."

State Police

The industrial states learned from the Pennsylvania experiment and created their own state police agencies. With the end of the era of labor unrest, these organizations evolved into fully functioning police agencies with statewide jurisdiction.

Generally speaking, state police agencies have full police powers and are responsible for vehicular traffic on state highways and criminal investigation in rural areas or in conjunction with municipal law enforcement. Additionally, the state police usually maintains and operates a state criminalistics laboratory and maintains the state's criminal records unit. The growth of state police agencies was due primarily to the increased mobility of American society and the resultant increase in nonurban crime. Also, state administrators and legislators found it necessary to respond to increased requests for police agencies not allied with local political interests.

Highway Patrol

The *highway patrols* were created in nonindustrial states. Lacking the labor unrest that caused the creation of the state police, these states saw no need for a

Photograph 3–2   Missouri Highway Patrol Officer

full-blown police force with statewide jurisdiction. As a result of the increasing intrastate and interstate automobile traffic, however, there was a need for an agency to provide uniform control of the state highways. The highway patrol was created to perform this function.

Most highway patrols have limited jurisdiction. They were designed to monitor and control traffic. Their authority, in many states, is limited to traffic-related problems. This limited authority of some of the highway patrol forces is becoming a source of increasing concern in many states, where the highway patrol is seen as a means to enhance the law enforcement and investigative capabilities of rural areas.

State Investigative Services

The lack of adequate investigative resources in rural areas of several states has led to the creation of special *state investigative agencies.* The organizations may work in conjunction with the state police or highway patrol, or they may be independent. The state of Kansas, for example, created the Kansas Bureau of Investigation (KBI) to take on major cases in those jurisdictions lacking adequate resources. Similar agencies exist in other states. Even the Texas Rangers are now organized as such an agency within the Texas Department of Public Safety.

The development of such investigative agencies was also a by-product of the Wickersham Report (see Chapter 2). This commission recognized the need for a state agency capable of bringing substantial resources and expertise to the scenes of major crimes in rural areas.

FEDERAL AGENCIES

The federal government maintains numerous law enforcement agencies. Unlike local police agencies with their broad powers of general jurisdiction, the federal agencies have a narrow focus and limited jurisdiction. The reason for this lies in the manner in which these agencies have been created. Over the years, federal offices were created to address specific problems related to federal law. This has led to a proliferation of agencies, sometimes with competing and overlapping duties.

Federal Bureau of Investigation

Probably the most famous of the federal agencies is the *FBI*. Created in 1870 with the establishment of the Department of Justice, it initially used private investigators borrowed from either the Secret Service or the Pinkerton Agency. The FBI was first called the Bureau of Investigation. In 1935 the name was changed to the Federal Bureau of Investigation.

The original mission of the FBI was to investigate crimes against the United States. In 1917, with the passage of the Espionage Act, this mission was expanded to include subversion and espionage. Some of the most controversial actions of this agency came in response to these added duties. During World War I, the FBI was used to track down men believed to be avoiding military duty, an activity they were also involved in during the Vietnam War. They were also directed to ferret out subversion during the 1919, also an activity that caused harm to their reputation in the 1960s and 1970s.

In 1924, John Edgar Hoover was promoted from assistant director to director of the FBI, a position he held until his death in 1972. With this appointment, the FBI shed its poor image and began a climb to respectability, and ultimately to an international reputation for effectiveness. Additionally, the FBI was given more responsibilities. By World War II, this agency was empowered to investigate interstate transportation of stolen vehicles, bank robbery, interstate fugitives, and kidnapping.

Today, the FBI has jurisdiction for over 200 types of criminal activities, including civil rights violations by other police agencies. Of equal importance to their investigative function, the FBI is also engaged in criminalistics, records, and training. The FBI has the most extensive criminalistics laboratory in the world. This laboratory analyzes every conceivable type of evidence for the nation's police agencies, at no cost. The National Crime Information Center (NCIC) is managed and maintained by the bureau. This center is responsible for a national file of known felony warrants and missing persons and property. Also, the FBI maintains the world's largest fingerprint file.

The FBI National Academy provides training for police managers throughout the United States. Additionally, the FBI provides instructors for a vast array of special schools established to assist law enforcement agencies with training on specific topics. These services are provided at no cost to the police agencies and

Photograph 3-3 FBI Training Center

allow law enforcement administrators access to analytical and training resources beyond their capacity to acquire on their own.

Bureau of Alcohol, Tobacco, and Firearms

The Bureau of Alcohol, Tobacco, and Firearms (ATF) was a by-product of the Whiskey Rebellion of 1794. Secretary of the Treasury Alexander Hamilton introduced a tax on spirits. Later the tax was abandoned, but was reintroduced during the Civil War. The director of Internal Revenue hired three persons to investigate the illegal manufacture of distilled spirits. The introduction of prohibition caused a surge in the importance of this agency. In the 1920s it was renamed the Prohibition Bureau. With the repeal of prohibition, this agency was renamed the Alcohol Tax Unit. As recently as 1962, over 90 percent of this bureau's resources were committed to investigations of moonshining in the southeastern portion of the United States.[4]

In 1942, this agency was given responsibility for administering the federal firearms laws. Their responsibility was increased in 1969 with the passage of the Gun Control Act. This law made the ATF responsible for licensing the nation's 250,000 firearms dealers. The assumption of the duties regarding firearms has taken the ATF into investigations of drug traffickers and outlaw motorcycle gangs, both of which have also been involved in the manufacture and sale of explosives and weapons.

In 1982, the Anti-Arson Act increased the agency's jurisdiction over arson. The bureau now has four National Response Teams (NRTs) that investigate cases of arson and bombings in conjunction with state and local agencies. As a result of reorganization in 1972, ATF was transferred out of the Internal Revenue Service and made a bureau within the Department of the Treasury. Today, ATF enjoys a sound reputation among law enforcement professionals.

Drug Enforcement Administration

This agency is responsible for enforcing federal statutes related to narcotics and dangerous drugs. Originally created under the Department of the Treasury's Bureau of Internal Revenue in 1914, the agency evolved through several distinct phases. In 1930, this agency became the Federal Bureau of Narcotics (FBN) and was given responsibility for drug enforcement. In 1968, this agency was taken out of the Treasury Department, merged with the Department of Health, Education, and Welfare's Bureau of Drug Abuse Control and placed in the Department of Justice as the Bureau of Narcotics and Dangerous Drugs (BNDD). Finally, in 1973, the BNDD was changed to its current title, the *Drug Enforcement Administration (DEA)*.

Not all DEA activities are related to illicit drugs. They are also responsible for regulating the manufacture and distribution of controlled substances. This requires working closely with pharmaceutical companies, physicians, and pharmacists. This agency establishes quotas for foreign distribution of controlled substances and registers all handlers of such substances.

When investigating the traffic in illicit drugs, the DEA functions primarily as an undercover operation. Few major drug cases are made through standard investigation. Most require penetration of the smuggling network by an undercover operative. This aspect of the DEA makes it substantially different than other law enforcement organizations.

U.S. Secret Service

The precursor of today's Secret Service was the Pinkerton Agency. During the War Between the States, this organization, led by Allan Pinkerton, was the first to take responsibility for the protection of the president, and was, for awhile, the primary intelligence organization for the United States. During the tenure of George McClelland as Commander in Chief of the Army, Allan Pinkerton's organization was the Secret Service.[5]

Following the war, Congress officially created the Secret Service as a bureau in the Department of the Treasury. It was created in 1865 to investigate crimes involving counterfeiting and forgery of government checks, bonds, and securities. Being the only general law enforcement agency in the federal government, its duties were quickly expanded to deal with smuggling, piracy, mail robbery, and land fraud. The Secret Service was also called into action against the Ku Klux Klan.[6]

The assassination of President William McKinley in 1901 resulted in the Secret Service being assigned the responsibility of protecting the president. Although the legislation authorizing presidential protection was passed in 1907, it was not until the attempted assassination of President Truman in 1951 that the Secret Service was granted permanent protection authority.

In 1922, the White House Police Force was created and given responsibility for protection of the persons and grounds of the White House. In 1930, direction of this organization was transferred from the military to the Secret Service. This force represents the only uniformed element of the Secret Service. In 1970, this force was expanded to include protection of foreign diplomatic missions located in the Washington, D.C. metropolitan area.[7]

U.S. Marshal's Service

President George Washington appointed the first U.S. Marshals in 1789 as a result of the Judiciary Act of that same year. The first marshal was Isaac Huger of South Carolina. The duties of these early marshals remained unchanged for many years. They were assigned to jurisdiction of the federal courts, where they enforced the laws of the federal government and orders of the court.

As the nation underwent westward expansion, these officers provided law enforcement. Frequently, the marshal was the only symbol of law and order for thousands of miles. The life of the early marshal was not an easy one. In the Oklahoma Territory alone, 65 marshals were killed within a five-year period.[8]

The marshals have been used for a variety of duties. With the civilizing of the west, the marshals were called on to handle other problems of civil disturbance. They have occasionally been used as a paramilitary force in riot situations. They were called in to deal with the Whiskey Rebellion of 1794, the Pullman Strike of 1894, the Homestead Riot of 1892, and the Indian demonstration at Wounded Knee in 1973.

Currently, the *Marshal's Service* serves the nation's 94 judicial districts. There is one U.S. Marshal for each district. These people supervise over 1400 deputy U.S. Marshals. The U.S. Marshals are presidential appointees. The deputies are under the federal civil service system. This agency is under the Department of Justice.

The primary duties of today's marshals are concerned with the safety and security of the federal courts and court personnel. They are also responsible for the safety of federal prisoners not in the custody of a corrections agency. Within the purview of these responsibilities are included administration of the federal government's witness protection program. The investigative responsibilities of the Marshal's Service are focused on violations of federal bail, probation, parole, or escaping from a federal prison. They are also responsible for the security of some federal property other than the courts.

U.S. Customs Service

Customs was established by the U.S. Congress on July 31, 1789. Customs officers were made responsible for collecting duties on certain imports. On March 3, 1927, the Bureau of Customs was established as a separate agency within the Treasury Department. On August 1, 1973, it was renamed the U.S. Customs Service.

Special agents of the Customs Service investigate smuggling, currency viola-

Photograph 3–4 Deputy U.S. Marshal

tions, criminal fraud against the revenue system, and major cargo thefts. An inordinate amount of time and resources expended by this agency is in the investigation and apprehension of drug smugglers. Other items, such as weapons, jewelry, plants, and food products, also require constant attention by Customs agents. Additionally, Customs is responsible for enforcing certain export laws. Most notably, weapons technology and monetary instruments (anyone taking more than $10,000 from this country must make a disclosure of this fact).

Customs personnel can be found in a variety of locations. Customs inspectors search baggage and persons entering the country. In addition to the special agents and inspectors, there are also Customs patrol officers (CPOs), a uniformed branch that works at border crossings.

Immigration and Naturalization Service

The *Immigration and Naturalization Service (INS)* was created by an act of Congress on March 3, 1891. It is responsible for administering immigration and naturalization laws relating to the admission, exclusion, deportation, and naturalization of aliens. Personnel responsible for fulfilling these duties are the uniformed *Border Patrol* officers and plainclothes criminal investigators.[9]

Photograph 3-5 Customs Agents

The more than 8000 miles of border are patrolled by the Border Patrol using land, air, and water craft of all types. Additionally, sophisticated electronic sensing devices are used to detect illegal border crossings in remote, often rugged terrain. On the southern border alone, the Border Patrol makes over 1 million apprehensions annually.

In 1984, INS recognized another problem that required a solution. Illegal immigrants were being attacked by organized gangs along the California–Mexican border. In conjunction with the San Diego Police Department, the Border Patrol created the Border Crime Prevention Unit (BCPU). This unit provides armed patrol groups of 10 to 12 officers along the dangerous border zones each night.[10]

U.S. Coast Guard

The Coast Guard was created by an act of Congress in 1790. Initially, this service was called the Revenue Cutter Service by founder Alexander Hamilton. It was this terminology that led to the naming of Coast Guard ships as "cutters."[11]

The U.S. Coast Guard was under the Department of the Treasury for most of its existence. Today, it is under the Department of Transportation, except in time of war, during which it is under the Department of Defense.

The Coast Guard is entrusted with the responsibility of enforcing the laws of the United States on the waters under U.S. jurisdiction. This includes detection and investigation of smuggling, enforcement of antipollution laws, monitoring of fishing treaties, and enforcement of safety regulations.

Photograph 3–6   Border Patrol

Photograph 3–7   U.S. Coast Guard

Coast Guard personnel are federal law enforcement officers rather than military personnel. They have, therefore, enforcement powers not granted to the military. The following ballad provides some indication of the Coast Guard's powers of search and seizure:

Of Search and Seizure on Your Boat

Wherever She May Be Afloat

In Inland Waters

If inland waterways you sail
the Coast Guard any time may hail
you, even without cause,
may board you and may make you pause
to show your documents and gear.
But more than that you need not fear,
unless there's reason to suspect
that crime aboard they may detect.
When that is true, then search they may
through fore and aft, all night and all day.

In Territorial Waters

When you are out, three miles all told,
the Coast Guard even may be bold
enough to make you hold
your vessel for a brief detention
and even board you for prevention
of smuggling crimes, especially dope,
which you won't have on board, we hope.
They'll stop you cold in any season
and board you without further reason.
Regardless of the vessel's flag
They search you and will haul you back
if dope they find in any measure
and you will forfeit ship and treasure.

In the Contiguous Zone

If in contiguous zones you are,
from land it is just twelve miles far,
no matter what flag you flew
the Coast Guard orders you to heave to
when they suspect with some sound reason
that crime aboard is then in season.
Yet if on board they think is pot,

they make you stop right on the spot.
They'll board you for much lesser proof:
Heave to, drop sail, and be aloof.

On the High Seas

When on the open sea you cruise,
and if the Stars and Stripes you use,
it's probable cause the Guardsmen need
which to a boarding then may lead
to check on whether Uncle Sam
has suffered from a fiscal scam.
For ships of foreign registry,
the rules are tough, they're telling me.
While hail they may you out at sea,
and board you if you so agree,
or if your country will accord
a right to them that they board.
But if aboard that foreign boat
conspiracy there is afloat
of crime to flaunt our codes and laws,
the Coast Guard may, on proper cause,
board and inspect that suspect ship
and ascertain her charted trip
to safeguard our land and shore.
There's too much dope, we need no more.

Stateless Vessels

And if you're stateless or display
the Jolly Roger on your stay
the Coast Guard may at any time
board, and investigate your crime.
For pirates have no rights at sea.
They are the sailor's enemy.[12]

Internal Revenue Service

The Internal Revenue Service (IRS) is responsible for administering and enforcing the laws and regulations relating to a variety of taxes. This agency was created
by Congress on July 1, 1865. This mission of the IRS is to encourage the highest
possible voluntary compliance with the nation's tax laws. When enforcement action
is necessary, however, it is handled by the Criminal Investigations Division (CID).

The CID deals primarily with income, excise, and employment taxes. Their
function is to determine the true income of an individual or organization that is
suspected of providing false tax information or for failing to provide any infor-

mation as required by law. They accomplish this through interviews, intensive review of financial records, and by locating other sources of information on the financial transactions of the person or organization involved.

The ability of the IRS to detect tax fraud has made this agency of prime importance in the investigation and conviction of organized crime figures. Al Capone was one of the first such gang leaders to fall from power through the efforts of the IRS. There have been others; today, much of the focus of the war on drugs is IRS inquiries into drug-related income. Since the majority of drug dealers do not declare this income for tax purposes, the IRS is in a strong position to shut down their operations.

General Services Administration

Federal Protective Officers of the General Services Administration (GSA) are responsible for the protection of federal property and facilities under the control of the GSA. Primarily, this pertains to storehouses and other facilities where supplies are stored and shipped. The officers provide security against both criminal activity and fires as well as enforcing federal laws and regulations at these facilities.

Postal Inspection Service

This agency is charged with the responsibility of protecting the U.S. mail. Postal inspectors investigate internal problems with the postal system. They conduct in-house audits and evaluate postal operations to ensure their compliance with federal regulations. Additionally, the postal inspectors conduct personnel investigations and evaluate the security and fire safety systems being used in postal facilities.

The best known service rendered by the postal inspectors, however, is in the area of criminal investigation. These officers investigate crimes committed against the postal service, such as robbery or burglary. They further investigate crimes such as theft of mail from private residences, or mailboxes. They are responsible for investigating mail fraud and the use of the mail to transmit illicit objects, such as illegal drugs, incendiary devices, and bombs.

Military Law Enforcement

Each branch of the military has its own investigative service. These agencies are not to be confused with the military police, which is an element of the army. The investigative units are responsible for investigating crimes committed by military personnel or civilians accused of committing crimes on military reservations.

The Naval Investigative Service. The U.S. Navy designates its investigative unit the Naval Investigative Service (NIS). This organization conducts the investigations above as they relate to navy or marine personnel. In addition, the

NIS functions as a counterintelligence unit. The NIS currently has about 900 special agents, composed of both military and civilian personnel. These officers work out of 150 offices and numerous shipboard assignments.

The Criminal Investigation Command.   The army's CID, so-called because it was once the Criminal Investigation Division, conducts criminal investigations of military personnel. When civilians are involved, this unit usually works in conjunction with local police. The CID also provides protective services to the Secretary of Defense and the Secretary of the Army. Occasionally, the CID assists the U.S. Secret Service.

The Office of Special Investigations.   The OSI of the U.S. Air Force consists of about 1900 special agents. Like the Navy, these agents may be either military or civilian. The OSI conducts investigations similar to those of the Navy and Army organizations. Additionally, the OSI is involved in counterintelligence activities. It also provides protective services for officials from the Department of Defense as well as for the Secretary of the Air Force.

Offices of the Inspector General

A number of investigative agencies have been established under the Inspector General. Created in 1978, these offices are responsible for investigating fraud against government programs. Most investigations by these agents concern embezzlement, kickbacks, filing false statements, mail fraud, and conspiracy.

The Department of Defense also has an Office of Inspector General. This agency has 6000 investigators responsible either to the Inspector General or to the military. These agents are responsible for investigating allegations of fraud in defense contracts.

INTERNATIONAL AGENCIES

There are no international agencies with true police jurisdiction. A number of agencies exist to enhance international cooperation. The International Maritime Commission, for example, was created to resolve issues concerning trade and jurisdiction on the high seas. A different type of international organization is Amnesty International, a privately funded organization devoted to investigating and protesting human rights abuses. The agency established for the express purpose of enhancing law enforcement in the international arena, however, is INTERPOL.

INTERPOL

In 1923, Johann Schober, police commissioner of Vienna, organized a conference of police officials from 20 countries to promote mutual assistance and cooperation. As a result of this conference a small office was created in Vienna under the name International Police Organization (INTERPOL). As a result of a worldwide counterfeiting problem that arose after World War I, INTERPOL, in conjunction with the League of Nations, became active in investigating and tracing organized counterfeiting gangs.

INTERPOL membership was extended beyond Europe in the following years. In 1938, legislation was passed that allowed the United States to join this organization. J. Edgar Hoover was thus permitted to accept membership in INTERPOL. The following year, Austria was annexed to Germany and the Gestapo perverted INTERPOL to help trace Jews fleeing Nazi Germany. The United States, as well as many other nations, withdrew from INTERPOL. This organization became dormant until after World War II.

In 1946, INTERPOL was reorganized, with Hoover elected one of the vice-presidents. The relationship between Hoover and other INTERPOL leaders was not a happy one. In 1950, the FBI withdrew from participation. The U.S. contact with this organization was, however, maintained through the Department of the Treasury.

In the mid-1970s, a turf battle ensued between the Treasury Department and Department of Justice. The Attorney General decided that the Justice Department should have the official connection with INTERPOL; Treasury objected. It was finally decided that Treasury and Justice would share the responsibility for representing the United States in INTERPOL. This agreement was subsequently amended with Justice gaining control over the INTERPOL–USNCB (U.S. National Central Bureau).[13]

By 1986 there were 138 INTERPOL members. Membership is accomplished by a nation merely stating its intention to join. There is no provision for expelling members. Members can resign if they so wish. Currently, there are no communist nations represented in INTERPOL.

The General Secretariat is now located at St. Cloud, France. Its major function is intelligence. INTERPOL has no criminal investigators. It gathers information on international criminal activities such as drug smuggling and white slavery. Currently, INTERPOL is not involved in investigating or tracking terrorist organizations. Their constitution prohibits investigating activities of a racial, military or religious nature.

PRIVATE SECURITY

The private security industry has been experiencing tremendous growth. These agencies are perceived to be more responsive than government law enforcement to the needs of its customer. The values of the security firm are clearly those of its employer. Moreover, private security can devote all of its energies to helping its clients, whereas the police must respond to every citizen concern.

It is estimated that by 1986, there were 1.1 million people employed in private security.[14] This figure indicates that private security is a larger force than the police. In fact, private security officers have consistently outnumbered the police since the 1950s.

The authority granted to private security operatives varies from state to state. Some states require licensing. Many others also have regulations controlling the activities of such firms. The problems associated with private security will become increasingly sensitive over the coming years. Private security personnel, because they are not government officials, are not subject to many of the legal restrictions imposed upon the police. For example, private security agents are not required to administer the *Miranda* warning prior to an in-custody interrogation. As private agencies become more active in the area of criminal investigations and apprehensions, the question of constitutional rights versus agency powers is likely to arise within the nation's courts.

Careers in private security are varied. The lowest-level position is usually the *security guard,* historically known as the "night watchman." These people are usually the least trained and have the lowest qualifications in the industry. Their function is to guard property or check identification at points of entry or exit for private businesses. Many of these positions are at minimum wage and frequently go to people who have difficulty finding work elsewhere. Some are frustrated police officers, people who want to be in law enforcement, but lack the qualifications.

A career level above that of security officer is the *hardware specialist.* People with backgrounds in electrical technology usually become involved in this portion of the business. There is a growing demand for electronic security devices. This includes not only the standard intrusion devices, such as burglar alarms, but also video monitoring equipment, motion detectors, and audio monitoring systems. It may be that the most profitable portion of the security industry is in the sale and installation of hardware.

Another career option is the *security consultant.* This person is part crime prevention specialist and salesperson. Sometimes these people work on commission, sometimes on salary; they are responsible for analyzing a client's security problems, proposing a solution, and contracting for the implementation of the security program. This person may or may not be involved in the management of the security system once it is in place. That is a function of *security management* and may be a specialty in itself.

At its highest and most expensive level, the *security specialist* provides intensive security for a specific purpose. Antiterrorist security for international firms, for example, has become a large and lucrative industry over the past 20 years.

Finally, let us not forget the private detective. Private investigations may be conducted through a corporation for a specific problem. For example, investigators for insurance companies serve such a purpose.

Another way of classifying these occupations is by proprietary security and contractual services. Proprietary security is the creation of the organization needing the security. In this model the organization will appoint a head of security to manage this organizational division or unit. Contractual services are provided by a security company. Anything from guards to electronic devices may be supplied as part of the contractual obligations. A national study found that about 450,000 people work in proprietary programs while 640,000 work in contract services.[15]

The study above, known as the *Hallcrest Report,* identified some real weaknesses in the private security industry. The major problem lies in the area of training and qualifications. Currently, there are few standards for selection and training of private security forces. Moreover, the expansion of the private security industry has generated additional work for the public police. It has been estimated that 10 to 12 percent of all police calls are false burglar alarms.[16]

To counter these problems, the Hallcrest Report formulated several recommendations. They urged the upgrading of employee qualifications, the creation of state regulatory bodies with powers to establish rules and regulations for this industry and the introduction of mandatory training standards. Furthermore, the report encouraged expanded interaction between police and private security, such as sharing of information, and the transfer of some police functions, such as responding to burglar alarms, to private security agencies.

SUMMARY

Law enforcement in the United States is multilayered and fragmented. The reason for this is due to the uneven development of a multilayered system of government. Several historical factors, some of which are contradictory, have caused this structure. First, Americans have little faith in a strong central government when it concerns life in the local community. There is now, and always has been, a strong tendency to want local control of law enforcement agencies. At the same time, Americans have more faith in a strong central government to provide a system of checks and balances on local politics. We assume local politics to be open to manipulation. We desire a central government that is above that kind of activity. The result is a local police force that is supposedly sensitive to the wishes of the community and federal and state agencies that are neutral. The result is fragmented law enforcement with duplication of effort and uneven standards and operational effectiveness.

This array of police forces start at the local level, which include municipal and county organizations. State agencies provide a number of services, including investigations, traffic control on state highways, and in some cases, rural law enforcement. The federal agencies are much more specialized, with a vast array of police elements with narrow missions.

On the international level there are several organizations that attempt to provide information and encourage international cooperation among the world's police agencies. Of these the most influential is INTERPOL, which is based in

France and maintains communications with more than 100 different member nations.

Finally, we have seen that private security in this nation is a rapidly growing industry. There are currently more people employed in the security field than in public law enforcement. This trend should continue with private security coming under the increasing scrutiny of the court system.

DISCUSSION QUESTIONS

1. Why are the most critical police services provided by municipal law enforcement?
2. What makes the county sheriff distinct from other law enforcement administrators?
3. Identify those federal, state, and local police agencies responsible for waging the war against illicit drugs.
4. Describe the ways in which the agencies in Question 3 interact to stop the traffic in illicit drugs.
5. What types of problems will the growth in private security create for the American court system?
6. Identify the problems specifically facing rural law enforcement in the United States.

NOTES/REFERENCES

1. *Report to the Nation on Crime and Justice*, 2nd ed. (Washingon, D.C.: U.S. Department of Justice, 1988), p. 63.
2. Howard Abadinsky, *An Introduction to Crime and Justice* (Chicago: Nelson-Hall Publishers, 1987), p. 155.
3. Thomas Reppetto, *The Blue Parade* (New York: The Free Press, 1978), p. 130.
4. Abadinsky, p. 250.
5. Richard Wilmer Rowan, *The Pinkertons: A Detective Dynasty* (Boston: Little, Brown & Company, 1931).
6. Philip H. Melanson, *The Politics of Protection: The United States Secret Service in the Terrorist Age* (New York: Praeger Publishers, 1984).
7. *Criminal Justice Careers Guidebook*, 1982, p. 62.
8. Abadinsky, p. 243.
9. *Federal Register*, 1984.
10. Carol Allen-Baley, "Border Patrol Officers Attempt to Stem the Alien Tide," *Police Product News,* Dec. 1984, pp. 30–49.
11. G. O. W. Mueller and Freda Adler, *Outlaws of the Ocean* (New York: Hearst Marine Books, 1985), p. 85.

12. *A Sailor's Guide*, as of 1984, as cited in Mueller and Adler, pp. 125–127.

13. Abadinsky, p. 269.

14. *Report to the Nation. . .,* p. 66.

15. William Cunningham and Todd Taylor, *The Growing Role of Private Security* (Washington, D.C.: U.S. Government Printing Office, 1984).

16. Joseph J. Senna and Larry J. Seigel, *Introduction to Criminal Justice,* 5th ed. (St. Paul, Minn.: West Publishing Co., 1990), p. 201.

Chapter 4

Recruiting, Selection, and Training

Key Terms

Recruiting strategies
Applicant pool
Affirmative Action
Civil Rights Act of 1964
Equal Employment Act of 1972
Equal Employment Opportunity
  Commission
Realistic job preview
Personnel interview

Oral board
Nonstress interview
Stress interview
Age Discrimination in Employment
  Act of 1967
Bona fide occupational qualification
Polygraph
Psychological stress evaluator
Field training officer

Chapter Objectives

At the conclusion of this chapter, students should be able to:

1. Understand the police selection process.
2. Understand the theory and application of Affirmative Action programs.
3. Assess their own potential for obtaining a position in law enforcement.

INTRODUCTION

The selection of competent personnel is crucial to the development of any organization. This is especially true for the development of an effective law enforcement agency. Unlike many other occupations, the police work almost exclusively with people, frequently under less than ideal circumstances.

All organizations need qualified employees. In addition to the reasons for competent personnel in private industry, four additional arguments for a competent police selection process have been identified as unique. First, police officers act alone, usually without supervision. Because of this, officers are given broad discretionary powers. They must utilize good judgment and have an innate sense of fairness and moderation. Second, the police agency is not only selecting police officers, but also hiring future police administrators. Lateral entry is the exception rather than the rule in law enforcement. It is from the new recruits, therefore, that future sergeants, captains, and chiefs will be selected. Bad police recruits ultimately are transformed into bad administrators. Third, the news and fictional media have put law enforcement in a spotlight. People currently expect more from their police than at any time in history. They expect efficiency, effectiveness, and compassion; many are unwilling to settle for less. Finally, the number of successful civil liability claims against the police has made poor policing too costly to accept. The court system has become much more willing to punish financially jurisdictions that allow their police to make poor decisions and take inappropriate actions.[1]

The problem becomes even more complicated for the police administrator because of the inability to test the applicant on police knowledge. Since the majority of applicants have no police background or training, they must be hired on their perceived ability to learn proper information and techniques. This need introduces a large amount of guesswork into the law enforcement hiring system.

No one has ever been able to identify specifically those characteristics that make some people better prospects for law enforcement careers than others. Also, many of the criteria for selection seem to be based more on the perceptions of police work than upon its realities. This chapter is devoted to helping the reader understand the police selection process. We discuss the relative merits of each of the screening factors used by law enforcement agencies. It should be understood, however, that not every police agency uses all, or any, of the following procedures. Cost factors and administrative philosophy will determine both the steps and the degree to which each procedure is used.

RECRUITING

Recruiting should not be confused with the selection process. The philosophy of recruiting is to get as many applicants into the process as possible. The screening process, on the other hand, is concerned with eliminating applicants that do not meet the agency's selection criteria.

Recruiting is therefore rarely assigned to personnel who are also involved in selection. There is a conflict of interest between these two operations; using the same people to do both jobs sets up an intolerable degree of goal confusion within the personnel unit. Sometimes, however, the size and resource limitations of the agency force it to integrate both recruiting and selection into one unit. Although this is a questionable practice, it sometimes cannot be helped.

There are a number of factors that affect the *recruiting strategies* used by police agencies. The first question is how far must an agency go to find suitable personnel. When assessing the *pool of potential applicants,* the police personnel director must know the size of the potential pool as well as the sexual and racial makeup of that group. Large departments have sometimes found it necessary to engage in nationwide recruiting campaigns, while smaller departments can usually find the personnel they need within a radius of 100 to 200 miles.

Cost is another factor that cannot be overlooked. Nationwide searches require expensive advertising campaigns as well as the capability of processing applicants from remote locations. Although it is not unreasonable to ask an applicant to appear at the agency for a series of tests and interviews, it is unreasonable to ask an applicant to make three or four long trips over a three- to four-month period for this processing. If we assume that the applicant is seeking employment, it is not safe to assume that this person has the money to pay for the cost of the travel and lodging necessary for these trips.

Equal Opportunity Employment

Affirmative Action programs are a fact of life for all organizations, but this is especially true of government agencies. Courts have consistently maintained that law enforcement agencies must strive to employ women and minorities. By definition, affirmative action means that employers must actively recruit, hire, and promote members of minority groups if minority groups are underrepresented in that agency.[2]

To deal with what appeared to be a serious problem of discrimination, Congress passed a number of laws regulating employment. The two most powerful of these acts are the *Civil Rights Act of 1964* and the *Equal Employment Act of 1972*. These laws make it illegal to discriminate on the basis of race, color, religion, national origin, or sex in hiring or promotional decisions.

The responsibility for enforcing federal law related to discrimination rests with the *Equal Employment Opportunity Commission (EEOC)*. This agency can take the organization to court for violations of the law. The more usual practice, however, is to attempt to persuade the offending organization to settle with the complainant by paying damages and changing the discriminatory policies.

Federal law. Since the promulgation of the foregoing laws, other regulations have been added to make the legislation stronger. Federal law relating to discrimination now addresses the following issues:

1. *Race, color, or national origin.* The law clearly states that it is illegal to dis-

criminate on the basis of race, color, or national origin. There are no exceptions.

2. *Sex.* In only a few cases is it legal to discriminate on the basis of sex. In such cases it is the responsibility of the agency to prove that, for example, a woman would not be able to perform the job in question. Law enforcement has not been identified as such a job.

3. *Appearance.* Many firms want their employees, especially those who deal with the public, to meet good grooming standards. Although there have been cases of "appearance" discrimination, organizations generally have the right to require their employees to meet appearance standards.

4. *Age.* It is no longer legal for employers, in most occupations, to force employees to retire at age 70. One exception is top executives with an income of $27,000 or more. In some states, forced retirement is now illegal in all cases. The age law also protects people between the ages of 40 and 70 from discrimination.

5. *Handicapped.* Every employer who has a contract with the federal government worth $2500 or more must actively seek to hire and promote handicapped people. A handicapped person is defined as anyone with a physical or mental problem that limits the person's normal activities. The law states, however, that the handicapped person must be qualified to perform the particular job for which he or she is being considered.[3]

The laws related to the handicapped have not been a problem for law enforcement at the federal level, but such is not the case at the state level. Wisconsin, for example, defines a handicapped person as someone who is excluded from employment because of a physical or mental impairment. When a law enforcement agency rejects an applicant due to that person's inability to meet specific physical requirements, the person is legally defined as handicapped. At that point, the burden of proof rests with the hiring agency to established that the requirements are reasonable. This law has already had an adverse impact on the vision requirements of at least one law enforcement agency; that case (*Brown County* v. *LIRC*) will be discussed more fully when we look at vision standards. Quite likely, this is only the start of a process wherein police physical standards are closely scrutinized by courts for job relatedness and fairness.

The realities of affirmative action. There is a disturbing trend developing among white college-age men. They seem to believe that Affirmative Action programs adversely affect white males. The hostility with which such programs are viewed threaten to disrupt the social harmony that has been developing between the races.

Although there is currently no research to support my theory, I believe that Equal Employment laws have been as beneficial to white males as to minorities and females. We tend to forget the past, especially those things that were unpleasant. There is no doubt that minorities and women were excluded from many occupations, including law enforcement, for many years. The first real impact of Equal Employment laws and regulations was breakdown of the employment barrier. This had an immediate impact on minorities and women. Over the long run, however, white men may well have benefited the most. This occurred because Affirmative Action programs required agencies to tie selection and promotion decision making to objective job-related criteria.

The procedural safeguards designed to protect minorities and women made it difficult for administrators to use the old system of personal loyalty and patronage to hire and promote officers. While white males had been admitted to law enforcement agencies, the existing employment standards were based on friendship and politics. Furthermore, once hired, they were subjected to a system of promotion based on preferential treatment. The "good ole boy" network worked only for good ole boys, men whose positions were based on family connections or mutual "backscratching." Those not so classified were excluded from the club. They were better off than minorities and females only in that they were allowed to work for the agency. Beyond that they were treated no better than minorities and women.

Affirmative Action has required fair, objective selection and promotion standards and procedures. No one, not even white males, were covered under these procedures in the past. The requirement that agencies select and promote fairly has improved the work environment for everybody, especially white males.

Recruiting strategies.   Research has found that while police agencies have not been highly successful in the recruiting of minorities, there are a number of specific practices that enhance the effectiveness of the Affirmative Action program.[4] The presence or absence of a minority hiring goal, for example, usually portends success or failure of the program. At the same time, it was found that maintaining high selection standards successfully reduced hostility to such programs by white male officers. This would indicate that fears of hiring unqualified officers because of an Affirmative Action program are unnecessary if handled correctly.

The foregoing study also recommended the elimination of numerical lists for hiring, arguing instead for a pass/fail system that gave administrators sufficient leeway to hire minorities without being required to jump over higher-rated applicants to employ those who are qualified but occupy a lower position on the list. Finally, it was observed that employee acceptance of an Affirmative Action program often rests with the perceived commitment of the agency administrators to the hiring of minorities.

Finding qualified applicants is often a problem. The fact that there are numerous people who might wish to apply for a job in law enforcement is irrelevant if these persons are unaware that job openings exist. There are a number of ways in which a police agency may make its needs known. The more common ones are newspaper advertisements, public employment agencies, private employment agencies, and institutions of higher education. The question, once more, is how

Irving Police
Recruiting
Career Officers

REQUIREMENTS

1. AGE: Minimum 21
2. U.S. CITIZENSHIP
3. EDUCATION: High School
4. HEIGHT AND WEIGHT in Proportion
5. VISION: 20/70 Corrected to 20/20 No Color Blindness
6. Valid Texas Drivers License and Acceptable Driving Record
7. Written Test, Physical Agility, Polygraph Exam, Background Investigation, Oral Interview, Physical, and Psychological Exam

CAREER BENEFITS

1. VACATION: 15 Days Per Year
2. SICK LEAVE: 15 Days Per Year
3. HOLIDAYS: 8 Days Per Year
4. INSURANCE: Life and Major Medical, Hospitalization, and Dental Plan
5. UNIFORMS AND EQUIPMENT: Furnished by the City
6. RETIREMENT: Municipal Retirement System
7. SALARY: A Six Step Salary Plan
8. STATE CIVIL SERVICE
9. INCENTIVE PAY PROGRAM: (College or Certification)

SALARY_____ PER MONTH

THE CITY OF IRVING, TEXAS, THE THIRD LARGEST CITY IN DALLAS COUNTY, TEXAS IS CURRENTLY SEEKING APPLICANTS FOR THE POSITION OF ENTRY LEVEL POLICE OFFICER. THOSE QUALIFIED PERSONS DESIRING A CHALLENGING CAREER IN LAW ENFORCEMENT SHOULD CONTACT THE CITY OF IRVING PERSONNEL OFFICE, 825 WEST IRVING BOULEVARD, IRVING, TEXAS 75060.

FOR ADDITIONAL INFORMATION, CONTACT THE POLICE DEPARTMENT PERSONNEL SECTION AT THE IRVING POLICE / FIRE TRAINING ACADEMY, 2603 ESTERS ROAD, IRVING, TEXAS 75062. TELEPHONE: (214) 594-1262.

Photograph 4–1   Recruiting Poster

far away from the jurisdiction of the agency should the recruiting officer go to publicize job openings. The answer is: as far as it is necessary to go to get a sufficiently large pool of qualified applicants. The final decision is usually determined by the combination of geographic density of applicant pool and the size of the budget allocated to the recruiting process.

THE SELECTION PROCESS

Personnel selection is seen by some as a game of chance.[5] Others see it the same way but seek to minimize the risks associated with chance. At the heart of personnel selection is prediction. The personnel officer attempts to predict whether or not a job applicant will become an effective employee. This decision is based on the results obtained in the process through which applicants are evaluated. The competence of the final decision is to a large degree determined by the ability of each step to predict accurately the future ability of the applicant on the criteria being examined.

The great difficulty with the police selection process is the lack of research dealing with precisely what police agencies should seek to identify in their applicants. By and large, most law enforcement agencies have adopted a general agreement on qualifications, based on traditional theories of policing. Some of these concepts are probably valid; others, unfortunately, are based on inappropriate stereotypes and will, in all likelihood, be tested in court within the next 5 to 10 years.

There may be as many as nine different stages in the selection process. These steps may or may not all be used by a specific agency. There is also no definite order in which the applicant may be processed. The possible stages are: application, written examination, interviews, physical agility tests, background investigation, medical examination, polygraph examination, psychological examination, and probationary period.[6]

Generally speaking, the number of stages used and the order in which they are administered depends on the philosophy of the police administration and cost factors. The more the chief executive is committed to intensive screening of applicants, the greater will be the utilization of possible techniques. Since cost is always a prime consideration in any organization, most agencies also use budgetary information when deciding how many steps to include in the screening process. Moreover, police agencies attempt to order the screening process in such a way as to eliminate as many unqualified applicants as possible as early in the process as possible, using the least costly of the techniques. For example, a good written exam is very cost-effective and eliminates many who do not meet basic intellectual requirements; thus this step will usually be found early in the screening process. Psychological examinations, on the other hand, are very expensive and, by and large, eliminate very few applicants. This procedure will therefore usually be found at or near the end of the selection process.

The Application

One of the most underrated steps in the selection process is the written application. Private industry has found that applicants can help both themselves and their employer when they self-select themselves out of consideration because the job is not what they expected.[7] Research has demonstrated the effectiveness of a *realistic job preview* (RJP) in reducing unrealistic job expectations and turnover.[8] Selection decisions are therefore enhanced when both parties share, rather than conceal, relevant information for making the person–job match.[9]

The application form represents the second step in the application process. The job advertisement is the first. It is at that point that the RJP is most effective. The potential applicant should have a good idea of what the job entails and can decide whether or not to proceed.

If the decision is made to apply for the position, the application form should be constructed in such a way as to further refine what the agency wishes. For example, most law enforcement agencies are reluctant to employ ex-felons. Asking for criminal history information on the form and including a cover sheet explaining what type of history will automatically eliminate an applicant can result in some applicants voluntarily removing themselves from the process. The same is true of physical limitations, educational requirements, or any other requirement where the candidate is capable of making a candid self-assessment.

Many departments include a short interview with the applicant at this stage. A personnel officer simply goes over the application with the candidate. This will sometimes result in the removal of an unqualified candidate from the process. This usually occurs in cases where the applicant was unable to make a realistic self-appraisal and needs the aid of someone familiar with the screening process.

Written Examination

The written exam has been a standard part of the police selection process since the creation of Civil Service. Until the early 1960s this was accepted as a legitimate step in applicant screening. This screening device is still used heavily in law enforcement, but the courts have begun to take a hard look at it to determine if written exams are discriminatory.

The question of court concern deals with job relatedness. To date there is no research that has established a correlation between scores on a police entrance exam and successful job performance. The difficulty in designing a written exam comes from the fact that most applicants have no police background. What would appear to be a valid test, one with law enforcement-related questions, would eliminate anyone without police experience. This is obviously nonproductive. The questions of concern, therefore, are: What capabilities are being tested, how do they relate to the job, and is the test designed in such a way as not to discriminate against minorities?

Police civil service entrance exams have, therefore, taken on the appearance of college entrance exams. General information-type questions are asked that test the applicant's level of reading comprehension, deductive ability, and memory. By and large, these tests have been upheld in court, even though there is still little certainty of their relationship to the job.

As a screening device, however, written examinations offer police agencies an objective means of eliminating applicants who are functionally illiterate, undereducated, or intellectually weak. It adds the further dimension of ranking applicants. Most other steps are pass/fail. The written exam, however, allows the personnel officer to list the candidates in order of test performance. Although, as mentioned earlier, this is not conducive to effective affirmative action programs, for many departments it provides an early means of establishing hiring priorities.

Most police entrance examinations are objective, multiple-choice tests. Some, however, are essay exams. The objective tests are much more common, although the essay format can provide a better understanding of the applicant's ability to write concise, coherent reports (absolutely necessary for effective law enforcement). The problems associated with the subjective nature of essay exams, however, make them especially susceptible to charges of discrimination. Also, a large body of applicants taking the written exam would require vastly more time and effort on the part of the test graders to evaluate essays, when multiple-choice tests are graded quickly and accurately.

Interviews

One of the procedures most susceptible to abuse is the interview. This is because of its less structured approach and the inherent secrecy of the interviewer's deliberations.[10] Oral interviews often allow the agency a pretext with which to discriminate. This not only happens to minorities and women, but other factors are sometimes involved. For example, if the interviewing officers believe police officers should be a certain size, short people, who are successful in the other phases, may fail to pass the oral interview. Despite these problems, however, an oral interview is usually a good idea. Law enforcement is a high communication occupation. At some point in the selection process it is necessary to determine if the candidate can speak coherently.

There are a number of different types of interview, each with its own purpose. One we have already discussed is the *personnel interview*. Usually conducted by an individual personnel officer shortly after the candidate submits the application, this interview is designed to verify the information on the form and to eliminate those individuals who are obviously not qualified.

Another form of interview is the *oral board*. This interview is conducted by a group of people who are usually members of the agency, although this is not absolute. The idea behind this interview is to have the perspective of several individuals concerning the ability of the candidate to interact with a group. Observations are not only made about the candidate's knowledge, but also concerning professional appearance, ability to put thoughts together in a meaningful way, and ability to articulate ideas.

Two strategies have evolved concerning oral boards. One, the more common, is the *nonstress interview*. In this form, the board asks nonoffensive questions in an attempt to learn something about the person, such as their goals and ethics. The typical interview using this format lasts from about 20 to 90 minutes. The second strategy, the *stress interview,* is designed to test the candidate's ability to think under pressure. In this format, which may last several hours, the applicant is subjected to a fierce cross-examination. The intent is to see if the candidate will break down, resulting in some form of emotional outburst. The theory is that police officers must be able to maintain their poise in stressful situations.

The nonstress interview is the most widely used, although some elements of the stress interview have been known to be inserted into this type as well. Whether good or bad, the oral interview is usually a standard fixture in the police selection process, and is likely to continue as such.

Physical Agility Tests

The belief that law enforcement sometimes requires physical activities, such as moving the injured from hazardous areas or taking hostile individuals into custody, has led to the creation of the physical agility course. The proliferation of

Photograph 4-2 Physical Agility Course

such tests is a by-product of the deemphasis of height and weight restrictions, which is related to the increased number of female and small male candidates for law enforcement. Since police officers are perceived as sometimes needing above average strength and dexterity, such tests are deemed necessary.[11]

The question, yet to be addressed in court, is whether or not these tests are valid in departments that have no requirement that officers maintain their physical condition after being hired. The argument for having the physical agility test rests on the need for officers to be able to perform certain physical acts. This would seem to be as necessary for 5- and 10-year veterans as for new recruits, but thus far, physical agility tests have survived challenge.

To be effective, this type of test should be the result of a thorough job analysis of the specific agency's routine, nonroutine, and emergency duties. While some tasks are common to all law enforcement agencies, there are usually some that are specific to individual jurisdictions. State agencies, for example, are more likely to be required to push a stalled vehicle from an interstate highway than are municipal officers. Still other departments may provide push bars on patrol vehicles to handle this type of problem. Job requirements, as we see, can differ greatly from agency to agency.

The areas generally found to be job related to law enforcement are reaction time, grip strength, coordination, and balance.[12] A variety of tasks that measure one or more of these areas are usually included in the overall test. To be truly job related, the agency should provide instruction on technique and allow the candidates an opportunity to practice. By doing this, the agency can be certain it is testing the true physical ability of the candidate, rather than their familiarity, or lack of familiarity, with the course.

Background Investigation

The only effective means that a law enforcement agency has to determine the true character of an applicant, as well as to discover how that person relates to others, is through the background investigation. Many applicants look good "on paper"; that is, they can manipulate the application information so as to enhance their strengths and eliminate or deemphasize their weaknesses. The background investigation seeks to discover that information the applicant would not like the agency to know.

It would be nice to think that the purpose of this portion of the process is neutral, to get both positive information as well as negative. To a small extent that is the case, but truthfully, the investigator is seeking negative information. The investigative assumption is that the candidate provided sufficient positive information to justify selection to the agency. Lacking the capacity to rebut the candidate's application, the presumption is that the candidate should be hired. Unless the choice is between several good candidates for a single position, the police agency does not need further positive information to make the decision to hire the candidate. The presence or absence of negative information, therefore, is often the factor upon which the decision to hire or reject will be made.

For an in-depth assessment, the agency needs information on the following areas: criminal history, employment record, credit record, sociability, mental and emotional condition and history, personal integrity, education history, and medical history.[13] By obtaining information concerning these areas, the selection board seeks to verify the information contained on the application form as well as to discover those not-so-easy-to-find personality traits that might indicate future job-related problems.

The fact that most police candidates are young both complicates and simplifies the investigative process. It is simplified because there are fewer places to go and people to contact concerning the applicant than would be expected of an older person. At the same time, fewer contacts limits the ability to determine the relative merits of the candidates. Although the process for young candidates is simpler, it is also prone to be less effective.

Law enforcement agencies have discovered that the only means to ensure effectiveness is with thoroughness. The person assigned to background investigations must be provided sufficient information with which to conduct a complete check of the candidates. Each candidate should be asked to provide both an application form and a personal history. The investigator should have a copy of both. The forms should contain the following information (not necessarily in this order):

1. Privacy Act release statement signed by the applicant, which gives the law enforcement agency access to school records, credit records, employment records, and medical records
2. A signed statement by the applicant that the facts contained in the two forms are correct, and an acknowledgment that falsification will automatically disqualify the applicant from consideration
3. Date and place of birth
4. Full name and address
5. A list of all past employers with dates of employment, salary, position held, duties, and reasons for leaving
6. A list of all schools attended, dates, degrees, and grades
7. Personal character references, with addresses and telephone numbers
8. A list of addresses of all the locations where the applicant has resided
9. Marital status and past marital history
10. A financial statement listing all debts and obligations as well as assets, holdings, and business interests
11. Medical history, including illness, injuries, nervous disorders, medication being taken, and so on
12. List of doctors attended, names, addresses, reason, and other pertinent information

13. List of all arrests and convictions for traffic violations and criminal conduct (local law may restrict this information to convictions only)

14. Special skills, accomplishments, awards, hobbies, and interests

15. A list and explanation of any civil court action in which the applicant was a named party[14]

Once this information is gathered, it becomes the duty of the selection board, or personnel director, to perform an evaluation of the data. The background investigator rarely performs this task; this person maintains the position of neutral gatherer of facts.

A number of factors that lead to elimination are obvious: felony convictions, dishonorable discharge, falsification of the application. Other facts may indicate a physical or mental deficiency that requires screening by a medical board. Still other information—poor work habits, lack of social adaptability—must be examined by the board and a decision made. These decisions are the most difficult because they are the most subjective.

When a candidate is rejected, it is essential the board/director state the reasons clearly and place such information in the candidate's permanent record. At some time this record may become evidence in a civil suit; it is mandatory that the reasons for the decision be well thought out and supported with evidence. Additionally, the decision must be fair and consistent; one applicant should not be rejected for a poor driving record if another candidate, with an equally poor record, is selected.[15]

Medical Requirements

The object of medical screening is to select healthy personnel free of physical defects, neurological defects, or pathological conditions that would interfere with the full performance of duties or would cause progressive physical deterioration.[16] It is critical that a competent medical examination be performed by a physician who understands the police occupational requirements. The physician(s) must also be prepared to deal with deception. Some applicants will go to amazing lengths to obtain a position with a law enforcement agency. For example, candidates have been known to memorize eye charts and submit fraudulent urine samples.

Although many physical standards are controversial, there appears to be agreement among law enforcement agencies that an effective medical screening process includes the following:

1. Administering a comprehensive medical questionnaire covering the family health history and current health habits, such as smoking, alcohol intake, physical activity, and medications. Special emphasis should be placed on primary risk factors of coronary heart disease, such as high blood fat levels

(cholesterol and triglycerides), obesity, physical inactivity, and family history of heart disease.

2. Taking the following recommended laboratory tests (budget permitting):

   a. Chest x-ray

   b. Physical inspection of the spine and limbs for bone and joint abnormalities and of the neck, chest, abdomen, eyes, ears, nose, and throat

   c. Auscultation (listening) of the heart and lung sounds for identification of possible cardiac murmurs, dysrhythmias, or chronic lung disease

   d. Measurement of resting heart rate, blood pressure, and respiration

   e. Chemical analysis of blood for levels of serum cholesterol, triglycerides, glucose, and uric acid

   f. Resting 12-lead electrocardiogram

   g. Exercise stress EKG

   h. Height and weight[17]

Age.   There is no absolute consensus as to what range of age is most suitable for police work. This is as true of when a person starts the career as of when an officer ends one. Most law enforcement agencies require candidates to be 21 years of age. Some police departments, however, have experimented with hiring people between 18 and 21 years of age. The Houston, Philadelphia, and Louisville police departments successfully incorporated younger officers and reported no ill effects of this procedure.[18] By and large, however, the typical law enforcement agency hires only applicants 21 or older.

The majority of law enforcement agencies also have maximum age limits for hiring. Commonly, the age of 35, or somewhere in that vicinity, appears to be fairly standard. This requirement has been upheld in court.[19] The basis for that decision, and similar ones, was that police work was a special case in which the officer must have agility, alertness, and dexterity. The idea of maximum hiring ages, therefore, seems well established at this time.

The *Age Discrimination in Employment Act of 1967,* amended in 1974, is the primary federal legislation dealing with people between the ages of 40 and 65. This law states that a person between these ages cannot be treated differently in hiring, discharge, or retirement. The only exception is in those cases where age is a bona fide occupation qualification, in which it can be used as an employment standard.[20] Since the majority of age-related hiring caps are set below 40, this law does not affect most police agencies.

A greater controversy exists concerning mandatory retirement age. As long as the courts accept the idea that police work is physically taxing and that age is a legitimate concern for police agencies, this law will probably not adversely affect the police selection process. Thus far the courts have held age to be a *bona fide occupational qualification* (BFOQ) of law enforcement. As a result, mandatory retirement age requirements have been found legally valid. So far, the youngest required retirement age accepted by the courts appears to be 50.[21] In this case the court held that there is a relationship between advancing age and decreased physical capabilities. The court accepted the assumption that police work is a physically taxing occupation. It should be pointed out, however, that this case was argued on constitutional grounds and did not address the issue of mandatory retirements as it relates to age discrimination. It remains for future court action to decide that issue.

   Vision.   Vision requirements have undergone modification in the past 10 to 20 years. There was a time when candidates were required to have perfect uncorrected vision (20/20) to be accepted into law enforcement. A study conducted in 1984, however, suggests that while there is general agreement that police officers should have corrected vision at or near 20/20, there is no consensus among police agencies concerning uncorrected vision requirements.[22]
   The courts have also begun to look at physical requirements to determine if they are discriminatory. The state of Wisconsin, for example, has rejected at least one such standard based on state laws prohibiting discrimination against the handicapped:

Brown County v. *Labor & Industrial Review Commission*
124 Wis. 2d 560 (1985)

In May, 1974, John Toonen applied for a job as a deputy sheriff with the Brown County Sheriff's Department. He was well qualified by experience and education for the position. He had served as a military police officer and had received an associate degree in police science. Before applying for employment with Brown County, he had served without any difficulties as a jail deputy, a dispatcher, and a traffic patrolman in Shawano County. He was told by the Brown County Sheriff's Department that upon the basis of his preliminary examination and experience, he would be hired as a traffic patrol officer by the county if he passed the physical. The physician examining for the county reported, however, that Toonen's uncorrected vision in each eye, 20/400, failed to meet the county's uncorrected vision requirement of 20/40 in the better eye and 20/100 in the poorer eye. By use of glasses or contact lenses, Toonen's vision was corrected to 20/20. Because his uncorrected vision did not meet the hiring standard, Toonen was not hired.
   In March 1980, Toonen filed a complaint with the Department of Industry, Labor and Human Relations (DILHR) alleging that Brown County had discriminated against him on the basis of a handicap. The record developed at a hearing in March 1981 before a DILHR hearing examiner reveals that Toonen never had any difficulty in performing his duties as a traffic officer because of his vision—that he had on occasion in the course of duty been in fights, sustained blows to

the head, but had never lost his contact lenses. There was expert testimony that modern contact lenses were very unlikely to be dislodged, and that even if one were lost, a person could see adequately with one lens. There was also evidence that patrolmen on the job with Brown County were not required to maintain the entrance level of uncorrected visual acuity and that serving traffic officers had visual acuity that did not meet the hiring standard.

In May 1981, the hearing examiner issued her decision. The hearing examiner found that Toonen was handicapped because of his visual impairment, that he had met the required burden under the act to show that he had been denied employment because of his handicap, and that Brown County had failed to meet its burden of showing that Toonen's handicap was reasonably related to his ability to perform on the job. The examiner held that Brown County had discriminated against Toonen in violation of WFEA and ordered Brown County to offer Toonen the next available position and to pay him back pay from January 1, 1980.

This decision was ultimately upheld by the Wisconsin Supreme Court.

As can be gleaned from the case, vision standards for law enforcement are currently in a state of flux. Historically, when a case such as the one above is decided against the police, it opens the floodgates for further litigation. Quite likely, future police vision requirements will be determined by the courts.

Color blindness is another area of police vision standards. It is safe to say that most law enforcement agencies require normal color vision. This is not an absolute standard with all agencies but one that has not been challenged in court. Whether or not it will be challenged and the likely outcome of such a challenge are open to speculation. As with visual acuity, the last word on color perception has yet to be written.

Dental requirements.   Dental problems alone have not been found to be grounds for denial of employment in a police organization. Sometimes, however, gum and teeth disorders are related to other areas of health, which might be sufficient for disqualification. The mere absence of teeth is not relative to the duties of the police officer, and we can only hope that the time is passed when such a test is used to make employment decisions.[23]

Hearing.   Hearing standards for the police have not been the subject of either research or litigation. An argument can be made that law enforcement, especially patrol, requires good hearing. The human ear can hear sounds ranging from 10 to 140 decibels. Above 100 decibels, sounds are painful; therefore, policing urban areas with the noise produced by aircraft, traffic, and construction can be damaging over a long period of time. It can be argued that since all personnel will eventually probably suffer from hearing loss, recruits should have the best possible hearing at the start of their career. Some authorities believe that the younger generation, with its tendency to listen to rock music at about the 130-decibel level, is subject to greater than normal hearing loss. Research has tended to confirm hearing deterioration across the entire population, especially among the younger members.[24] We may argue, therefore, that hearing standards may become increasingly important in law enforcement screening.

Height and weight. Areas that have received an inordinate amount of attention by the courts are requirements concerning height and weight, mostly height. Traditionally, police agencies have had minimum height requirements of between 5 feet 7 inches and 6 feet. The rationale for this is the belief that bigger people are harder to intimidate than smaller ones and are more able to complete successfully the physical tasks required of police officers. There is also a stereotype of the smaller man as having a constant "chip on his shoulder," the so-called Napoleon complex (the need to overcompensate for a lack of physical stature).

Law enforcement agencies have also had maximum height requirements, usually around 6 foot 6 inches. This was based on the assumption that anyone larger would have difficulty riding around in an automobile for long periods of time. There was also some concern about the availability and cost of uniforms for exceptionally large people.

We should take note of the fact that research conducted by Kenneth R. Willoughby and William R. Blount has shown that shorter officers score higher in aggression than do their taller counterparts.[25] The study, conducted in a southern state, looked at 125 officers. These officers were divided into three groups: short (those below 5 feet $9\frac{1}{2}$ inches), medium (between 5 feet $9\frac{1}{2}$ inches and 6 feet $\frac{1}{2}$ inch), and tall (over 6 feet $\frac{1}{2}$ inch). Using Spielberger's Trait Anger Scale, the researchers found that both short and medium-height officers scored significantly higher on aggression potential than did the taller officers.

Interestingly, although this study found no differences between the groups in number of arrests, a linear relationship was found between the groups and warning citations. The shorter group issued an average of 129.02 warnings while the medium-height group issued an average of 110.66 warnings and the tall group issued an average of 88.83 warnings.

The researchers concluded that the aggressive tendency was being spent on warnings, thus indicating that the shorter officers were successfully curtailing their potential for aggressiveness. In summary, while the aggressive tendency did exist in the shorter officers, it was not being manifested in a dysfunctional manner.

The legal challenges to height requirements have, as one might suspect, been aimed at job relatedness. Additional ammunition for those attacking these requirements has been the effect of height requirements on female applicants. Not surprisingly, many of the people attacking height requirements in court were female applicants who were rejected because of height.

The courts have taken a consistent stand on this issue. Height requirements must be job related and must not discriminate against women or ethnic minorities. By and large, the results of court challenges have led law enforcement agencies to abandon height requirements, opting instead for physical agility testing.

As a general rule, weight requirements have always been tied to height. A common policy among police agencies is that weight must be in proportion to height. There has been little court action regarding weight requirements for police applicants, but that could change. Nationwide, overweight people are fighting bias and employment discrimination. Law enforcement is not exempt from this attack, although the courts have regularly supported the idea that police agencies have a right to issue and enforce weight control directives.[26]

Polygraph Examination

The *polygraph,* sometimes incorrectly referred to as a lie detector, has been used extensively in applicant screening for law enforcement. Although not utilized universally, it is safe to say that the vast majority of police agencies rely heavily on the polygraph for preemployment screening. Interestingly, although the polygraph has been under increasing attack in the private sector, its use has not been the subject of attack within law enforcement. This is especially surprising in light of the court's steadfast refusal to allow polygraph testimony in criminal cases without permission of both prosecution and defense.

The theory behind the polygraph examination is that when a person has a psychological reaction to a stimulus, it produces a measurable physiological reaction. The term *polygraph* refers to a multipen system that measures instrumental responses on a roll of chart paper. The equipment provides simultaneous measures of breathing, blood pressure, and skin resistance to external electrical current (galvanic skin response). The stimulus producing the measurable effects may be the applicant's attempt to hide information or attempt to deceive the inter-

Photograph 4–3   Polygraph Examination

viewer. Another stimulus may be a reaction to a specific question or word due to a past traumatic experience.

The attacks on the polygraph and its use have come as the result of studies indicating that this instrument is not absolutely accurate. The possibility for error has made some industries reluctant to use the instrument in personnel decisions. The correct use of the polygraph, however, greatly reduces the chance of error. For the most part, police agencies use this device well and have benefited from a number of practical advantages from its use.

Law enforcement agencies have discovered, for example, that when they widely publicized their use of the polygraph, there were fewer undesirable applicants for police positions. The use of this instrument also makes a public statement regarding the police agency's determination to screen stringently those wishing to become police officers.[27]

Finally, research has uncovered some remarkable facts concerning applicants and the polygraph. In both private industry and law enforcement, the polygraph examination has uncovered startling information about potential employees, not obtainable through a normal background investigation. For example, among 190 candidates for police officer in the Chicago area, only 43 percent were considered qualified, while the remaining 57 percent indicated deception, found to include 35 burglaries and serious thefts, 3 robberies, 13 admitted use of narcotics, and 31 bribes to police officers. A later study of 225 applicants (in 1975) from the Chicago area again showed only 44 percent considered acceptable, with the remaining 56 percent showing deceptions, including 80 burglaries or serious thefts, 39 uses or sale of narcotics, 38 bribes to police officers, 30 instances of buying or selling stolen merchandise, and 6 admissions of indecent exposure, car theft, or hit-and-run accidents.[28]

The polygraph examination is a natural complement to the background investigation. Ideally, information gathered through either background investigation or the polygraph should be cross-checked through the other. This makes the two methods mutually reinforcing. Typically, the polygraph examination uncovers more extensive admissions than are found in the background check. Considering the cost and time factors involved, the polygraph is probably more efficient and effective.[29]

The following list is fairly typical of questions asked in the polygraph interview:

1. Have you ever been discharged from a job?
2. Do you want to become a police officer for dishonest purposes?
3. Do you intend to stay with this police department on a long-term basis?
4. Did you intentionally falsify or omit any information on your employment application?
5. Do you suffer from any condition that would hinder your performance as a police officer?
6. Are you currently being investigated for any criminal offense?

7. Have you ever been arrested or sentenced to jail?

8. Have you ever been involved in any criminal activity?

9. Has your driver's license ever been revoked or suspended?

10. Have you ever used marijuana?

11. Have you ever used or sold illegal drugs?

12. Are you delinquent on any of your financial obligations?

13. Have you ever been involved sexually with a child or with a member of your own sex?[30]

14. Have you ever participated in any activity for which you could be black-mailed?

It should be obvious that the polygraph examination is used as a check against all information supplied by the candidate, including motivation and job history.[31]

Voluntary admissions, both before and during, the formal polygraph examination are a normal part of the procedure. Any conclusions reported by the polygraph examiner are usually reviewed by an appropriate member of the screening committee. Not all admissions or disclosures disqualify a candidate; therefore, the decision concerning what should or should not disqualify an applicant is crucial to an effective selection procedure.

Psychological stress evaluation.   A measuring device, related to the polygraph, is the *psychological stress evaluator* (PSE). This device was developed by two retired Army intelligence officers and has been available since 1970. This instrument capitalizes on the principle of involuntary physiological changes that are related to psychological stress. It is designed to display graphically certain stress-related components of the human voice's two modulations, the audible and inaudible.[32]

This device has several advantages over the traditional polygraph. First, it is not necessary to "wire" the subject to the machine, as is required of the polygraph. All that is needed during the interview is a tape recorder. It is even possible to tape a telephone interview. The tape is then played through the PSE, where the analysis takes place. The instrument provides a chart of the voice pattern; areas of high stress stand out clearly from the normal voice pattern.

There is currently some controversy as to which instrument is most effective. One wonders why manufacturers of polygraph machines have not included voice analysis as an additional component of newer model polygraphs. In the future, I suspect, that is a likely development.

Psychological Screening

The components of the psychological screening process include a battery of psychological tests, a background analysis, and an in-depth or "clinical" interview by a psychologist knowledgeable in law enforcement. Some of the more frequently used tests are the Minnesota Multiphasic Personality Inventory (MMPI), the Sixteen Personality Factor Questionnaire (16PF), and the California Psychological Inventory (CPI).

Research on the MMPI and CPI found that by using these instruments, psychologists could reasonably predict academy attrition (candidates who later dropped out of the police academy) and low ratings of emotional suitability. The researchers point out, however, that they did not attempt to evaluate the effectiveness of the psychological instruments in terms of potentially good or bad police officers. They merely looked at the two areas of academy success and emotional suitability.[33]

A review of research on psychological testing discovered mixed results. It was found that these tests failed to predict job performance, either good or bad. Even when the primary purpose of the test was to discover some mental anomaly, it was not totally accurate given the individual's ability to provide untruthful responses to test questions. In this case, the author recommended that psychological testing had some value but should not be used as the sole basis for either rejection or selection.[34]

The use of psychological testing as a screening instrument has gained acceptance over the past 20 years. The movement toward this form of screening was introduced due to the recognition that law enforcement can ill afford officers who are mentally or emotionally unstable. Unfortunately, this type of screening process has not been the panacea that proponents originally believed. Part of the difficulty with psychological testing lies with the competing philosophies of administrators. Some have accepted the premise that there is an ideal police type. Under this theory, the tests are used to *select-in* applicants—to hire only those fitting the police mold. The second philosophy is the reverse, or *screen-out* concept—to reject those not mentally suited to police work. Both ideas are flawed. The select-in model is based on a false presumption—that there is an ideal police type. Research has failed to discover such a person. The second is more useful, but only when the applicant has a precisely identifiable disqualifying mental problem. Psychological tests are therefore useful when used in conjunction with other screening techniques. Used alone, they lack the sensitivity to screen candidates adequately.

Bilingual Requirements

With the extensive Hispanic migration into the southwest, California, and Florida, knowledge of the Spanish language is of increasing importance. The time has passed when a police officer can get by with knowledge of only one language. The realities of multilanguage communities are forcing law enforcement agencies in these areas to require police applicants to be bilingual. Moreover, as Hispanics migrate northward, agencies in those areas will find it necessary to hire Spanish-speaking officers. With every year that passes, the United States becomes more and more a multilingual culture. That fact alone should make Spanish a required part of public school curriculum. At the very least it will be become a requirement for employment in many police agencies.

TRAINING

Although crucial to effective law enforcement, the selection of capable personnel is only the first step in the process of staffing the agency. Even good people must be trained. The days of simply swearing in the new officers and turning them loose on the street is gone forever. The complexities of modern life make extensive training a necessity for all police officers.

There are a variety of levels of training, as well as a number of different types. The first training the new officer will encounter is *basic training*. This will probably be administered at a police academy. The larger agencies have their own academies; smaller departments usually rely on either a state or a regional police academy.

The topics covered vary from state to state, depending on the training requirements. Currently, there is tremendous variance in the number of hours required of new police officers. Even within some states, the requirements will vary, depending on the size and type of the agency. Generally speaking, most academies present training in firearms, criminal law, constitutional law, traffic law, self defense, and criminal investigation. The longer the academy, the more topics as well as the increased depth of coverage.

The next level of training is *field training,* usually conducted by a *field training officer* (FTO). This training occurs on the job. The FTO starts out by assuming many of the duties, but slowly begins to introduce the new officer to the job. Eventually, the FTO steps back and merely watches the new officer, offering advice when necessary. The purpose of this training is to introduce the recruit gradually to the realities of the job.

The FTO is a position of critical importance. Frequently, a mentoring relationship forms between the FTO and trainee. When this occurs, the new officer often looks upon the training officer as the most knowledgeable person on the force. As a role model, the FTO becomes the one person whose advice is always listened to, whose behavior is routinely internalized, and whose attitude is incorporated into the psyche of the new officer. It is difficult to overestimate the impact of the FTO on the attitude, performance, and career of a new officer.

Later training takes the form of *in-service training.* This tends to be specialized training provided to keep officers current with changes in the field of law enforcement. Topics such as changes in law as well as changes in procedure may be addressed here. Additionally, many departments require their officers to undergo periodic firearms training and evaluation. Also, specialized schools have been created around the nation to teach such specialities as death investigation, accident reconstruction, and mid- and upper-level management training.

Because society changes, learning is a never-ending process. Police training is a continuous affair. There is no point in an officer's career where the necessity for training ends.

The Probationary Period

The last step before an officer is fully accepted is the probationary period. During this period, which may vary from 6 to 18 months, the agency may dismiss the officer without stating a cause and with little or no due process protection.

The purpose of the probationary period is to allow the agency to observe the officer's performance under real-life conditions. Police administrators have acknowledged the fact that some people perform very well in a classroom only to self-destruct on the street. Ultimately, it is less important to hire people who study well than those who perform their duties with compassion, respect, and competence.

The problems associated with probationary periods, especially short ones, is the random nature of police service. It is possible for a police officer to complete a probationary period without once facing a situation that genuinely tests an officer's abilities. Once the probationary period is passed, the decision to terminate the officer for improper conduct becomes much more difficult. It is important, therefore, that every effort be made to use the probationary period to its maximum usefulness.

Promotions

The promotion process in many respects is a repeat of the selection process. Most agencies require a period of service prior to competing for promotion. This period may run from two to five years, depending on the department. As a general rule, only the smallest of agencies have no such requirement. Additionally, if the agency turnover is low, or if the agency is stable or shrinking in size, there may be a low number of openings for supervisory or administrative positions. When that happens, competition may drive the waiting period upward. In some state police agencies, for example, it is not uncommon for an officer to wait 8 to 12 years before being truly competitive for promotion.

The promotion process varies from department to department. Like the selection process, however, there are only so many steps that can be implemented. The least accepted method is that in which the chief administrator appoints the supervisory and administrative positions. This occurs without any objective selection criteria. This method was used extensively in the past. Affirmative Action requirements have rendered this method illegal in all but the smallest agencies, where the number of applicants is low and they are all well known by the chief administrator.

In most cases the promotion process will include one or more of the following: written examination, oral board, performance appraisal, and simulation exercises. The written examination is usually a multiple-choice test in which the questions are taken from departmental materials such as policies, procedures, and laws. Test material may also be taken from textbooks on management or supervision. The primary guideline in the construction of such tests is that they have high content validity. They must test material that is job related.

The *oral board* may either focus on the same types of material used in the written exam or may require the applicant to respond to hypothetical situations where they must demonstrate how policy and procedures would be implemented.

Performance appraisal is the review of applicants' performance in their present capacities. In these cases it is assumed that someone who demonstrates competence at a lower level has a better chance of success at a higher rank than does someone who does poorly at the lower rank.

Simulation exercises are designed to evaluate an applicant's ability to perform under the pressure of a real situation without the dangers inherent in real-life situations. The format used is generally referred to as the in-basket test. Applicants are given a stack of problems and are granted only so much time in which they must provide a written response detailing how they would solve the problems. They are graded on how many problems they solve and on the quality of those responses.

The most extensive promotion process, which uses all of the steps, is known as the *assessment center*. This format is used by midsized to large departments and is fairly expensive to operate. It has the advantage of testing the full range of abilities of those seeking promotions. The only serious drawback is the cost and the fact that the process is time consuming.

BECOMING A POLICE OFFICER

There is no deep, dark secret to becoming a police officer. The informal rules for seeking any job apply equally well to law enforcement. The process listed above is designed to eliminate unqualified applicants. There are two primary elements to obtaining a position in law enforcement: qualifications and image.

If a person has been convicted of a felony or has been diagnosed as being mentally unstable, he or she can probably forget law enforcement as a career. Furthermore, while popular fiction leads us to believe that most people will abuse drugs during their youth, many police agencies will immediately reject applicants who have had *any* experience with illicit drugs, including marijuana. Even poor driving records can have an adverse effect on being hired by a police agency.

Serious medical problems will also eliminate a person's chances with major agencies. This includes physical characteristics that do not pose a problem to the applicant but fail to meet the agency's stated criteria. The potential applicant would be well advised to obtain a detailed list of the agency's medical and background requirements. If the person does not meet those criteria for employment, they are probably wasting their time applying at that department.

Should a person have all of the qualifications for employment, he or she must still convince the agency to hire him or her rather than those other candidates who also meet the standards for employment. This is where image management becomes important.

First, the applicant should dress like the job is important. The first impression is made when the applicant walks through the door. Judgment and taste are closely correlated. Clothing, hair style, and general appearance make a powerful statement about a person. A solid positive appearance is critical for job applicants.

Second, police agencies are looking for people with strong self-esteem, which is not to be confused with egomania. Police officers must walk into volatile situations and take command. Shy, self-conscious, withdrawn persons do not present an image that would lead police administrators to have confidence in the person's ability to take charge. Applicants should show self-assurance and try to relax. It is normal to be nervous during job interviews, but the less apparent the stress, the more confidence the person will appear to possess.

Third, it is normal for job interviews to start out by asking applicants to provide a brief history of themselves. This is the opportunity for the candidate to shine. The applicant should give the interviewers some insight into his or her family, interests, and aspirations. The applicant is not a prisoner of war who is expected to provide only name, address, and social security number. To do so will frustrate the interviewers and set a negative tone for the entire process.

Fourth, the applicant should be cheerful (not giggly or silly). People prefer working with others who have a good sense of humor and are personable. A good personality can cover a multitude of other flaws. Positive, cheerful candidates have a tremendous advantage over the competition.

Finally, applicants should be honest. Nothing destroys an interview quicker than being caught in a lie. Many of the questions may be subjective. In those cases applicants should not attempt to outguess the interviewers. Questions such as these tend to lead down a pathway of logic. When applicants guess at the answer, they become tied to that answer. As the questions continue to probe the imaginary situation to its conclusion, the applicants find themselves locked into a progression of responses alien to their natural tendencies. Frequently, the result is disastrous; the applicants end up looking foolish. Answers should be given honestly and to the best of the applicant's ability. The answers may not be correct (in many such cases there is no right answer), but the applicant will be comfortable with the responses. Confidence and sincerity are sometimes what the question is truly testing.

Law enforcement is a challenging and exciting career. For those who anticipate applying at a police agency, pay close attention to the information in this chapter, and good luck (it always helps to have a little luck).

SUMMARY

Police selection is a multilevel process consisting of steps designed to evaluate specific aspects of the applicant's capabilities. The process really begins with recruiting. Recruiting strategies determine the type of person sought by the agency. Additionally, the advertisement process and application form provide a mechanism for self-selection and screening which are cost-effective. Recruiting and screening, however, are different functions requiring different personnel. The duties are such that using the same personnel for each function is likely to create a conflict of interest.

Affirmative Action is a program under the auspices of the Equal Employment Opportunity laws. It is designed to accelerate the movement of minorities and females into the mainstream of the modern workplace. In reality, Affirmative Action programs have been equally beneficial to white males in that procedures instituted under Affirmative Action have required objectivity and fairness in the selection and promotion process.

The screening process may consist of any of the following steps: application, written examination, interviews, physical agility tests, background investigation, medical examination, polygraph examination, psychological examination, and probationary period. In theory, each step is designed to eliminate unqualified applicants. Hopefully, by the time the applicants reach the last two or three steps, the most expensive procedures, there is a low probability of failure.

The ultimate goal of the selection process is the hiring and retaining of qualified personnel. Law enforcement is a human endeavor requiring intense interpersonal contact between the officers and the public they serve. The selection process is designed to bring the best possible personnel into the law enforcement occupation. To the degree this process is successful, law enforcement is successful.

DISCUSSION QUESTIONS

1. Why is the selection of good personnel mandatory for effective law enforcement?
2. In your opinion, which steps in the selection process eliminate the most unqualified candidates? Why?
3. Discuss the impact of Affirmative Action on police professionalism.
4. What are the problems associated with some of the physical requirements currently mandated by law enforcement agencies?
5. What are the strengths and weaknesses of psychological testing?
6. Why is image management important to a person seeking employment with a law enforcement agency?

NOTES/REFERENCES

1. Vance McLaughlin and Robert L. Bing III, "Law Enforcement Personnel Selection: A Commentary," *Journal of Police Science and Administration,* Vol. 15, No. 4, Dec. 1987, pp. 271–276.

2. Ramon J. Aldag and Timothy M. Stearns, *Management* (Cincinnati, Ohio: South-Western Publishing Company, 1987), p. 357.

3. Aldag and Stearns, pp. 357–358.

4. Ellen Hochstedler, "Impediments to Hiring Minorities in Public Police Agencies," *Journal of Police Science and Administration,* Vol. 12, No. 2, June 1984, pp. 227–240.

5. B. S. Schneider, *Staffing Organizations* (Pacific Palisades, Calif.: Goodyear Publishing Company, 1976); R. D. Arvey, *Fairness in Selecting Employees* (Reading, Mass.: Addison-Wesley Publishing Company, Inc., 1979).

6. Richard N. Holden, *Modern Police Management* (Englewood Cliffs, N.J.: Prentice-Hall, Inc., 1986), pp. 212–229.

7. Robert Albanese, *Management* (Cincinnati, Ohio: South-Western Publishing Co., 1988), p. 363.

8. W. H. Mobley, *Employee Turnover: Causes, Consequences, and Control* (Reading, Mass.: Addison-Wesley Publishing Company, Inc., 1982); S. L. Premack and J. P. Wanous, "A Meta Analysis of Realistic Preview Experiments," *Journal of Applied Psychology,* Vol. 70, 1985, pp. 706–719.

9. Albanese, pp. 363–364.

10. Holden, p. 224.

11. Keith N. Haley and Richard M. Dinse, "Medical, Physical and Residence Requirements," in *The Police Personnel System,* Calvin Swank and James A. Conser, Eds., (New York: John Wiley & Sons, Inc., 1983), pp. 136–138.

12. Charles R. Swanson, Leonard Territo, and Robert W. Taylor, *Police Administration: Structures, Processes, and Behavior,* 2nd ed. (New York: Macmillan Publishing Company, 1988), pp. 200–201.

13. Jack Gregory, "The Background Investigation and Oral Interview," in *The Police Personnel System,* Calvin J. Swank and James A. Conser, Eds. (New York: John Wiley & Sons, Inc., 1983), pp. 185–202.

14. Gregory, pp. 188–189.

15. Gregory, pp. 189–190.

16. Leonard Territo, C. R. Swanson, Jr., and Neil C. Chamelin, *The Police Personnel Selection Process* (Indianapolis, Ind.: Bobbs-Merrill Educational Publishing, 1977), p. 53.

17. Haley and Dinse, pp. 129–130.

18. Haley and Dinse, p. 130.

19. Ridaught v. Division of the Florida Highway Patrol [314 So. 2d 140 (Fla. 1975)].

20. Haley and Dinse, pp. 130–131.

21. Massachusetts v. Murgia [49 Law. Ed. 2d 520 (1976)].

22. Richard N. Holden, "Vision Standards of Law Enforcement: A Descriptive Study," *Journal of Police Science and Administration,* Vol. 12, No. 2, June 1984, pp. 125–129.

23. Haley and Dinse, p. 133.

24. Diagram Group, *Man's Body* (New York: Bantam Books, 1976), p. E32.

25. Kenneth R. Willoughby and William R. Blount "The Relationship between Law Enforcement Officer Height, Aggression, and Job Performance," *Journal of Police Science and Administration,* Vol. 13, No. 3, Sept. 1985, pp. 225–229.

26. Haley and Dinse, pp. 134–135.

27. Swanson, Territo, and Taylor, pp. 201–203.

28. John E. Reid and Fred E. Inbau, *Truth and Deception: The Polygraph Technique,* 2nd ed. (Baltimore: Williams & Wilkins, 1977), p. 359.

29. Robert B. Mills, "Psychological, Psychiatric, Polygraph, and Stress Evaluation," in *The Police Personnel System,* Calvin J. Swank and James A. Conser, Eds. (New York: John Wiley & Sons, Inc., 1983), p. 175.

30. Although some agencies no longer reject homosexuals for jobs in law enforcement, the majority of police agencies still consider such candidates unsuited for police work. Many agencies further believe that questions concerning sexual preference are an invasion of privacy except when and if the behavior is illegal. This question is therefore controversial.

31. Mills, pp. 177–178.

32. Territo, Swanson, and Chamelin, pp. 113–114.

33. George E. Hargrave, "Using the MMPI and the CPI to Screen Law Enforcement Applicants: A Study of Reliability and Validity of Clinicians' Decisions," *Journal of Police Science and Administration,* Vol. 13, No. 3, Sept. 1985, pp. 221–224.

34. Elizabeth Burbeck and Adrian Furnham, "Police Officer Selection: A Critical Review of the Literature," *Journal of Police Science and Administration,* Vol. 13, No. 1, Mar. 1985, pp. 58–69.

Chapter 5

The Police Organization

Key Terms

Law-oriented policing
Community-oriented policing
Problem-oriented policing
Mission statements
Value statements
Classical management theory
Frederick W. Taylor
Division of labor
Span of control
Unity of command
Exception principle

Methods of patrol
Nondirected patrol
Directed patrol
Location-oriented patrol
Perpetrator-oriented patrol
Solvability factors
Specialized units
Administrative services
Staff inspections
Line inspections
Technical services

Chapter Objectives

At the conclusion of this chapter, students should be able to:

1. Identify the basic principles of organizing.
2. Describe and understand the structure of the police organization.
3. Identify basic strengths and weaknesses in police organizational design.

130

INTRODUCTION

Like all organizations, law enforcement agencies, are designed to deliver the services they are mandated to deliver. Not every police officer drives a car or motorcycle, and a surprisingly small percentage of the sworn police personnel are criminal investigators. The police mission represents a broad array of functions, ranging from the primary delivery of police services to the public to support for the police activities themselves.

Given the complex nature of the police mission, the organizational structure of law enforcement agencies must allow for the provision of services in an ever-changing society. The focus of this chapter is on the structure of police agencies; that is how they are designed to fulfill their mission.

THE POLICE MISSION

The police do so many things at the behest of society that it becomes difficult to identify their mission clearly. The public assumes that the police exist to enforce the law. While this is certainly a portion of their mission, in reality they perform a vast array of other services, some of which they do more often than enforcement.

The reason for the proliferation of police duties can be identified with relative ease. The police are the only public service that works 24 hours a day, seven days a week. Moreover, the police will respond to any call, maintain confidentiality about the information they obtain, and more important, will not bill the citizen for the services. As a result of their willingness to provide fast, free, and usually effective service at any time of the day or night, the police have become society's caretaker.

If we must define the police mission, therefore, we must start with order maintenance. Most of the services performed by the police fall into this category. The police are called to break up fights, keep traffic moving, and in general, keep the peace.

The second aspect of the police mission involves law enforcement. Within this broad category we must include arresting or citing law violators when the event is seen by the officer, investigating criminal activity not observed by an officer, and the process of obtaining warrants and arresting suspected offenders.

The third aspect of the police mission is the delivery of emergency services. The police are dispersed across time and space; they are not only assigned by shift throughout the day, but also by beat, so that the jurisdiction receives equal police coverage. Frequently, the police officer is the first official to arrive at a scene where medical attention is required. In the majority of cases where police officers are cited for saving a life, it is through their efforts with first aid that the life is saved.

Finally, the police respond to all calls for service. These calls vary from people who wish to complain about a neighbor to requests to rescue cats from trees. Police officers have been asked to kill poisonous snakes, break down doors to rescue a child who has become locked in a bathroom, provide advice on preventing a basement from flooding, actually stop a basement from flooding, and escort a frightened citizen to his or her home. It is impossible to list everything that on-duty police officers have been requested to do by citizens. Everything requested and accomplished by the police, it might be added, is done so at taxpayer expense.

The problem of identifying the police mission is an important one. All organizations must have goals and objectives. Goals and objectives stem from the mission. An agency that cannot define its mission will have difficulty identifying its goals. The mission statement is really nothing more than the organization's reason for being.

Only recently have police organizations begun to identify their mission. As is usually the case, once the discussion of an organization's purpose begins, new ideas come to light about that purpose. When all is said and done, we discover that there are only two general philosophies of policing currently in vogue today among American police administrators. The large majority of agencies are either law oriented or community oriented.

The Crime-Fighting Orientation

The values of police agencies that have developed over the years are related to a movement toward professionalism. The values are rarely stated but have become implicit in organizational decision making. According to Robert Wasserman and Mark H. Moore, these values include the following:

1. Police authority is based solely in the law. Professional police organizations are committed to enforcement of that law as their primary objective.
2. Communities can provide police with assistance in enforcing the law. Helpful communities will provide police with information to assist them (the police) in carrying out their mission.
3. Responding to citizen calls for service is the highest police priority. All calls must receive the fastest response possible.
4. Police, being experts in crime control, are best suited to develop police priorities and strategies.[1]

These authors also believe that other values reflect the common belief among police officers that police departments exist to advance the profession of policing, not to serve as an important part of maintaining democratic values and improving the quality of life in their communities.

By its very nature, the crime-fighting agency is a highly technical organization. The emphasis is on *law-oriented policing:* solving crime and prosecuting criminals. Rules and procedures are rigid; the command structure is centralized and autocratic.

Community-Oriented Policing

Community-oriented policing operates from a broader set of priorities. This approach is based on the assumption that policing a city's neighborhoods is best done at the individual neighborhood level rather than by centralized command. Moreover, this approach commits the police to a problem-solving partnership: dealing with crime, disorder, and the quality of life.[2]

In contrast with the crime-fighting orientation, departments moving toward the community policing, or *problem-oriented policing,* model have begun to focus on value statements rather than mission statements as a means to direct and control officer behavior. Community-oriented agencies are more flexible than their crime-fighting counterparts. They maximize decision making at the lowest levels of the organization, where officer and citizen meet face to face. The community-oriented agency strives to act as consultant and partners with the citizens of the community. The role of the individual police officer is broadened to include a number of functions that extend well beyond that of traditional police work.

Mission Statements versus Value Statements

Mission statements are a clearly delineated statement of purpose for the organization. It explains why the organization exists. *Value statements,* however, are a new concept. For example, the Houston Police Department, during the tenure of Lee Brown, publicly issued the following value statements:

1. The Houston Police department will involve the community in all policing activities that directly impact the quality of community life.
2. The Houston Police Department believes that policing strategies must preserve and advance democratic values.
3. The Houston Police Department believes that it must structure service delivery in a way that will reinforce the strengths of the city's neighborhoods.
4. The Houston Police Department believes that the public should have input into the development of policies that directly impact the quality of neighborhood life.
5. The Houston Police Department will seek the input of employees into matters that impact employee job satisfaction and effectiveness.[3]

While the foregoing values reflect a tendency toward the movement to community policing, it must be noted that the trend is still in its infancy. Officers readily accept the values of the crime-fighting orientation. They have accepted the newer values reluctantly or, in some cases, not at all. Still, the old ways have not served the nation that well. Perhaps the community-orientation model will work better.

THE POLICE STRUCTURE

Law enforcement agencies are organized primarily along classic military lines. In principle this provides a tight system of control from the top of the organization to the bottom. The chief, or sheriff, sits at the top of the organization and deftly directs the operations to achieve and maintain a high level of efficiency and effectiveness. In reality, it does not achieve what most police administrators would like, but no one has yet to find a suitable alternative to this structure. We can assume with some confidence that the current structure of law enforcement organizations is going to be with us for a long time.

The Authority Structure

The police authority structure is best described as a pyramid with the chief executive at the top. Below the chief, the lower administrators occupy ever-expanding levels of authority until the bottom of the organization is reached. A command from the chief executive is passed downward until every member of the organization has been informed. Information or requests submitted from below are passed upward in a straight line until they reach the chief executive's desk.

The organizational format described above is a by-product of *classical management theory,* first advocated by men such as *Frederick W. Taylor* early in the twentieth century. Two basic assumptions permeate this approach to management. First, it is assumed that workers are inherently disinterested in their work and will avoid it if possible. Second, since work itself is of no importance, economic incentives should drive the management–labor relationship. Good management, it was believed, linked productivity to financial rewards.[4]

Using classical theory, police administrators adopted the basic principles that were a product of this thinking: division of labor, unity of command, and span of control. Police administrators attempted to routinize and standardize police work, especially patrol. Police work was simplified to mean "law enforcement." Attempts were made to tightly limit discretion; entire generations of police officers were taught that they merely enforced the law. If special problems arose, the typical response was to create special units (vice, tactical, etc.) rather than assign them to patrol. The creation of these centralized units further eroded the already weakened precinct or lower commanders, while it enhanced the control and authority of the central administration.[5] Until the riots and crime problems of the 1960s, it was believed that this was the way departments should be managed. By the mid-1970s, police experts were not sure. Still, despite a variety of experiments, the classical organization format is still the primary organizational structure among law enforcement agencies.

Division of Labor

Law enforcement agencies have multiple tasks. To accomplish what is expected of them, police agencies are structured so as to provide services as effectively as possible. To this end, law enforcement organizations assign personnel to specific tasks accompanied with specific responsibilities. It is in the fulfilling of these specific tasks by organizational elements that allows the agency to fulfill its overall mission.

Many police duties require officers to be able to respond to a vast array of situations, requiring basic knowledge of possible solutions, without necessarily being experts. Still other situations require a high amount of expertise. For this reason, law enforcement agencies generally employ a *division of labor* into generalists and specialists.

Generalists. A police generalist is an officer with multiple responsibilities. The most obvious example of such a person is the patrol officer. Uniformed patrol provides services on call. Since the person calling the police determines what particular service is desired, the patrol officer must be able to respond to almost anything. Patrol officers have been asked to provide first aid, rescue stranded animals, destroy injured animals, find lost children, resolve personal and business disputes, and take a wide array of reports concerning real or imagined crime.

To accomplish these tasks, the patrol officer must be well trained, possess a

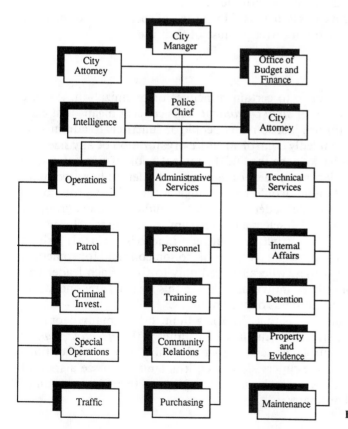

Illustration 5-1 Police Organization

good sense of humor, and be comfortable in the role of "jack of all trades but master of none." Officers who spend many years in this role eventually attain a large amount of expertise in many areas. In a sense, the generalists are the most visible arm of the police, since it is they who arrive at all calls. Frequently, it is the generalist who determines whether or not the specialist is needed at the scene.

Specialists.   When incidents arise that are beyond the capabilities of the generalist, the specialist is called. This person—usually a sworn officer, but not always—has the substantial training and expertise necessary to address the problem at hand. Personnel such as homicide investigators, crime scene specialists, traffic accident reconstructionists, and legal advisors examplify the types of specialization necessary for the effective delivery of police service.

Specialists are a necessary part of law enforcement, but there are drawbacks to their use. As a person gets more proficient at the delivery of one type of service, other knowledge and skills are lost. Specialists become occupationally narrow, and eventually lose much of their ability to function as generalists. There is also a tendency for specialists to develop a feeling of superiority over the generalist arm of the agency. This is a destructive tendency that causes isolation of the various elements as they stop communicating with each other.

Overall police effectiveness is increased by the use of specialists. At the same time, morale and teamwork often suffer because of their use.

Span of Control

All formal organizations adhere to certain principles of organization. Among these principles is the concept of *span of control.* This concept means that each supervisor or administrator has just so many people or functions to administer. No one person can singlehandedly control an entire organization of any size.

This principle dates back to the the Old Testament book of *Exodus,* where the tribes of Israel are divided into leaders of thousands, leaders of hundreds, and leaders of tens. Every 10 families would have a single leader. Every group of 10 such leaders would select a single leader, the leader of hundreds. Each group of 10 leaders of hundreds would also select a leader from among them. This would be the leaders of thousands. This structure would continue to build in this fashion until every member of all the tribes was responsible to someone and for someone. Ultimately, at the top sat Moses, who answered only to God. Each leader was therefore responsible for only 10 individuals. Using this format, any one leader can command hundreds of thousands or even millions.

The other side of this coin is that there is a limit to how many people or functions one person can effectively manage. This limit is the *effective span of control.* The true span of control represents the actual number of personnel or functions assigned. At the first-line supervision level, it is unusual to see a span of control above 10 personnel. A general rule of thumb places the effective span of control at around six subordinates.

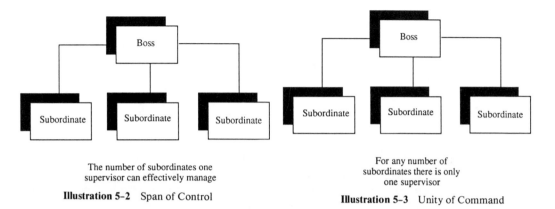

The number of subordinates one
supervisor can effectively manage

Illustration 5–2 Span of Control

For any number of
subordinates there is only
one supervisor

Illustration 5–3 Unity of Command

Unity of Command

A corollary to span of control is the idea of *unity of command*. As span of control is measured from the top of an organization downward, unity of command looks up from the bottom. The fundamental guideline in this principle is that no person can effectively serve more than one master.

Unity of command, simply stated, means that each member of the organization answers to only one supervisor or manager. Each sergeant may have responsibility for six or seven patrol officers, but each of those officers answers only to that single sergeant. This principle seeks to prevent the confusion inherent in a system of multiple bosses and contradictory commands. Unity of command keeps the lines of communication and responsibility clear and uncomplicated.

Delegation

The principle of *delegation* states that each level of the organization has duties and obligations for which it is responsible. Even though the chief executive of the organization is ultimately responsible for all actions of the organization, sufficient authority must be delegated to other people and subunits to meet the goals of the organization. As no one person can personally oversee every decision or action, it is also true that no one person can make all the decisions for the organization. Sufficient authority must be given to others so that effective decisions and actions can be taken in a timely manner.

Delegation means that the chief executive allows others in the organization to make decisions, and stands behind those decisions. A general guideline regarding which decisions will be made at the top of the organization and which at the top is called the *exception principle*. Routine decisions are made by the people or elements dealing with those particular routine situations. Exceptional, out-of-the-ordinary decisions are made higher up in the organization.

OPERATIONS

Police service is delivered through the operations elements of the organization. All other units exist to support this function. Operations is where the police agency meets the public. The major elements of the operations segment are patrol and investigations.

Patrol

In an attempt to respond as rapidly as possible to the needs of its citizens, the law enforcement agency distributes a portion of its personnel over the jurisdiction. The terrain features of the jurisdiction plus the population distribution determine both the type of the patrol force used and the level of concentration of patrol officers. Patrol may be of any form of vehicle or foot. The purpose of patrol, however, never varies. It is designed to get police service to those who need it, as fast as possible, while also providing a force that can act on its own when the need arises.

Patrol is the most important police element. Other units may be created or disbanded as the size or philosophy of the organization changes. Patrol, however, is the one constant in police organizations. Whether the agency has one officer or 30,000, patrol will comprise a major part of the delivery of police services.

The decision concerning the *methods of patrol* to be utilized depends on a number of variables. Geographic size is a major determinant. Generally, cities on the eastern seaboard tend to be confined to a relatively small area. They have grown upward rather than outward. Western cities, on the other hand, have spread outward over a much larger area. The result is that population density is greater in the eastern cities than in the west. This means that effective patrol deployment will differ between the regions. The east will have more foot patrol and horse patrol, whereas the west will have a greater reliance on motor vehicles, both automobile and motorcycle. Both coasts will use a variety of forms of patrol, but the area size and population density will be a controlling factor in the importance of each patrol format.

Weather and closeness to a body of water will also determine the type of patrol force deployed. A water patrol unit would make little sense in Elko, Nevada. New York City, however, would be hampered without such a unit. Similarly, motorcycle patrol will be of little benefit in Fairbanks, Alaska. The use of snowmobiles, however, would be a practical means of providing police services in that location.

Other factors in patrol deployment include cost, special problems, tradition of the agency, and attitude of the community. The decision as to which type of patrol should be implemented is rarely a simple one. Rather, it requires careful analysis of the problem to be addressed, the geography of the area, and the feasibility of the plan. The formats that may be adopted are numerous. The various types of patrol are discussed below.

Auto.   By far the most widely used form of patrol in today's law enforcement is auto patrol. The police car, both marked and unmarked, is a mainstay in the delivery of police service. The automobile is to the modern police what the horse was to the cavalry of the nineteenth century.

That the automobile should be so popular among the police comes as no surprise. We live in an automobile society. The police must control such a society on its own terms. Traffic control alone mandates extensive use of automobiles. Additionally, the automobile allows each officer to act as a self-contained force. The storage space in the trunk of a police car allows the officer to carry rescue equipment, evidence collection equipment, first-aid instruments, rope, flares and myriad other items necessary for a vast array of situations.

Locked inside the temperature-controlled environment of the vehicle, the office can maintain the police presence in all but the most intemperate weather conditions. The speed and range of the automobile allows a single officer to cover a large geographic area quickly. The police radio provides constant communication with the dispatcher and other officers. In short, the automobile is the ideal instrument of the modern police officer.

Motor patrol has changed over the years. As more is learned about law enforcement, patrol techniques adjust to meet the newly discovered needs. Originally, police cars were put on the street to provide responses to calls for service and to provide an equal dispersion of police personnel throughout the city. The first motor patrol beats were designed to be about the same size, geographically. It then became apparent that different regions of the jurisdiction had different levels of activity. This required a redesign of the beats so that each officer would experience roughly equal workloads. Ultimately, computerization and statistical modeling have resulted in even more sophisticated patrol techniques.

Undoubtedly the greatest catalyst in the evolution of motor patrol has been technology. The first cars lacked radio. Officers had to go to a telephone to communicate with police headquarters. From that era law enforcement has progressed to automobiles that are equipped with the most modern technology. Everything from cellular phones to mobile computers can be found in police vehicles. The one thing that has not changed is the importance of the patrol vehicle to the police mission. This is still the most effective element of the police organization.

Foot.   Foot patrol dates back to the first law enforcers. Long before the advent of vehicles, officers walked their assigned areas seeking to protect their communities. The modern police force still has some use for such a patrol format. There are areas of the community where cars cannot go. There are also concentrations of people so dense that foot officers represent the only practical method of delivering police service. In these situations, foot patrol serves a vital purpose.

In the past 20 years it has been argued that motorized patrol has led to a distancing of the police from the citizens. Some have argued that law enforcement has suffered as a result of the reliance on automobiles. Because of theories such as these, police researchers have attempted to ascertain the various strengths and weaknesses of foot and motorized patrol. The Flint Neighborhood Foot Patrol Program is such an attempt.

The Flint Neighborhood Foot Patrol Program

In 1979, the Flint, Michigan Police Department began its foot patrol program. This program was financed by the Charles Stewart Mott Foundation and evaluated by the School of Criminal Justice at Michigan State University. Unlike earlier foot patrol strategies, with the emphasis on random patrol of a specified beat, the Flint program focused on specific crime prevention objectives. The foot patrol officers also served as crime prevention officers in that they initiated and maintained Neighborhood Watch programs, conducted crime prevention surveys, and gave crime prevention presentations in schools, businesses, and homes. The Flint foot patrol program heavily emphasized citizen involvement in the practices and decision making of the foot patrol elements.

Flint divided both motor and foot patrols into four sectors of roughly equal size. Researchers, using a stratified random sample, compared foot officers, four from each sector, with an equal sample of motor officers. Only the first and second shifts were compared since foot patrol did not work the third shift. Because the foot patrol was a permanent assignment, the same foot officers were used throughout the research, whereas motor officers, whose shifts and assignments changed, varied (25 different motor officers were actually used).

The months of October 1983 and May 1984 became the period of study. These months avoided peaks in activity customary in the summer months and the lulls that usually occur in winter. The sample foot and motor officers comprised over 1200 eight-hour tours of duty for the two-month period.

In an effort to compare the the two forms of patrol, the researchers categorized and tabulated the activities of the officers as reflected in their daily report forms. The dailies were checked against monthly activity reports to verify data and to establish a quality control mechanism.

The categories of activity common to both foot and motor patrol were: felony arrest, misdemeanor arrest, investigations initiated, value of property recovered, investigations assigned, premises found open, suspicious persons, parking violations, and public services rendered. There were seven categories relevant only to foot patrol. These were: meetings attended, speaking engagements, business visits, home visits, juvenile activities, business security checks, and home security checks. Categories relevant only to motor patrol were: hazardous tags (citations), nonhazardous tags (other than parking violations), injury accidents, and property accidents.

A comparison of comparable activities of foot and motor patrol revealed the following statistics:

Activity	Motor patrol	Foot patrol
Felony arrests	2.06	13.18
Misd. arrests	2.75	14.12
Investigations assigned	97.87	304.12
Investigations initiated	203.5	106.87
Premises open	.63	3.12
Suspicious persons	12.88	96.31
Parking violations	4.25	11.18
Services rendered	100.81	13.37
Recovered property	1100.00	3046.87

Figures are rates per officer.

Source: Dennis M. Payne and Robert C. Trojanowicz, *Performance Profiles of Foot Versus Motor Officers* (East Lansing, Michigan: National Neighborhood Foot Patrol Center, School of Criminal Justice, Michigan State University, 1985) p. 17.

Illustration 5-4   Police Activities Chart

Additionally, the researchers identified contacts as adversarial and nonadversarial. In adversarial contacts, the officer is viewed as a threat by the citizen. Such contacts are usually terminated with the issuance of a summons, citation, or with the person's arrest. Nonadversarial contacts included amiable interchanges between officer and citizen. An analysis of foot versus motor patrol revealed the following:

Contacts	Adversarial	Nonadversarial	Total
Foot patrol			
Contacts	351	3,613	3,964
Percentage	8.85	91.14	99.99
Motor patrol			
Contacts	2,531	247	2,778
Percentage	91.10	8.89	99.99

Source: Dennis M. Payne and Robert C. Trojanowicz, *Performance Profiles of Foot versus Motor Officers,* Community Policing Series No. 6 (East Lansing, Mich: National Neighborhood Foot Patrol Center, School of Criminal Justice, Michigan State University, 1985), p. 19.

Illustration 5-5   Public Contact Chart

Statistically, the foot patrol program was a success. As the graphs clearly indicate, the foot patrol officers were more effective in every comparable aspect except services rendered and investigations instigated. This should be expected, given the superior mobility of the motor patrol elements. Similarly, foot patrol was far superior to motor patrol in nonadversarial contacts. Again, this should come as no surprise considering the public relations emphasis of the foot patrol versus the traffic control aspects of the motorized units.

In closing, the researchers warned against overstating the strengths of foot patrol. They accurately state that in a highly technical and mobile society such as ours, motor patrol will always be the primary mode of police service delivery. The utility of programs such as the Flint foot patrol project, however, has been more than amply demonstrated by this program.[6]

Some of the locations most likely for foot patrol are the downtown areas of cities, large shopping malls, public parks, and housing projects with dense populations and limited street accessibility.

Motorcycle.   One of the most expensive and dangerous forms of police patrol is the motorcycle patrol. This force is utilized mostly for traffic control. The theory behind the motorcycle is that it can weave in and out of traffic congestion that automobiles are unable to navigate. Motorcycles can also be hidden more easily, allowing the police to monitor traffic with radar in areas unavailable to police cars. The same reasoning applies to catching traffic violators in heavy traffic. Where police cars would bog down in traffic, the motorcycle can wend its way through the congestion until the violator is apprehended.

The motorcycle represents a special utility form of police vehicle. Its use is limited, but valuable in those situations where needed. It is expensive because, unlike automobiles, it cannot be handed from officer to officer, shift after shift. The seat and handlebar settings are made for an individual officer, which means that it can operate only when that officer is on duty. The motorcycle is also limited by weather. In some parts of the country there are only a few months when this vehicle can be used effectively. Moreover, the officers require special clothing, such as boots, leather jackets, and heavy-duty pants, which are also expensive, not to mention the special training required.

It might also be noted that in departments using motorcycles, the highest injury rate is among the motorcycle officers. In summary, motorcycles have some important uses but are a high cost–high risk form of patrol.

Air.   Air patrol comes in two forms, plane and helicopter. As a general rule, large metropolitan areas will use the helicopter, while state police forces will rely more on the plane. When there are exceptions, it is usually the state that will also have helicopters; cities have little use for police planes. The helicopter is an excellent tool for a variety of functions. By being able to look down on the city, the helicopter crew can aid in the isolation of the scene of a crime in progress, patrol a wide area of the city while hovering in the same spot, conduct chases

Photograph 5–1   Motorcycle Officer

Photograph 5–2   Police Helicopter

involving fleeing vehicles from the safety of the air, assume responsibility for actions occurring on the rooftops of the city's buildings, and aid in search and rescue missions.

The primary use of planes is in the traffic function. The flow of automobiles and trucks can be monitored from high above the traffic. Law enforcement vehicles can be directed to violators or problem areas by the crew of the aircraft. Additionally, the plane is a useful tool in searching a large uninhabited area for either fleeing suspects or people who are lost.

The primary drawback to aircraft is cost. Planes and helicopters are expensive to buy and operate. In areas where they are needed, however, these vehicles may be well worth the expense.

Horse.   The use of horses in law enforcement has been with us since the early settlers. Unlike in the frontier days, however, mounted police officers no longer chase bandits through the badlands. Today's mounted police officers are used mostly in the larger cities. Sitting atop a horse allows an officer to oversee developing problems in either traffic or pedestrian areas. Large eastern cities have made extensive use of mounted police officers in downtown areas. Moreover, cities that have large urban parks, such as Central Park in New York City, have found that police officers mounted on horseback are better prepared and equipped to patrol within the confines of that area. Other uses of horses include ceremonial functions. The Texas Rangers routinely appear in parades mounted on horseback. The same is true for many sheriff's agencies, especially in the west and southwest.

The utility of the horse in law enforcement operations is well proven. The horse is likely to be with policing for many years to come.

Water.   Only law enforcement agencies adjacent to a body of water have or need water patrol. Those who do have this need may have a wide variety of watercraft to fulfill their mission. The size of the watercraft will vary with the type of agency and type of water to be patrolled. By far the largest water patrol force is the U.S. Coast Guard. This force has everything from large cutters to smaller craft for inland waters. Customs also has a fleet but is more likely to use smaller, high-speed pursuit craft for its mission. Cities, states, and counties may have anything from fairly substantial cabin cruisers to outboard fishing–type vessels.

There are multiple purposes for watercraft. First is for traffic control. As with highways, traffic on the nation's waterways must also be monitored and controlled. Drunk boaters pose as much a threat to the safety of the public as do drunk drivers. Second, water patrol elements are useful for search and rescue as well as to promote water safety. Basically speaking, wherever there are people, there is a need for police officers. Watercraft allow the police access to people on the water.

Photograph 5-3 Missouri Water Patrol

Directed versus nondirected. Originally, patrol was designed to be random. The idea was that by distributing patrol officers over a wide area and allowing them to meander through their beats with no aforethought, criminals would be unable to predict police movement. It was felt that this would allow the police some element of surprise and give them an advantage over their adversaries.

Of course, the assumptions behind *nondirected patrol* were badly flawed. First, the vast majority of burglars and other thieves do not plan with police movement in mind. In fact, being amateurs, most do not plan at all. Second, it assumes that a single police car is likely to stumble blindly across a crime in progress while in between other required duties and while patrolling a beat that takes over an hour to cover effectively. In fact, the average burglary takes less than a minute to complete, with many taking as little as 15 seconds. Grab-and-run thefts take even less time. Moreover, most violent crime takes place indoors and is out of sight of passing patrol officers. In short, many of the assumptions on which random patrol was based were simple, and perhaps even silly.

A new form of patrol has now been introduced that seeks to eliminate some of the problems of random, nondirected patrol. The newer form, *directed patrol,* is self-explanatory. Rather than merely turning a police cars loose on the street to wander aimlessly, directed patrol uses computer technology to predict criminal episodes and assign police officers accordingly.

Highly specialized police crime analysis units use probability theory to predict these actions. The old M.O. (modus operandi or method of operation) files have become remarkably sophisticated. By keeping a detailed and precise record of criminal events, a crime analysis unit attempts to detect pattern of behavior. These patterns can then be used to predict when and where the criminal will strike again. Police officers are then directed to locations at specific times in an attempt to outguess the criminal.

Although not absolutely accurate, directed patrol has been more successful than nondirected patrol. Unfortunately, there is a negative side effect. Patrol officers, tied to the computer by an electronic leash, have lost some of their autonomy. Morale and job satisfaction have suffered as freedom of movement has been curtailed. No one likes being a puppet on a string, even if the string is electronic.

There are other types of directed patrol; some allow a little more freedom for officers than the tightly controlled model described above. *Location-oriented patrol* (LOP) and *perpetrator-oriented patrol* (POP) offer two such versions. Location-oriented patrol focuses on areas or places with a high probability of criminal attack. Perpetrator-oriented patrol places likely suspects under surveillance, or at the very least, requires some monitoring of these persons. The LOP method is useful when a location is high-risk and there is no known suspect. The POP methods are useful with a person who has a record of criminal acts but whose targets may vary over a wide area.

A broader catch-all term that encompasses both LOP and POP is *problem-oriented policing,* in which the resources of the operations elements are directed at identifiable problem areas and people. The strength in this model is the utilization of planning with goals and objectives in defining and delivering police services.

While random patrol is by no means dead, increased sophistication in data collection and analysis has made this approach less desirable. The day is rapidly approaching when random patrol may become obsolete.

Investigations

When we think of investigations we often conjure up names such as Sherlock Holmes, Miss Marple, Sam Spade, and maybe even Dirty Harry. Most people assume that investigations are the sole territory of plain-clothed officers, seeking to detect crime, mystically and logically, from the microscopic and fragmentary pieces left at the scene. Nothing could be further from the truth.

Most crimes are solved by uniformed patrol. The overwhelming majority of investigations involve uniformed officers, especially the preliminary investigations. Detectives do solve crimes, but usually only when the uniformed officer who completed the preliminary investigation provides a solid lead that the detective can follow.

Solvability factors determine whether or not a crime will be investigated or merely filed away for future reference. Also, the amount of attention given to an investigation is a by-product of these factors. Case screening is based on the belief that there are three type of cases: those already solved where the investigator need only locate an identified suspect, cases that can be solved where there is a good probability that the investigation will produce a suspect, and cases unlikely to be solved.[7]

Factors looked at to determine how a case should be handled include such variables as whether there was an eyewitness, how traceable the stolen items are, and how much publicity the case has generated. Clearly, if there are no leads and no means of finding missing items, the chances of solving a crime are slim. Valuable resources are wasted on investigations with a low probability of solution. This is true in terms of both budgetary loss and personnel frustration. Case screening is a mechanism by which investigators can more effectively manage their case load.[8]

Still, the reality of criminal investigation is that it is boring, unglamorous, and highly unproductive. Detectives spend most of their time writing reports.[9]

Specialized Units

There are certain police tasks that require an inordinate amount of training and specialization. These *specialized units* are found almost exclusively in larger police organizations. These units are problem oriented; that is, they are created to address a narrow range of situations requiring police action.

Tactical teams.   Tactical, or SWAT (Special Weapons and Tactics or Special Weapons Assault Teams), units are the result of law enforcement reaction to incidents involving snipers, terrorists, and hostage situations. The 1960s presented law enforcement with a series of events that they were neither equipped nor trained to handle. The tactical team seemed the ideal solution.

Tactical teams have a much stronger military orientation than other police units. They combine intensive weapons training with sophisticated technology. Unfortunately, these teams are frequently detrimental to departmental morale. Members of these teams often perceive themselves as elite and act as though that were the case. Hostility and resentment toward these officers often follow.

Another drawback is cost. These teams are expensive to train and equip. Because they must always be prepared for any tactical situation, they must spend spare time in training rather than on patrol. This means that such units are used only for tactical situations. In large jurisdictions this is an acceptable expense because there are sufficient tactical incidents to require their services. Smaller jurisdictions, however, have little use for such units; the cost is simply prohibitive.

Hostage negotiation teams.   Created for purposes similar to that of tactical teams, hostage negotiation units are designed to deal specifically with situations involving hostages. Unlike tactical teams, however, these units are designed to resolve such situations without violence. Usually, hostage negotiations units go hand in glove with tactical teams. If at all possible the negotiators bring an incident to a peaceful conclusion. Failing that, the tactical team steps in.

Like tactical teams, hostage negotiation units require extensive training and careful personnel selection. Fortunately, these units do not require the high-cost equipment necessary for tactical operations. Still, usually only the largest agencies can afford such units.

Decoy units.   Decoy units are designed to trap criminals in the act of committing the crime. Police officers dress and act like people who have been at risk in high-crime areas. The idea is to deceive the criminal into believing that the officer is an easy victim. This type of police activity can be very effective in areas where purse snatchings or strong-arm robberies occur. They have also been used for many years in the vice units of police organizations. This is just about the only practical method of catching prostitutes, drug dealers, and gamblers.

Unlike tactical teams, decoy units are ad hoc. They can be organized and disbanded on whim. Personnel in these units also require little in the way of training; most are from detective units. By and large these units are relatively inexpensive to operate and very effective for the limited range of crimes for which they are created.

Intelligence.   The police intelligence units do very little in the arena we think of as police work. They make few, if any, arrests and rarely testify in court. Their function is to gather information about possible criminal activity. They may gather this information by assigning personnel to undercover activities that put the officers in a location where they are likely to overhear conversations relating to criminal activities. Or, personnel within these units may review information gathered in police reports, field interrogation cards, and other places, and use that as a frame of reference for intelligence-gathering activities.

The difference between the kind of information gathered by intelligence officers and normal police information is that intelligence is always very sensitive. It is rarely used in court or appears in any public document. Intelligence is gath-

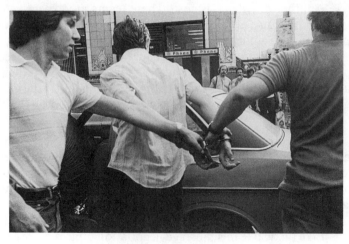

Photograph 5-4   Decoy Unit

ered for decision-making purposes. It allows the organization to stay one step ahead of criminal operations. The sensitivity of such information results from the fact that intelligence, unlike other information, will have large doses of hearsay, rumor, and sheer speculation. Also, it may involve information about people that would be very harmful to those people if released. Intelligence is not bound by the normal rule of police information gathering. It is important but always has the potential for misuse and can sometimes result in embarrassment for innocent people as well as the police. Because of this potential for harm, intelligence operations must be carefully structured and controlled. The information must also be considered highly secret.

ADMINISTRATIVE SERVICES

Service divisions are usually subdivided into two different types. There are services aimed at supporting the police administrative function and services that focus on aiding operations. *Administrative services* are those police functions that support police administration. Among these elements will be found such areas as personnel, research and planning, data analysis, inspections, and internal affairs.

Personnel

The personnel unit, or division depending on the agency's size, has the responsibility for managing the process of recruiting, selecting, and hiring personnel. They further manage the promotion process as well as maintain policies and records on vacation, sick leave, benefits, and personnel assignment. This is a vital aspect of the administrative function. Law enforcement is a "people" business. Hiring and keeping good people is crucial to effective law enforcement. Similarly, the promotion and transfer process must be fair and impartial. The way in which the personnel officers do their job can have a pronounced impact on the morale and job satisfaction of the entire department.

Research and Planning

Over the past 20 years police administrators have begun to realize the necessity for planning. It is no longer sufficient to send officers into the streets with no idea of what demands the jurisdiction will make. Administrators need an idea of where the problem areas are and what resources will be needed for a period of up to at least five years.

The research and planning unit provides this information. Planning involves studying social, political, and technical trends so that future needs can be predicted. This element also looks at police supplies and equipment to determine which brands and models best serve the agency's needs at present. The research and planning unit is the chief administrator's oracle. It exists to guide police policymaking for the present and the future.

Data Analysis

Data analysis is sometimes associated with research and planning. It also supports the crime analysis unit. The major purpose of this element, however, is making sense out of the massive amounts of information that are fed into the police department. Unlike the research and planning unit, which studies social and political trends, data analysis looks at police-generated information. Calls for service, arrests, traffic complaints, and time required to deal with the various problems are all fed into the data analysis computers.

This element attempts to make sense of what is currently happening so that managerial decisions can be made accurately and in a timely manner. Beat design and distribution of officers are just two of the organizational decisions that rely on this unit. It is not sufficient merely to gather data; there must also be a competent method of deciphering what the information means. That is the duty of the data analysis unit.

Inspections

The inspections function is spread over a number of different units. Not all inspections are the domain of a services division. Line, or operational, elements sometimes have an inspection function as well. The two most common types of police inspection are the staff inspection and the line inspection.

Staff inspections. The purpose of the *staff inspection* is to determine to what degree of effectiveness a particular police element is operating. These inspections are rarely conducted as a surprise. They are more effective when the unit being examined knows of the inspection in advance and is operating at its best. Only in this manner can the inspections unit determine where the real problem areas are.

Staff inspections are conducted by personnel not attached to the unit being inspected. Sometimes this is a function of the internal affairs unit; sometimes the inspection is conducted by an ad hoc inspections team directed by a command-level officer. The inspection may be very detailed or may focus on only one or two areas. The final report of the inspection is delivered to the chief executive as well as the commander of the unit inspected. This form of inspection is an instrument of administrative control. It provides the administration with information on how well a unit is operating within the agency guidelines and identifies deficiencies that require correction. The staff inspection is very close to the military concept of the inspector general's evaluation.

Line inspections. The *line inspection* is normally an operations function. This inspection is handled by the command and supervisory staff of the element being inspected. There are a number of purposes for this inspection, as well as a number of different types. Supervisors might inspect officers to ensure the proper wearing of the uniform. Paperwork is often inspected for accuracy and completeness. Weapons may be inspected, as well as policy manuals. The line inspection is similar in nature to the military personnel inspection.

Internal Affairs

A concern for members of any society is who shall police the police. The function of the internal affairs (IA) element is to ensure compliance with department policy and law. The IA unit has the responsibility for conducting investigations into police misconduct.

Organizationally, internal affairs is usually located close to the office of the chief executive. Because this element will be involved in sensitive investigations, the organization can ill afford to have too many people between the chief executive and this vital unit. The internal affairs unit must be protected from internal pressures not to pursue problem officers vigorously. At the same time it is unwise for communications between the chief executive and this unit to be filtered through multiple layers of bureaucracy.

In a sense, internal affairs is an inspection unit. It is not so classified, however, because unlike inspections, the internal affairs unit is reactionary. This element responds to complaints and allegations; it rarely initiates its own investigations without cause.

TECHNICAL SERVICES

Those organizational elements that directly support line functions are classified as technical and, therefore, are found within the technical services division. *Technical services* involve such functions as criminalistics, crime prevention, communications, records, jail operations, and maintenance.

Criminalistics

The crime laboratory has become part of the media mystique of policing. Criminalistics is the science of criminal investigation and provides the police with an important set of instruments and procedures for solving and prosecuting criminal cases.

There are two parts to the criminalistics process, however, and not every department is equipped to handle both. The first step is the identification and processing of the crime scene. Crime scene technicians, whether police officers or specialists, systematically identify and collect items from the scene that may later be determined to be evidence. These items are then submitted to the criminalistics laboratory.

The laboratory represents the second part of the process. Every department, whatever its size, is responsible for the search of the crime scene and the subsequent collection of evidence. Only the largest departments, however, are equipped with criminalistics laboratories. In those cases where the department does not have its own laboratory, a number of options are available.

The largest and best equipped crime laboratory in the nation is that of the Federal Bureau of Investigation. Any law enforcement agency may use this laboratory for a wide array of analytical services. Most states also have a centralized crime lab for the use of agencies within that state. Additionally, the larger departments frequently make their laboratory services available to smaller departments. There are also a number of independent laboratories around the nation, some established in conjunction with private industry, others on college or university campuses. Some of these labs charge fees, others provide the service for no charge. The important fact is that all law enforcement agencies have access to a crime lab of some type.

The key factor in criminalistics is the collection of the evidence. The quality of the various criminalistics laboratories is generally very good. No lab, however, can process nonevidence. The items must be collected and stored properly if they are to be analyzed. In cases where there was physical evidence and the crime lab was of no help, it has invariably been due to the failure of the personnel at the crime scene to do their job properly.

Photograph 5–5   Criminalistics Lab

Crime Prevention

There may be some dispute over where a crime prevention unit should be located in the organization. Certainly, there is no single place where it can be located. I have chosen to place it within technical services because the crime prevention officers work more closely with line than with staff elements. The philosophy of crime prevention is that certain types of crime can be better prevented than later investigated. The concept was developed in England, where it is believed that citizens have some responsibility for protecting themselves and their property.

Crime prevention units attack crime in a number of ways. The first tactic is through the process known as *target hardening*. It is widely believed that much property crime occurs through opportunity. Thieves steal those items that are easy to steal and burglars break into buildings that are easy targets. Target hardening means making it more difficult to steal and burgle; it means lessening the

Photograph 5-6 Crime Prevention Officers

opportunities for crime. Police tactics aimed at target hardening include teaching people about physical security techniques and organizing neighborhoods into mutual aid societies. Neighbors band together to watch out for each other's safety and property.

The police have also adopted education as a tactic for preventing crime. There are police programs in schools that teach about the danger of drugs and alcohol. Other programs are aimed at teaching small children about techniques for protecting themselves from child molesters. Still other educational programs teach business people about various confidence games and counterfeiting schemes, to name just a few.

Crime prevention is proactive policing at its best. Programs such as these have the added benefit of providing positive police citizen communication, which itself can lead to improved police performance. Unfortunately, the concept of crime prevention has only been given lip service in many organizations. At the heart of the problem lies the inability to measure nonbehavior. A crime prevented is a nonaction, an unmeasurable quantity. Also, many law enforcement organizations are still caught up in the notion that crime prevention is not "real police work."

To fight this attitude, crime prevention has been altered in some agencies. You might say that it has been given a face lift. To a very real extent, community policing is a variation of crime prevention. Rather than be identified as a crime prevention officer, police personnel now refer to themselves as community police officers or police community problem solvers. The techniques of community policing and problem-oriented policing closely resemble those of the earlier crime prevention officer. This tactic may be working. In many organizations community-oriented policing is being given more status and resources than were the earlier crime prevention programs. The increased commitment to this idea is a good sign.

Communications

Communications provide the lifeblood of the law enforcement organization. The days of the lone police officer walking rounds are long gone. Today's police agency is a high-tech, high-mobility team, interlinked with sophisticated communications equipment. Many of the larger agencies have *computer-aided dispatch* (CAD); still others have the means of constant electronic monitoring of the positions of police vehicles. The police cannot function effectively without high-quality communications.

The modern police communications center is located adjacent to the records unit. We are discussing communications alone for the present. In reality, records and communications are frequently combined into a single element of the organization. The purpose of the communications element is to effectively and efficiently direct police units in the street to the locations requiring police service. The dispatcher serves as a pivot point between the police and the public. Citizens requiring police help are rarely in a position to contact a police officer directly. Instead, they call the police department. The dispatcher, or person handling the phones, receives the information, assesses its priority status, then contacts the appropriate officer(s) for handling the situation. If the officer needs further information, the request is routed back to the dispatcher, who then attempts to obtain that information from the person calling.

Speed of response, appropriateness of which units respond, and thoroughness of information provided to responding elements are all under the control of the dispatcher. Moreover, in situations requiring multiple-unit response, the dispatcher may act as an electronic chess master, carefully assigning police units to appropriate locations to intercept fleeing felons or to find missing children.

The role of communications is vital to the police mission. Good communications frequently results in good law enforcement. Bad communications can be disastrous.

Records

Law enforcement agencies store volumes of records. Every official contact between a police officer and a citizen is documented and filed. Moreover, each record must be cross-referenced for easy access. Record keeping is therefore a major task in all police organizations. The types of records used in law enforcement are: arrest reports, offense reports, juvenile reports, incident reports, accident reports, field interrogations, photograph records, fingerprint files, M.O. (modus operandi) files, investigative reports, follow-up reports, damage to public property reports, warrant files, internal investigative reports, and police vehicle damage reports, to name some of the types of records stored.

Frequently, officers conducting current investigations need information regarding a past similar occurrence or possible suspect. It is the function of the records section to locate this information and provide it to the officer. As mentioned in the section of communications, the records element is often a part of an overall communications and records unit. As it is true in civilization that the past is often the key to the future, so is it true that the past often provides the key to the solution of current and future crimes. It is the duty of the records section to act as librarian and departmental historian so as to safeguard the past.

Jail Operations and Management

Not every law enforcement organization has a jail, but most have some form of holding facility. County sheriffs and large municipalities, however, often have substantial jail operations. The jail provides a true challenge for law enforcement organizations. Police officers by temperament and training are not prepared to manage jails. Some law enforcement organizations have realized this and hired corrections personnel to manage and staff the jail. Others make do with what they have, and what they have are police officers.

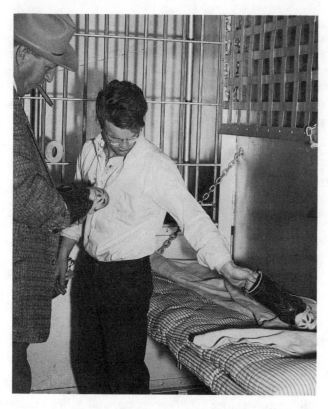

Photograph 5-7 Jail

The difficulties that arise with jail management relate to cost and liability. Jails are expensive. The building materials required for security drive construction costs out of sight. Prisoners must be clothed, fed, and their medical bills must be paid by the jurisdiction housing them. Personnel are required to monitor the prisoners, which increases personnel cost. Prisoners must be protected from other prisoners. Visitation must be allowed, but monitored. Friends and relatives may attempt to smuggle weapons and contraband into the jail. Prisoners and guards are subject to attack by violent prisoners or by those seeking to escape.

In addition, there are a variety of rules, regulations, laws, and court decisions regulating jail operations that must be followed. Failure to adequately follow the regulations or inappropriate response to problems can lead to civil suits, injuries, and even death. Jail management is a difficult but important function of the technical services division.

Maintenance

Mundane as it may seem, even in law enforcement agencies someone must ensure that the equipment performs as it should. Vehicles must be serviced, tires replaced, windows cleaned. Radios, spotlights, and emergency equipment must be repaired or replaced as needed. Weapons must be cleaned, as must buildings. Proper maintenance is critical to effective law enforcement. Computers, automobiles, and radios must work consistently or the officers are left without information, transportation, or communication.

Normally, sworn personnel do not perform most of the maintenance functions of the agency. That is usually the duty of civilians hired for this purpose. Still, the sworn officers are dependent on those who perform these vital tasks. Moreover, sworn administrative personnel are usually responsible for the management of these functions. Maintenance is therefore a major element in the police organization.

SUMMARY

Law enforcement organizations are designed along traditional lines of authority and structure. They are pyramid shaped, with each level accountable to the level above. This has led to a semimilitary orientation often manifested in uniforms and insignia of rank.

Within organizations of any size, there are certain elements that will always be found. Patrol, in its many configurations, is the mainstay of all agencies. Other elements, such as investigations and services, depend on size and resources. As the agency grows, so too does the need for specialization. With specialization comes problems, but the problems do not outweigh the necessity for specialization in most cases.

While the provision of police services is the primary reason for the existence of the police, the police agency must also provide administrative and technical assistance to the line elements. For this reason law enforcement agencies must do more than patrol and investigate. They must also recruit, hire, fire, promote, discipline, and reward personnel. They must provide supplies, equipment, and housing for the agency. In short, the officer on the street is merely the visible representative of a large, complex, sophisticated organization. Like the proverbial iceberg, the public sees but the tip of the organization. The effectiveness of the unseen portion, however, often determines the effectiveness of the line elements.

DISCUSSION QUESTIONS

1. Distinguish between span of control and unity of command. Why are these concepts important?

2. Why is patrol the most important element of a police organization?

3. What are the advantages and disadvantages of organizational specialization?

4. Why do police organizations use the pyramid structure? What are its strengths and weaknesses?

5. Why are the communications and records units so important to police operations?

NOTES/REFERENCES

1. Robert Wasserman and Mark H. Moore, ''Values in Policing,'' *Perspectives on Policing,* Vol. 8, Nov. 1988, p. 4.

2. Wasserman and Moore, p. 5.

3. Wasserman and Moore, p. 4.

4. George L. Kelling and Mark H. Moore, ''The Evolving Strategy of Policing,'' *Perspectives on Policing,* No. 4, Nov. 1988, p. 6.

5. Robert M. Fogelson, *Big-City Police* (Cambridge, Mass.: Harvard University Press, 1977).

6. Dennis M. Payne and Robert C. Trojanowicz, *Performance Profiles of Foot versus Motor Officers,* Community Policing Series No. 6 (East Lansing, Mich.: National Neighborhood Foot Patrol Center, School of Criminal Justice, Michigan State University, 1985).

7. John E. Eck, *Solving Crimes: The Investigation of Burglary and Robbery* (Washington, D.C.: U.S. Department of Justice, National Institute of Justice, 1983), pp. xvii–xviii.

8. Paul B. Weston and Kenneth M. Wells, *Criminal Investigation: Basic Perspectives,* 5th ed. (Englewood Cliffs, N.J.: Prentice-Hall, Inc., 1990).

9. Samuel Walker, *Sense and Nonsense about Crime,* 2nd ed. (Pacific Grove, Calif.: Brooks/Cole Publishing Co., 1989), p. 136.

Chapter 6

Police Socialization

Key Terms

Police subculture
Socialization
Ritualism
Mentoring
Police values
Police as buffoons
Police as dullards
Police as sadists

Police as heroes
Police as wizards
Police as harassed professionals
Police media image
Police public image
Police self-image
Occupational danger
Occupational stress

Chapter Objectives

At the conclusion of this chapter, students should be able to:

1. Understand the internal dynamics of police organizations.
2. Identify those factors that shape the police image.
3. Understand the complexity involved in police socialization.

INTRODUCTION

Police officers are not born, they are made—created through a process of training, interaction with other officers, and perceptions formed over a lifetime. It is quite likely that no other occupation creates such monumental expectations as in police recruits, only to crush them under a mountain of reality. The harsh truth is that no one outside police work knows what police officers really do.

This inaccurate perception is partially the fault of the literary media. Cops and robbers stories have been a major portion of the pop literature for well over a century. Television and motion pictures also rely heavily on police stories to attract audiences. Crime is an interesting topic; exciting crime is more fascinating. Writers play fast and loose with the truth. We should expect this, for the media sells excitement. For law enforcement stories to be salable to the general public, they must be fast moving and thrilling.

The police themselves are also partly responsible for their inaccurate image. The police would like to have people think their job is as exciting and fulfilling as they are portrayed in the media. There is a tendency toward martyrdom among police officers. They like to be viewed as long-suffering defenders of the innocent and preservers of law and justice.

Most of this is nonsense. Mythology, however, is part of every occupation. Moreover, every occupation has its own value system and its own methods of teaching those values. Socialization is a process whereby new members of the organization are introduced to, and ultimately absorbed into, the occupation. All organizations socialize their members.

Police socialization is one of the most rigidly enforced processes within all work groups. The new officer must accept the values of the agency or not thrive as a member of the group. In this chapter we will look at the values and myths of the police. Hopefully, we will develop an understanding of how the world is viewed from the perspective of law enforcement officers.

THE POLICE SUBCULTURE

The term *subculture* denotes a culture within a culture. We are familiar with other types of subcultures. The juvenile gangs of the ghetto, prison inmates, even immigrants living in close confinement qualify as subcultures. To identify an occupational group as a subculture, however, requires some justification. As mentioned previously, all organizations socialize their employees into the desired value system. We do not classify stockbrokers, doctors, lawyers, or even priests as members of a subculture. What is it about the police, therefore, that leads us to such a classification?

The police operate in an aura of isolationism, secrecy, strong in-group loyalties, sacred symbols, common language, and a sense of estrangement. These are almost axiomatic subcultural features underpinning a set of common understandings among police in general which govern their relationships with one another as well as with those who are not police.[1] Such a perspective emphasizes the necessity to view the world from the eyes of an outsider. This perception of an outsider looking in at, and isolated from, the remainder of society is what causes the *police subculture.* The actual creation of this phenomenon is a steady, time-consuming process.

The police subculture is a clearly defined world populated only by those charged with the authority to enforce the law. No one is admitted into this world who has not accepted the values of the occupation. *Socialization* actually begins in the selection and screening process, is refined in the police academy, adapted and modified in the field training period, and finally, absorbed through years of police work.

Entrance into the world of the police is like few other employment experiences. The vast array of interviews, tests, and inspections provide the applicant with a feeling of awe. At each step the potential officer is made to feel that entry into the police world is like acceptance into an elite organization. This feeling is enhanced by the observed dropout rate. Indeed, in many major departments as few as 3 to 5 percent will complete the screening process successfully.

Upon completing, or maybe we should say "surviving," the screening procedures, the new recruit is introduced to the first *rite of passage.* The new officer is sworn in. There are few occupations that require the taking of an oath. The new recruit will be familiar with some of those, such as elected officials and military personnel, and will feel that now he or she is also truly exceptional. Of course, there is the warning that goes with the ritual. The new officers are informed that until the probationary period is completed, they may be discharged at any time without warning, explanation, or appeal. In effect, the new officer has been given authority above and beyond that of the vast majority of citizens. The probationary process makes it clear to recruits, however, that they owe total obedience to the organization or that authority will be unceremoniously stripped from them. Simultaneously, they become both powerful and powerless. Then they are sent to the academy.

The Academy Experience

For most urban and state officers, the first real contact with the police subculture occurs at the academy. Surrounded by other recruits, the new officer is subjected to the harsh and sometimes arbitrary discipline of the organization. The recruit is taught absolute obedience to departmental rules and regulations, undergoes rigorous physical training, and is bored to tears with uninspired lectures on the technical aspects of the job. Moreover, every aspect of the recruit's life is overlaid with *ritualism.*

Solidarity is stressed through group rewards and punishments. Group cohesion is further enhanced by intergroup competition, identifying garments for each class and cajoling newcomers. Evidence suggests that such tactics work. Regular

Photograph 6–1   Police Academy Class (Photograph courtesy of the Missouri Highway Patrol.)

academy reunions in many agencies are well attended. This happens even though the members of a class may be transferred far apart and not see each other for years, if at all. For many officers, the academy experience results in a career-long source of identification.[2]

The formal content of the academy stresses the technical aspects of the job. Simultaneously, however, the recruit is introduced to the traditions and values of the agency. Interspersed in the formal, dry lectures are police fables, or *war stories*. Various instructors relate real-life incidents, often embellished over years of telling the story. During these interludes, the recruits are allowed to relax. The instructor ceases to be a stern task master and becomes one of the class. Laughing and joking are allowed as the older officer allows the recruits to be one of the insiders. The recruits begin to value these times in much the same way as children view a trip to the ice cream parlor. More important, during unsupervised periods, the recruits discuss these incidents, developing their own responses and reactions. In a sense, the recruits live out the incidents vicariously, then test their responses with those of the other recruits. Often these incidents become part of the agency's folklore, retold again and again by these officers, as if the situations happened to them.

The importance of war stories cannot be overemphasized. This is the information the recruits desire. They want to know how to survive, both on the street and in the organization. It is only through informal interactions with senior officers that this information is obtained. The recruits are also still under a false impression concerning their chosen occupation. Having no street experience, they still believe the media-created police image. War stories tend to reinforce this image because the most popular tales are those involving life-threatening situations. The recruits come to believe that the world is a jungle in which only the strong survive. Story content focuses on emotions such as fear, injury, and death. Distrust of the public plays a major portion in many of the object lessons of the tales. Ever so subtly the recruits are taught that it is only other officers that can be relied on; no one else is to be trusted.

Field Training

For most new police officers, graduation from the academy means trading a classroom instructor for a field training officer (FTO). The field training experience is critical to the effective development of new officers. This experience is intended to allow the new officer to integrate the information learned in the classroom with real-life situations on the street. The FTO supervises the process, allowing the recruit to grow into the job while being protected from the results of mistakes (see Chapter 4).

A concern to police administrators is that academy training may be undermined by field training. It is almost a police cliché that older officers tell recruits to forget what they have learned in the academy. The danger in this admonition is that the new officer will take the message seriously, thus lose the self-confidence carefully developed in the academy. Also, the senior officer's so-called *real police procedures* are invariably the result of corner cutting and sloppiness developed over a long period of time. This can be damaging to young officers.[3]

Typically, the field training period lasts from 30 to 90 days. Ideally, the new officer should still be on probation when released from field training. This is so that the officer can be evaluated on the merits of individual performance, without the crutch of a training officer. The field training program is usually conducted in three or more phases. First is the introductory phase, followed by several training and evaluation phases. The last component of this program is usually pure evaluation, as the training officer merely observes the recruit's handling of calls.[4]

The selection of field training officers is also of critical importance. These people should be good officers and good teachers. They should have a keen sense of both the duties required and the evaluation process used by the administration. The FTOs are involved extensively in training and evaluation. Both should be in line with the needs of the agency. Undoubtedly, some form of *mentoring* process takes place in the socialization of new officers. Ideally, the FTO should become the young officer's mentor. This may not always happen. A mentoring relationship requires that both parties accept the role of mentor and student. If the FTO becomes merely another training officer, the recruit will most likely seek out a mentor when assigned to his or her first duty station. The choice will probably be based on personality factors. Like a puppy seeking a master, the recruit will seek someone in whom trust can be placed. The relationship that develops will determine the values and style that the recruit adapts, for good or bad.

Reality

The reality of police work is a far cry from the myths. Research has consistently found that police officers spend a minimal amount of time on crime-fighting duties. If they do not fight crime, one might ask, just what is it that police do?

According to a study of a major city's police, John A. Webster found that police officers spend their time as follows:

Activities	Percentage of Consumed Time
Crimes against persons	2.96
Crimes against property	14.82
Traffic	9.20
On-view	9.10
Social service	13.70
Administration	50.19

Source: John A. Webster, "Police Time and Tasks," in *Thinking about Police: Contemporary Readings,* Carl B. Klockars, Ed. (New York: McGraw-Hill Book Company, 1983), pp. 232–238.

Illustration 6–1   Police Time and Tasks

The categories selected are, for the most part, self-explanatory. Crimes against persons and property certainly need little in the way of definition. The larger groups, social service and administration, however, are aggregates and require further discussion.

Webster included such incidents as family crisis, drunkenness, suicides, mental illness, ambulance calls, and public nuisances as social service. Administration activities include coffee breaks, meals, community relations, taking reports, running errands, attending court, serving warrants, and performing as police technician. The category "on-view" refers to actions initiated by the police themselves, other than events in the other categories. For example, stopping a suspicious person on foot or in a vehicle and security checks of buildings fall into this category.

Even the time spent on crime-related incidents is inflated. Included in this category is the time spent on burglar alarms. It was estimated by the police of the city under study that in excess of 90 percent of all alarms were false. Some of the time spent on crimes against property, therefore, was spent responding to a false alarm.

What these statistics mean, of course, is that the new officer will not be chasing robbers and rapists, and defending the city from evil, but will be an *order taker:* someone who answers calls for service, writes reports, and sends those reports to headquarters.[5] The enthusiasm and dedication of the new officer will come under a severe and continuous assault by the realities of the job. Instead of facing new challenges and solving serious crimes, the officer will be confronted with petty problems, boredom, and mindless bureaucracy.

Police Values

Police officers, for the most part, come from the lower-middle-class spectrum of society. Therefore, *police values* are relatively easy to identify. Officers come from the societal group that is the most law and morality oriented. Generally speaking, it is the middle class that has more fully bought into the ideas espoused in the Judeo-Christian ethic system. Politically, the police are conservative by nature. They believe in structure. Structure, they feel, comes from rules, regulations, and law. They believe fully in the validity of punishment, be it capital, corporal, imprisonment, or fine. Frequently, they use the amount of punishment administered by the court as a measure of their worth. We should not be surprised, therefore, that many police officers complain bitterly about the leniency of the courts.

The police are self-oriented. They believe that only other officers understand the job and understand them as people. This has two effects. First, it builds into the police psyche distrust of outsiders. Second, it forces officers into a strict cohesion that demands unity to a degree that becomes pathological. The police world thus becomes one of *us versus them,* with the dysfunctional corollary that the worst of us is better than the best of them. The orientation toward rigid compliance with rules coupled with the strict unity also has a negative impact on the police value system. It builds and constantly reinforces conformity while stifling creativity. Police officers can easily fall into the pattern of the inflexible bureaucrat.

Other aspects of the value system are manipulated by the police image. Much of the difficulty women officers face has little to do with police work itself but is related to their relations with male officers. It has only been in the past 25 years that women have been allowed to participate as equal members of law enforcement organizations. For over 5000 years law enforcement had been *man's work.* The modern male police officer is faced with a dilemma that earlier officers did not have to confront. To accept women into the ranks means that the job may not be as glamorous or dangerous as it has been portrayed. It lessens the male officers' self-image because they believe it is a not-so-subtle statement that *anyone* can be a police officer. It is not so much the women themselves that cause the problem as it is what women in policing represent. For many it is an assault on perceived notions of manhood.

THE POLICE IMAGE

The police image is not under complete control of the police. Everyone has some idea of what constitutes police work. The law enforcement image is also fair game for writers of both fiction and nonfiction, as well as anyone who has had contact with a police officer. Almost everyone has an opinion of the police. It is the composite of all those beliefs that make up the police image.

Elements of the police image are part fiction and part fact. There are myths, legends, and realities. To understand policing it is necessary to peel back the layers of misinformation. This is not an easy task. Police imagery surrounds the occupation like a thick fog.

The Fictional Police Officer

Let us start this discussion by saying that we do not truly know to what extent fiction influences the police image. Some police officers seem to revel in the image projected by the media, especially when the image is one of dedication and competence. It might even be said that for many in the field of law enforcement, life imitates art. Some officers pattern their own behavior after that of fictional characters. For other officers, the media are merely an uncomfortable distraction, providing the public with unrealistic expectations. For example, some police agencies routinely send an officer to search for fingerprints at crime scenes where the officers know there is little chance of finding such prints. This is done because the public, having seen such behavior on television, expects this service and would be upset if it was not provided. From these observations, we can surmise that the media do have an impact on the police image. We simply do not know the strength of that influence.

The police officer in fiction is almost invariably a stereotype of one form or another. Rarely is he or she presented as more than a one-dimensional character. At worst, the officer may be used for comic relief or as a foil to the more sophisticated private detective or attorney. Officers are sometimes portrayed as corrupt or ignorant, or both. At best, the police are heroes, showing intellectual capacity nearing the genius level. Rarely is the officer treated honestly. Few such books or films would sell. It is from the works of fiction, however, that most people obtain their first glimpse of law enforcement. This is quite likely where the image building begins. Whether the police are forced to overcome this image or bask in its glow depends on the nature of the fiction.

By and large there are six distinct classes of fictional police officer. There are sometimes found a variety of subclasses, but ultimately the vast majority of fictional officers are buffoons, dullards, sadists, heroes, wizards, or harassed professionals.

Buffoons.   In all probability this stereotype was created in the first silent movies. The *Keystone Kops* portrayed the police literally as clowns. Television added its own version with such family favorites as *Car 54 Where Are You?* and *Sledge Hammer*. It is quite likely that this fictional image of the police is the least harmful. Laughter is healthy—for both society and the institution that is the focus of the humor. The characters portrayed are so obviously comic caricatures that they have rarely been mistaken for reality. Still, the police officer as clown is a major source of entertainment, a fact attested to by the success of movies as the *Pink Panther* series or *Police Academy 1-?*.

Dullards.   The police officer as dullard is almost as popular as the clown. Over the years law enforcement officers have played the fool to highlight the protagonist's genius. Almost all private detective stories have at least one police character who is unbelievably stupid. The unintelligent police officer is as stereo-

Photograph 6–2 Keystone Kops

typical as the unintelligent athlete. This image was made popular by Sir Arthur Conan Doyle's police officers in the Sherlock Holmes stories. Slow-witted police officers have been popular in fiction ever since.

It is difficult to determine what impact this portrayal has on the police image. We do know that most people see the police as blue-collar, lower-middle-class individuals. That is not the image of well-educated and trained professionals. It may also be true that the public is not comfortable with the notion of police officers as either highly educated or well trained. Given the power that police officers possess, the notion that they might be intelligent enough to use those powers fully could be frightening to some people. This is only speculation, however; we truly do not yet know the impact of fictional police characters on the public's perception of the police. Since the public has far more contact with the police of fiction than they have with the real thing, we must conclude that there is an impact.

Sadists. The corrupt or sadistic officer is another mainstay of modern fiction. One need only look at ancient literature to find the "little guy" facing an antagonist who epitomizes power and corruption. Even before the creation of police organizations the literature was replete with *David and Goliath* stories. It seems only natural that the police, the most visible and powerful arm of government, should be the natural enemy of the weak and powerless.

Also, sufficient true corruption among the police has emerged to enhance the corrupt image of the media cop. Stories such as *Serpico* and *Prince of the City* have helped establish the tainted image of large eastern police agencies. Moreover, daily reports of police corruption or misbehavior by the nonfictional media adds support to the negative image portrayed in fictional stories.

Bad cops in fiction have several possible negative side effects. First, whether intended or not, such stories implant the seeds of mistrust. It is easy to believe in real-life corruption when one sees so much fictional corruption. Second, it reinforces the idea that the police are the enemy. Not everyone has the ability to divorce truth from fiction. The blurring of right and wrong that takes place in "bad cop" stories confuses those who lack this capacity.

I am not arguing for censorship. Writers should be able to develop stories in any way they see fit. I merely wish to point out that any occupation's image is often in the hands of others. Writers of both the printed and electronic media affect the image of the police with what they write. No one can control this, but police officers should be aware of potential sources of negative imagery. The fictional officer who is sadistic or corrupt provides such a source.

Heroes.   Some of our first media heroes were the men and women of the Saturday morning western. These characters rode into town, cleaned up the place, and rode into the sunset. They did not curse, drink, or dally with the opposite sex; they were pure of heart and soul. The western was probably the most pure of the American morality plays. Good always won, evil always lost. The innocent rarely got hurt—the maiden was always saved, her honor intact; the money was always recovered. So strong were the beliefs by those who made the movies of

Photograph 6-3   The Lone Ranger

that era that even off the set, the actors and actresses were expected to behave as their characters behaved. Why? Because movie producers believed that people, especially young people, modeled their behavior after their heroes on the giant screen. Heroes were created as role models and no one questioned the validity of this idea.

What effect does this have on the public's perception of the police? I have seen well-educated adults ask why the police shoot to kill rather than wounding the suspect or shooting the gun from a suspect's hand. The question itself shows how little the public understands the dynamics of an incident involving the exchange of gunfire. It takes very little investigation to determine where these ideas come from. Today's adult grew up with *the Lone Ranger, Hopalong Cassidy,* and *Roy Rogers.*

Even the modern, more sullied, hero provides a false impression of the police. Police characters such as *Dirty Harry,* for example, routinely kill 11 or 12 people in the course of a two-hour movie. Of course, all of those killed richly deserved such a fate, but one wonders at the true effect of constant combat on the psyche of the officer doing the killing. It should be mentioned that not once in any movie did Inspector Harry Callahan exhibit one ounce of either uncertainty or regret at having killed any of his victims.

As a result of movies such as these, police officers who speak with schoolchildren are almost always asked how many people they have killed. Chil-

Photograph 6–4 Dirty Harry

dren are usually amazed to learn that in most cases, the officer has not killed anyone. Even adults are shocked to learn that a very small percentage of the police ever discharge a firearm at another person.

In movieland, policing is war. Every day each officer goes to work not knowing if this will be the day that he or she kills or gets killed. It makes one wonder why anyone would want to be a police officer. Equally important, it makes one wonder about the mind set of those who wish to be police officers precisely because of this image.

Wizards.   The 1950s saw the creation of the television supercop. The great private detectives of literature, Sherlock Holmes, Sam Spade, and Hercule Poirot, had reigned supreme until the advent of television. Private detectives, with only their wits and fists to rely on, had to make room for the police detective, who had not only wits and fists, but also the law as a weapon. The private investigators retained their popularity but were often forced to compete with a police show on another channel. Such fare as *Highway Patrol* and *M Squad* competed successfully with *Meet Boston Blackie* and *The Thin Man.* In more recent times *Kojak, Columbo,* and *Miami Vice* have maintained the police position within the realm of serious drama.

The important aspect of these police stories is the return to the morality play. The police always get the criminal. Through brilliant insight or hard work, the stars are always successful. The only change is that sometimes the innocent get

Photograph 6–5   Kojak

hurt and sometimes the heroes cry. Other than that, there is little difference between the Saturday evening star and the earlier Saturday morning hero.

The impact of these stories on the police image is probably positive. Certainly, it may lead young people to investigate the possibilities of a police career. That the media have such an impact can easily be established when one considers the effect the movie *Top Gun* had on the U.S. Navy's efforts to recruit young men for pilot training. This became one of the hardest positions for a young person to obtain, due to the huge number of applicants that appeared immediately following the release of the movie.

There is a downside to the image provided in detective stories. In reality, the police do not always catch the criminal. Innocent people are raped, robbed, and murdered at a frightening rate. The public may well expect more than the police can give. This expectation could be based on fictional law enforcement rather than on reality. Overcoming the fiction-produced expectations can be an impossible task.

Harassed professionals. The newest of the fiction-produced police images is that of the harried professional. Competent, but overworked and underappreciated, this character usually manages to solve the case in some way. This character is portrayed as a sensitive human being. He or she has personal problems and makes mistakes. Things usually work out in the end, although sometimes they do not. Joseph Wambaugh has ended a number of his best-selling books by killing off the protagonist through suicide. In fact, Wambaugh's characters are sometimes so human, they are what psychologists formerly referred to as neurotic. The enemies of these characters are the bureaucracy, political system, and courts. The police do what they can in a cesspool of governmental incompetence and interference.

While these police officers are sympathetic characters, I am not certain that the image is necessarily healthy. While providing the public with an image of policing that is positive, these stories often do so at the expense of other institutions. Even more problematic, some police officers may accept these situations as accurate, further inflaming what may already be a tenuous relationship between police officers, their supervisors, and the courts. To portray police officers constantly as competent, while courts or police management are described otherwise, is both inaccurate and harmful.

The Real Police Officer

The image of the police is determined by a number of factors, some over which the police have little or no control. Undoubtedly, the image created by fictional police officers plays a role in the creation of this imagery, but other factors also come into play. The news media have a tremendous impact on the police image. In reality, a local newspaper or broadcast news station can hound a police chief or sheriff out of the community. Similarly, the entire police organization can suffer or prosper as a result of editorials and news stories. Individual citizens also develop an image of the police. Usually, this is a combination of information they have received from the media, friends, and relatives as well as the opinion they form from their own contacts with the police.

Media perceptions.   The media know very little about the realities of law enforcement. Despite the fact that the majority of stories broadcast during any given time span will be police-related, media personnel rarely have either sufficient training or contacts with the criminal justice system to be considered well informed. The result is that some articles and stories are inaccurate, ill informed, and based on myth rather than fact.

We often forget that behind the makeup and slick electronic imagery, those professional, sincere men and women reporters are reading scripts. The scripts are put together hurriedly, with an eye toward putting the story on the air in a short time span. Often, important information is left out because of time restraints. The television crew opts for visual stimulation as opposed to information processing.

Despite the problems with the news media, the overall *police media image* appears to be good. Most news stories are crime related; therefore, the police are presented as sources of expertise, information, and dedication. It is usually when allegations of police misconduct arise that the news media take on the role of adversary to the police. The danger posed by the media lies in their tendency to measure the competence of other organizations by how they affect the media. Police organizations sometimes have the need to keep information secret. The media views their role as that of protectors of the public interest. They often view any attempt at secrecy as corrupt at worst, incompetent at best.

There are problems inherent with the police–media relationship. The press is a powerful institution that is itself subject to the same problems as those of any social institution. Large news organizations are as bureaucratic as any other large organization. Furthermore, the motives and practices of news personalities are not always altruistic. The news industry is competition driven. Big money and numerous large egos are involved. It is a cutthroat business, with market share and subscription rates determining success or failure.

The unfortunate aspect of all this is that people and organizations can be made or destroyed by a well-designed media campaign. In summary, the media, to a very large extent, create the police image for either good or ill. This is especially true at the local and state levels, where people have direct access to the politicians.

There is a positive side to the media's power. Where there is corruption and brutality, the press are far more likely to expose it than are the police or courts. A good news organization tends to keep government officials, including the police, honest.

Citizen perceptions.   The individual citizen forms a perception of the police based on what he or she sees and hears. The *police public image* is formed when a good experience with the police leaves the citizen with a good feeling for all police officers. Similarly, a negative police–citizen contact leaves the person with the perception that all police officers are bad.

We should also remember that bad stories travel further and faster than do good ones. A person who has experienced brutality, discourtesy, or callousness will tell everyone within earshot about that incident. Often, the story will be repeated for years to come. Moreover, because people willingly believe anything bad about another person, the story will be repeated by those hearing it, in an effort to highlight a point about how bad the police are. Sadly, incidents involving courteous and competent officers are rarely broadcast with as much enthusiasm. Courtesy and competence are not news and not worthy of gossip. The result is that a single bad officer can destroy the image of an entire police agency.

Another citizen perception, of some annoyance to municipal police officers, is the amount of variance found between types of agencies, based on nothing more than their employer. As a general rule, the public has a higher regard for federal law enforcement agencies than they have for state organizations. At the same time, citizens usually think more highly of state agencies than they do of local police organizations. Tracing the source of these perceptions is difficult. It is most obvious when viewing law enforcement. In reality, however, people generally have the same feelings toward all governmental agencies. The federal government is seen as more competent and professional than the state governments, which are more respected than are local governments. The fact is that only a small percentage of law enforcement personnel are employed by the federal government and the states. The large majority of police officers in the United States are employed locally. Furthermore, the 50 or so federal agencies have limited jurisdiction and responsibilities while some of the state agencies are also limited in their enforcement powers.

The majority of the duties delegated to law enforcement organizations by society are the responsibility of local law enforcement. Many of these functions, especially order maintenance, are not handled by either the state or federal government. Police work, as we know it, is almost the exclusive realm of local police agencies. The federal and state agencies are specialists whose assigned duties support the general jurisdiction of the local police. To phrase it somewhat more harshly, most state and federal agencies could be disbanded tomorrow with no great impact on either crime or society in general. The same cannot be said of municipal agencies. Nevertheless, the local police do not receive the same respect afforded those at higher levels of government. Whether this is simply the by-product of their association with a lower level of government or because of that old adage "familiarity breeds contempt" is not known. What we do know is that the local police receive a somewhat lower level of respect than their state and federal counterparts.

The police self-image.   The police see themselves as society's last line of defense. The term "thin blue line" accurately represents this perception. They also view themselves as unappreciated and unrespected. This appears to be true of police everywhere. Studies of police in Europe report the same findings.

Conservative by nature, the police have little patience with or understanding of the liberal point of view. They identify with the victims of crime and see little need for a progressive penal philosophy. They believe that they have a better understanding of human nature than anyone else, especially sociologists.

Not realizing that their viewpoint is skewed by the kinds of contacts they have with the public, they generally believe everyone to be corrupt. This cynicism is not new to the modern American police. During the reign of Napoleon, Joseph Fouché (see Chapter 2) concluded that with few exceptions the world was composed of scoundrels, hypocrites, and imbeciles. In 1939, Reid Bane found that police officers were committed to the belief that the citizen was always trying "to get away with something," and that all men would commit crimes were it not for fear of the police.[6]

The police tend to identify outsiders as either friend or foe. Those who agree with the police value system are friends, those who do not agree are the enemy. Sensitive to any criticism, the police consider anyone who publicly contradicts their views or actions as an enemy. It might be said that the police view themselves as the last knights of an unappreciative civilization. It is not coincidental that Joseph Wambaugh titled his first two police novels, *The New Centurions* and *The Blue Knight*. This is the *police officer's self-image*.

POLICE PROBLEMS: MYTHS AND FACTS

The two areas that have seemed to attract the most attention for those who observe the police are *danger* and *stress*. It is widely believed that policing is both dangerous and stressful. An entire array of assumptions are based on these beliefs. The foundation for these ideas is based on the perceptions of the police themselves, as well as those who observe the police.

This is an area of some confusion. Neither the amount of danger nor the amount of stress has been subjected to intensive inquiry. They are assumed to be part of the law enforcement occupation. Recent research, however, appears to dispute these assertions. Policing may not be as dangerous or as stressful as we believe. Still, the research is sketchy. We are only beginning to understand this complex area of the police occupation. We attempt to gain a better understanding of both danger and stress through a review of both.

Danger

Police officers see danger everywhere. From the moment new officers enter the academy they are bombarded with tales of danger. They are warned to beware of crimes in progress, where most police deaths occur. They are told to be careful when investigating domestic disturbances. Even the traffic stop can become a tale of terror. Finally, they are admonished to be wary even when completing such mundane familial tasks as grocery shopping, because if a robber identifies a person as a police officer, the officer is certain to be assassinated.

Interestingly, police officers do not believe that there are many job-related injuries in law enforcement. They do believe, however, that police work is dangerous.[7] On the one hand, they recognize that they are not likely to be injured but believe they are in a dangerous occupation. This comes from the belief that danger is ever present, even though unlikely.

In terms of actual death and injury, the statistics do not support the notion that policing is excessively dangerous. Between 1975 and 1984, 971 officers were killed in the line of duty. This averages out to a rate of around 97 per year. The total number of law enforcement officers during that time period was 467,117. This means that police officers were killed at a rate of slightly more than 1.5 per 10,000.[8] Moreover, the number of police officers killed has been declining. From a high of 134 deaths in 1968, line-of-duty deaths has decreased to 66 in 1986. This despite the increase in the overall number of police officers during that period.

To place this in proper perspective, law enforcement deaths in 1986 averaged 1 for every 9542 officers employed. During the same time, miners died at the rate of 1 per 3405; people employed in the construction industry died at the rate of 1 per 5590; and people employed in agriculture, forestry, and fishing died at the rate of 1 for every 7309.[9]

During 1986, 64,259 officers were assaulted, for a rate of approximately 10 out of every 100 officers. Eighty-four percent of these assaults took place without the use of a deadly weapon; most were by use of feet or fists. Approximately three officers in a hundred received personal injury.[10]

Occupation	Number of Employees	Fatalities	Rate per 100,000
Mining	681,000	200	1:3,405
Construction	681,000	670	1:5,590
Transportation	4,481,000	800	1:6,051
Agriculture	804,000	110	1:7,309
Law enforcement	629,745	66	1:9,542
Manufacturing	18,358,000	770	1:23,842
Finance	5,267,000	190	1:27,721
Trade	19,423,000	510	1:38,084
Services	18,617,000	370	1:50,316

Sources: U.S. Department of Labor, Bureau of Labor Statistics, May 1989, and *Sourcebook of Criminal Justice Statistics,* 1987.

Illustration 6–2   Comparative Death Rates - 1986

Most officers killed, about two-thirds, were in uniformed patrol. This seems obvious since it is patrol that makes the initial response to a call and is most vulnerable, due to the lack of information concerning the situation. The situations in which officers were killed varied somewhat, but we can identify a number of general categories that give us some idea of which situations were most dangerous. These categories are: arrest situations, domestic disturbances, traffic situations, and assailants.

Arrest situations.   The largest single category of police officers killed in the line of duty were the result of arrest situations. In the study cited above, 44 percent of all deaths in the line of duty occurred in such incidents. While this category was most responsible for officer deaths, it was only third in number of nonfatal assaults on police officers. Nineteen percent of the officers assaulted were attacked while attempting to make an arrest.

Domestic disturbances.   The so-called "family fight" accounted for the largest single category of assaults on the police. Thirty-three percent of all such assaults occurred during these incidents. Seventeen percent of line-of-duty deaths occurred during such disturbance calls.

Traffic situations.   Traffic pursuits and stops accounted for 13 percent of the police deaths and 10 percent of the assaults. An unexpected aspect of these situations is that a number of officers killed as a result of a traffic stop died from wounds inflicted with their own weapon.

Assailants.   This category includes such incidents as crimes in progress, civil disorders, ambushes, and transportation of prisoners. Assailants were responsible for 11 percent of the deaths and 25 percent of the assaults.

Stress

Writers commenting on police work have proclaimed law enforcement either the most stressful or one of the most stressful occupations in America today.[11] This is done despite a lack of empirical data verifying this conclusion and significant methodological problems in studies supporting the assertion.

The factors that have led police observers to proclaim law enforcement a high-stress occupation are beliefs about police involvement in suicides, divorce, alcoholism, and physiological problems. We will look at the available evidence on each of these topics.

Suicide.   There is uncertainty regarding the extent of the police suicide problem. Many believe suicide to be an occupational hazard. One study, conducted in Wyoming, found that police suicides between 1960 and 1968 were twice as high as the second highest group.[12] Still another study, conducted in Los Angeles, California, between 1970 and 1976, found that police suicide rates were considerably below average for Los Angeles County.[13] Moreover, a study of the British police found a very low suicide rate.[14]

A factor complicating the accumulation of statistics on police suicides is the likelihood that they are underreported. The police are often the first officials to arrive at the scene of a death. There are two reasons why they might deliberately misclassify a suicide. The first is religion. The New England states have large Catholic populations. Suicide is a mortal sin for Catholics. A suicide cannot receive the blessings of the church. This increases the trauma of the suicide's family. The police could quite conceivably wish to save the family that grief.

The second reason is related to insurance. Many insurance companies will not pay the beneficiary in cases of suicide. The family is thus left without the means to survive. The police, in an effort to take care of the family of one of their own, could classify the suicide as an accident, resulting in the payment of the policy. There is little doubt that suicides have been misrepresented by the police. A common subterfuge is to report that the officer was accidentally killed while cleaning a gun.

While acknowledging the underreporting of police suicides, we must also realize that suicide in general is also underreported. People wishing to die, but also wanting their surviving family members to benefit from their deaths, have a veritable catalog of means to make the death appear accidental. Auto accidents, gas leaks, industrial accidents, and even the manipulation of police officers into a shooting incident—all have been used to fake a suicide. The question is: How much more underreported are police suicides than other suicides? That is something we have no way of knowing. At the present time we must admit that we simply do not know if the police have a higher suicide rate than other occupations.

Divorce.   This is another area that is undergoing revision. It was formerly believed that the police had exceptionally high divorce rates.[15] However, later research has cast doubts on that assertion. It is now believed that the divorce rate for police is no higher than the rate for most Americans.[16]

There is also a belief that the police occupation affects the police family negatively in ways other than divorce. The rotating shifts and weekend and holiday work schedules all force the family to adjust. What is unknown is whether these adjustments are more difficult for police families or for families of other occupations forced to make identical adjustments. Firefighters, military personnel, doctors, nurses, and flight crews all face similar problems. To date no study has linked the stresses in police marriages to those of people with similar life-styles. In all likelihood there is little difference in the pressures placed on such families.

Alcoholism.   It has been widely believed that the police suffer from an inordinate amount of alcoholism.[17] To date there is no research supporting this assertion. Alcoholism may or may not be a problem. At this time, we simply do not know the extent of alcohol abuse among police officers.

Medical problems.   There is a substantial body of research indicating that police officers suffer from a wide variety of physical disorders. One study in Tennessee found that between 1972 and 1974, police officers were admitted to general hospitals at rates significantly higher than average. Almost 66 percent of these cases were for disorders of the digestive or circulatory systems, compared to approximately 48 percent for all occupations combined.[18] A 1972 study found that police officers experience headaches and ulcers more frequently than does the general population of males. Moreover, the researchers discovered that cigarette smoking is more prevalent among police officers than among males in general.[19]

Despite these findings, serious questions remain concerning the effects of stress on police officers. There is no doubt that over time stress produces physiological problems for the person afflicted. It is also true that research such as that cited above indicates that the police have an unusually high rate of physiological disorders. It seems a simple matter of adding two and two and reaching the conclusion that police work is stressful, thus debilitating over time.

Unfortunately, relating cause and effect in this case is not so easy. Stress is not the only factor that causes heart and gastrointestinal problems. Cigarette smoking is now known to contribute to such problems, as is excessive weight and high cholesterol levels. Researchers found that 15 percent of the police officers studied had cholesterol levels that doubled the risk of coronary heart disease. This study also found that 56 percent of the officers were from 6 to 20 pounds overweight and that 28 percent were more than 20 pounds overweight.[20]

The question that begs an answer is whether police medical problems are the product of stress or the by-product of a sedentary life-style coupled with poor dietary habits. Long hours of riding in a patrol car, massive consumption of junk food, excessive smoking, and low amounts of exercise may be more deadly than an armed felon. There is at least an even probability that this, rather than stress, is the cause of chronic physiological problems.

Some police agencies are hedging their bets. They are addressing both problems. A number of stress reduction programs have been introduced to police training seminars. At the same time police administrators in a number of agencies have begun mandating weight control and exercise programs. Still other police agencies have issued policies prohibiting officers from smoking.

In summary, we do not know how much stress there is in police work or what its ultimate effects may be. There is sufficient concern, however, to have resulted in policy initiatives addressing the issue.

SUMMARY

The police socialization process occurs in a pressure cooker. The recruit is subjected to a number of forces that converge to force that person's self-image and value system to conform to those of the police subculture. Organizational survival requires that the new officer accept the unwritten code and obey its rules. From initial selection, through the academy, and on into the organization, the officer is molded into a symbol of conformity. The officer either fits the mold or does not fit into the organization.

The factors that combine to shape the police value system and image vary. Some of these factors are mythical or fictional. Law enforcement abounds with mythology. The Matt Dillons and Wyatt Earps of the Old West represent the image of the lone gun-toting police officer, holding the line of civilization against barbarianism. Fictional police officers created by the various forms of media also have an impact on the police image. The result is that neither police officer nor citizen is certain of what the police are or what they can accomplish.

Research has demystified many of the police perceptions. The occupational danger associated with law enforcement, for example, has been found to be much lower than expected. Moreover, there is little statistical support for the belief that law enforcement is a high-stress occupation. While there is still much to learn about these areas, it appears that policing is no more stressful than any other occupation.

DISCUSSION QUESTIONS

1. Identify factors that affect the police image.
2. What is the relationship between real police officers and those in fiction?
3. Compare the amount of danger that actually exists in police work with the amount of danger perceived by the police.
4. What factors are used to measure stress in police work?
5. What factors, other than stress, may affect the foregoing measures?

NOTES/REFERENCES

1. P. H. Bayley and H. Mendelsohn, *Minorities and the Police* (New York: The Free Press, 1969), as cited in John Van Maanen, "On the Making of Policemen," *Human Organization,* Vol. 32, 1973, pp. 407–418.
2. John Van Maanen, "On the Making of Policemen," *Human Organization,* Vol. 32, 1973, pp. 407–418.

3. Geoffrey P. Alpert and Roger G. Dunham, *Policing Urban America* (Prospect Heights, Ill.: Waveland Press, Inc., 1988), p. 52.

4. Michael S. McCampbell, "Field Training for Police Officers: State of the Art," in *Critical Issues in Policing: Contemporary Readings,* Roger G. Dunham and Geoffrey P. Alpert, Eds. (Prospect Heights, Ill.: Waveland Press, Inc., 1989), pp. 111–120.

5. John A. Webster, "Police Time and Tasks," in *Thinking about Police: Contemporary Readings,* Carl B. Klockars, Ed. (New York: McGraw-Hill Book Company, 1983), p. 237.

6. Arthur Neiderhoffer, "Police Cynicism," in *The Ambivalent Force: Perspectives on the Police,* 3rd ed., Abraham S. Blumberg and Elaine Neiderhoffer, Eds. (New York: Holt, Rinehart and Winston, 1985), p. 208.

7. Francis T. Cullen, Bruce G. Link, Lawrence F. Travis III, and Terry Lemming, "Paradox in Policing: A Note on Perceptions of Danger," in *The Ambivalent Force: Perspectives on the Police,* 3rd ed., Abraham S. Blumberg and Elaine Neiderhoffer, Eds. (New York: Holt, Rinehart and Winston, 1985), pp. 351–356.

8. Alpert and Dunham, pp. 134–135.

9. *Occupational Injuries and Illnesses in the United States by Industry, 1987* (Washington, D.C.: Bureau of Labor Statistics, May 1989).

10. *Law Enforcement Officers Killed and Assaulted, 1986,* FBI Uniform Crime Reports (Washington, D.C.: U.S. Government Printing Office, 1987), p. 47, Table 7.

11. W. Clinton Terry III, "Police Stress: The Empirical Evidence," in *The Ambivalent Force: Perspectives on the Police,* 3rd ed., Abraham S. Blumberg and Elaine Neiderhoffer, Eds. (New York: Holt, Rinehart and Winston, 1985), p. 364.

12. Marilyn J. Davidson and Arthur Veno, "Police Stress: A Multicultural, Interdisciplinary Review and Perspective, Part I," *Abstracts on Police Science,* July–Aug. 1978, pp. 190–191.

13. J. Dash and Martin Reiser, "Suicide among Police in an Urban Law Enforcement Agency," as cited in Gail Goolkasian, Ronald W. Geddes, and William DeJong, "Coping with Police Stress," in *Critical Issues in Policing: Contemporary Readings,* Roger G. Dunham and Geoffrey Alpert, Eds. (Prospect Heights, Ill.: Waveland Press, Inc., 1989), p. 503.

14. Gisli H. Gudjonsson, "Life Events Stressors and Physical Reactions in Senior British Police Officers," *The Police Journal,* Vol. 56, Jan. 1983, pp. 60–67.

15. John Stratton, "The Law Enforcement Family: Programs for Spouses," *FBI Law Enforcement Bulletin,* Mar. 1976, p. 16.

16. Davidson and Veno, p. 192; John G. Stratton and Barbara Tracy Stratton, "Law Enforcement Marital Relationships: A Positive Approach," *FBI Law Enforcement Bulletin,* May 1982, p. 6; Arthur Neiderhoffer and Elaine Neiderhoffer, "Policemen's Wives: The Blue Connection," in *The Ambivalent Force: Perspectives on the Police,* 3rd ed., Abraham S. Blumberg and Elaine Neiderhoffer, Eds. (New York: Holt, Rinehart and Winston, 1985), p. 386.

17. Joseph J. Hurrell, Jr. and William H. Kroes. "Stress Awareness," in *Job Stress and the Police Officer,* W. H. Kroes and J. J. Hurrell, Jr., Eds. as cited in Gail Goolkasian, Ronald W. Geddes, and William DeJong, "Coping with Police Stress," in *Critical Issues in Policing: Contemporary Readings,* Roger G. Dunham and Geoffrey Alpert, Eds. (Prospect Heights, Ill.: Waveland Press, Inc., 1989), p. 503.

18. Ronald Fell, Wayne C. Richard, and William L. Wallace, "Psychological Job Stress and the Police Officer," *Journal of Police Science and Administration,* Aug. 1980, pp. 139–144.

19. William H. Kroes, Bruce L. Margolis, and Joseph J. Hurrell, Jr., "Job Stress in Policemen: Research Paper," Behavioral and Motivational Factors Branch, National Institute for Occupational Safety and Health, Cincinnati, Ohio, undated, as cited in Gail Goolkasian, Ronald W. Geddes, and William DeJong, "Coping with Police Stress," in *Critical Issues in Policing: Contemporary Readings,* Roger G. Dunham and Geoffrey Alpert, Eds. (Prospect Heights, Ill.: Waveland Press, Inc., 1989), p. 502.

20. Judith M. Grencik in Peter Pitchess, "The Psychological Fitness of Deputies Assigned to the Patrol Function and Its Relationship to the Formulation of Entrance Standards for Law Enforcement Officers," *LEAA Final Report,* 1973.

Chapter 7

Crime and the Police

Key Terms

Crime rates
Uniform Crime Reports
Index crimes
National Crime Survey
Unreported crime
Serial killer
Mass murderer
Spree murderer
Simple assault
Aggravated assault

Career criminals
Clearance rate
Clearance techniques
Kansas City Preventive Patrol
    experiment
Reactive patrol
Proactive patrol
Response-time studies
Rand Study of Detectives

Chapter Objectives

At the conclusion of this chapter, students should be able to:

1. Understand the problems associated with gathering and analyzing crime data.
2. Understand the problems associated with the investigation of crime.
3. Understand the mechanics and uses of the Uniform Crime Reports.
4. Appreciate the limitations of law enforcement in the prevention and investigation of criminal acts.

INTRODUCTION

In 1829 Sir Robert Peel stated that the primary role of the police was to prevent crime. This has been a basic philosophy of law enforcement ever since. In reality, the police may not have that much of a deterrent effect. Indeed, there is some question as to whether or not the entire criminal justice system truly has any impact on crime or criminality.

To resolve the issue, we need to look at a number of factors. First, we must look at the nature of crime. We must understand the issues involved in gathering and evaluating crime statistics. Second, it is necessary to look at the realities of crime: what factors actually control crime, and equally important, what factors do not affect crime. Finally, we must look at the police themselves. What do we know about police work, and how does this affect crime?

THE NATURE OF CRIME

The study of crime and its causes is a full-time job for many people. Those who study crime causation exclusively are called *criminologists*. It would be nice to say that we know conclusively what causes crime. Unfortunately, the number of theories devoted to this issue are well beyond the scope of this book. Rather than present an exhaustive review of crime theories, we will focus on what we know about crime. That means we will discuss the data available on the various crime problems. In that way we may develop some understanding of what is happening throughout the United States.

Understand, also, that crime has two sides, statistical and emotional. For those who study crime, the process is largely one of number crunching. How many murders, rapes, and robberies are committed in a certain year? In what ways can those numbers be lessened? What causes the numbers to increase? There are times when academic discussions of crime sound as though criminal episodes are the product of mathematics. For the victims and their families, however, crime has a radically different meaning. Numbers are meaningless to those devastated in a criminal attack. Those who study crime and justice must always keep this in mind.

Crime versus Crime Rates

Before embarking on a review of the nation's crime statistics, we must first realize that there is a major difference between crime and crime rates. The term *crime* will be used to denote the entire amount of criminal activity committed within the United States. *Crime rates* refer to those criminal acts that are reported to the police. Currently, it is estimated that only about one-third of all crimes are reported to the police.[1]

This means that there can be tremendous fluctuations in crime rates even

Violent Crimes	1,327,440
Murder	18,980
Forcible Rape	87,340
Robbery	497,870
Aggravated Assault	723,250
Property Crimes	11,102,600
Burglary	3,073,300
Larceny-Theft	6,926,400
Motor Vehicle Theft	1,102,900
Total	12,430,000

Note: Offenses may not add to totals because of rounding.[1]
Report to the Nation on Crime and Justice, 2nd ed., p. 12

Illustration 7-1   Reported Crime—1985

though actual crime may remain constant. Since both crime studies and policy decisions are based primarily on reported crime, we must conclude that the data used are often suspect. Indeed, the crime data are subject to manipulation, as we will see when we discuss the politics of crime rates.

Gathering Crime Statistics

The two major sources of crime statistics are the Uniform Crime Reports and the National Crime Survey. Neither source attempts to document all crimes. Instead, they each focus on a limited number of well-defined crimes. Both sources use commonly understood definitions instead of legal definitions of crime.

The *Uniform Crime Reports* (UCR) focus on eight major crimes. The system was created by the International Association of Chiefs of Police (IACP) in 1927. The system originally listed only seven *index crimes:* homicide, rape, robbery, assault, burglary, larceny, and motor vehicle theft. In 1978, arson was added as the eighth category. The index crimes are those actions deemed so serious that they represented a measure of the nation's crime situation. These crimes are also referred to as part I offenses. This is because the UCR is divided into two parts, the first of which is the index crimes. The second part is devoted to lesser offenses such as gambling and prostitution, as well as a variety of misdemeanors. As the information gathered for the UCR is compiled from police reports, the UCR records only crimes reported to the police. No further distinction is made. The UCR tabulates crimes against both people and businesses.

The *National Crime Survey* (NCS) was begun in 1973 in an attempt to obtain a clearer picture of the nation's crime problem. The NCS measures the same crimes as the UCR, except homicide and arson. Moreover, the NCS counts only crimes committed against people over the age of 11. Information for the NCS is gathered through a nationwide survey. It does not discriminate between crimes reported or unreported to the police. It attempts further to obtain information about the victims and locations of the criminal events.

Both methods have limitations. Those factors that discourage the reporting of crimes to the police cause the UCR to be seriously underreported. Similarly, the NCS is known to underreport crimes committed by persons related to the victim. Still, the combination of these two techniques give us some data from which to study the crime picture.

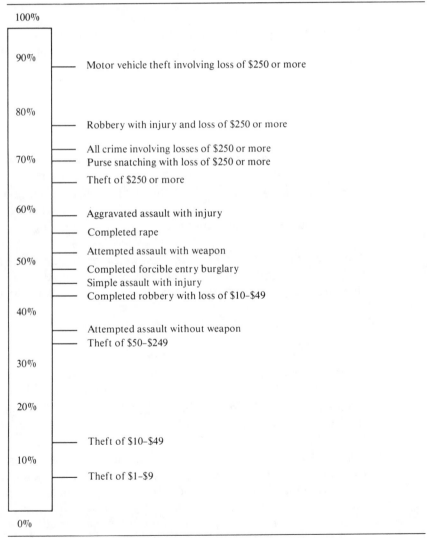

Source: Reporting Crimes to the Police, BJS Special Report, December 1985.

Illustration 7-2 Crime Reporting Rates

Unreported Crime

Unreported crime is sometimes called the "dark figure" of crime. The sad fact is that most crime is unreported. The reasons for this are varied. Generally speaking, violent crimes are more likely to be reported than property crimes, and the greater the loss of property, the greater the likelihood of reporting.

The reasons why people do not report criminal attacks are as varied as the reasons why they make such reports. We know that there are three general major reasons for the reporting of crime:

1. *Economic:* to recover property; to receive insurance money
2. *Obligation:* because it was a crime; because it was the victim's duty; to keep it from happening again
3. *Deterrence/prevention:* to deter others; to punish the offender

There are six major reasons why people do not report crimes to the police:

1. *Not serious enough.* Many victims believe the crime was not sufficiently serious to warrant the time and effort required to make a report.
2. *Nothing could be done.* Some victims believe there is nothing that can be done, regardless of how hard the police try. In these cases they believe that what is done is done and cannot be undone. They see no need for further action.
3. *Police would not do anything.* In these cases the victim lacks confidence in the police. Regardless of the seriousness of the crime, the perception exists that they are disinterested, incapable, or unsympathetic to the victim's plight.
4. *Personal disadvantage.* Some victims will not report a crime because to do so places them at a further disadvantage. For example, embezzlements of funds may prove too embarrassing to a financial institution in terms of public image. Similarly, many rape victims feel that the rape was bad enough without the added humiliation of an investigation and public trial.
5. *Personal/private.* Persons victimized by family or friends frequently believe the crime is a private affair. They are unwilling to expose the family to public humiliation by making a formal complaint.
6. *Reported to someone else.* In some cases the victim may report the incident to someone other than the police. Schoolchildren, for example, will often report victimizations to the school officials. Crimes in apartment complexes may be reported to the complex manager or security guard. Incidents at places of work may be reported to the supervisor or administrator. Often these crimes are not reported to the police by the person receiving the complaint.

Once again it should be noted that each of the factors controlling the decision to report or not report has little to do with crime itself. These are factors affecting the victim's decision to report, not the criminal's decision to commit the crime.

In the following discussion we provide the statistical information available on specific crimes for the year 1985. For ease of discussion we focus on seven of the index crimes (murder, forcible rape, robbery, aggravated assault, burglary, larceny–theft, motor vehicle theft).

Homicide. The crime of homicide is defined as "causing the death of another person without legal justification or excuse."[2] Crimes included in this category are murder, nonnegligent manslaughter, and negligent manslaughter. Statistically, 58 percent of the known murderers were relatives or acquaintances of the victims. Another 20 percent of the murders occurred as the result of some felonious activity. Most often, murder was the result of an argument. Some 39 percent of all murders were preceded by such an event. The weapon most used was a handgun (43 percent), with cutting or stabbing instruments the second most used weapon (21 percent).

When the murder was the result of another felony, most often it was robbery (9 percent). The other crimes producing murder were narcotics (3 percent), sex offenses (2 percent), and arson (1 percent), with other crimes at 3 percent.

Photograph 7–1   Henry Lee Lucas (Photograph courtesy of David Schleve)

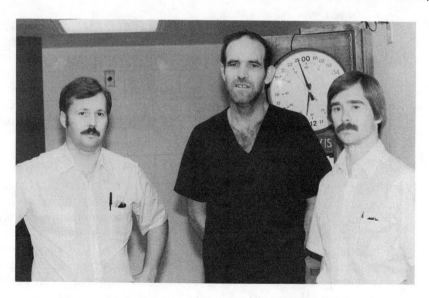

Photograph 7-2   Otis Toole (Photograph courtesy of David Schleve)

Two percent of the murders were involved with suspected but unsubstantiated felonies. In 18 percent of all murders there was a motive besides arguments and felonies. In 23 percent of the cases, the police were unable to establish a motive.[3]

The police are occasionally faced with multiple murders. Although these tend to generate tremendous publicity, they are, thankfully, rare. There are three different types of multiple murderer. The type receiving the most publicity lately is the *serial killer*. These individuals kill several victims in three or more events. The killings may take place over weeks, months, or years and usually follow a pattern. Examples of serial killers are Henry Lee Lucas and Otis Toole, who over a span of several years murdered a large number of young boys and girls.

A second type of multiple murderer is the *mass murderer*. This person kills four or more victims in a short time span at one location. Examples of mass murderers are Charles Whitman (killed 16 people with a rifle while atop a tower at the University of Texas), Richard Speck (killed 8 student nurses in Chicago) and James Oliver Huberty (killed 21 people at a MacDonald's restaurant in San Diego).

The third form of multiple murderer is the *spree murderer*. These killings involve murders at two or more locations with almost no time break between murders and are the result of a single criminal episode. An example of such a person is Daniel Remeta, who during a robbery and aided by two others, killed the manager of a Stuckey's restaurant in Grainfield, Kansas, then killed a deputy sheriff an hour later, and finally, seized hostages in a grain elevator, whom he subsequently killed before his capture. Other examples are Charles Starkweather and Carol Fugate, who terrified the Nebraska countryside.

Photograph 7-3   Charles Whitman

Photograph 7-4   Charles Starkweather (Photograph courtesy of David Schleve)

Photograph 7-5   Carol Ann Fugate (Photograph courtesy of David Schleve)

Two different aspects of homicide rates tend to generate public pressure on the police. The multiple murder attracts such media coverage that public fear and outrage demand a police response. Otherwise, the public appears unresponsive to murder, unless the death rate rises to become a news event in and of itself. Increased murder rates as a result of gang-related violence are especially apt to generate a public demand for action.

Since homicides are either spontaneous or planned, the police are almost always in a reactive mode when dealing with this crime. It is quite likely that they do prevent homicides through intervention in disputes. In any case, the police cannot be held responsible for homicide rates.

Forcible rape.   Rape is defined as "unlawful sexual intercourse with a female, by force or without legal or factual consent."[4] The majority of rapes involved a lone offender and lone victim. About 32 percent of the rapes occurred in or near the victim's home. The majority, about 73 percent, occurred between 6:00 P.M. and 6:00 A.M. A majority of the victims were young: about 58 percent were under the age of 25. Moreover, most rapes were intraracial; that is, whites raped whites and blacks raped blacks. The average rapist was 28 years of age. Slightly more than half were white (52 percent), and as one would suspect, the vast majority were male (99 percent).

Like homicide, rape may be either spontaneous or planned. Neither type occurs in front of police officers. Once more, the ability of the police to do anything but investigate the crime after the fact is severely limited.

Robbery.   This crime is defined as the "unlawful taking or attempted taking of property that is in the immediate possession of another, by force or threat of force."[5] Robbery differs from other property-oriented crimes because of the direct confrontation with the victim. We know the following about robberies committed in 1985. In almost half the robberies committed, weapons were displayed by the attacker. Guns and knives were the most frequent weapons brandished, but the weapons least used in a physical assault during the robbery. The use of guns as weapons resulted in the greatest likelihood that the robbery would succeed.

Robbery is the most violent of property-oriented crimes. One in three victims were injured during the robbery; 1 in 10 were so badly injured that they required medical treatment. Furthermore, robbery victims were more likely than rape or murder victims to face two or more assailants. Robberies occurred most frequently on the street and next most frequently at or near the victim's home. A higher proportion of victims were injured during nighttime robberies than were injured during daylight hours. The average robber is male (92 percent), black (62 percent), and 24 years of age. Robberies were more likely to occur in August and December and least likely to occur in February and April.[6]

Crime prevention techniques have proved somewhat useful in moving this crime around. No technique for truly preventing robberies has been discovered.

Assault.   There are two forms of assault, simple and aggravated. *Simple assault* is usually a misdemeanor and occurs when one person inflicts less than serious bodily injury on another or threatens injury without the use of a weapon. The more serious charge is *aggravated assault,* which requires the inflicting of serious bodily injury or the threat to inflict such injury with a deadly weapon.[7]

Statistically, we know the following: Simple assaults occurred more frequently than aggravated assault. The majority of assaults involved one attacker and one victim. The average person committing an assault was 29 years of age, male (87 percent), and white (58 percent).

This crime is somewhat more problematic than other crimes because of our inability to control for intent. Many aggravated assaults were really attempted murders, while still others were simple assaults that got out of control. Additionally, any time that two or more people come into conflict, there is the possibility of an assault. In cases where there is also alcohol consumption or drug use, the possibility of assault increases.

Two factors contribute to the relationship between aggravated assault and homicide. First, medical technology has increased significantly over the past decade. It is more difficult to kill someone today than it was 25 years ago if medical personnel are available quickly. Even the absence of medical personnel does not preclude the lifesaving capacity of the citizenry at large. In some cities a significant portion of the population is trained in cardiopulminary resuscitation (CPR) and basic first aid. This was not true 25 years ago.

A second but competing factor is the evolving weapons technology. As sophisticated firearms become more available to the general public, we can expect more assaults to become homicides.

Burglary.   A burglary is committed whenever there is "unlawful entry of any fixed structure, vehicle, or vessel used for regular residence, industry, or business, with or without force, with the intent to commit a felony or larceny."[8]

The majority of burglaries are residential (66 percent). A large minority of these cases (42 percent) occurred without forced entry. About 37 percent of the nonforced residential burglaries occurred during the day (6:00 A.M. to 6:00 P.M.). The average burglar was 22 years of age, male (92 percent), and white (70 percent).

Burglary is a crime of stealth. The criminal has at his disposal entire cities. Despite more than a decade of intensive crime prevention programs, no evidence could be found that the increased use of burglar alarms, sophisticated locks, or other security devices has had any effect on burglary rates at all. In fact, these rates have remained relatively constant over time.[9] This crime represents immense frustration for the police. The low clearance rate for this crime bears this out.

Larceny.   Larceny, also called theft, is the "unlawful taking or attempted taking of property, other than a motor vehicle from the possession of another, by stealth, without force or deceit, with intent to permanently deprive the owner of the property."[10]

The average thief was white (67 percent), male (69 percent), and about 25 years of age. Less than 5 percent of all personal larcenies involved contact between the victim and the offender. Those larcenies that involve such contact are usually *purse snatching* and *pocket picking*. Unlike most crimes, these two criminal events affect the elderly as much as other age groups. Again, the police can do little but investigate after the crime has occurred.

Motor vehicle theft.   This crime is defined as the "unlawful taking or attempted taking of a self-propelled road vehicle owned by another, with the intent of depriving him or her of it, permanently or temporarily."[11]

Motor vehicle theft is a relatively well-reported crime. In 1985 it is estimated that 89 percent of all completed thefts were reported. The stolen property in these cases is also much more likely to be recovered than that of any other property offense. Car theft appears to be mainly a young man's crime. The average car thief was 22 years of age, predominantly white (66 percent) and male (91 percent).

The Politics of Crime Rates

Crime rates are subject to manipulation. For whatever reason, and there are compelling ones, such statistics can be partially controlled. The ability to manipulate crime rates, however, does not equate with an ability to control crime. Statistical manipulation can occur through a variety of mechanisms. First, there is sufficient flexibility in the definitions of offenses to allow leeway in data collection. For example, the Uniform Crime Report measures only aggravated assault. The difference between aggravated and simple assault is frequently nothing more than a police decision as to which charge to file. If the police wish to increase the crime rates, they may file the higher charge. A decision to show lower rates may result in the police consistently using the lesser charge. The same thing can occur when burglaries are reduced to trespassing and felony thefts are reduced to misdemeanor thefts. These actions remove criminal events from the UCR's part I category of index crimes and places them in the part II category of lesser crimes. Remember that it is part I crimes that determine a jurisdiction's crime rate (crime rates are computed by dividing the number of Part I crimes by the number of people in the jurisdiction; the result is expressed as rate of serious crimes per 100,000 people).

A second type of manipulation can occur through the assignment of personnel. If a law enforcement organization is experiencing a growing crime problem in a specific area, the normal response is to increase the number of police officers working that area, unless the goal is a quick reduction in the crime rate. Should the administrator decide to remove police personnel from the high-crime area, the immediate impact would be a reduction in *reported crime*. Real crime would remain constant or possibly increase. Reported crime would drop for three reasons. First, on-view arrests by officers would cease to exist in that area. This would represent a dramatic change in the number of reported crimes if a significant portion of the crime problem was occurring on the streets or in the open. Second, many crimes are reported by convenience. A victim sees an officer on the street and because the officer is there, reports the crime: no officers—no convenience reporting. Third, the lack of police translates to a lack of caring by the police, thus creating the impression that the police will not do anything anyway, so why report the crime.

There is sometimes an unintended manipulation of crime rates that can be harmful to reform-minded police administrators. In those areas where citizen regard for the police is low, crime reporting may also be low. The introduction of a new police administration, one striving for professionalism and close police-public cooperation, can dramatically alter the community's crime picture, for the worse. A probable early effect of the new administration is an increased crime rate. One of the measures of public confidence in law enforcement is the public's willingness to report crimes to the police. As confidence grows, so will rates of reported crime. If the municipal administration and news media do not understand this phenomenon, the new administration can quickly lose the confidence they gained. Sadly, the results can be circular; with the public's confidence lagging, the reporting rates can also dip once more, returning the community to the original status quo. In summary, crime rates are dangerous mechanisms for policy review and analysis.

Public Perceptions of Crime

It can safely be stated that the majority of Americans believe crime to be a serious problem. This belief is held so strongly that crime is often a major issue in elections at all levels. Sometimes, however, what the people believe differs widely from the facts. An excellent example can be found in the near hysteria that surrounds missing children.

For the past decade we have been exposed to a nationwide campaign to find missing children. Photographs of children adorn everything from milk cartons to the side panels of trucks. Why? Because it had been estimated that thousands of children a year were being kidnapped by strangers and murdered.

The reality of the stranger abduction homicide of children is a far cry from these estimates. In January 1989, a comprehensive review of studies on this topic was released. The findings indicate that this phenomenon happens infrequently. Between 1976 and 1984, a total of 1378 children were reported kidnapped and murdered by strangers. This averaged about 153 cases per year.[12] This study further found that the 14- to 17-year-old age group was most vulnerable to this crime. Adolescents accounted for about two-thirds of the victims of stranger abduction homicides. Females were also at greater risk. Different studies place female victimization at between two and four times that of males. The sexual nature of stranger abduction cases probably accounts for this difference.

What the research indicates is that the number of cases in which strangers kidnap and murder a child is so small as to be statistically insignificant. This does not make the cases that do occur insignificant, for the kidnapping and murder of a child is traumatic for the entire community. Statistically, however, only 1.7 per million children die in this manner each year. The number is so small that it can in no way be called an epidemic. Moreover, a crime committed that infrequently is very difficult to prevent.

The discussion above merely illustrates a portion of the problem. The fact is that fear of crime limits the freedom of a full 40 percent of the public. Many limit their activities to "safe" places or "safe" times. Still others spend money for security devices. One survey found that two-thirds of the population reported doing something to prevent crime.[13]

Television may also have an impact on citizen fear of crime. The tendency to sensationalize major crime stories gives the appearance that crime is rampant. In fact, major crime stories are news because they are unusual. Still, intense coverage of such events keeps the topic on the minds of the public. They may begin to believe the crime problem as worse than facts indicate.

The fear of crime is also somewhat abstract. People are more afraid of street crime than of other forms. More important, research has shown that people are sensitive to their surroundings.[14] The atmosphere of a neighborhood provides cues upon which individuals assess their safety. A deteriorating neighborhood gives off an aura of danger. It radiates the image that no one cares and no one will help a person in trouble. Well-kept neighborhoods, on the other hand, provide an image of warmth and safety. It is clear here that people care; here there are people willing to help someone in trouble.

POLICE AS CRIME FIGHTERS

If the preceding discussion is true, what can the police do to control crime? To answer that question, we must distinguish between overall crime and specific criminal acts. While crime may be in perpetual motion, ever evolving and fluctuating through society, individual criminals are a different matter.

It may not be desirable for the police to capture all juveniles engaged in criminal acts. The same may be true for some adults. For even though transient criminals generate a great deal of crime, these are not the people causing the great fear of crime. That distinction belongs to the nation's repeat offenders, the so-called *career criminals*. These individuals commit crimes over a long period of time and are responsible for much of the serious crime. This is as true of juveniles as it is of adults. For example, studies in Philadelphia, Pennsylvania, Racine, Wisconsin, and Columbus, Ohio, found that 23 to 34 percent of the juveniles involved in crime were responsible for 61 to 68 percent of all the crimes committed by juveniles. Similarly, a Washington, D.C., study found that 24 percent of all the adult arrests were attributable to just 7 percent of the adults arrested.[15]

The implications are clear. Many criminals pose no lasting threat to society, while a smaller number create the majority of society's crime problem. Does this mean that effectively getting the career criminals off the street will eliminate crime? No, it does not, for we would still be faced with an army of transient criminals. Also, new career criminals are evolving daily. It does tell us that focusing police efforts at the career criminal is the most effective means of addressing this problem.

Also, even though the police are not likely to have a great impact on overall crime, they can, and often do, have an impact on individual lives. When a serial killer is arrested, lives are saved. We cannot know which lives are saved, but we do know that serial killers do not stop themselves. As long as they are free, people die. The same is true for career burglars and robbers. While they are off the streets their potential victims are safe. These facts are not measurable but are valuable just the same. The police do, therefore, have an affect on the lives and property of citizens. Unfortunately, we have no means measuring this impact. It must suffice us to acknowledge that this impact exists.

Clearance Rates

The *clearance rate* is computed as the number of crimes solved by the police compared to the number of crimes committed. This figure is usually expressed as a percentage of cases cleared. Clearing a case does not necessarily mean that the culprit was arrested. A variety of *clearance techniques* are available.

The first means of clearing a case is by *arrest*. This means that a suspect was arrested and charged with the crime. This does not mean that the person was convicted, nor does it necessarily mean that the correct suspect was arrested. An arrest in a case automatically classifies that case as cleared, regardless of what happens after the arrest. Additionally, when a person is arrested for one crime, then admits to others, those cases may be cleared by arrest, even though no charges are filed in the particular case.

The second form of clearance is by *exception*. When a case is cleared by exception, it means that the suspect was identified but for some reason was not arrested. If the suspect is dead or not available for arrest because that person is out of the country or in a mental hospital, the case is cleared by exception. This category means simply that the police know who committed the crime but are unable to prosecute due to events beyond their control.

Cases that are *unfounded* are also classified as cleared. A case is unfounded when it is determined that the crime did not actually occur. Since the crime is listed on the UCR once it is reported, there is no mechanism for its removal. Clearing a case by marking it unfounded solves this problem.

The majority of crimes are not cleared by arrest. The highest clearance rates are for crimes against the person. The following table represents cases cleared by arrest in 1985.

The reason for the variance in clearance rates should be obvious. The police are more likely to clear crimes in which there is an eyewitness who can identify the criminal. In cases involving stealth and secrecy, there are few witnesses and therefore fewer clearances. The blunt truth about law enforcement's ability to solve

Murder	72%
Aggravated assault	62%
Forcible rape	54%
Robbery	25%
Larceny–theft	20%
Motor vehicle theft	15%
Burglary	14%
All UCR index crimes	21%

Source: Crime in the United States (Washington, D.C.: FBI, 1985).

Illustration 7–3   Cleared by Arrest Rates (1985)

crimes is that the police solve a crime when someone tells them a crime has been committed and someone points out the guilty party.

We should also note that clearance rates are a measure of police productivity only. Neither the courts nor statisticians rely on clearance rates as a measure of the effectiveness of the criminal justice system. Police administrators use these statistics as a relative measure of police effectiveness. Even then, such rates are only a vague measure. There are too many uncontrolled factors in criminal investigations for these rates to provide much in the way of evaluation.

The Kansas City Preventive Patrol Experiment

The assumption that random patrol was a feasible method of preventing or reducing crime has been a major element of police folklore since the creation of the first patrol units. Police management experts studied ways to make patrol better; numerous deployment models were devised and proposed. The question unasked until 1962 was whether patrol really did prevent or reduce crime.

That question was asked in Kansas City, Missouri, and resulted in the *Kansas City Preventive Patrol experiment.* The city was divided into 15 areas, or beats. Each area received one of three different types of patrol service. Five beats received *reactive patrol;* routine patrol was eliminated and officers responded only to calls for service. Five other beats were designated *control beats;* they received the same type of service they had received prior to the experiment. The remaining five were designated for *proactive patrol;* these received intensive patrol, at two to three times the normal level of patrol for those areas.

The variables the researchers studied were amount of crime, police response time, citizen satisfaction with the police, citizen fear of crime, and traffic accidents. The researchers stated: "Given the large amount of data collected and the extremely diverse sources used, the overwhelming evidence is that decreasing or increasing routine preventive patrol within the range tested in this experiment had no effect on crime, citizen fear of crime, community attitudes toward the police or the delivery of police services, police response time or traffic accidents."[16]

Although there were criticisms of the methodology used in the study, no research conducted since has been able to challenge its findings. The point to be remembered is that the previous assumptions about the preventive nature of patrol have yet to be substantiated.

Response Time

Conventional wisdom has held that the faster the response time, the greater the likelihood that the police will identify and arrest the criminal. *Response-time studies* deal with the elapsed time between when the criminal event begins and the moment the first police officer arrives at the scene.

The reality appears to be somewhat different than conventional wisdom suggests. Research in a number of cities indicated that arrests attributable to fast response time occurred in only 2.9 percent of reported serious crimes.[17] The study above found that 75 percent of the serious crimes were *discovery crimes.* That is, they were discovered well after the fact, and well after police response time had become irrelevant. Furthermore, the average length of time before the victim called the police in these crimes was 10 to 10 $\frac{1}{2}$ minutes, extending the response time even further. In discovery crimes, the police had virtually no chance of response-related arrest.

The other 25 percent were *involvement crimes,* in which the victim confronted, or was confronted by, the offender. In these incidents we might conclude that response time can make a difference. We must remember, however, that the assumption is that the police will be notified about the crime as soon as possible. The validity of our assumptions about a rapid police response rests on the speed with which they are notified. It is generally believed that police can make an arrest only if they arrive within 2 to 3 minutes of the completion of the crime. This study found that the average reporting time for involvement crimes was between 4 and 5 minutes. Thus, even for involvement crimes, the possibility of response-related arrest is very low.

How critical is the time element in these crimes? This study found that in those incidents where the victim waited 5 minutes or more to call the police, they might as well have waited an hour.[18] Even in those cases where the crime was reported while still in progress, the chances of a response-related arrest, although much better, were still only 35 percent.

There is a natural inclination for citizens to delay their call to the police. The study above found that there are three basic reasons for not calling the police immediately. First is uncertainty. The citizen may not be certain what is happening is a crime. Sometimes the person will want additional information or advice. This may come from either calling someone other than the police or talking to someone else at the scene.

The second reason is that people sometimes take actions to help themselves cope with the effects of the crime on themselves. In these cases the witness may leave the scene and call later when composure has been regained. Others may seek the support of a family member or friend, in which case that person will be called prior to calling the police. Still others may personally chase or constrain the suspect. The person may also render first aid to the injured.

Third, many citizens experience conflict over whether or not to call the police at all. These people may procrastinate in the hope that someone else will take action, or they may wish to get support for their decision by seeking advice from another.

Even when citizens wish to call the police, it is not always that easy to do so. They must have access to a telephone; if there is a phone present, they must know or have access to the police phone number. Even when communication is established, the police complaint taker and the citizen must quickly establish clear communication. This study found that in 10 to 12 percent of the cases researched, a communication problem developed at this point, with an average resulting delay of 35 seconds.

In essence, it would appear that police response time has little effect on the clearance rates for criminal acts. Even though there are methods available for improving response time (i.e., better training of police complaint takers, 911 phone service, etc.), the impact on the police likelihood of making response-related arrests is low.

The Rand Study of Detectives

Police detectives enjoy a mystique bordering almost on the magical. Both fiction and nonfiction media have painted the detective with an image of near invincibility, as a hard-working individual with an unsurpassed intellect and infallible intuition. Such is the image of this group that even other police officers have a love–hate relationship with detectives. Every young officer wants to be a detective; every officer who has been around awhile comes to resent the perceived wall of arrogance that surrounds the investigative units.

The truth, it seems, is a far cry from the legend. In 1972, the Rand Corporation began a monumental study called the *Rand Study of Detectives*.[19] From this study we have learned a great deal about what detectives can and cannot do.

Only 2.7 percent of all part I offense clearances were attributable to special techniques used by investigators. The remaining 97.3 percent of the clearances took place no matter what the investigators did, as long as normal follow-up procedures were used. Of course, the real impetus behind the detective mystique comes from those high-publicity cases where the perpetrator is unknown. What are the realities of these crimes? Despite all the time spent by investigators on these cases, only 2.7 percent were cleared through detective work.

The most important elements in deciding whether or not a case would be solved were the contributions of victims, witnesses, and patrol officers. In fact, the detectives spent about 93 percent of their time on activities that did not lead directly to solving previously reported crimes. Within these activities we find that only 12 percent of the time was spent on cases that were eventually solved; another 40 percent was spent on cases that were never solved, and 48 percent of the time was spent on cases after they had already been cleared.

Detectives may be viewed as a support element for the prosecutor. As the previous time breakdown shows, a great deal of the detective's time was spent in postarrest processing. It is the detective who becomes responsible for assembling the witnesses and physical evidence for presentation in court. The researchers concluded that there was a strong likelihood of a relationship between police documentation of a case and the final disposition of the case (i.e., rate of dismissals, heaviness of plea bargaining, and type of sentence imposed).

The case preparation function may therefore be the most important aspect of the detective role. Yet it gets less attention than the investigative aspect, which is largely insignificant. In the final analysis, the researchers advised a shifting of resources away from traditional investigative functions toward other operations elements. They also advocated the creation of strike forces to address specific crime problems. Moreover, they recommended studying the feasibility of assigning postarrest investigations to the prosecutor's office, with sufficient personnel to function effectively. This study further indicated that better crime scene processing offered the potential for increased clearances. The current utilization of crime scene technicians is erratic, to say the least.

What this comes down to is that the detective has little impact on case clearances. It is patrol that effectively solves the vast majority of cases cleared. The detective's function appears to be primarily case preparation for prosecution.

SUMMARY

Right or wrong, the police are held accountable for the amount of crime within a community. To determine the effectiveness of the police crime prevention function, data are collected to allow statistical analysis. The primary measurement used by the police are the Uniform Crime Reports. The information gathered for the UCR consists of those crimes reported to the police by victims. The UCR provides some indication of criminal activity, but is flawed by its dependency on victims, many of whom do not report crimes to the police, for any number of reasons.

In an attempt to gain a more accurate view of criminal activity, the National Crime Survey was instituted. Information gathered for the NCS is collected in a format similar to that of the census. A random sample of a community is surveyed to determine the amount of criminal victimization that has occurred. The NCS reports have indicated that the UCR reports are indeed based on a mere fraction of the crime committed. Unfortunately, even the NCS reports fail to measure all crime.

The police dependency on public reporting has other implications for law enforcement. Where public faith in the police is low, there is not only a low report rate but also a lack of willingness on the part of many citizens to participate in the justice process, even as witnesses. It is clear that both the prevention and investigation of criminal acts are not totally in the hands of the police. The public has a much greater impact than the police on the level of crime.

Police myths have also been exploded over the past two decades. The Kansas City Preventive Patrol experiment questioned the effectiveness of random patrol as an agent of crime prevention. Studies on police response time have demonstrated that a rapid police response is important in only a small number of cases. Finally, the Rand Study of Detectives found that criminal investigation was largely ineffective in solving crimes.

Overall, it appears that the police are not nearly as effective in crime control as most people think. The fact is that the police solve crimes when a citizen tells them that a crime has been committed and then tells them who to arrest.

DISCUSSION QUESTIONS

1. Distinguish between crime and crime rates.
2. Why do victims of crime fail to report the crime to the police?
3. What factors contribute to low clearance rates among property crimes?
4. What did the Kansas City Preventive Patrol experiment discover about uniformed police patrol?
5. Discuss the realities of detective work.
6. How important is response time to the successful investigation of crimes?

NOTES/REFERENCES

1. *Report to the Nation on Crime and Justice,* 2nd ed. (Washington, D.C.: U.S. Department of Justice, Bureau of Justice Statistics, 1988), p. 34.
2. *Report to the Nation . . . ,* p. 2.
3. *Report to the Nation . . . ,* p. 4.
4. *Report to the Nation . . . ,* p. 2.
5. *Report to the Nation . . . ,* p. 2.
6. *Report to the Nation . . . ,* p. 5.
7. *Report to the Nation . . . ,* p. 2.
8. *Report to the Nation . . . ,* p. 2.
9. *Report to the Nation . . . ,* p. 6.
10. *Report to the Nation . . . ,* p. 2.
11. *Report to the Nation . . . ,* p. 2.
12. "Preliminary Estimates Developed on Stranger Abduction Homicides of Children," *Juvenile Justice Bulletin,* Jan. 1989.
13. Wesley G. Skogan, "On Attitudes and Behaviors," in *Reactions to Crime,* Dan A. Lewis, Ed. (Beverly Hills, Calif.: Sage Publications, Inc., 1981), p. 29.
14. James Q. Wilson and George Kelling, "Broken Windows: The Police and Neighborhood Safety," *Atlantic Monthly,* Mar. 1982, pp. 29–38.
15. *Report to the Nation . . . ,* p. 44.
16. George L. Kelling, Tony Pate, Duane Dieckman, and Charles E. Brown, "The Kansas City Preventive Patrol Experiment," in *Thinking about Police: Contemporary Readings,* Carl B. Klockars, Ed. (New York: McGraw-Hill Book Company, 1983), p. 160.

17. William G. Spelman and Dale K. Brown, "Response Time," in *Thinking about Police: Contemporary Readings,* Carl B. Klockars, Ed. (New York: McGraw-Hill Book Company, 1983), p. 161.

18. Spelman and Brown, p. 162.

19. Jan Chaiken, Peter Greenwood, and Joan Petersilia, "The Rand Study of Detectives," in *Thinking about Police: Contemporary Readings,* Carl B. Klockars, Ed. (New York: McGraw-Hill Book Company, 1983), pp. 167–184.

Chapter 8

Criminal Investigation and the Law

Key Terms

Substantive law
Case law
nullum crimen, nulla poena, sine lege
Ex post facto laws
Actus rea
Mens rea
Elements of the crime
Probable cause
Search warrants
Plain view doctrine
Warrantless search
Search incident to arrest
Stop and frisk

Exclusionary rule
Good faith exception
Inevitability of discovery exception
Totality of circumstances test
Lineups
Showups
Photo lineups
Confession
Miranda warning
Spontaneous utterance
Admission
Hearsay
Dying declarations

Chapter Objectives

At the conclusion of this chapter, students should be able to:

1. Understand the legal factors involved in a criminal investigation.
2. Describe a criminal act through the identification of the legal elements of the crime.
3. Understand the legal limitations involved with police search and seizure.
4. Understand the legal requirements for the admissibility of confessions and statements.

5. Relate the Fourth and Fifth Amendments of the U.S. Constitution to the process of criminal investigation.

INTRODUCTION

Police interaction with the court system occurs well before a case is presented for trial. The courts, through the evolution of case law, have provided law enforcement with a series of procedural limitations and instructions designed to keep police operations within the mandate of the constitution. Thus, the police, in developing a criminal prosecution, must follow a carefully laid set of guidelines or risk having the case thrown out of court.

Despite the much believed theory that the courts unfairly limit the police while protecting the guilty, these guidelines are based on well-established legal principles. It is true that the constitution limits police behavior. We should stress, however, that the police behavior most limited is that behavior which is least desired in a democratic society. Also, these limitations are hardest on those departments with poor training and a low understanding of the function of law enforcement in a democracy.

What is also not usually recognized, even by the police themselves, is that the courts have done more to bring about professionalism within law enforcement than any other agency or social trend. It has been the courts, through both case law and civil suits, that have forced increases in police training and education. The same can be said for the development and refinement of police policy and procedures. Whatever bad results can be credited to the requirements that police issue the Miranda warning prior to questioning or the use of the exclusionary rule to disallow illegally obtained evidence from a criminal trial, the fact remains that law enforcement has benefited greatly from both court-ordered requirements. As citizens, we have benefited in equal measure.

With these thoughts in mind, we will examine the influence of the courts on law enforcement. The elements of police procedure most affected by the courts are definitions of crime, seizure of evidence, and confessions.

PREPARING THE CASE

The process of criminal investigation is not the focus of this chapter. Instead, we will concentrate on those activities defined and restricted by legislative enactment (*substantive law*) and court decision making (*case law*).

The first step in the investigative process is to determine whether or not a crime has actually been committed. To make this determination, the officer must match the facts of the case to the statutes described in the criminal code of the jurisdiction (local, state, or federal). To know with certainty that there is a match between the person's actions and the legal code requires the officer to accurately place the elements of the suspect's actions within the context of the criminal statute. This is more commonly referred to as *establishing the elements of the crime.*

Elements of the Law

To grasp the complexities involved in criminal law, we will look at two major legal ideas involved with law and its enforcement. First, we examine what elements are necessary to define an action as criminal. Second, we look at the precision with which actions are determined to meet the criteria for prosecution.

There are seven major elements of a crime in Western law. Each of these must be present or the actions of the individual are not considered criminal. In addition, the criminal statute will be written in such a way as to provide precise definitions so that the police and courts can act fairly and consistently when enforcing these statutes. The elements necessary for an act to be defined as law are legality, actus rea, causation, harm, concurrence, mens rea, and punishment.[1]

Legality. An act cannot be a crime unless it is so proclaimed by law. There must be a legislative enactment prohibiting the actions or a person cannot be prosecuted for that action. This is a major principle of American law that is derived from the Romans. It is perhaps best defined by the Latin phrase, *nullum crimen, nulla poena, sine lege,* which means: no crime, no punishment, without law. In our court system, as in most of Europe, this means that there must be an act of the lawmaking body specifying actions as criminal. Moreover, the law must be "on the books" at the time it is committed or it does not constitute a crime. The Constitution prohibits *ex post facto laws* (laws enacted to cover past actions).

Actus rea. The legal term *actus rea* means that there must be an action or failure to act by the individual in violation of the statute. Bad intentions are insufficient for prosecution. For example, intending to rob a bank does not constitute a crime until some action is taken by the person toward completion of that goal.

The most obvious examples of illegal behavior concerning the *failure to act* relate to the tax and selective service laws. Failure to file an income tax return or failure to notify the Selective Service that the person has reached the age of eligibility for military service both constitute criminal behavior.

Causation. There must be a causal relationship between the action of a person and the harm suffered. For example, if one person shoots another, but the victim dies from pneumonia while in the hospital, there is little chance for a successful prosecution for murder. The legal question would be: What was the relationship of the shooting to the subsequent death of the victim? Since there is only a remote connection between the shooting and the cause of death, there is no crime of murder, although the crime of assault remains. On the other hand, should this victim die six months later of complications resulting from the gunshot wound, the causal relationship would be firmly established and the allegation of assault could be changed to one of homicide.

Harm.   The action must cause some harm to someone. The damage may be to a person, property or reputation. If there is no harm, there is no crime. There has been a social movement in this country to legalize certain behavior because it is believed to harm only the person engaging in that behavior. These so-called *victimless crimes* are believed to be the result of society's attempt to legislate morality rather than provide sound law. The counter legal theory is that harm is still the result of the act, even if it is self-inflicted. Furthermore, it is commonly accepted that even though the direct harm is to the person engaging in the prohibited behavior, others, such as relatives, may also suffer emotionally from inappropriate actions of a loved one.

Concurrence.   The intent to commit the crime must occur simultaneously with the act itself. For example, suppose that a person is visiting a friend and while in the friend's house, decides to steal a portable radio. The culprit may be charged with theft, for clearly he took it with the intent to deprive its owner of its use. The thief cannot be charged with burglary, however, for when he entered the house he did so legally, without intent to commit the crime. There must be an identifiable connection between intent and act or there is no crime.

Mens rea.   The term *mens rea* refers to a guilty state of mind. More clearly, this is the legal phrase for intent. Under the philosophy of Western law, a person committed the act intentionally and of his or her own free will. Involuntary behavior is therefore not illegal behavior.

This is the area of the law in which we find the concept of not guilty by reason of insanity. The insanity defense is based on the belief that even though the suspect committed the act, there was no intent. A person who cannot determine right from wrong cannot be said to have the intention of doing wrong. Needless to say, this is a highly controversial area of the law.

Punishment.   The legislative enactment must specify a punishment or range of possible punishments for the violation of the act. A law without punishment is worthless; it cannot be enforced or prosecuted. The final element in the law, therefore, is the specified price to be paid by the person convicted under the statute. The price may be the loss of property (i.e., money, real estate, vehicles), it may be through reduction in or loss of freedom for a specified time, or it may be the ultimate sanction, loss of life. Whatever the sanction, some punishment is required or there is no law.

Elements of the Crime

For the police officer the elements of law discussed above are less important than the *elements of the specific crime* under investigation. The criminal case, to be properly presented in court, must be developed so that each part of what constitutes a crime is proven beyond a reasonable doubt. For example, the Model Penal Code's definition of criminal homicide reads:

Section 210.1 Criminal Homicide:

1. A person is guilty of criminal homicide if he purposely, knowingly, recklessly, or negligently causes the death of another human being.
2. Criminal homicide is murder, manslaughter or negligent homicide.

Section 210.2 Murder:

1. Except as provided in Section 210.3(1)(b), criminal homicide constitutes murder when:

    a. it is committed purposely or knowingly;

or

    b. it is committed recklessly under circumstances manifesting extreme indifference to the value of human life. Such recklessness and indifference are presumed if the actor is engaged or is an accomplice in the commission of, or attempt to commit, or flight after committing or attempting to commit robbery, rape, or deviate sexual intercourse by force or threat of force, arson, burglary, kidnapping or felonious escape.
2. Murder is a felony of the first degree (but a person convicted of murder may be sentenced to death, as provided in Section 210.6).

Section 210.3 Manslaughter:

1. Criminal homicide constitutes manslaughter when:

    a. it is committed recklessly; or

    b. a homicide which would otherwise be murder is committed under the influence of extreme mental or emotional disturbance for which there is reasonable explanation or excuse. The reasonableness of such explanation or excuse shall be determined from the viewpoint of a person in the actor's situation under the circumstances as he believes them to be.
2. Manslaughter is a felony in the second degree.

What must an officer establish in order to file a charge of murder? First, it must be established that the victim died. Second, the death must be the result of an action by another. Third, there must be evidence that the action was intentional. Fourth, it is not sufficient to prove intent alone; criminal intent must be established. Self-defense, for example, fulfills the criteria for murder when intent is substituted for criminal intent. Self-defense is an example of justifiable homicide.

We must also recognize that intent may be inferred from the actions of the suspect. A person who aims a gun at another and pulls the trigger can be presumed to have the intention of shooting the victim, whether death is or is not the intended result. Consequently, when an act is so flagrantly reckless that a reasonable person could predict that the action is likely to cause death or injury to another, intent to cause harm can be inferred. For example, discharging a firearm in the general direction of a group of people or into an occupied building is so likely to cause injury that the court can draw a legal presumption that any harm resulting from that act was intentional.

Each and every criminal act is designed in a manner similar to that of criminal homicide. Each and every law has a series of elements that must be established beyond a reasonable doubt and within the rules of evidence. Also, terminology used in the writing of the law may not always conform to dictionary definitions. The legislature writes the law, but the definitions and interpretations are provided by the courts through case law. It is not sufficient to know only how the law is stated; the officer must also know how specific words and phrases are defined by the courts.

PHYSICAL EVIDENCE

Once it has been determined that a crime has occurred, the next steps in the investigative process are the identification and collection of evidence. Frequently, evidence must be gathered in an adversarial environment. That is, the officer must go into a place where the police are neither welcome nor wanted to recover an item that is the property (legal or otherwise) of another, who does not wish to part with that particular item.

Under our constitution there are limitations on how and when the government can take property from private citizens. When that property is to be used as evidence in a criminal trial, the procedures are very strict. The legal restrictions on search and seizure are found in the wording of the Fourth Amendment to the Constitution: "The right of the people to be secure in their persons, houses, papers, and effects, against unreasonable searches and seizures, shall not be violated, and no warrants shall issue, but upon probable cause, supported by oath or affirmation, and particularly describing the place to be searched, and the persons or things to be seized." This amendment would appear to be fairly straightforward and simple. The reality, however, is that human behavior is very complex. The myriad situations in which the police find a need to search for evidence greatly complicate the problem of interpretation. To obtain a good understanding of what the Fourth Amendment really means, we are required to look at case law.

Fourth Amendment Requirements

Simply stated, the Fourth Amendment requires the police to obtain a search warrant prior to searching private property. It also requires that this warrant be based on probable cause. *Probable cause* is best defined as a set of facts that would lead a reasonable person to believe that a crime is being committed or is imminent and that the suspect is the person committing that crime. In cases requiring a search warrant, probable cause would mean that the officer has a set of facts that would lead a reasonable person to conclude that specific evidence of a crime is likely to be found at a specific location. The determination of whether or not the the conclusion truly is reasonable is made by a neutral magistrate.

Not all searches require a warrant. The police may search any place in which they have been given permission by the owner or the person having lawful control of the property to be searched. Also, in some exigent circumstances, a police officer may search without either permission or a warrant. We discuss each of these searches below.

Search warrants.   *Search warrants* are issued by a magistrate. This is a court order permitting an officer to search a specified location for specific evidence. How specific? Some courts have held that a warrant to search a house does not necessarily permit officers to search an unattached garage for that house. The police must therefore clearly specify the address of the building or a sufficient description of that building or buildings to be searched. The locations specified on the warrant are the only places that can be searched. The warrant must be applied for through a formal application process. The usual method is for the police to submit a sworn affidavit stating the known facts justifying the search and identifying the location to be searched and items to be seized. It is also customary for the police officers serving the warrant to notify the court issuing the warrant of the outcome of the search—what was recovered.

It is possible for the police to recover evidence other than that specified in the warrant. The *plain view doctrine* allows a police officer to seize any evidence open to plain view. The only requirement is that the officer observe the item from a place in which he or she is lawfully present. Since a search warrant allows the officers to enter the building legally, any evidence observed by an officer while in that location may be seized as evidence.

The warrant cannot, however, be a ruse to conduct an exploratory search. The item must be either in the open where anyone can see it or in a location that is a likely area for the officer to search for the item listed in the search warrant. For example, if officers are searching for narcotics and find an illegal weapon in a dresser drawer, it may be seized because a dresser drawer is a reasonable place to search for illegal drugs. Conversely, if the officers are searching for illegal weapons and find drugs within a mislabeled aspirin bottle in a medicine cabinet, that may not be seized. It is not reasonable to search for weapons in an aspirin bottle.

Thus, even a search warrant is not a license for an unlimited ransacking of a person's residence. It is a court order allowing for a reasonable search based on sound information.

Warrantless searches.   As mentioned previously, there are two types of *warrantless search*. A search may be conducted with the permission of the person controlling the area to be searched, and a search may be conducted when there is sufficient probable cause to obtain a warrant but insufficient time to do so. The difficulty with searching by permission is the requirement that the permission be voluntary. The search cannot be the result of coercion, real or imagined. The person in control of the property must knowingly allow the police to search the premises or the search is illegal. Since the permission is given freely, it can be withdrawn freely. The police may receive permission to search and then find contraband, only to discover that when they get to court the defendant denies giving the permission. Lacking solid proof of the permission, the search may be declared illegal.

Some departments have attempted to eliminate this problem by requiring people to give written permission for a search. This reduces the problem of proving that there was permission, but still leaves the possibility of a claim that coercion was used to obtain the signature. Coercion need not be physical. Merely the perception of intimidation, however slight, can invalidate the search. Permission searches, although often the easiest to execute, represent a potential legal minefield for the police.

Probable cause searches conducted without a warrant are also potentially troublesome in court. The reason lies in the legal presumptions of the court. A search executed with a warrant is presumed valid. The defense has the legal burden of proving such a search illegal. Searches conducted without a warrant, however, are presumed illegal. It is the prosecution that bears the burden of proving that the search was reasonable. Any search conducted without a warrant therefore automatically means more difficulty in getting the evidence into court.

There are a number of different types of warrantless search. The most common of these is the *search incident to arrest*. Whenever a person is arrested, the officer has the right to search the arrestee for the purpose of removing weapons, contraband or evidence. This is the safest of the warrantless searches since it has been uniformly accepted as reasonable by the courts.

The second such search is similar to a search incident to arrest, except that it allows for a search of the area within the immediate reach of the subject. Again, this search is to prevent the person from seizing a weapon or destroying evidence.

Chimel v. *California*
395 U.S. 752, 89 S. Ct. 2034, 23 L.Ed.2d 685 (1969)

Late in the afternoon of September 13, 1965, three police officers arrived at the Santa Ana, California, home of the petitioner with a warrant authorizing his arrest for the burglary of a coin shop. The officers knocked on the door, identified themselves to the petitioner's wife, and asked if they might come inside. She ushered them into the house, where they waited 10 or 15 minutes until the petitioner returned home from work. When the petitioner entered the house, one of the officers handed him the arrest warrant and asked for permission to "look around." The petitioner objected but was advised that "on the basis of a lawful arrest," the officers would nonetheless conduct a search. No search warrant had been issued.

Accompanied by the petitioner's wife, the officers spent 45 minutes to an hour searching the entire three-bedroom house, including the attic, garage, and a small workshop. They opened and searched closets. They also opened drawers and removed the contents. As a result of the search, the officers seized coins, medals, tokens, and other items as evidence.

The U.S. Supreme Court reversed the lower court decisions authorizing this search. The Court ruled that application of sound Fourth Amendment principles in this case produces a clear result. The search here went far beyond the petitioner's person and the area from within which he might have obtained either a weapon or something that could have been used as evidence against him. There was no constitutional justification, in the absence of a search warrant, for extending the search beyond that area. The scope of the search was therefore "unreasonable" under the Fourth and Fourteenth Amendments, and the petitioner's conviction was not allowed to stand.

A further extension of this concept is the *stop and frisk*. Under this concept a police officer is allowed to conduct a pat-down search of a person when circumstances indicate a possibility of danger to the officer. It should be noted that the officer need not have probable cause to conduct a stop and frisk. Such a search can only be a pat-down of the outer clothing and only to feel for weapons.

The final warrantless search occurs when a warrant is called for but there is insufficient time to obtain such a warrant. Usually, this situation occurs when the police unexpectedly confront a situation involving criminal behavior and the suspects are aware of the police presence. Often, any delay in searching and seizing the evidence will result in the destruction of those items. Drugs may be flushed down a toilet, weapons may be removed and hidden, and documents may be burned. The police must either act quickly or lose the evidence. Such searches are considered reasonable by the court, but the police will be required to prove that such an emergency did in fact exist.

In all situations such as these, there is a temptation by the police to attempt to justify emergency searches when there really was time and opportunity to obtain a warrant. This is a mistake. The police should always seek a warrant unless there truly is an emergency. Laziness in this regard usually only manages to get the search declared illegal.

Terry v. Ohio
392 U.S. 1, 88 S.Ct 1868, 20 L.Ed.2d 889 (1968)

At 2:30 P.M. on October 31, 1963, Detective Martin McFadden of the Cleveland Police Department observed Mr. Terry and Mr. Chilton acting suspiciously at the corner of Huron and Euclid in downtown Cleveland. Officer McFadden had been a police officer for 39 years, assigned to work shoplifting in downtown Cleveland for 30 of those years.

The officer testified that the men did not look right to him. He saw one of the men leave the other and walk to a store where he looked in through the window. That man then returned to the location of the other man, who, after conferring with the first man, repeated the same series of steps. They continued this ritual, about a dozen times over a 10- to 15-minute interval, until they were joined by a third man. After conferring with this person, they once more returned to their pacing and watching. The third man left. Terry and Chilton resumed the ritual once more for several more minutes. They then began to walk in the direction taken by the third man.

Officer McFadden, based on his extensive experience, believed that these men were "casing a job, a stick-up." He considered it his duty to investigate further. Stopping them in front of Zuckor's store, where they met the third man, a Mr. Katz, Officer McFadden inquired as to the nature of their behavior. Believing as he did that these two were preparing to commit a robbery, he believed them to be armed. To protect himself, McFadden spun the men around and felt along the outer clothing. He felt what he believed to be a gun in Terry's coat pocket. Repeating the procedure, the officer removed a gun from Chilton as well. All three men were taken to the station, where Terry and Chilton were charged with carrying concealed weapons.

Terry challenged the legality of the search on the basis that it was not based on probable cause, nor was it pursuant to a lawful arrest. The Supreme Court ruled the search admissible. They ruled that an officer has the right to protect himself with a reasonable search to determine if weapons are available. This search is limited to a pat-down of the person's outer clothing. Only if the officer feels an item that can reasonably be considered a weapon can the search be extended into or under the clothing. The search is therefore then based on the probable cause produced by the frisk. Any weapons seized in such a search may be used as evidence against the person subjected to the search.

The exclusionary rule.   A tool used by the court system to protect people from unreasonable searches is the *exclusionary rule.* The federal courts have used this rule since 1914. Only since 1961, however, has it been applied to state courts (see *Mapp* v. *Ohio*). The method by which this rule protects people is the exclusion of any and all evidence obtained illegally.

Proponents of this rule argue that it merely returns the facts of the case to their original condition prior to the illegal search. That is, it denies evidence to the prosecution that had the police obeyed the law, they would not have had anyway. It is further argued that this is the only practical means of controlling police behavior concerning constitutional protections against illegal searches.

Mapp v. *Ohio*
367 U.S. 643, 81 S.Ct. 1684, 6 L.Ed.2d 1081 (1961)

On May 23, 1957, three Cleveland police officers arrived at the home of the appellant, Dollree Mapp, pursuant to information that "a person was hiding out in the home, who was wanted for questioning in connection with a large amount of policy paraphernalia being hidden in the home." Miss Mapp and her daughter by a former marriage lived on the top floor of a two-family dwelling. Upon their arrival at the house, the officers knocked on the door and demanded entrance, but appellant, after telephoning her attorney, refused to admit them without a search warrant. They advised their headquarters of the situation and set up a surveillance of the house.

Three hours later four more officers arrived at the scene, at which time they once more sought entrance. When Miss Mapp did not respond immediately, at least one of the several doors to the house was forcibly opened. Meanwhile, Miss Mapp's attorney arrived but was denied entrance to the house and was not allowed to see his client. Miss Mapp confronted one of the officers on the staircase in her home and demanded to see the warrant. The officer produced a piece of paper, which Miss Mapp seized and placed in her bosom. A struggle ensued during which time the officers recovered the piece of paper. Miss Mapp was then handcuffed and forcibly taken upstairs, where officers searched her bedroom. Ultimately, the entire house was searched, including the basement, where the obscene materials that led to her conviction were found.

At the trial no search warrant was presented and no mention of such a warrant was made by the prosecution. There was, in fact, serious doubt that such a warrant ever existed or was even applied for by the police.

The appellant argued that the search was unjustified and violated her constitutional rights prohibiting unreasonable search and seizure. The Supreme Court agreed. Applying the exclusionary rule to the states, the Court proclaimed that evidence illegally seized from a person may not be used against that person in court.

The exclusionary rule is not without numerous opponents. The major arguments against the use of this instrument center around the price paid by society. It is asserted that the exclusionary rule does not protect innocent people from illegal searches, only the guilty. Allowing people who are clearly guilty to go free in order to punish the police is seen as socially self-destructive. Moreover, the general public sees the exclusionary rule as further evidence that the American court system coddles criminals at the expense of the victims. The exclusionary rule is apparently not a good public relations tool for the American system of justice. This is all the more so when we consider that the United States is virtually the only nation, now or in the past, to frequently exclude physical evidence from a trial.

Like all legal principles, the exclusionary rule is constantly evolving. Two major court decisions have altered some of the negative aspects of this rule. In *United States* v. *Leon* (1984), the U.S. Supreme Court instituted a *good faith exception* to the exclusionary rule. In this case, police officers served a search warrant issued by a detached and neutral magistrate. The probable cause upon which the search was based was later found to be faulty, calling into question the legitimacy of the search. The Supreme Court held that despite the magistrate's mistake, the police had acted in good faith; therefore, the evidence was to be admitted.

The second major case, *Nix* v. *Williams* (1984), established the *inevitability of discovery exception* to the exclusionary rule. Under the findings of this case, evidence that can be reasonably expected to have been discovered regardless of the actions of the police can be used in court.

Nix v. *Williams*
—U.S.—, 104 S.Ct. 2501, 81 L.Ed.2d 377 (1984)

This case summarizes the legal issues involved in what is sometimes known as the "Christian Burial Case" and is the conclusion of two separate trials and Supreme Court reviews for the same incident. The facts of the case are as follows. On December 24, 1968, 10-year-old Pamela Powers disappeared from the YMCA building in Des Moines, Iowa, where she had accompanied her parents to watch an athletic contest. Shortly after she disappeared, Robert Williams was seen leaving the YMCA carrying a large bundle wrapped in a blanket. A 14-year-old boy who had helped Williams open his car door reported that he had seen "two legs in it and they were skinny and white."

Williams' car was found the next day 160 miles east of Des Moines in Davenport, Iowa. Later several items of clothing belonging to the child, some of Williams' clothing, and an army blanket like the one used to wrap the bundle that Williams carried out of the YMCA were found at a rest stop on Interstate 80 near Grinnell, between Des Moines and Davenport. A warrant was issued for Williams arrest.

Police surmised that Williams left Pamela Powers or her body somewhere between Des Moines and the Grinnell rest stop, where some of the young girl's clothing had been found. On December 26, the Iowa Bureau of Investigation initiated a large-scale search. Two hundred volunteers divided into teams began the search 21 miles east of Grinnell, covering an area several miles to the north and south of Interstate 80. They moved westward from Poweshiek County, in which Grinnell was located, into Jasper County. Searchers were instructed to check all roads, abandoned farm buildings, ditches, culverts, and any other place in which the body of a small child could be hidden.

Photograph 8-1 Robert Williams
(Courtesy of UPI/Bettmann.)

Meanwhile, Williams surrendered to local police in Davenport, where he was promptly arraigned. Williams contacted a Des Moines attorney, who arranged for an attorney in Davenport to meet with Williams at the Davenport police station. Des Moines police informed counsel they would pick Williams up in Davenport and return him to Des Moines without questioning him. Two Des Moines detectives then drove to Davenport, took Williams into custody, and proceeded to drive him back to Des Moines.

During the return trip, one of the policemen, Detective Leaming, began a conversation with Williams, saying:

I want to give you something to think about while we're traveling down the road. . . They are predicting several inches of snow for tonight, and I feel that you yourself are the only person that knows where this little girl's body is . . . and if you get a snow on top of it you yourself may not be able to find it. And since we will all be going right past the area [where the body is] on the way into Des Moines, I feel that we could stop and locate the body, that the parents of this little girl should be entitled to a Christian burial for the little girl who was snatched away from them on Christmas Eve and murdered. . . After a snow storm we may not be able to find it at all.

Leaming told Williams that he knew the body was in the area of Mitchell-ville, a town they would be passing on the way to Des Moines. He concluded the conversation by saying, "I do not want you to answer me. . . . Just think about it. . . ." Without further prompting, Williams eventually directed the police to where he had hidden the child's body.

In 1969, Williams was convicted of first-degree murder. This conviction, however, was overturned by the Supreme Court on the grounds that Detective Leaming's comments to Williams constituted an interrogation. They ruled, there-fore, that the evidence, including both Williams directions and the child's body, was inadmissible. The case was sent back for retrial [see *Williams* v. *Brewer,* 430 U.S. 387 (1977)].

In 1977, a second trial was held, in which the prosecution made no mention of Williams' statements and directions. Once more Williams was convicted; once more the defense appealed, asking that the child's body be excluded as evidence.

The U.S. Supreme Court, reversing the ruling of the Circuit Court of Ap-peals, ruled that the body could be admitted as evidence. They held that if Wil-liams had not directed the police to the child's body, there was a strong possibility that the police would have found the body on their own. In fact, the police were conducting a thorough sector search and presented evidence that they would have systematically moved into the area where the body was found and that their search technique would have succeeded in finding her.

The Court thus ruled that where evidence exists that evidence uncovered il-legally by the police would have been found later by the police on their own, legit-imately, that evidence may be used as evidence.

The reasoning behind these cases is that the exclusionary rule is designed to protect people from police misconduct. These two exceptions clearly show that where there is no police misconduct or where the wrongdoing would have had little or no impact on the outcome of the case, the exclusionary rule will not be used. The focus of this rule is on police behavior and police behavior only.

The Use of Informants

There are certain types of crimes that require *inside information,* information gathered by undercover police officers or through the use of informants. Crimi-nal activity involving victimless crimes or any kind of conspiracy are best attacked from the inside. Where possible, the police prefer to use police officers in an un-dercover role. That is not always practical. Frequently, informants offer the only possible method of evidence gathering.

The use of informants is fraught with pitfalls. People who are willing to give evidence against an acquaintance do so for a variety of reasons, mostly selfish. One of the most common informants is one who decides to provide evidence against another, in trade for personal consideration. This consideration may consist of money paid for the information, or it may involve an agreement that reduces or drops charges against the informant. Still others provide information to gain revenge against a former associate or lover. Occasionally, those engaged in an illegal activity provide such information for the purpose of inflicting damage on their competition.

Some informants have honorable motives. Sometimes a person, merely through contacts at home or work, gains knowledge of a crime and seeks to aid the police because the person believes that such activities are wrong. Others get involved with a criminal gang for one crime, but become aware of other crimes in which they are unwilling to participate.

Whatever the reason, the information provided by informants must be treated with a certain amount of skepticism. Even people who inform for the best of reasons may be very unknowledgeable about the crime or what information is valid evidence. The others, those whose motives are suspect, may provide good information only to become witnesses with low credibility.

Informants are generally classified in three ways. The first and most common form is the informant who provides evidence and testifies in court. The second type is the secret informant, who provides evidence to the police but who does not testify and whose name does not appear in the court records. The third type, the anonymous informant, is unknown, even to the police.

Informant testimony.   The first type of informant is required to testify in the criminal proceeding. In these cases, this person will provide firsthand testimony of criminal activity on the part of the defendant. As was mentioned earlier, this testimony is usually suspect, due to the character of the witness. Informant testimony can be enhanced, however, by supporting information provided by the police through the investigative process.

Informant testimony is provided in the same manner as that of other witnesses. Like other witnesses, informants are subject to cross examination. The primary means by which many defense attorneys attempt to impeach informants is by showing the weaknesses in their character. This is especially so when the informant has a criminal background or was a participant in previous criminal episodes. Most people have an aversion to traitors, even when the person is providing testimony of criminal activities. This fact allows the defense to portray the informant as a person of little honor. The judge and jury are then invited to dismiss the testimony of such a person.

Informant testimony is, therefore, problematic. It may be necessary, but is a likely target of an aggressive defense. As a general rule, the police use such testimony only when there is no other means of getting the evidence into court.

Secret informants.   Secret informants are used primarily to provide baseline information from which further evidence can be obtained. For example, such a person may be used to introduce a police undercover officer to key members of the illicit operation. In this case the officer, who is vouched for by the informant, can become a member of the organization and gather sufficient evidence without the necessity of identifying the original informant in court.

There are other times, however, when the informant provides information necessary for a search warrant but cannot be identified in court, for safety reasons. When this happens the court must weigh the possible danger to the witness with the defendant's right to confront witnesses.

In the past, two aspects of the information provided by an informant had to be evaluated before such information could be used as the basis for a search warrant. First, the police were required to verify the veracity of the informant. This could be done in various ways. The best was to establish that the informant had provided accurate information in the past. This was especially true if the informant had a poor character. Other ways included establishing that the informant had a strong character and no reason to lie.

The second assessment was of the information provided. The judge needed some reason to believe that the information was true, independent of the information provided by the informant. This meant that the police were required to provide intelligence that supported accusation of the informant. This need not have been evidence in and of itself. For example, if the informant provided information that a person involved in the distribution of cocaine received a shipment of cocaine every Thursday at 1:00 P.M., this was not sufficient for a search warrant. If, in addition, however, the police discovered that a known cocaine dealer visited this location at 1:00 P.M. every Thursday, a search warrant was more likely to be obtained.

This was known as the two-pronged *Aguilar test*. Any time a search warrant was based on informant testimony, this test had to be administered by the judge and both inquiries satisfied. This was especially true when the informant was to be kept secret from the court. Establishing the credibility of a secret informant was difficult, due to the inability of the judge to assess the integrity of such a witness.

In *Illinois* v. *Gates,* however, the Supreme Court abandoned the two-pronged Aguilar test in favor of the *totality of circumstances test*.

Illinois **v.** *Gates*
462 U.S. 213, 103 S.Ct. 2317, 76 L.Ed.2d 527 (1983)

On May 3, 1978, the Bloomingdale Police Department received an anonymous letter by mail stating the following:

> This letter is to inform you that you have a couple in your town who strictly make their living on selling drugs. They are Sue and Lance Gates, they live on Greenway, off Bloomingdale Rd. in the condominiums. Most of their buys are done in Florida. Sue his

wife drives their car to Florida, where she leaves it to be loaded up with drugs, then Lance flies down and drives it back. Sue flys back after she drops the car off in Florida. May 3, she is driving down there again and Lance will be flying down in a few days to drive it back. At the time Lance drives the car back he has the trunk loaded with over $1,000,000.00 in drugs. Presently they have over $100,000.00 worth of drugs in their basement.

They brag about the fact they never have to work, and make their entire living on pushers.

I guarantee if you watch them carefully you will make a big catch. They are friends with some big drug dealers, who visit their house often.

Lance & Susan Gates
Greenway
in Condominiums

The letter was referred to Detective Mader by the chief of police. Mader decided to pursue the tip. He discovered that there was a Lance Gates residing at the location identified in the letter. He further discovered that L. Gates had made a reservation on an Eastern airlines flight to West Palm Beach, Florida.

Mader made arrangements with an agent of the Drug Enforcement Administration to set up a surveillance of that Eastern Airlines flight. The DEA reported that Gates boarded the flight. Other agents, in West Palm Beach, reported that Gates went to a room registered to Susan Gates at the Holiday Inn. At 7:00 the next morning, Gates and an unknown woman were seen getting into a station wagon identified as belonging to the Gates. They drove north on an interstate highway frequently used by travelers going to and from the Chicago area. Based upon this information, Mader requested a search warrant for the Gates' residence and automobile. The judge, based on the aforementioned facts and in possession of the anonymous letter, approved the warrant.

Upon their arrival at 5:15 A.M. on March 7, the Bloomingdale police were waiting. Found in the vehicle were 350 pounds of marihuana. In the house, police found marihuana, guns, and other contraband. The items seized in evidence were suppressed by the trial court judge, who after applying the two-pronged Aguilar test, found that there was no factual basis for establishing the credibility of the writer of the letter. This decision was sustained by the Illinois Appellate Court and Supreme Court.

The decision was overturned by the U.S. Supreme Court, which ruled that the Illinois courts were using too strict a standard for determining the reliability of the informant's information. Judge Rehnquist, writing for the majority, stated: "This totality-of-the-circumstance approach is far more consistent with our prior treatment of probable cause than is any rigid demand that specific 'tests' be satisfied by every informant's tip. Perhaps the central teaching of our decisions bearing on the probable cause standard is that it is a 'practical, nontechnical conception.' [*Brinegar* v. *United States,* 338 U.S. 160, 176 (1949)]. "In dealing with probable cause, . . . as the very name implies, we deal with probabilities. These are not technical; they are the factual and practical considerations of every-day life on which reasonable and prudent men, not legal technicians, act" (Id., at 175). "Our observation in *United States* v. *Cortez* [449 U.S. 411, 418 (1981)]. regarding 'particularized suspicion,' is also applicable to the probable cause standard:

> The process does not deal with hard certainties, but with probabilities. Long before the law of probabilities was articulated as such, practical people formulated certain com-mon-sense conclusions about human behavior; jurors as factfinders are permitted to do the same—and so are law enforcement officers. Finally, the evidence thus collected must be seen and weighed not in terms of library analysis by scholars, but as understood by those versed in the field of law enforcement.

The Court concluded that the totality of circumstances in this case was such that probable cause did exist upon which a search warrant could be issued. Despite the fact that the writer of the letter was unknown, a series of future actions was accurately predicted by the writer. These actions would be difficult to predict had not the writer had close contact with the Gates family. The corroboration of the major portions of the letter provided the police with a good probability that the remainder of the letter was accurate as well. It is the opinion of the court, therefore, that sufficient probable cause existed to search the Gates' home and car. The judgment of the Supreme Court of Illinois was therefore reversed.

IDENTIFYING THE SUSPECT

At some point in a criminal investigation the police must identify a suspect. The methods by which this can be accomplished vary from apprehension at the scene of the crime, identification by an eye witness, identification through the matching of physical evidence, to identification by means of a confession or admission by the suspect. The rules of evidence differ with each method. Identifying the suspect and sustaining that identification through the court process is a necessity for obtaining a conviction.

Eyewitnesses

In a criminal case, the eyewitness is a double-edged sword. Far more convictions are obtained through the testimony of an eyewitness than through other forms of evidence. One need only look at the clearance rates for various crimes to learn how important an eyewitness is. The downside of eyewitness testimony is the in-herent unreliability of such witnesses. Generally, there are three types of eyewit-ness. First, and most reliable, is the witness who actually knows the suspect. In such cases there is no doubt as to the ability of the witness to recognize the suspect. The longer the relationship, the more reliable the witness.

The second type of eyewitness is the person who does not personally know the suspect but has seen that person on occasion. This will sometimes happen in robbery or rape cases, where the suspect has, in the process of planning the crime, come into contact with the victim. In these cases the witness is reasonably reliable but much less so than the witness who knows the suspect.

The third type of eyewitness is the least reliable. This is the victim who is accosted by a total stranger. In these cases the attack may last from a matter of a few seconds to a little less than an hour, with the shorter times being more predominant. The victim is not just frightened, but usually terrified. The lighting is often poor and the culprit frequently uses some form of disguise. These are the kinds of cases where there is a good likelihood of erroneous identification. This is especially true when the criminal is of one race and the victim of another. People are simply more sensitive to specific elements of facial structure among members of their own race. The statement ''they all look alike'' can be applied by a member of any race to members of any other race. What must be acknowledged is that this type of eyewitness is *inherently unreliable* and that any information obtained from such witnesses must be used with great care.

Lineups. A technique used by law enforcement to help an eyewitness identify a suspect is the *lineup*. The format for a lineup requires that a suspect be placed in a room with a number of other people and that the witness be required to select the suspect from that group. Generally, the group will be placed on a stage-like setting and asked to face the witness, who is usually screened from the suspect by lighting or the use of one-way glass. Each person in the lineup may be asked to turn various ways and may be asked to say something so that the witness can hear their voices. This is a legitimate means of identification as long as the proper procedure is followed.

There are rules of fairness, which are mostly common sense. If the suspect is a short black man, it is not proper to surround him with tall white men. In other words, the people selected to stand with the suspect must fit the same general

Murder	72%
Aggravated assault	62%
Forcible rape	54%
Robbery	25%
Larceny-theft	20%
Motor vehicle theft	15%
Burglary	14%
All UCR Index Crimes	21%

Includes only cases cleared by arrest. Actual clearance rates will be slightly higher.

Illustration 8-1 Clearance Rates (1985)

characteristics as the suspect. They should also wear similar clothing. It is not required that they wear exact clothing, but it should be of a similar type. For example, if the suspect wears jail-issue overalls, so should the others. If the suspect wears street clothing, so should the others. If clothing was a major consideration in the original description, either that type of clothing should be worn by everyone in the lineup or by no one.

The suspect has the right to have an attorney present at a lineup. Neither the suspect nor the defense attorney can refuse to participate, but the defense attorney may observe the proceedings to ensure the fairness of the process.

The lineup may be used for one or numerous witnesses, but no two witnesses should be permitted to view it at the same time. When more than one person is asked to provide information or an identification, there is a tendency for those people to seek group support. Rather than getting two or three positive identifications, it is possible to get one identification, seconded and voted on by the others, who themselves may not be so certain.

Show-ups. A *show-up* differs from a lineup in that the witness or witnesses are shown only the suspect and are asked to make an identification on that basis. The show-up is the weaker of the methods legally but has some utility in some situations. It is most used when a suspect has been stopped on the street shortly after the commission of the crime. The victim is then transported to the suspect, or vice versa, and asked to make an on-site identification. This method is necessary when the description provided to police is the only information they have available. Lacking probable cause to make an arrest, the police detain the potential suspect temporarily until the witness can verify or exonerate that person.

The strength of this approach lies in the short period between the actual crime and attempted identification. The memory of the victim or witness is still fresh and the suspect has not had time to change his or her appearance. Some very solid identifications can be made in this fashion.

The danger lies in the urge that all witnesses have to aid the police. False identifications have been made simply because the witness wanted to be helpful but was not really certain that the person examined was the culprit. Also, because the person is not under arrest, there is no chance to contact an attorney, thus no possibility for legal representation at such a procedure. While a lineup is a straightforward procedure with built-in safeguards, the show-up is an ad hoc on-the-scene police tactic.

Show-ups may also be conducted in the same manner as a lineup, with the defense attorney present at the police station. These cases are rare, however, since it is a format likely to increase the possibility of a false identification. When given a choice between a lineup and a show-up, good police procedure always calls for the former.

Photo lineups. A variation of the lineup is the *photo lineup*. In this procedure, the witness is shown photographs rather than being asked to look at living people. The rules for this procedure are the same as for a normal lineup. The pictures must be of the same type. For example, if the suspect's picture is a police "mug shot," the other photographs should not be from a high school yearbook. The photographs should be about the same size, format, and all color or all black and white.

The photo lineup is especially useful when the police have numerous suspects, no specific suspects, or a suspect they do not yet have in custody. A time-honored procedure is to let witnesses look at photograph albums of people arrested for similar offenses. By allowing the witnesses to move through a large array of photographs at their own pace, the danger of the police influencing the decision is minimized. By and large, this is a reasonably safe procedure, as long as the police do not provide hints as to which photograph should be selected.

The danger in this procedure is the problem associated with the photography process. Looking at a miniature, two-dimensional facsimile of a person is just not the same as looking at the real person. Fortunately, there is a greater chance of failing to identify the correct suspect than in identifying the wrong one. Most of the failures in photographic lineups are due to the inability of the witness to make any identification, even when the culprit's picture is present.

Confessions

A *confession* is a statement by a person or persons, accepting full responsibility for a criminal act. Many cases are brought to a successful conclusion because the suspect confesses. Emotional scenes in which the murderer bares his or her soul before the entire court are standard fare on television shows such as *Perry Mason*. The reality is somewhat different. The court is the least likely place for a person to originate a confession. The process of police interrogation is far more likely to produce such a result. The law concerning police interrogations is fairly rigid, and for good reason.

Despite the fact that people have known for centuries that torture produces false confessions, torture is still used for such purposes. There are criminal justice systems in the world today that allow torture for obtaining convictions. Similarly, there are police officers in this country who use such methods even though they know it to be improper and invalid.

The right to be free from self-incrimination is stressed in the Bill of Rights. This means that the police may not coerce information from a suspect that will be used against that person in court. The rules that spell out these rights are found in the U.S. Supreme Court decision in the case of *Miranda* v. *Arizona*.

Miranda v. *Arizona*
384 U.S. 436 (1966)

On the night of March 2, 1963, 18-year-old Barbara Ann Johnson left her job at the Phoenix Theater to catch a bus. She was accosted by a man who shoved her into his car, tied her hands and feet, then took her to the edge of the city, where he raped her. He then drove the victim to a street near her home, where she was released. The man asked the young woman to say a prayer for him, then drove away.

After hearing Miss Johnson's story, the Phoenix police picked up Ernesto Arthur Miranda and asked him to answer some questions voluntarily. At the station, Miranda was identified in a lineup. Barbara Johnson thought he was the man who had raped her; another woman identified him as the man who had previously robbed her at knifepoint.

Miranda gave the police a handwritten statement confessing to the crime and stating that he was voluntarily waiving his constitutional rights. At the trial Miranda's attorney asked that the confession be withheld because, he argued, Miranda did not know what his rights were. The police admitted that at no time did they ever advise Miranda of any rights. The judge overruled the request and Miranda was found guilty.

The U.S. Supreme Court agreed to hear the case and on June 13, 1966, Chief Justice Earl Warren delivered the Court's decision. This landmark case established clear procedural requirements for police interrogations. The Chief Justice said: "The current practice of incommunicado interrogation is at odds with one of our Nation's most cherished principles—that the person may not be compelled to incriminate himself. Unless adequate protective devices are employed to dispel the compulsion inherent in custodial surroundings, no statement obtained from the defendant can truly be the product of free choice."

The Court thus overturned the Miranda decision and sent the case back for retrial. After this decision, the police were required to advise suspects of their constitutional rights prior to custodial interrogation.

The first right that must be stated is that people in police custody have the right to have an attorney present to advise them prior to police interrogation. This means that when a person is taken into police custody, no questions concerning criminal activities may be asked until the person in custody has spoken with an attorney. This does not mean that the police are prohibited from obtaining basic information unrelated to a crime, such as name and address. The prohibition is for crime-related information.

The concept of in-custody interrogations is also specified. For this right to take effect, it is not necessary that the person be under arrest. People in situations where they feel they may not leave if they wish to do so are considered to be in custody. Atmosphere has a great deal to do with the assessment of whether or not the person is in custody. Interviews in the home of the suspect have been held not to be an in-custody interrogation. The same interview held in the police station, however, is considered an in-custody interrogation. Still, questions posed that provide the person an opportunity for self-incrimination will be closely scrutinized.

Second, but more important, no one is required to provide self-incriminating statements whether or not an attorney is present. This rule possesses the same elements as the right to have an attorney present during the interrogation. Plainly speaking, no person may be forced to undergo a police interrogation. At the point when people say they do not wish to answer further questions, the police are obliged to stop the interrogation.

Should suspects wish to confess, they may do so. The requirement concerning the admissibility of confessions is that it is freely given with the full understanding that such a statement may be entered into court as evidence. Establishing that the confession is voluntary requires the prosecutor to show that the person was read, and understood, the *Miranda warning*. It must next be established that the person knowingly and voluntarily waived the rights established by the Fifth Amendment of the Constitution. This is accomplished through testimony by witnesses to both the reading of the *Miranda* warning and the waiving of such rights by the defendant. Often, the police provide a *Miranda* warning form with a signature space in which the suspect indicates in writing both understanding of the provisions of the warning and the waiver. Once this information is presented in court, it is still open to rebuttal, but the defense attorney bears the burden of proving that the confession was not voluntary.

There are some types of voluntary confession that take place without benefit of the *Miranda* warning. These cases occur when a person approaches a police officer and confesses without any prompting from the officer. While the police are required to warn a person who is in custody, there is no requirement that a police officer turn a deaf ear to an unsolicited confession or admission. There is, however, a line that may not be crossed concerning such cases. The police officer may not engage in a detailed point-by-point interrogation without administering the *Miranda* warning.

Some questions are allowed as long as the officer is merely attempting to clarify what the suspect is saying. Frequently, voluntary confessions are provided in a state of confusion for both the person and the officer. Attempts by the officer to slow down the rate of information flow or obtain a location, time of the incident, or names of others involved are legitimate. This is seen as information gathering necessary to investigate a crime that is being reported.

Another form that a voluntary confession may take is the *spontaneous utterance*. This occurs when a person, in a state of anxiety, blurts out a statement linking this person to a crime. For example, if a police officer comes upon a man standing over an apparently dead woman, it is reasonable for the officer to ask what happened. The response "I killed her" would be a spontaneous utterance. The legal theory supporting the validity of this statement is the belief that the crime has spoken through the person. The officer did not ask for an incriminating statement. The person felt no external coercion to make such an admission. Nevertheless, the statement is legal and can be used in court.

Admissions.   Unlike a confession, an *admission* is not a full acceptance of criminal responsibility. Rather, it is acknowledgment of a fact that may be used to associate a person with a criminal act. For example, if a man were accused of a burglary and told the police that he was in the neighborhood when the crime occurred, he has made an admission. Such an admission could be self-incriminating and thus is subject to the same protections as confessions.

Hearsay.   In the process of investigating a criminal case, the police officer will receive information from various sources and of differing quality. Witnesses or victims sometimes will provide the names of possible suspects based on what they have been told by someone else. Although this may provide a useful investigative lead, it is *hearsay* evidence and may not be used in court.

The confusing aspect of the rules regarding hearsay testimony revolve around the exceptions to this rule. *Dying declarations,* for example, are such an exception. Even then, there are strict procedures for the admittance of such evidence. The person making the declaration must know that death is imminent. The victim's statement must identify the attacker and be witnessed by a neutral party (i.e., police officer, nurse, doctor, priest, uninvolved witness, etc.). Finally, the victim must die. Only then can the statement be entered into evidence at a trial.

Also, third-party statements may be entered for the purpose of establishing that such statements were made, as long as the truthfulness of the statement is not the issue. For example, let us say that Jack Smith wanted to testify that Sarah Brown told him that Mike West was a thief. The statement could be entered to demonstrate Sarah Brown's opinion of Mike West. This statement could not, however, be used to establish evidence against Mike West. The truth of the statement is not reliable; it is hearsay. The fact that Sarah Brown made the statement to Jack Smith is reliable because Jack Smith was a party to the conversation in which the statement was made.

SUMMARY

The elements of police procedure most affected by the courts are definitions of crime, seizure of evidence, and confessions. A criminal investigation is not conducted in a vacuum where there are few rules or guidelines. It is a process of research and discovery limited by constitutional law, procedural law, rules, and regulations. The purpose of this array of laws, rules, and instructions is to guarantee, to the highest degree possible, that people will be treated in a fair and consistent manner.

The first set of definitions necessary for an investigator to understand is the elements of the crime. In our society there must be a written law, promulgated through the legislative process, that specifies what actions or inactions constitute a violation of that law. Furthermore, a penalty or range of penalties must be specified, and there must be evidence that the accused violated the act intentionally. To initiate a prosecution, it is necessary to establish clearly the existence of these factors. This initial investigation, concerning whether or not a crime has been committed, is the realm of criminal law.

The ability to establish that a crime has been committed does not automatically mean that the police then have a free hand to obtain confessions and seize evidence. The collection of evidence, both physical and oral, is constrained by procedures formulated in accordance with the Fourth and Fifth Amendments of the Constitution. Evidence collection and submission in a court of law are, therefore, within the realm of constitutional law.

The failure of the police to function within the guidelines of criminal and constitutional law is not without a price. The U.S. Supreme Court established several guidelines for the admission of certain evidence. The *Miranda* warning must be given to a suspect during any custodial interrogation. Failure to do so results in inability to use in court the statement itself or any information derived from that statement. Similarly, the exclusionary rule prohibits the introduction of evidence into court that was obtained in violation of constitutional guidelines. Although there is some criticism of these court-imposed measures, the purpose of both is to pressure law enforcement personnel to act in accordance with the Constitution and other legal mandates while fulfilling their obligations. There is little doubt that these requirements have had a positive influence on police procedures.

In fulfilling the law enforcement role, police agencies are vastly more restricted than when they fulfill other aspects of the police mission. It must be remembered, however, that the law enforcement role offers a greater potential for the injury of an innocent person than does any other aspect of policing. For this reason the courts and legislators are more sensitive to police actions in this arena than in the other, less limited areas of the police role. Such sensitivity and control are likely to be a permanent part of the law enforcement mission, and that is as it should be.

DISCUSSION QUESTIONS

1. What constitutes the elements of a crime?
2. What factors are necessary for an action to be a crime?
3. Identify the various types of search, and describe the legal requirements for each.
4. Discuss the process by which a search warrant may be obtained.
5. Discuss the use of informants and the legal issues concerning their use.
6. Describe the various types of lineups and the situations and legal limitations of the use of each type.
7. What are the legal requirements for a confession or admission to be admissible in court?
8. Discuss hearsay and the exceptions to this rule.

REFERENCE

1 Jerome Hall, *General Principles of Criminal Law,* 2nd ed. (Indianapolis, Ind.: The Bobbs-Merrill Company, Inc., 1947), p. 18.

Chapter 9

The Court and Its Officers

Key Terms

Municipal courts
Limited jurisdiction
Justice of the peace
State courts
De novo
Real objectives of the court
Stated objectives of the court
Judicial review
Federal magistrates
Federal district courts
U.S. circuit courts of appeal
U.S. Supreme Court
Special federal courts

Rule of four
Friends of the court
Per curium
Dissenting opinion
Concurring opinion
Opinion of the court
Advise and consent
Impeachment
Legislative enactment
Prosecutorial discretion
Plea bargaining
Bailiff
Court clerk

Chapter Objectives

At the conclusion of this chapter, students should be able to:

1. Understand the structure and purpose of various courts.
2. Understand the appellate structure of the American court system.
3. Identify the duties and functions of the courtroom working group.
4. Understand the various processes by which judges are selected and removed.
5. Understand the controversies surrounding plea bargaining.

INTRODUCTION

When we think of justice, the image of the courtroom often comes to mind: a place where learned men and women strive to discover the truth and protect the innocent. Frequently, we imagine a large Greek style building with marble pillars, adorned with carvings of figures representing truth and justice. While the shape and design of the buildings vary, it is nice to think that the ultimate goal of the courts is justice.

Unfortunately, there is another image that comes to mind when thinking about American courts. The fictional media have not been kind to our courts. We are bombarded with the image of a system ineffective and inefficient to the core, a system too bogged down in bureaucratic trivia to accomplish even a semblance of justice. We also see corrupt and inept judges confusing the system even more, judges intervening in every aspect of American life, interposing their own ideology into the social and political fabric of the nation.

Which is the real court system: the men and women seeking justice, or the stagnant pond of ideologues and martinets? The answer is both and neither. The American court system is, like other court systems, people doing the best they can in an incredibly complicated society. Ours is just possibly the most complex and diversified court system in the world. That may well be due to the fact that ours is the most complex and diverse society in the world.

Part of the problem with describing the American courts lies in the fact that while our courts are all within a single court system, they are also in different systems. There is a single federal court system with multiple layers of courts. Each state also has its own court system, although they ultimately answer to the federal courts. At the same time there are city and county courts that are independent, yet answer to the state courts. You see the problem. The lower courts are independent but must operate under guidelines imposed both by law and by the higher courts. Each court has a specific function but is controlled by other courts with different functions.

The best approach to describing the courts is just to describe them. That is the purpose of this chapter. We start with the lower courts and work our way upward.

THE AMERICAN COURT SYSTEM

The American courts are multifaceted. The various strands of the court system weave through the fabric of our society like a finely manufactured garment. Through the halls of justice march an army of litigants, each seeking reward or vindication. The larger the amount to be won or lost, the higher the level of the court to make the decision.

Municipal Courts

Municipal courts, also called city courts or police courts, deal only with misdemeanors. Though not identified by the same name, county courts serve the same purpose for counties as these courts serve for towns and cities. Through these courtrooms pass the vast majority of criminal cases filed by the police. With their *limited jurisdiction,* municipal courts rarely deal with cases requiring incarceration, never send anyone to prison, and typically handle individual cases at high speed. They are by far the most efficient, but also the least encumbered with elaborate, time-consuming prosecutions. This is the courtroom of the petty offense: the traffic violation, the minor assaults, the breech of the peace. While the cases handled at this level are rarely complex, they are nevertheless crucial to the municipal and county systems of government. Because the majority of citizens who have contact with the courts do so at this level, these courts are the most visible to the most people. This means that for most people, the quality of American justice is evaluated here.

Objectives. Municipal courts exist for a variety of reasons. Primarily, they provide a mechanism by which minor problematic behavior can be controlled. I use the term "problematic" because it seems somewhat harsh to think of traffic offenses as criminal. There are two types of municipal court. The first is the court described above. It has limited jurisdiction and handles the vast majority of ordinance violations. The second type is the justice of the peace court. This office may be county or municipal. It has even less jurisdiction than does the municipal court. The *justice of the peace*, or J.P., is a holdover from frontier days. This office has been subject to dwindling responsibility over the past two decades and is not likely to regain it former prominent stature. Many legal scholars regard the J.P. as the dinosaur of the American court system. It is seen as an idea whose time is long past.

Municipal courts strike at inappropriate behavior in two ways. First, the mere act of bringing a person before such a tribunal is believed to have some impact on that person's behavior. Second, this court has an array of punishments that can be inflicted on a person convicted of a violation. Although somewhat limited in the types and amount of punishment that can be inflicted, it is thought sufficient for the minor offenses they address. By far the most used instrument of punishment is the fine. This may range from $1 to as much as $1000 in some courts. Many states limit this amount to considerably less. Maximum fines of $200 are not uncommon.

The fine system has more than one purpose. First and foremost, it is thought to be an effective means of getting an offender's attention. It is a form of behavior modification, wherein the fine represents a negative reinforcement against the inappropriate behavior. Second, there is a longstanding belief that the community would prefer to have those who violate the law make a contribution to the betterment of the society they offended. As a result, city and county officials regularly base their budgets on both tax revenues and estimated fine revenues. Most people would be surprised at how much money is taken in regularly by courts at this level.

Limitations.   The obvious limitations have to do with jurisdiction. Municipal courts are limited not only to the geographic boundaries of the city limits or county lines, but also in the types of offenses they can adjudicate. In short, these courts handle violations of city ordinances within the city limits (or county ordinances within the county lines).

Historically, the municipal court has not had a solid image of either fairness or effectiveness. In the past too many small towns let "out-of-town" motorists pay the city taxes. The infamous speed traps, especially popular in many of the less populated areas, gave both city police and courts a bad name. The very fact that local governments rely heavily on court revenue, even today, is a sore spot for many citizens. A legitimate concern by thoughtful people everywhere is whether or not budget needs dictate either police activity or judicial decisions concerning the size of various fines. This is a concern expressed occasionally by the police, who sometimes wonder whether or not pressure to enforce traffic regulations strictly is motivated by a concern for driver safety or by a shortfall in the city's coffers.

There is no question that city and county legislators depend on court revenue. The question is: How much pressure do these people place on police administrators or judges to maintain a steady cash flow? As with so many other areas of controversy, there is no real answer to that question. It depends on the professionalism and ethics of the individual legislators.

State Courts

State courts come in shapes and sizes. Even the names of the court change from state to state. They may be called superior courts, district courts, or even supreme courts. Their function, however, does not vary significantly from jurisdiction to jurisdiction. These are the major trial courts of the state, indeed of the nation. The vast majority of serious criminal and civil cases will be handled here.

Primarily, these tribunals are courts of original jurisdiction. They handle cases presented for the first time. State trial courts do, however, have some limited appellate jurisdiction. Cases heard in municipal court may be appealed in the higher state trial courts. When this happens, the case is heard *de novo,* which means that it is handled as if it were a new case, with little regard for the earlier court decision.

Objectives.   As with all institutions, there are real and stated objectives. *Real objectives* are those that the organization is seriously addressing, while *stated objectives* are those primarily for public consumption. The stated objectives of the state courts are to protect the people from illegal governmental intrusions while protecting the innocent from predatory criminals.

The real objectives of the state trial courts are to provide a forum wherein

complaints and evidence can be weighed to determine if wrongdoing has occurred. If such has occurred, the objective shifts to providing the appropriate
legal response. In addition, the courts review and evaluate governmental procedures and establish future legal guidelines for the processing of such cases.

The means by which these courts accomplish these tasks are varied and complex. State courts deal with serious issues, occasionally including decisions of life
and death. The major weapon of the courts, for good or ill, is procedure. The
major state courts, as well as the federal courts, rely extensively on procedure. To
a very great extent, process guides the court system in much the way that railroad
tracks determine the destination of a freight train.

Appellate structure.   There is some variance in appellate court structure,
but this is due primarily to the effects of population density. It is a principle of the
American system that only one court be the final arbiter of points of law. This is
as true of the state courts as it is of the federal system. Thus with the same number
of high courts as North and South Dakota, the states of Texas and California are
required to handle the final appeals for a vast population.

The larger states have addressed this problem in several ways. Texas, for
example, has separated the appellate function into two distinct arenas, criminal
and civil. The Texas Supreme Court is the final state court for civil appeals, and
the Texas Criminal Court of Appeals handles cases involving criminal actions.
Still other states have created intermediate courts of appeal to handle cases before
they reach the state supreme court.

By definition, appellate courts have appellate jurisdiction. Most do not have
original jurisdiction. The function of these courts is to review the decisions of
lower courts to ensure that proper procedures were followed and that the decisions were compatible with constitutional and substantive law. That these courts
are critical elements in the legal structure can be verified by the fact that almost 80
percent of all appeals are handled by state appellate courts.[1]

Federal Courts

The federal courts sit at the top of the American judicial structure. Although
these courts handle fewer criminal cases than do the state courts, they establish
the guidelines within which all courts must sooner or later operate. This was not
the original purpose of these courts. The initial idea for the federal court system
was to hear cases involving federal crime, in much the same manner that states
dealt with state crime. The development of the concept of *judicial review* changed
the focus of the American courts.

Judicial review, a by-product of *Marbury* v. *Madison,* proclaims the federal
court system as the keeper of the Constitution. After this decision, courts were
empowered to declare acts of the other government bodies unconstitutional and
therefore illegal. Eventually, the development of civil rights legislation and evolv-

ing interpretations of the constitutional concepts of due process and equal protection provided the federal courts with oversight power concerning state courts.

Federal courts now spend a large portion of their time involved in the activities of the state criminal justice systems. They have become involved in almost every aspect of American life. To a very real extent, the overloading of the federal court system is due more to oversight of the states and review of state court decisions than to an increasing federal criminal case load.

Other than for the overview function, the federal courts are structured in a way that is very similar to the state courts. *Federal magistrates* deal with the minor violations of federal law in much the same way as the municipal courts, while the *federal district courts* represent the major trial courts of the federal system. The *U.S. circuit courts of appeal* are intermediate appellate courts assigned to geographic regions of the country. At the top of the entire legal pyramid sits the *U.S. Supreme Court,* which is the final court of appeal for all American legal decisions.

Objectives.   The objectives of the federal court system are essentially the same as those of the state court. Like their counterparts at the state level, these courts have real and stated objectives. The real objectives, like the state courts, is to ensure that the cases before them are processed in accordance with proper substantive and procedural law.

Stated objectives are linked to the symbolic mission of the federal courts. They wish to protect all people from unconstrained governmental intrusion while protecting individuals from the ravages of crime. The federal courts sit between the government and the people. They want to protect the people from the effects of an overzealous government, but also wish the people to be safe from avaricious felons.

The courts know, although sometimes the police forget, that police abuse is a far greater threat to society than are criminals. The courts, therefore, seem destined to stand forever between these two forces, ever attempting to maintain a balance within which honest people can prosper.

In reality, of course, the courts deal only with cases brought before them. The mission may be monumental, the walls may be marble, the expectations of the people may be high, but in the final analysis, the federal courts really attempt to do about the same thing as the state courts. The federal courts have more power at their disposal, which means that they have a greater impact on the overall legal system. The result, therefore, is that the federal court system is the most important institution in the American court structure.

Special courts.   Besides the better known courts within the federal system, there are some lesser known *special,* or *extraordinary, federal courts* that act only on certain types of law. They are located mostly in Washington, D.C., and hear only special cases. These courts exist for custom and patent appeals and for claims against the federal government. They also hear appeals of administrative decisions in much the same manner as higher courts hear appeals from the lower courts.

Another extraordinary federal court is the three-judge district court. This is an *ad hoc* tribunal specially convened in exceptional circumstances. Litigants who wish to use this court must make a special application of the senior judge of the district court. If the application is granted, the senior judge convenes the court, which has three judges, one of which must be a district court judge and one a judge from the court of appeals. This court hears controversial issues in an attempt to deal effectively with them prior to the case being sent up on appeal.[2]

Structure.   The structure of the federal court system is the model on which the state court systems are based. In order of ascending hierarchy, the federal court system is composed of the federal magistrates courts, federal district courts, U.S. circuit courts of appeal and U.S. Supreme Court. Of these courts the circuit courts of appeal and Supreme Court have primarily appellate jurisdiction; only the magistrates courts are limited to original jurisdiction. The others have both original and appellate jurisdiction, albeit limited in most cases.

The federal district courts are the workhorses of the system, handling the majority of criminal cases. Additionally, the district courts review appeals from federal magistrate's court and habeas corpus review of state court decisions as well as governmental policies and actions. Judges in these courts sit alone but are not confined to one location. Usually, the federal district court judges conduct most of their business in one location, usually the federal court building for that district. They may, however, conduct trials and other court business at any location within the district.

There are 12 circuit courts of appeal, which review cases appealed from lower federal courts and from some administrative and regulatory agencies. In 1980, for example, 19,259 cases from federal district courts as well as almost 3000 appeals from administrative agencies were heard by the courts of appeal.[3] Cases heard by this court are not heard by all of the judges in the court. Three judge panels decide issues brought before the bench. This is not to say that each court has only three judges. On the contrary, the largest court has 23 judges, while the smallest has only four.[4]

The circuit courts of appeal must hear all appeals brought before them from federal district courts. Under our legal system every person brought before the bar of justice has a right to one appeal. The circuit courts of appeal provide this service for the litigants of the district courts. Historically, about one in four cases will be appealed from a district court to a court of appeals.[5]

Supreme Court decisions affect the entire system, states as well as federal. For it is at this level that ultimate interpretations of law and process are determined. Appellate cases may reach the Supreme Court in several ways. They may be appealed from state courts, federal courts, or from the special three-judge federal courts. Unlike the other appellate courts, the Supreme Court may choose the cases it wishes to hear. Because of the potential for an overwhelming caseload, the Supreme Court carefully selects which cases it will hear. The mechanism by which cases are selected is known as the *rule of four*. This means that four of the nine judges must vote to review a case or it is rejected.

The process by which a litigant may appeal to the Supreme Court varies depending on the type of case. Each request for a hearing, whether by writ of appeal, certiorari, or certification, is sent to the office of the Chief Justice. Since almost half of the petitions come from poor people or convicted prisoners, these must be investigated and evaluated by the Chief Justice's law clerks.[6] This is because the petitions are frequently poorly written and lacking evidence necessary for review. After an investigation by the clerks, if there is sufficient information to review the case, it is sent to the other eight associate judges for their review.

Those petitions that are submitted with appropriate trial transcripts and preparation are sent from the Chief Justice's office directly to the other eight judges. Each associate justice, or the judge's clerk, then reviews the petition and determines whether or not it is suitable for a review of the full court. If four judges vote to review the case, it is scheduled for review by the entire court.

When a case is accepted for review by the Supreme Court, the appropriate attorneys are notified so that they may prepare materials for submission. Special-interest groups, with permission of the litigants or the Court, may file information as *friends of the court* and present whatever relevant information they wish to bring to the Court's attention. Most cases are handled in this manner, without oral arguments. The Court decides in closed session, basing their opinions on written briefs and trial transcripts. In these cases they render their decision briefly, with a short statement citing relevant supporting cases providing the reason for the decision. These are known as *per curium* decisions.

The Court may also set a time and date for oral arguments. In these cases, the procedure is somewhat different. Each side will be given a specified time limit for presentation of its case. Attorneys for each side will be asked to emphasize what they believe are the strongest legal points of their position. They must also be prepared to respond to questions posed by the judges. Sometime after oral arguments the judges will meet and debate the relative merits of the case. Discussion will be opened by the Chief Justice and will proceed along lines of seniority. When the Chief Justice believes that it is time to make a decision, he or she will call for a vote. A simple majority is needed for a decision on any and all cases. The senior judge on the majority side then decides who will write the opinion of the court. The Chief Justice is always the senior judge in cases where he or she is on the majority side.

Each judge is free to issue a *dissenting opinion, concurring opinion,* or join with the *opinion of the court*. Moreover, judges may join in either of these options. Dissents are presented by judges on the minority side of the vote. Concurring opinions are usually prepared by a judge who voted with the majority but does not agree with some or all of the arguments presented in the formal opinion. In these cases a judge is saying, "I agree with the decision, but for different reasons."

The written opinions of the Supreme Court justices are, in some respects, as important as the legal decisions. Case law is the product of such deliberations. Future cases will be deliberated using the arguments and precedents established in these cases. The need for clarity in the opinions rendered is paramount. Both law and procedural issues are based on such opinions. Ambiguous or vague opinions often lead to confusion or misinterpretation by attorneys and judges in lower courts. When this happens it becomes necessary for the Supreme Court to hear another case of a similar nature, in order to clarify their first decision. It is this process of fine-tuning legal decisions that gives American law its crazy-quilt appearance of overlapping cases and conflicting opinions.

The Supreme Court and law enforcement.   The decisions rendered by the Supreme Court often have a dramatic impact on law enforcement. As we saw in

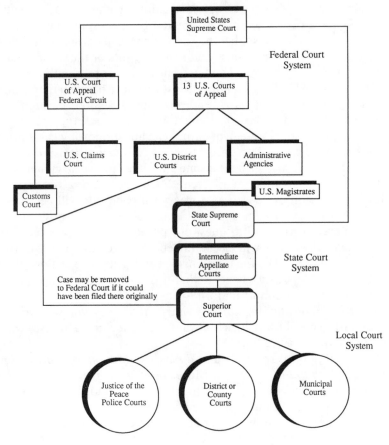

Illustration 9–1   U.S. Court System

Chapter 8, the decisions in *Miranda* v. *Arizona* and *Mapp* v. *Ohio* dramatically altered police procedures during interrogation and in cases involving search and seizure. Any time the Supreme Court declares a procedure unconstitutional, that procedure is immediately and permanently eliminated or changed significantly.

Over time the Court has, through case law, not only changed police procedures, such as those mentioned above, but has also altered the makeup of police agencies. It has been court decisions that have struck down height requirements and mandated hiring minorities and females. In a sense it is unfortunate that these actions have resulted from court intervention into law enforcement. I say ''unfortunate'' because all of these changes should have come from enlightened leadership within law enforcement itself. The sad truth is that it has been the courts, especially the federal courts, that have dragged American law enforcement, kicking and screaming, into the twentieth century.

OFFICERS OF THE COURT

There are a number of people that compose the courtroom work group. These people are vested with authority and responsibilities related to the orderly dispensing of justice. Among these are the judge, attorneys (both defense and prosecutor), bailiff, and clerks. It is upon the shoulders of these people, acting as both a team and, in the case of the opposing attorneys, occasionally adversaries, that the task of seeking out the truth in complex issues falls.

Judges

The key person in the courtroom is the judge. This is the person to whom all questions of law are addressed. In the lower courts, and to a degree in the felony courts, the judge will be the sole decision maker, the person who will determine if the accused is guilty or innocent, the person who will pronounce sentence. The judge may well be the ultimate authority figure in the judicial system. When people feel they received justice in the court, they praise the judge; if they are left bitter by their experience, they blame the judge.

Selection. The vast majority of *municipal judges* are appointed, with the exception of justices of the peace, who are usually elected. In larger jurisdictions selection guidelines usually require that the applicant have at least a law degree and be a member of the state bar association. Very little else is required, except that often the person selected be a member of the appropriate political party.

Smaller jurisdictions have even fewer requirements. Many require only that the person be willing to take the position. Not every state requires municipal judges to be attorneys. There are still far too many nonattorneys holding judicial office in this country. That is one of the major criticisms of the municipal court system:the inadequacy of the qualifications of the judges on those benches.

State	Selection[a]	State	Selection[a]
Alabama	PE	Montana	NE
Alaska	M	Nebraska	M
Arizona	H	Nevada	NE
Arkansas	PE	New Hampshire	G
California	NE	New Jersey	G
Colorado	M	New Mexico	PE
Connecticut	G	New York	PE
D.C.	M	North Carolina	PE
Delaware	G	North Dakota	NE
Florida	NE	Ohio	NE
Georgia	PE	Oklahoma	NE
Hawaii	M	Oregon	NE
Idaho	NE	Pennsylvania	PE
Illinois	PE	Rhode Island	G
Indiana	H	South Carolina	L
Iowa	M	South Dakota	NE
Kansas	H	Tennessee	PE
Kentucky	NE	Texas	PE
Louisiana	PE	Utah	M
Maine	G	Vermont	M
Maryland	M	Virginia	L
Massachusetts	G	Washington	NE
Michigan	NE	West Virginia	PE
Minnesota	NE	Wisconsin	NE
Mississippi	PE	Wyoming	M
Missouri	H		

[a]L, legislative appointment; M, merit; G, governor appointment; PE, partisan election; NE, nonpartisan election; H, hybrid.

Illustration 9-2   Selection of State Judges

The appointment of *state court judges* varies as much as the names of the courts themselves. The methods used to select judges range from appointment to election to a form of merit system. Within each option there also lies diversity. The appointment may be by the governor, state supreme court, or legislator. The election may be partisan or nonpartisan in format.

About one-half of the states select judges by way of popular vote. Some of these use a partisan election wherein the judge runs for office under the auspices of a political party that supports the person's election. Other states use a nonpartisan election in which the political parties play no role.

The appointment process also varies from state to state. Governors appoint some judges, and state supreme courts or legislative bodies appoint others. Even here, however, politics plays a major role in the selection process. Unlike some municipal judges, state trial court judges are required to be members of the state bar to qualify for appointment. Although this is no guarantee that the person is qualified to be a judge, it at least establishes a minimum standard of legal education. Generally speaking, state judges are better qualified than their counterparts in the municipal courts, although there are exceptions.

Federal judges are appointed for life. The process is one of *advise and consent.* The President of the United States appoints these judges, subject to approval by the Senate. Actually, selecting the person to be appointed is a process that varies from president to president. Traditionally, the senior senator of the majority party of the state in which the appointment is to be made makes the actual selection.

Other techniques have involved asking the state bar association for a list of suitable candidates from which the president makes the selection. There are no guidelines as to how the president makes this choice; it is totally up to the incumbent. Lately, the second procedure seems to have been preferred over the first, but that may change as presidents change. The senatorial review process, *advise and consent,* attempts to ensure the basic competence of the person selected. All federal judges must be attorneys. Further, most have established a record of accomplishments as either a sitting judge, a prosecuting attorney, or a teacher of law in a law school.

Removal.   The removal of a judge may be accomplished in several ways, depending on which type of judge one wishes to remove. Federal judges are considered constitutional judges, which means that they have life-long tenure. Removal of a federal judge must therefore be through the *impeachment* process. If a judge acts in such a manner as to present an image of impropriety, the Congress may vote to impeach the person, after which a trial will be held in the U.S. Senate. The Senate will then decide whether or not the judge will remain in office. Historically, it has proven very difficult to impeach a federal judge. In those cases in which this has occurred, the judge so removed had committed and was convicted of a violation of a serious law.

The removal of state court judges may be accomplished in one of several ways, one of which is impeachment. Another is by *legislative enactment.* More than half the states permit the removal of a state judge by a concurrent two-thirds vote of both houses, or by the governor with a concurrence of a majority vote in both houses.[7]

Still other states allow a judge to be removed by recall. This process requires the circulation of a petition, and if the required number of valid signatures appears on the petition, the judge's name appears on the ballot at the next election. The electorate may then vote for the judge's removal or for the judge to continue in office. A majority vote determines the outcome.

All states have *commissions* on judicial conduct that are responsible for investigating allegations of improper behavior by judges. This commission may recommend censure or removal from office. In those cases the state supreme court or another judicial tribunal makes the actual decision as to whether or not the judge remains in office.

Prosecutors

The prosecutor wears two hats; that is, this person plays a dual role in the legal system. The authority to select which cases will be prosecuted and which dismissed gives the person holding this office a great deal of power over the police. In a very real sense, the prosecutor is the chief law enforcement officer within any given jurisdiction. This power is narrow, being confined only to criminal cases, but in that arena the prosecutor's word is law (no pun intended).

The second role of the prosecutor is that of advocate for the people of the jurisdiction. This person represents the citizenry as a whole while also representing the victim. In this capacity the prosecutor is charged with seeing that justice is done. To do that, the prosecutor must vigorously pursue the truth. If the facts of a case do not support the police charges, the prosecutor must see that this case does not go to trial.

A common misconception is that the prosecutor's only duty is to prosecute cases brought by the police or citizens. The role is actually much more complex. This person is responsible for seeing justice done. Rather that merely prosecute police cases, the prosecutor must first ensure that the facts of the case are supportable by evidence and that there truly is a solid basis for pursuing the case further. Police officers would, in many cases, prefer a rubber stamp prosecutor; one who would accept any case for prosecution. That is not the way our system is designed. The prosecuting attorney represents a major checkpoint in the legal system. To get a case to court, this person must first be convinced that such a case exists.

Selection.   Prosecuting attorneys are either elected or appointed, depending on the jurisdiction. At the federal level, district attorneys are appointed by the president with the advice and consent of the Senate. At the state level, prosecutors are elected in all but five states.[8] Locally, city prosecutors are usually elected in larger areas. In smaller towns and cities, however, local attorneys are sometimes hired on a part-time basis. In these cases, the prosecutor is hired by a city administrator with advice and consent of the town or city council.

Even in the smallest communities, prosecutors are attorneys. This is true even in jurisdictions where the municipal judge may not be trained in the law. In these cases the prosecutor exercises even greater control and responsibility for justice in that community. Untrained judges lean heavily on the knowledge of the prosecutor for proper dispensing of law and justice.

Removal.   Prosecutors may be removed from office in much the same way as judges. Unlike judges, some of whom have tenure for life, no such protection exists for prosecutors. No prosecutor is either elected or appointed for life. Federal prosecutors hold political office and officially work in the Department of Justice for the U.S. Attorney General. The Department of Justice provides broad guidelines under which the district attorneys and the assistant district attorneys operate, but these guidelines are loose. In reality, the federal district attorneys are relatively independent when it comes to deciding which cases will and will not be prosecuted.

In theory, as political appointments, they can be removed by the U.S. Attorney General. In reality, federal prosecutors are almost never removed without cause. By and large, people holding this office have a considerable amount of discretion and job security.

At the state and local level, prosecutors may be recalled or fired, depending on whether they were elected or appointed. In most cases there must be just cause for either action. In cases involving dismissal of a contract prosecutor, cause is not always debated. As a contract employee, the prosecutor has only the job protection that is built into the contract. Lacking cause, the legislative body may still buy out a person's contract and hire someone else. In truth, this rarely happens. By and large, prosecutors tend to stay in office as long as they wish. Most of the turnover in prosecutors is voluntary.

Decision making. *Prosecutorial discretion* is a broad-based power inherent in the office of prosecutor. The actual decision to prosecute is somewhat more complicated. First, there are screening decisions that are reasonably consistent across all prosecutors. These include: evidentiary factors, the views of the prosecutor on key criminal justice issues, the political and social environment in which the prosecutor functions, and the resource constraints and organization of the prosecutorial operations.

In addition, studies have confirmed the existence of at least three policies that affect the screening decision:

1. *Legal sufficiency.* An arrest is accepted for prosecution if, on routine review of the arrest, the minimum legal elements of the case are present.
2. *System efficiency.* Arrests are disposed of as quickly as possible by the fastest means possible, which are rejections, dismissals, and pleas.
3. *Trial sufficiency.* The prosecutor accepts only those arrests for which, in his or her view, there is sufficient evidence to convict in court.[9]

The broad discretion authorized American prosecutors has led to accusations of prosecutorial misconduct in many instances. Although many such complaints are justified, it must be remembered that the police are often suspicious of any refusal to prosecute. Thus the prosecutor may make justifiable decisions only to face contempt and hostility from the investigating officers or, in some cases, the media. The point here is that while prosecutors have a great deal of authority, they also have great responsibility. Since their decisions are never secret, prosecutors are subject to a great deal of second guessing by others.

Plea Bargaining

Over 90 percent of all felonies are disposed by *plea bargaining*. Despite this, most people, including those who work for criminal justice agencies, believe that plea bargaining is a sordid process.[10]

The history of plea bargaining is relatively short. The practice began following the Civil War but did not become widely practiced until this century.[11] The reasons for the incredible expansion of use of this process can be traced to a number of factors. First, the complexity of the trial process itself, with its growing array of pretrial motions and increased focus on procedural detail, made trials both time consuming and expensive. If for no other reason than the economics involved in prolonged trials, it was necessary to find a less formal alternative. Second, the expansion of criminal law, especially in the era of prohibition, meant more cases filed. This expansion led to a greatly increased case load, requiring the courts to seek ways to alleviate the pressure on the courts. Third, an increase in crime rates meant ever-increasing case loads. This, of course, added to the pressure created by the expansion of the law itself. Fourth was the high level of political corruption within the urban criminal courts for several decades before and after the turn of the century. Wholesale plea negotiation served both sides well. Corrupt politicians and legal officials could wheel and deal with the prosecutor to get a reduced sentence. Prosecutors would negotiate a plea so that the case would not have to go before a corrupt judge. Finally, the increase in professionalization among law enforcement, prosecutors and defense led to more understanding of the pressures brought about by heavy case loads. As a result, plea bargaining became, if not reputable, an acceptable means of handling cases.[12]

There are two types of plea negotiation. The first is charge bargaining, where the defendant agrees to plead guilty to a specific charge. In exchange for this plea, the prosecutor may agree to drop other pending charges or may accept the plea to this offense rather than charge the defendant with the actual charge. For example, a burglar may agree to plead guilty to a charge of trespassing or theft; a rape charge might be changed to aggravated assault; capital or first-degree murder might be dropped to noncapital murder or manslaughter.

The second type of plea negotiation is sentence bargaining. The defendant agrees to plead guilty on the condition that the prosecutor recommends a lesser sentence than that which would normally be imposed.

It is not possible to totally separate these types of plea negotiation. An arrangement that leads to a lesser charge being filed in court will almost always result in a lesser sentence being imposed. The defendant may therefore achieve his or her goal of reducing the punishment through a variety of negotiation techniques.

Criticisms of plea bargaining focus on the impact of this process on justice. Since the strength of the negotiated plea is in its allowing the accused to escape with a reduced charge or penalty, those who opt for a full trial face the full force of the law, both in criminal charges and penalties. There is therefore a price to be paid for demanding one's constitutional right to a trial. This places considerable pressure on the defendant to plead guilty, even though the person may be innocent. From the public's point of view justice is also thwarted by this process. Those accused of serious criminal acts are sometimes allowed to slip through the hands of the legal system through deft negotiation. The critics claim, therefore, that plea bargaining serves neither the accused nor the public.

Those who support plea bargaining argue that case loads are so heavy that trying every case would result in such a backload that it would cause the legal system to break down. Moreover, the cost of full trials would tax the limits of both the government treasuries and the personal resources of the defendants. Furthermore, the police often have the right suspect but do not have sufficient evidence to win in a trial. Plea bargaining offers a mechanism whereby guilty persons receive some punishment, even though it is less than the criminal act warrants. Proponents argue, therefore, that plea bargaining serves the interests of both the public and the persons accused of crimes.

Defense Attorneys

The defense attorney's function is to protect the defendant's legal rights and to be the defendant's advocate in the trial process. In some cases defendants have chosen to represent themselves, but on the whole, most defendants are represented by attorneys. The right to have an attorney is protected by the Sixth Amendment to the Constitution. Such council must be provided in any case for which the penalty may be jail or prison.[13] Such representation must be allowed at every critical step in the criminal justice process.

Gideon v. *Wainwright*
372 U.S. 335 (1963)

Clarence Earl Gideon was 51 years of age when arrested for breaking into a pool room in Panama City, Florida. Gideon had spent the better part of his adult life in jails for theft and burglary. On June 4, 1961, he was arrested for the foregoing crime and charged with "unlawfully and feloniously" breaking and entering with intent to commit a misdemeanor—petty larceny.

At the time of Gideon's arrest the state of Florida had no provisions for granting defense attorneys for indigent suspects in anything but capital cases. Gideon requested assigned counsel and this request was denied. Acting as his own defense, Gideon did his best. Unable to interrogate witnesses adequately and unfamiliar with points of law, the outcome was never in doubt. A jury found him guilty as charged, and on August 25, Judge Robert L. McCrary sentenced him to five years in the Florida State Prison.

From his prison cell Gideon prepared and submitted a handwritten petition to the Florida Supreme Court. This appeal was denied without a hearing. Gideon then submitted a petition for review with the U.S. Supreme Court. On June 4, 1962, the U.S. Supreme Court granted Gideon's petition and Abe Fortas, later to be appointed to the Supreme Court, was appointed by the Supreme Court to represent Gideon.

Fortas argued that the accused cannot effectively defend himself and thus cannot receive due process and a fair trial. He further pointed out that the indigent defendant, lacking bail or bond, is almost always in jail during the pretrial preparation period and thus cannot interview potential witnesses or even prepare for the defense. Fortas further stated: "To convict the poor without counsel while we guarantee the right to counsel to those who can afford it is also a denial of equal protection of the laws."

On March 18, 1963, the Supreme Court, in a unanimous verdict, upheld Gideon's appeal. In this decision, the Court stated that Gideon was indeed entitled to a court-appointed attorney and that states were obligated under the Sixth Amendment to the Constitution to provide attorneys for indigents in all felony cases.

Speaking for the Court, Justice Hugo Black said: "In our adversary system of criminal justice, any person hauled into court, who is too poor to to hire a lawyer, cannot be assured a fair trial unless counsel is provided for him. This seems to us to be an obvious truth."

The right to counsel itself poses no problem for a jurisdiction. It is a relatively simple matter to allow an arrested person to phone a private attorney to obtain representation. When the suspect is indigent, however, we are faced with another problem. Who is to pay for the counsel guaranteed by the constitution, if not the defendant? The answer is, of course, the taxpayer. There are currently three different methods by which jurisdictions have addressed the issue of legal aid to indigent defendants: public defenders, assigned counsel, and contract systems.

Public defenders.   Public defender programs are public or private nonprofit organizations with full- or part-time salaried staff. There are two categories within the public defender classification—statewide and local. Under the statewide system one person is named public defender and charged with developing and maintaining a defender system in each county. Local public defenders, however, are independent and autonomous.

Assigned counsel.   This system involves the appointment of private attorneys by the court. There are two main types of assigned counsel. The first is the *ad hoc system*, wherein judges appoint practicing attorneys within the community on a case-by-case basis. The second is a *coordinated system,* which has an admin-

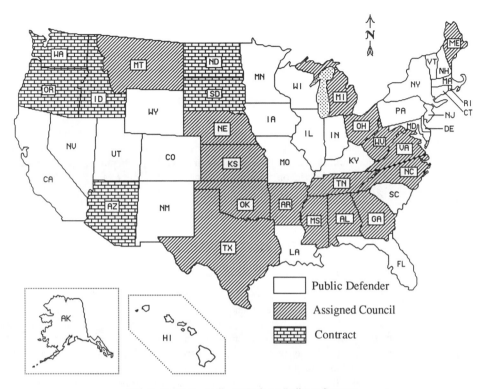

Illustration 9–3   Indigent Defense Delivery Systems

istrator responsible for the appointment of counsel as well as establishing a set of standards and guidelines for administering the program.

Contract systems.   The contract systems involve government contracting with individual attorneys, bar associations, or private law firms to provide services for a specified dollar amount. County agencies usually award the defender service contracts, and they are usually awarded to individuals rather than firms or organizations.

Argersinger v. *Hamlin*
407 U.S. 25, 92 S.Ct. 2006, 32 L.Ed.2d 350 (1972)

In this case the petitioner (Argersinger) was arrested in Florida on the charge of carrying a concealed weapon. Under Florida law a person could receive a sentence of up to six months in jail plus a $1000 fine. The trial was held before a judge. Argersinger, an indigent, was unable to afford legal counsel; therefore, he was forced to represent himself. Argersinger was found guilty and sentenced to six months of confinement. As with Clarence Gideon, Argersinger filed a habeas corpus appeal alleging that by failing to provide legal counsel, the state of Florida was violating his constitutional rights.

The U.S. Supreme Court agreed with Argersinger and reversed the conviction. Justice Douglas delivered the opinion:

> That picture is seen in almost every report. "The misdemeanor trial is characterized by insufficient and frequently irresponsible preparation on the part of the defense, the prosecution, and the court. Everything is rush, rush. [Hellerstein, "The Importance of the Misdemeanor Case on Trial and Appeal," 28 *The Legal Aid Brief Case* 151, 152 (1970)]"

> There is evidence of the prejudice which results to misdemeanor defendants from this "assembly-line justice." One study concluded that "[m]isdemeanants represented by attorneys are five times as likely to emerge from police court with all charges dismissed as are defendants who face similar charges without counsel. [American Civil Liberties Union, Legal Counsel for Misdemeanants, Preliminary Report 1 (1970)]

> We must conclude, therefore, that the problems associated with misdemeanor and petty offenses often require the presence of counsel to insure the accused a fair trial. Mr. Justice Powell suggests that these problems are raised even in situations where there is no prospect of imprisonment. We need not consider the requirements of the Sixth Amendment as regards the right to counsel where loss of liberty is not involved, however, for here petitioner was in fact sentenced to jail. And as we said in *Baldwin* v. *New York,* 399 U.S., at 73, "the prospect of imprisonment for however short a time will seldom be viewed by the accused as a trivial or 'petty' matter and may well result in quite serious repercussions affecting his career and his reputation."

> We hold, therefore, that absent a knowing and intelligent waiver, no person may be imprisoned for any offense, whether classified as petty, misdemeanor, or felony unless he was represented by counsel at his trial.

> Under the rule we announce today, every judge will know when the trial of a misdemeanor starts that no imprisonment may be imposed, even when local law permits it, unless the accused is represented by counsel. He will have a measure of the seriousness and gravity of the offense and therefore know when to name a lawyer to represent the accused before the trial starts.

Bailiffs

The *bailiff* acts as sergeant at arms in the courtroom. This person may be a deputy sheriff or may be a court employee. In either case, the bailiff's function is to see that the judge's orders are carried out. The various duties of the bailiff include calling the court to order, escorting defendants and witnesses to and from the court, and escorting the jury to and from the court as well as to the location in which they conduct deliberations. The bailiff also ensures that the jury is not disturbed during deliberations. Other duties include administering oaths to witnesses and taking appropriate action to ensure the security and safety of all participants in the courtroom.

Clerks

Although a number of court employees might be classified as clerks, there is only one *court clerk*. This person is responsible for scheduling cases, receiving fines, and recording court orders. This person is the court's bookkeeper. Under the general heading "clerks," one might also find the court reporter. This person takes detailed notes, usually with the aid of a tape recorder or specially designed typewriter that utilizes a form of shorthand. The notes are then transferred into a written formal report which becomes the court record. It is this record that both prosecutor and defense attorney will use when one side appeals the court's decision.

SUMMARY

The American legal system is a multifaceted array of local, state, and federal courts. At the bottom of this structure are the municipal courts, which handle only misdemeanors and other local problems of a minor nature. Felonies are dealt with through either the state courts or federal district courts, depending on the nature of the crime. Both state and federal governments have appellate courts that exist to review decisions made at lower levels of their respective court systems. At the top of the legal hierarchy sits the U.S. Supreme Court, which has final authority on all federal issues and interpretations of the constitution. In its role as interpreter of the constitution, the Supreme Court also greatly influences actions of state courts.

Judges within these various courts are selected in a variety of ways. Federal judges are selected through a process of advise and consent. The president appoints the judge, subject to approval by the Senate. All such judges must have law degrees and, by and large, have sufficient experience in the judiciary or as a law professor to provide a basis for their selection. State court judges are selected by several different methods. Some are appointed, either by the governor or by a committee or board designed to oversee the court system. Some are elected. Still others are selected through a multifaceted approach: a combination of appointment and, later, election. All states require that state court judges have a law degree and be a member of the state bar association. Municipal judges may be either appointed or elected. At this level, the smaller jurisdictions do not always require the judge to be an attorney.

Other participants of the trial process include the attorneys representing the prosecution and defense. These people are usually attorneys, although there are occasions where a defendant may represent himself or herself. The prosecutor is a government employee who represents the state or federal government. The defense attorney may be hired by the defendant at the defendant's expense. Or the defense attorney may be appointed by the state. If defense is appointed, the expense may be covered through one of several ways. The public defender may be a state employee in the same manner as the public prosecutor. The judge may also appoint a local attorney as defense counsel. The taxpayers also pay this attorney's bill, which may be a set fee or may be subject to some limited negotiation. In this system the judge may appoint any local attorney or may select from a list of attorneys who have indicated a willingness to serve in such a capacity.

The court working group also includes the court clerk and bailiff who serve as court functionaries. The clerk maintains the record system, and the bailiff maintains order, decorum, and security within the courtroom. These offices exist at courts at all levels.

DISCUSSION QUESTIONS

1. Describe the various methods by which judges are selected.
2. Discuss the duties and responsibilities of the prosecutor.
3. When is it necessary for an indigent to be provided an attorney?
4. Describe the various systems for providing court-appointed attorneys.
5. Identify the strengths and weaknesses of the municipal court system.
6. Trace a case from a lower state court through the appellate process.
7. Argue the pros and cons of plea bargaining.

NOTES/REFERENCES

1. George F. Cole, *The American System of Criminal Justice,* 5th ed. (Pacific Grove, Calif.: Brooks/Cole Publishing Co., 1989), p. 461.
2. Herbert Jacob, *Justice in America: Courts, Lawyers, and the Judicial Process,* 4th ed. (Boston: Little, Brown and Company, 1984), p. 166.
3. U.S. Bureau of the Census, *Statistical Abstract of the United States, 1981* (Washington, D.C.: U.S. Government Printing Office, 1981), Table 320, p. 185.
4. Jacob, p. 232.
5. Jerry Goldman, "Federal District Courts and the Appellate Crisis," *Judicature,* Vol. 57, 1973, pp. 211–212.
6. Jacob, p. 240.

7. Howard Abadinsky, *Law and Justice* (Chicago: Nelson-Hall Publishers, 1988), p. 119.

8. *Report to the Nation on Crime and Justice,* 2nd ed. (Washington, D.C.: U.S. Department of Justice, Bureau of Justice Statistics, 1988), p. 71.

9. *Report to the Nation on Crime and Justice,* p. 72.

10. Nick Schweitzer, "A Prosecutor's View of Plea Bargaining," in *Criminal Justice: Annual Editions 90–91, John J. Sullivan and Joseph L. Victor, Eds., 14th ed. (Guilford, Conn.: The Dushkin Publishing Group, Inc., 1990), p. 133.*

11. Sue Titus Reid, *Criminal Justice,* 2nd ed. (New York: Macmillan Publishing Company, 1990), p. 376.

12. Albert W. Aschuler, "Plea Bargaining," in *Enclycopedia of Crime and Justice,* Sanford H. Kadish, Ed., (New York: Macmillan Publishing Company, 1983), Vol. 2, p. 830.

13. Gideon v. Wainwright [372 U.S. 335 (1963)]; Argersinger v. Hamlin [407 U.S. 25, 37 (1972)].

Chapter 10

Criminal Procedure

Key Terms

Preliminary hearing
Grand jury
No bill
True bill
Indictment
Information
Presentment
Arraignment
Motion to suppress evidence
Change of venue
Motion to quash a search warrant
Motion for severance
Motion for pretrial discovery
Motion to dismiss due to delay in
bringing the case to trial

Speedy trial laws
Voir dire
Challenge for cause
Peremptory challenge
Presumption of innocence
Burden of proof
Direct examination
Cross examination
Redirect examination
Prima facie case
Presentence investigation
Determinate sentencing
Indeterminate sentencing
Habeas corpus

Chapter Objectives

At the conclusion of this chapter, students should be able to:

1. Understand how a case proceeds through a criminal court.
2. Understand the legal mechanisms involved in a prosecution.
3. Identify the problems associated with criminal trials.
4. Describe the steps from arrest to sentencing.

INTRODUCTION

The process for guiding a criminal case through the courts is remarkably similar across the state and federal legal system. That should not be surprising. Since court procedures are refined and approved at the federal level, the states pretty much follow their lead. In this portion of the chapter we trace a felony case through trial and appeal. As stated above, this process will be followed by most courts. There are some exceptions. Those we discuss as appropriate.

PRETRIAL PROCEDURES

Bringing a criminal case before a court is not a simple process. The ability of the trial court to carry out its function satisfactorily is often determined by the series of procedures that take place well before that time. Issues concerning the proper criminal charges, validity of proposed evidence and location of the trial, and a number of other issues must all be worked out beforehand. Handled smoothly and fairly, the major areas of disagreements between the opposing attorneys can by alleviated so that the trial itself is uncomplicated and calm. Handling the tough arguments before the trial is designed to both speed up the trial and make it fairer. These pretrial procedures encompass such elements as preliminary hearings, indictments and informations, arraignment and pretrial motions.

Preliminary Hearings

The *preliminary hearing* is designed to allow a judge to evaluate the evidence and determine if there are sufficient grounds on which to base a criminal prosecution. This is the first screening of charges against a defendant.[1] About half the states use this step in their criminal process.

This hearing is much like a trial in miniature, with participation by both prosecution and defense. Sometimes it is similar to a sparring match between the contending attorneys, with the defense attempting to learn as much about the prosecution's case as possible, while the prosecution attempts to reveal only enough to justify taking the case to trial.

In states requiring a grand jury, the preliminary hearing takes place prior to indictment. Similarly, this hearing takes place prior to the filing of informations. The accused may waive the preliminary hearing, however, thus clearing the way for either indictment or information. An important distinction between these procedures is the ability of the defense to present its own evidence and attack that of the prosecution during the preliminary hearing. This does not occur during a grand jury proceeding.[2]

Indictments and Informations

The *grand jury* is an old common law institution created as a device to gain knowledge from local people about matters of interest to the crown.[3] It has since been used to allow an impartial panel of citizens the opportunity to assess the validity of complaints before the suspect is actually charged with a crime.

The grand jury operates as a kind of inquisitorial body where witnesses are summoned before it to answer questions or provide information the panel sees fit to request. The hearings are conducted in private. The objectives of the grand jury are to determine if sufficient evidence exists to take the accused to court. There are two possible findings that may be made by this panel. If the grand jury believes that there is not sufficient evidence to proceed, they issue a *no bill*. If, however, they believe probable cause exists to send the case to trial, the grand jury issues a *true bill*. The true bill is also known as an *indictment*. When a person is indicted, formal charges will be filed in that case. If the suspect is not currently under arrest, the indictment serves as grounds on which a judge may issue a warrant for that person's arrest. In a grand jury proceeding the accused does not have a right to be present or to provide evidence. The grand jury is also not bound by all the rules of evidence required at a trial.[4]

The Constitution requires the use of a grand jury in federal trials. Currently, however, four states require a grand jury for all cases, with 15 requiring it for felonies and six requiring this process for capital cases only. As this demonstrates, the constitutional requirement for a grand jury is applicable only to the federal government. State constitutions determine the use of this institution within their individual jurisdictions.

While supposedly an investigative body, the grand jury has evolved primarily as a tool of the prosecutor. This panel, which usually consists of around 23 citizens, hand-picked by the prosecutor, sits for a much longer period of time than the vast majority of petit, or trial, juries. One of the major concerns of those who study the legal system is dependence of the grand jury on the prosecuting attorney. This person is the only attorney present and thus defines law and procedure for the citizen panel. One study in the Philadelphia metropolitan area found that indictments were issued in 95 percent of the cases.[5] This may be due to good police work or may be the result of an assembly-line process under the almost complete control of the prosecutor. Whatever the reason, it is true that prosecutors have a strong influence on grand jury decisions.

Those states not using the grand jury have an alternative format for determining the validity of criminal charges. In these states, the police take their evidence directly before the prosecuting attorney. The prosecutor evaluates the information and if this person believes the evidence is sufficient to proceed, an *information* is issued. The information serves the same function as an indictment. Upon presenting the information before a judge or magistrate, an arrest warrant may be issued for the suspect.

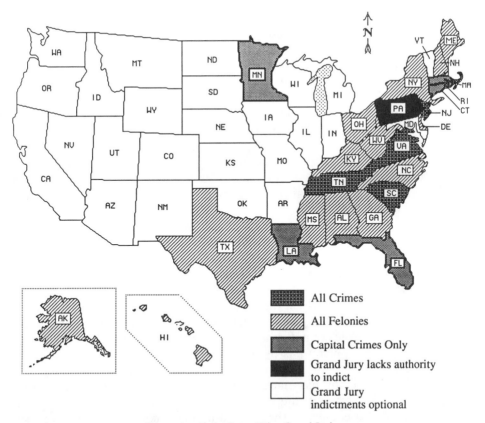

Illustration 10–1   States Using Grand Juries

As we can see, in either system the prosecutor is the key person in determining whether or not criminal charges should be filed. It might be argued that given the strong influence of the prosecutor over grand juries, it is much faster, and certainly more cost-effective, to use the information system. There is little evidence that grand juries have any impact on decisions to file criminal charges.

There is one aspect of grand juries, however, that bears further consideration. The grand jury is empowered to call witnesses and investigate any human endeavor they see fit. In this role this tribunal becomes a very powerful committee, rivaling senate investigating committees. Sometimes grand juries have the power to obtain information that a prosecutor, acting alone, would be unable to get. When it functions in this capacity—begins an official prosecution without the indictment presented by the prosecutor—it returns a *presentment*. This is an official document asking for the prosecutor to prepare an indictment.[6] The grand jury in its investigative capacity is often a useful tool for law enforcement because of its extensive investigative powers. This tribunal has the power to compel witnesses to appear and present evidence of any matter under investigation.

Arraignment

The point at which the defendant is formally brought before a judge, has the charges explained, and enters a plea is called *arraignment.* The accused may enter four possible pleas. The first is *guilty,* which means that the accused admits to the charges and accepts whatever sentence the court chooses to hand out.

The second plea is *not guilty,* which means that the accused denies the charges or is arguing that the act occurred but there should be no blame due to extenuating circumstances. An example of the latter would be not guilty by reason of insanity.

The third possible plea is *nolo contendre*, which means "no contest." In this plea the accused accepts the judgment of the court but does not admit to guilt. This is tantamount to saying: "I am not admitting to anything, but choose not to defend myself." The fourth plea is really a nonplea. It is called *standing mute*. The accused simply refuses to respond to the judge's question: "How do you plea?"

In practical terms, the results of the various pleas can have only two outcomes. The official plea is either guilty or not guilty. The person who "stands mute" has a plea of not guilty entered and the trial proceeds from there. The only advantage a person has by pleading *nolo contendre* is civil. A plea of guilty subjects the accused to possible civil action, such as a law suit. By pleading guilty the person has made a public statement that he or she is responsible for the criminal act and all injuries that resulted from that act. A plea of no contest cannot be used against the accused in a civil court because this person has not admitted responsibility for the act or the results. This is a significant option, in many cases involving traffic accidents, especially with injuries involved. The person causing the accident can plead no contest to any traffic charges stemming from the accident without jeopardizing the subsequent lawsuit. In fact, it is sometimes more advantageous to plead no contest to the charges than to run the risk of eventually being found guilty and having that information used in the civil court.

Arraignment is also the point in the process where jeopardy sets in. Up to this point, the police or prosecutor can drop or make changes in the charges. Once the accused has been arraigned, however, the charges must either stand as presented or fall. Once dismissed they cannot be reinstated without violating the prohibition against double jeopardy.

At this point the decision may also be made concerning whether or not the case will be heard before a jury or just the judge. The defendant may waive a jury trial and accept the verdict of the judge. The prosecutor may not compel the defendant to waive a jury trial but in most cases can require one. Thus both defense and prosecution can request a jury trial, but only the defense may waive this right. As a result of the plea, the judge either sets a trial date or sets a date for sentencing.

Pretrial Motions

Prior to going to trial there are a number of motions that may be filed with the court requesting a specific action. The purpose of this action is to ensure that the trial is conducted in a fair and impartial manner. Such motions include:

1. Motion to suppress evidence
2. Change of venue
3. Motion to quash a search warrant
4. Motion for severance
5. Motion for pretrial discovery
6. Motion to dismiss due to delay in bringing the case to trial

Probably the most used pretrial motion is the *motion to suppress evidence.* This motion states that some or all evidence was obtained in violation of the Fourth Amendment of the Constitution and therefore is inadmissible as evidence. The defense may also argue that statements were obtained in violation of the Fifth Amendment and that these statements should be suppressed as well. Should the judge find that the evidence or statements were illegally obtained, those items or statements will be barred from presentation at the trial. That is, the jury will never be allowed to know that those items or statements even exist.

The cases where this motion is used most involves illegal drugs, and for a very good reason. The mere possession of illicit drugs is sufficient to support a conviction for possession of such drugs. In a large enough quantity, there is a legal presumption of intent to sell the illicit drugs. To beat the overwhelming majority of drug cases therefore requires preventing the drugs from being introduced as evidence. Failure to suppress drug evidence frequently leads to a guilty plea. In these cases the entire prosecution is either won or lost in the motion to suppress hearing.

Other cases may also utilize this motion. Any crime where there is physical evidence seized by police or where there is a confession or statement of guilt is subject to this pretrial motion. The sole purpose of this process is to evaluate the legality of police procedure in obtaining evidence or statements.

Another often used pretrial motion is the request for *change of venue.* This motion requests that the location of the trial be changed. The reason for this request is usually that pretrial publicity is so intense as to make it virtually impossible to find a fair and impartial jury in that area. It is usually the defense that makes such a request, but not exclusively. Prosecutors sometimes make such a motion when there appears to be overwhelming sympathy for the suspect, based on publicity.

Requests for change of venue are most likely in small jurisdictions when there is a spectacular case, such as a gruesome murder. The court is likely to honor such requests, thus simplifying the jury selection process.

The *motion to quash a search warrant* is similar to a motion to suppress evidence. Since evidence seized in accordance with such a warrant is presumed legal, the defense must first discredit the search warrant to suppress the seized evidence. Grounds for such a motion are usually based on insufficient probable cause as a basis for original issuance of the warrant or a flaw in the document itself, such as incorrect address listed on the warrant.

The *motion for severance* occurs when there are multiple defendants in a single trial. The defense attorneys may wish to have individual trials for each defendant. This is especially so when the evidence of guilt is much stronger for one defendant than the others. Not wishing to have a client found guilty through association, the defense attorney is likely to ask for a separate trial.

The *motion for pretrial discovery* focuses on prosecutorial evidence. There is no such option for the prosecutor to seek defense evidence. In this motion the defense may request that physical evidence be submitted to an independent lab for analysis, at the expense of the defense, or may request all police reports and witness statements. The theory behind this concept is that the defendant cannot adequately answer the charges without knowledge of what is going to be used as evidence. It should also be noted that this motion came into being as a result of prosecutorial misconduct and represents a safeguard against such misconduct in the future.

The *motion to dismiss due to delay in bringing the case to trial* is a result of laws passed to speed up the legal process. *Speedy trial laws* are designed to get a case into court as fast as possible once charges have been formally filed. Ideally, accused persons should not have to wait years for their day in court. Considering the negative impact such a delayed process can have on a person's home life and occupation, such a law is reasonable. The motion to dismiss occurs when the delay between arrest and trial is such that either the statutory time limit is violated or the defense argues that the delay is unreasonable. In such cases neither the amount of evidence nor the seriousness of the crime are factors. The question is one of the amount of time it takes to bring the case to trial.

THE TRIAL

The trial itself represents the forum in which guilt or innocence is officially established. This forum may be informal, as when a traffic matter is heard before a judge, or it may be extremely formal. The latter occurs during a trial in which a serious felony is charged. If the trial is to be heard before a jury, the first step is the selection of the jury.

Jury Selection

The jury selection process is a multistage affair designed to provide the court with a group of impartial citizens. The idea of the jury dates back to old English common law. The use of the jury has pretty much fallen into disuse among most of the nations of the world; even the British use it much less than in earlier times. This institution is still widely used in the United States, however, with no indications that its popularity is waning.

The first step in the process is the selection of a jury pool. In most states this pool is formed by drawing names from voter registration lists. This method has been criticized for its lack of representativeness of the general population. The U.S. Bureau of Census estimates that the percentages of those registered to vote range between 40 and 70 percent of the those eligible to vote, depending on the area.[7] Thus the pool of possible jurors excludes many people and may be discriminatory if the voting patterns in an area tend to group around people with similar characteristics to the exclusion of others with different characteristics. For example, white middle-class people tend to vote more than do minorities, especially lower-class minorities.

After the pool is selected, jury panels are randomly selected from this group. A standard-size jury panel is around 30. This panel will be brought into the court room to face the trial participants. At this stage in the process, the judge and opposing attorneys will conduct *voir dire*. This means that the panel members will be asked a variety of questions to determine the suitability of each member to participate in the trial.

The number of jurors selected for the trial will vary from six to 12. Traditionally, the number is 12 and major felony cases will always require this many jurors. Misdemeanors and some lesser felony cases may function with a six-person jury, depending on the laws of that state.

The attorneys will attempt to assess the potential juror's attitudes toward crime and punishment in general, and toward the accused and attorneys in particular. The panel will be asked about their backgrounds, whether or not they know any participants in the trial, what kind of publicity they have heard about the case, and whether or not they think they can be impartial.

There are two means by which jurors can be removed from this panel. The first is *challenge for cause*. If either attorney can show some reason why a juror is partial to either side, that juror can be dismissed by the judge. There are no limits on the number of allowable challenges for cause. The purpose of the process is to impanel an impartial jury. If this requires going through numerous 30-person panels to get the required jurors, so be it.

The second method of removing jurors is the *peremptory challenge*. There are individual panel members that either side may see as undesirable for that particular jury, but not have sufficient grounds to have the person dismissed for cause. Each attorney is given a specified number of peremptory challenges which allow the attorney to dismiss the juror without explanation. The number of allowed peremptory challenges depends on the jurisdiction and nature of the trial. The more serious the charges, the more such challenges the attorneys are likely to get.

Many attorneys believe that the jury selection process is the most important step in the trial. The realities of human nature make it unlikely to get a truly impartial jury. The secret to success sometimes lies in the ability of an individual attorney to select people who are already leaning toward that attorney's position. This has been recognized as so important that there are now professional jury selection consulting services that use psychology, social history, and body language techniques to help attorneys select jurors. Thus far these techniques have been highly successful, which has raised the question among some scholars as to whether or not this is a sophisticated form of jury fixing. The debate still rages and this is not the proper forum to conduct this debate. The point is that jury selection is a critical part of the trial process.

Jury size.   While historically 12-person juries have been the rule, the Supreme Court has allowed some deviation. The number 12 is believed to come from the early influence of the church. It was believed that the Holy Spirit would hover over the court proceedings to ensure that justice was done. It was also felt that since there were 12 apostles and 12 tribes of Israel, the number 12 would be especially well received by God.[8]

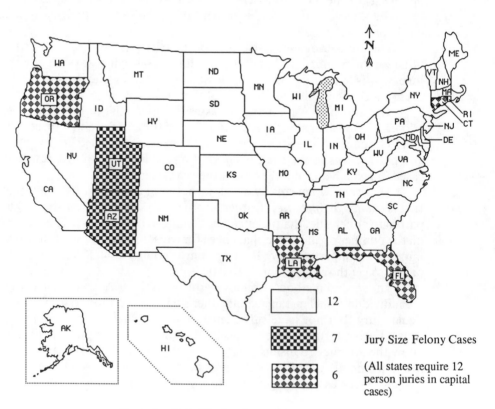

Illustration 10–2   The Jury System in the United States

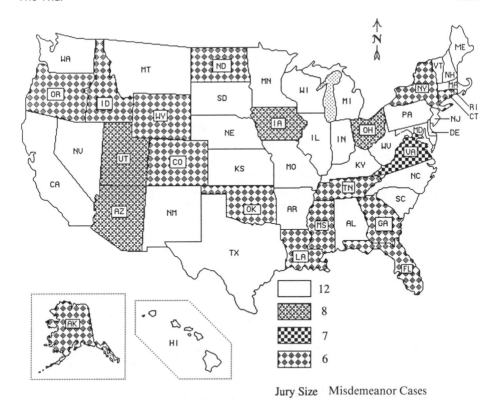

Jury Size   Misdemeanor Cases

Illustration 10–2   Con't

The Supreme Court has subsequently ruled, however, that juries as small as six persons are allowable in some cases. So far no state having capital punishment has used any jury of less than 12 in capital cases. Lesser felonies, however, have been tried in some states with six, seven, and eight persons.

The Supreme Court has also ruled that unanimous juries are no longer necessary in 12-person juries.[9] As the number of jurors drops below 12, however, there is a strong belief that fairness demands a unanimous verdict. This is especially true in six-person juries. The Court has presented the states with a trade-off. They no longer need unanimous verdicts if they stay with a 12-person jury. Should they wish to reduce the size of the jury, the states face an increased possibility of deadlocked juries. Still, each state can make its own choice. As the illustration shows, some states have taken advantage of the choices.

Case Presentations

The trial begins with opening statements. The prosecutor has the option of beginning the proceedings by describing the crime and telling the jury what the prosecution hopes to prove. The defense follows the prosecutor and tells the jury what kind of flaws to expect in the prosecution's case. The defense may also provide a hint of the strategy it plans regarding countering the prosecution's case.

For both the defense and prosecution, opening statements are optional. Either may choose not to make such a presentation, although the more complicated the case, the more necessity the prosecution has to provide some kind of introduction to the jury. The defense, usually better prepared to attack the prosecution's case after it has been fully presented, is the most likely to waive the opening statement. After the opening statements, the presentation of evidence begins. The prosecution goes first, followed by the defense.

Prosecution.   The prosecution presents first because there is a *presumption of innocence* that exists regarding the defendant. Since this person has yet to be convicted, the defense is not compelled to present anything until evidence presented in court indicates that there is something to defend against. The *burden of proof* for establishing *guilt beyond a reasonable doubt* rests with the prosecution.

The prosecutor begins by calling the first witness. This is usually someone who is familiar with all major aspects of the case. Most of the time this will be the investigating officer or officer originating the report. This allows the prosecution to lay the foundation for the entire case. Other witnesses will add important bits and pieces of the case, but it is important to provide the jury with a broad overview of the case as well as appropriate background information.

Upon completion of the prosecutor's questions, called *direct examination,* the defense begins the *cross examination.* The cross examination is limited to information discussed on direct examination. The defense attorney may not open new topics unless the witnesses introduce those topics during the response to the attorney's questions. The purpose of the cross examination is to challenge or verify information presented on direct examination.

After the cross examination by the defense, the prosecutor may engage in a *redirect examination,* in order to repair damage done by the defense attorney. Redirect examinations are limited even further. The prosecutor may only address issues raised in the cross examination. New topics may not be introduced.

The defense attorney may then be afforded the opportunity for continued cross examination, which is limited to those issues raised in the redirect examination. This back-and-forth redirect and cross examination may last until one side has no further questions.

At this point the prosecutor calls the second prosecution witness and the process begins again. This witness, as well as defense witnesses, are usually not in the courtroom during the questioning of other witnesses or the entering of evidence. At the beginning of the trial the decision is made concerning what has come to be phrased as *the rule. Invoking the rule* means that all witnesses are excluded from the courtroom until they are called to give testimony. Either prosecution or defense may request the judge to invoke the rule. Such a request is almost always granted. The only exceptions to the rule are the major antagonists.

The defendant is not asked to leave the court room. In civil cases neither party to the suit is required to leave.

The prosecution calls all witnesses and presents all evidence necessary to establish beyond a reasonable doubt that the defendant committed the specified crime. This does not mean the prosecutor presents all witnesses or all evidence. Sometimes information will be held out for rebuttal purposes. We discuss that later in this chapter. When the prosecutor announces "prosecution rests," the prosecutorial phase of the trial ends. The ball then rests in the defense attorney's court.

Defense. Almost invariably the first motion the defense attorney will make is a motion to dismiss the case due to a failure by the prosecution to establish a *prima facie case*. This means that the defense is claiming that the prosecution has failed to establish the minimum amount of proof necessary to justify the trial. Unless the prosecution has badly blundered in the presentation of the case, this motion will be denied.

At this point the defense begins the presentation of its case if the defense attorney so wishes. There is no requirement that the defense present a case. If the defense feels that the prosecution case is obviously weak, it may not want to run the risk of inadvertently strengthening it by the admission of more witnesses or evidence. Also, sometimes the defense has no witnesses and no evidence. In these cases, the defense will rest immediately.

In most cases, however, the defense does have a presentation to make and this follows the same format as with the prosecution introduction of evidence, with the roles reversed. At the end of this presentation, the defense attorney announces "defense rests," and this stage of the trial comes to an end, maybe.

Rebuttals. Cases in which the evidence portion of the trial does not end are those in which the prosecutor chooses to present rebuttal witnesses or evidence. This form of presentation is limited in much the same manner as redirect examination. Rebuttal witnesses cannot open new topics, or as the phrase goes, "cannot break new ground." Their purpose is to undermine the evidence presented by defense witnesses.

These witnesses are subject to cross examination and the defense attorney may also present witnesses to rebut the rebuttal witness. In these circumstances previous witnesses may be called back to the witness stand for this purpose. After the last of the rebuttal witnesses, the evidentiary portion of the trial closes. The attorneys then deliver their closing statements.

Closing Statements

The closing statements, also known as *summations,* present prosecution and defense with the opportunity to both summarize and finalize the meaning of the evidence.

The prosecution states emphatically that the evidence proves the case beyond a reasonable doubt. The defense emphasizes weaknesses in the prosecution's case.

Procedurally, the prosecutor goes first and last. The judge will specify how much time may be spent on summation. Each side has no more than the time thus allocated. The defense uses this time in one block. The prosecutor, however, must decide how to divide the allocation most appropriately.

The prosecutor will open the closing statements with a summation of the prosecution's case. Emphasis is usually on the evidence presented by the prosecution. At the conclusion, the prosecutor will sit down and yield the floor to the defense attorney.

The defense will attack the prosecution's case and make a plea for the jury to find the defendant innocent. The defense attorney will once more yield the floor to the prosecution. The prosecution will then use the remainder of the time allocated disputing the defense assertions and conclude by a plea that the jury bring in a verdict of guilty. When the prosecutor sits down, the formal presentation by the opposing attorneys is over.

Jury Instructions

Prior to sending the jury into a closed to room to determine its verdict, the judge issues these people their instructions. This is sometimes referred to as the *charge to the jury*. The charge is made to inform the jurors as to their task and what procedures to employ in reaching the verdict. These instructions usually include the statement that the jurors should consider the defendant innocent until proven otherwise and the burden of proving otherwise rests with the prosecution. The instructions may also describe what constitutes reliable evidence, how to assess the credibility of witnesses, and what inferences may reasonably be drawn from testimony. The judge will usually also provide the jury with legal definitions or similar information with which these people can better understand the law. Terminology, such as reasonable doubt, may also be defined. Finally, the judge will provide a complete list of possible verdicts, from which the jury will be required to choose one.[10]

There are also occasions when the judge determines that the prosecution has failed to established sufficient evidence to justify a finding of guilty. In these cases the judge may instruct the jury to bring in a verdict of not guilty.

Deliberations

After the jury is charged, they are ushered to a closed room where they deliberate the relative merits of the case and attempt to make a decision based on the evidence and the charge. The first step is to elect a foreman, unless the trial occurs in a state in which the foreman is automatically the first juror selected.[11]

Although the jury has a charge, there is no legal mandate concerning how juries make their decisions. The proceedings are secret and no member of the court, media, or public is allowed access to the jury during deliberations. On occasion the jury may request clarification of a legal point from the judge or may request copies of statements to reread or physical evidence to examine. The judge hears these requests and determines whether or not they are reasonable. If so, which is usually the case, the request is granted.

The objective of the jury, in most states in felony cases, is to reach a unanimous verdict, either for guilt or acquittal. In those cases requiring a unanimous verdict, anything less results in a *hung jury*. If this happens, the judge declares a *mistrial* and the prosecution decides whether or not to retry the case. Not guilty verdicts end the legal process immediately. If the verdict is guilty, however, the process enters the next phase, sentencing.

At this point the jury is dismissed with the thanks of the judge, unless they are required to deliberate the sentence. Some states use jury sentencing; others place this responsibility with the judge. If they are dismissed, the jury is no longer required to maintain secrecy about the trial. They may discuss any aspect of the process with anyone they choose.

Sentencing

A verdict of guilty requires a sentence. In some states the actual passing of sentence cannot be pronounced until completion of a *presentence investigation* (PSI). In other states the presentence investigation is optional.

The presentence investigation serves several purposes. First, it provides the judge and opposing attorneys with information from which they can debate and, hopefully, derive at a just sentence. Second, this information is useful to corrections personnel in inmate classification or for purposes of probation supervision.

The presentence investigation usually includes information based on interviews with the defendant, family, friends, employers, and any others who might have information pertinent to the sentencing decision or defendant's case.[12] Additionally, information from medical personnel, psychiatric experts, and social workers might also be included in such a report.

The presentence investigation is usually prepared by probation officers, and this time-consuming activity requires a significant portion of their work load.[13] One study also found that courts do not always follow the recommendations of the PSI. The researchers felt that this was due to the lack of faith by judges that the PSIs are accurate predictors of who is a good probation risk.[14]

The sentence itself will follow one of two formats. Some jurisdictions use *determinate sentencing,* which means that the convicted person is sentenced to a specific period of time in prison or on probation. The second format is *indeterminate sentencing,* which means that the defendant is given a sentence expressed by a range of time, such as one to five years. In the latter system, the actual time served is determined by corrections officials and parole boards.

The judge also has other options available. The defendant may have all or part of the sentence suspended or may be placed on probation. Probation may be either supervised or unsupervised. If there were multiple convictions, the judge also has the authority to make sentences run concurrently—at the same time, or consecutively—back to back.

Through sentencing, society attempts to express its goals for the corrections process. There are five objectives of corrections. These are reflected in the sentences handed down by the courts. The objectives are:

1. *Retribution:* giving defenders their "just desserts" and expressing society's disapproval of criminal behavior.
2. *Incapacitation:* separating offenders from the community to reduce the opportunity for further crime.
3. *Deterrence:* demonstrating the certainty and severity of punishment to discourage further crime by the offender and by others.
4. *Rehabilitation:* providing aid to offenders in such areas as psychology, vocational training, and education to provide them more access to legitimate

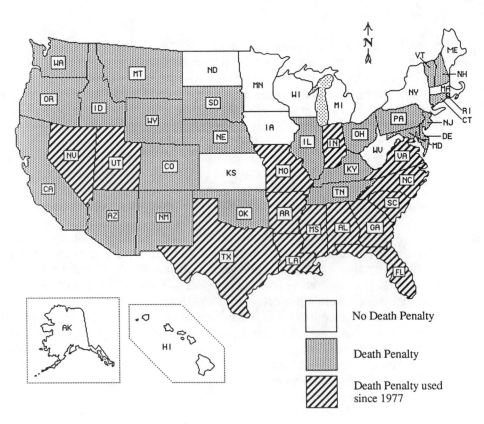

Illustration 10-3 States Using Capital Punishment

occupations and to help them adapt better to society's expectations for proper behavior.

5. *Restitution:* having the offender repay the victim or the community for damages suffered as a result of the offender's actions. The repayment may be in either money or service.

The objectives of sentencing are sometimes in conflict. A frequent complaint of prison reformers is that rehabilitation and retribution are clearly incompatible. The same may be said for rehabilitation and restitution or rehabilitation and incapacitation. The reason for these contradictions is that all of the objectives are not suitable for all cases. Restitution may be reasonable for a juvenile vandal but is hardly logical when dealing with a sadistic rapist. Using the same logic, one would hardly expect to rehabilitate a serial killer, although a person convicted of possession of drugs would be a reasonable candidate for such an approach. Simply stated, the selection of the appropriate sentencing goal is a by-product of the different types of cases and offenders brought before the court.

APPEALS

The end of the trial does not necessarily mark the end of the legal process. The defense always has the right to appeal to a higher court. In some limited cases the prosecution also has the right to an appeal, but not of the verdict. In those cases, the prosecution may appeal a ruling by the trial judge. This ruling may or may not affect that particular trial, but may affect future trials in which a similar issue is raised. The majority of appeals are by the defense. The process for appeal is always to the next-highest level in the court system.

State Appellate Review

There is a time frame in which appeals must be presented. Failure to present the appeal to the court before the end of the specified time can result in a dismissal of the appeal without a higher court review.

Appeals in the state courts may be on either points of law or fact. The points of law may also be on either state or federal constitutional issues. During the course of the trial, attorneys are allowed to raise objections to decisions and procedures they feel are incorrect. This allows the trial judge to make a determination based on the objection and make corrections at the trial itself. Appeals are based on these objections. In many cases, failure to raise an objection eliminates appeals based on that point.

In the appeals court, the case is not retried. Instead, the transcripts of the trial are sent with the appeal and appeal rebuttal, where a panel of judges considers the issues raised by the appellant. Juries are not used in appellate courts. Similarly, judges do not make individual appellate decisions. In some cases, such as a temporary stay of execution, a single appellate court judge may make a decision. Final decisions, however, are always made by a panel of judges.

The appeals court considers the merits of the appeal and renders a decision. The decision may be to *affirm* the judgment of the trial court or to *reverse* the decision. If the lower court decision is reversed, the case may be sent back for retrial, or it may be dismissed or some portion may have to be changed to meet the criteria of the appellate court's findings. If it is sent back for retrial, it will officially be *reversed and remanded.*

This process will be followed all the way to the highest state appellate court. If the case is reversed, however, the prosecution may then appeal as if it were the defendant. In fact, the prosecution becomes the appellant in those cases. If there is no federal question, the case officially ends with the highest state court of appeals.

Federal Appellate Review

If the party losing the case at the state level can argue that a federal issue is involved, the next step in the appeals process is the U.S. Supreme Court. Appeals from the state courts do not have to work their way up the entire federal court structure. There is a straight appellate line from a state supreme court to the U.S. Supreme Court.

The normal process for getting a state case to the Supreme Court is through a process wherein the appellant requests a *writ of certiorari.* This asks the Supreme Court to accept the case for review. The justices of the Supreme Court review such requests and vote on their relative merits. Following the rule of four, the justices decide what cases merit their attention (see Chapter 9).

An appeal to the U.S. Supreme Court is the final step in the normal appeal process. For the vast majority of cases that get this far, there is no judicial option left. Sometimes, however, there is another means of attacking the verdict. This process, known as a *collateral attack,* uses the writ procedure.

Habeas Corpus.   Inmates of jails or prisons can use the writ of *habeas corpus* to argue that their confinement is illegal. In effect, this allows an inmate to appeal the legality of the arrest and trial procedure through the federal court, starting at the bottom and working up to the Supreme Court once more.

Originally, the writ of habeas corpus was designed to force law enforcement agencies to produce the defendant before a court, and either charge or release this person. The federal courts later began using it to protect people from unscrupulous local police and courts. It has evolved into a format for federal court supervision of the entire state and local criminal justice structure.

The habeas corpus process is time-consuming, and relatively few cases are appealed in this manner. Most notable of these are capital cases, which almost always follow this path. This is one of the reasons for the long time period required to execute a condemned prisoner.

The habeas corpus process is not unlimited. The Supreme Court has ruled that it will no longer hear such appeals based on Fourth Amendment complaints where the state appellate court has ruled on the case. Still, sufficient arguments are open to the habeas corpus process to add even more time and complexity to an already time-consuming complicated process.

Executive Appeal

The last hope for the convicted prisoner is the executive appeal. The foundation for such an appeal lies deep in ancient history. The king in every realm was always empowered to grant clemency to convicts. In fact, in many lands, religious holidays or times of great celebration frequently were used as reasons to grant freedom to prisoners.

Every industrialized nation in the world currently has a form of executive appellate procedure. Some have more formal systems for dealing with such appeals. Great Britain, for example, has a special council that advises the Queen on such matters.

The United States does not have a formalized process. Inmates or their legal counsel merely submit a written request for a review by the chief executive. At the federal level this is the President of the United States. At the state level it is the governor. The president cannot pardon state prisoners, and governors cannot pardon federal prisoners.

If the chief executive of the jurisdiction agrees to hear a case, the result may be a decision not to intervene, a pardon, or a commutation of sentence. The commutation of sentence converts a sentence of death to life imprisonment. Unlike a judicial reversal of a court verdict, the executive pardon is given simply by the grace of the chief executive. It does not speak to errors, procedures, or law, and it sets no precedents. It says simply that this person is forgiven and released from custody.

During the past 20 years there have been several actions of this type, both controversial. The most famous was President Ford's pardon of former President Nixon for alleged criminal actions during the events known as the Watergate scandal. The second event, or series of events, concerned the allegations that the former governor of a southern state was selling pardons to state prisoners. Although the actions of President Ford produced controversy, the pardon was well within his authority as president. The selling of pardons, however, overstepped the boundaries of ethical conduct. The pardons were legal and within the authority of the governor, but selling them out the back door of the governor's mansion stepped well beyond both the intent and letter of the law.

It might be mentioned that for whatever reasons, neither President Ford nor the governor in question were reelected. Executive pardons do carry a potential cost if not used carefully.

CRITICISMS OF THE COURTS

The creation of an institution of justice does not guarantee that justice will be achieved. No judicial system has been perfect; certainly the courts of the United States are not exceptions. There are a number of criticisms of the courts. Among those are the costs of justice, the politics of justice, and general inefficiency among the courts.

The Costs of Justice

Herbert Jacob has argued that the courts are controlled primarily by the upper and middle classes. The evidence for that, he points out, is that the criminal courts deal mostly with the problems of the poor, while the civil courts spend most of their time with middle-income and wealthy citizens.[15]

Whether the foregoing criticism is justified or not, one thing is certain about our justice system. It is very expensive. Some of the most highly publicized cases of the past 20 years involved celebrities and millionaires. The T. Cullen Davis murder trials in Texas and the John DeLorean drug trafficking trial in California attracted immense media attention. Both offer an interesting insight into the American court system. In both cases the prosecution was able to present video-taped evidence showing Davis apparently paying a man he thought was a hired killer for the murder of a judge (the murder was faked) and showing DeLorean apparently contracting for a shipment of cocaine. The point, in both cases, is not whether these men were guilty or innocent, but that by putting on a defense with a price tag well in excess of $1 million each, they defeated good prosecution teams with very powerful evidence. Could someone with fewer resources do as well in our court system? Not likely.

We may well have a two-tract court system with full rights and competent representation for the wealthy and a bargain basement version, complete with assembly-line processing and lip service representation, for the poor. That is not exactly what the Constitution means by equal protection of the law, but as yet no one has developed an alternative plan for equalizing the system.

The Politics of Justice

The American court system is designed so that the judiciary is independent of the other branches of government. The reality, however, is that while judges are independent after they are appointed or elected, they must be politicians to attain the position of judge. This adds some interesting aspects to our judiciary. It can be argued that the American court system is staffed by amateurs and is innundated with far too many theatrics.

By European standards, American judges are amateurs. In Europe, as in most parts of the world not blessed with the English common law, men and women enter the magistracy immediately following law school. They are judges all their professional lives, working steadily upward as they gain experience and distinguish themselves. Highly trained and able to work closely with other professional judges, their decisions are consistently based on sound legal principles.

In contrast, the American judge is only required to be an attorney. Sufficient contacts in the right places or loyal work for the right political party are the prerequisites for a position in the judiciary. In the federal courts, for example, approximately 90 percent of the judges were of the same political party as the president who appointed them.[16] American court decisions are also marked by flamboyance among judges, some of whom seem to believe they *are* the law rather than merely its interpreters.

The American trial can also occasionally be described as more a circus, or media event, than a calm, thoughtful quest for truth. Courtroom antics allowed in this country are unheard of among the courts of Europe and Scandinavia. This is partially attributable to the adversary system of justice, which pits the opposing sides against each other in verbal combat. Also, it may simply have developed as a result of a growing emphasis on oratory, rather than evidence (early European trials forbid oral testimony in an effort to minimize the advantages of the charismatic orator over a less eloquent adversary).

Whether we like it or not, the American court system is a political institution. From personnel selection to the decision of which cases an appellate court will hear, politics is a constant consideration. This may be unavoidable and may also be true in other countries. It may not even be too bad, but it does cast doubts on the judicial process. The element of politics in the judiciary always elicits the question: "Just who do the courts serve?"

Inefficient Courts

The American court system may well be the most inefficient court system in the industrialized world. Getting a case through court can be agonizingly slow. Court delays of a year or longer are commonplace. The court backlog is a source of continuing controversy among court administrators and other government officials as well.

Plea bargaining, always a controversial topic, is a direct by-product of court delays. We are told, with justification, that without plea bargaining the American court system would grind to a halt (see Chapter 9).

Why do we have these delays, and what can be done to decrease them? Those are two of the burning questions concerning our courts today.

The first problem lies with us as citizens. We are a nation of litigants. Americans go to court more than citizens of any other nation. We thrive on the court battle, the lawsuit, the criminal charges. In and of itself, this will produce an extensive work load for the courts. Once the work load becomes unmanageable, backlogs occur, creating even more delays, causing further backlogs. The answer would seem to indicate the addition of more courts. That does help, for a short period of time, until the ever-growing demand swamps the new judges as well.

Another solution, one not favored by attorneys, is legislation restricting either access to the courts or amounts of money collectible in civil suits. Reducing the number of civil suits would have a solid impact on the criminal courts by releasing judges and courtrooms from civil litigation so that criminal cases can be handled.

It has also been argued that decriminalization of certain so-called victimless crimes would also relieve the pressure on both courts and corrections. Not likely; the police control the court's work load. A shift in enforcement emphasis would not decrease the court's work load, merely change the type of cases presented.

Another major factor in court delays is the criminal process itself. Common law judicial systems worship the *gods of procedure*. Lost in the depths of antiquity is the fact that procedure was originally used to simplify judicial decision making and did not envision the rights of the participants in the process worthy of consideration. There is a long-held belief among American attorneys that somehow there is a connection between procedure and justice. In fact, there is no such connection. Flexibility, rather than rigid procedure, would appear to offer a better approach to obtaining the truth in any tribunal. Alas, the procedural quagmire grows rather than shrinks. More and more court delays are the result of an intricate and inviable process that focuses on dotted "i's" and crossed "t's" to the detriment of major issues. All other factors aside, the American court process is simply slow.

The speed issue is being addressed, but with limited effect. Speedy trial laws have attempted to address this issue. The Speedy Trial Act of 1974 (amended in 1979), for example, required the government to present an information or indictment within 30 days of the arrest or time in which the defendant was served with a summons. Trial must commence within 70 days from the filing date (and making public) of the information or indictment.[17] Some states have followed suit, but there are still areas where court delays in excess of a year occur.

Technical innovations could have an even greater impact on court efficiency, but attorneys and judges are notoriously tradition oriented. Many delays are unavoidable, due to the inability to get all the witnesses at the same place at the same time. The trials themselves sometimes drag on and on because of arguments by defense and prosecution over points of law concerning which statements of a witness should be admitted into evidence.

Both of the problems above are easily solved with the addition of videotapes. Witnesses can be examined and cross-examined by prosecution and defense in a private room close to the witness's residence. The judge can later edit the tape to remove unacceptable statements. The tape containing all evidence can then be shown to the jury in a much briefer period of time, producing several advantages.

First, it prevents witnesses and their attorneys from sneaking statements to the jurors, a common practice that entails a witness making an illegal statement that the judge, of course, orders the jurors to forget. The attorneys smile to themselves, for everyone knows the jurors probably will not forget that statement; thus the damage is done and cannot be undone short of a mistrial.

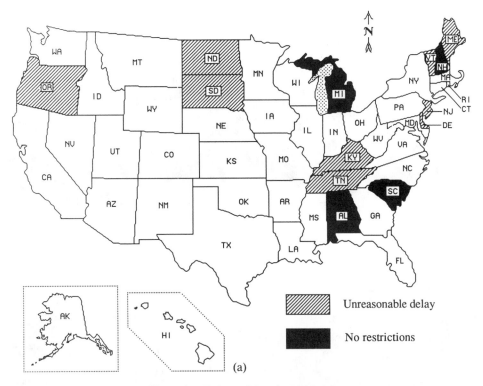

(a)

Illustration 10-4   A-C Speedy Trial Laws

Second, it allows witnesses who are physically unavailable to appear in court to testify, with full defendant benefits of cross-examination available. In fact, this problem could be solved without the taping option if the court allowed video teleconferencing in the court room. Using the same technology we see on the popular news show "Nightline" with Ted Koppel, witnesses could be displayed on a large video monitor, sworn in, and questioned as if that person were actually in the courtroom, when the witness need go no farther from home than to a studio set up for the teleconference.

Third, the taping procedure would speed up the actual trial dramatically, since the in-court arguments could be reduced or eliminated. The trial, in essence, is pretaped; there is no reason for delays.

Finally, with a videotape presentation, there is a permanent record for the court in the event that a new trial is ordered several years later, after some of the key witnesses become unavailable. In fact, should witness testimony be ordered stricken or altered, a simple editing job adjusts the offending portion and the entire trial can be replayed before a new jury with very little preparation on the part of the prosecutor, defense, or judge.

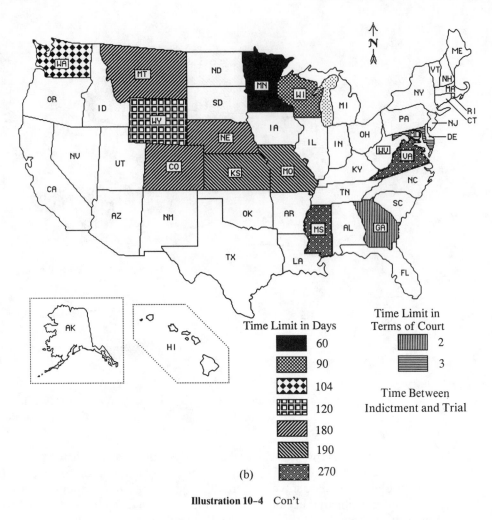

Time Limit in Days

▓ (60)	60
▒	90
◆	104
▦	120
▨	180
▧	190
▨	270

Time Limit in
Terms of Court

▥	2
▤	3

Time Between
Indictment and Trial

(b)

Illustration 10–4   Con't

All in all, technology will change the nature of the trial process. It will just take time for the legal profession to accept these changes.

SUMMARY

The American criminal trial is a multistage process. It starts with an accusation. This may either be made by the police as the result of a complaint or of a police investigation, or it may be the result of a grand jury investigation.

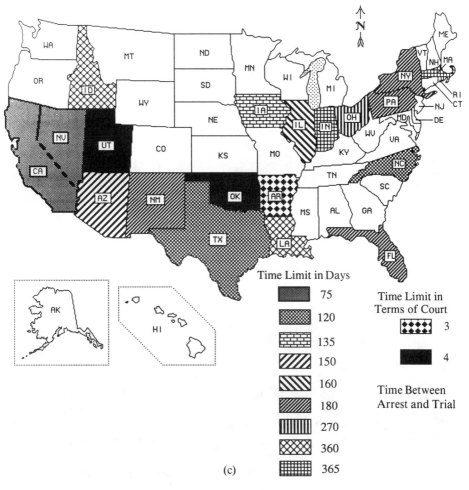

Time Limit in Days

(75 swatch)	75
(120 swatch)	120
(135 swatch)	135
(150 swatch)	150
(160 swatch)	160
(180 swatch)	180
(270 swatch)	270
(360 swatch)	360
(365 swatch)	365

Time Limit in
Terms of Court

(3 swatch)	3
(4 swatch)	4

Time Between
Arrest and Trial

(c)

Illustration 10-4 Con't

Once an allegation is made, it must be reviewed to assess the viability of prosecution. A preliminary hearing is often used to determine the validity of the accusation. Following this process, or without it if the preliminary hearing was waived, either a grand jury or a prosecutor (depending on the jurisdiction) evaluates the case. If the case warrants further review, a grand jury will issue a true bill or indictment, or the prosecutor will issue an information. Either of these leads to the formal issuing of an arrest warrant.

Prior to a formal trial, the defendant will be arraigned. The charges will be formally read and the defendant asked to enter a plea. If the plea is guilty, the

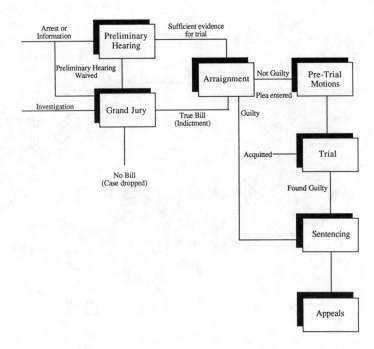

Illustration 10–5   Criminal Trial Process

process enters the sentencing stage. If the plea is other than guilty, a court date is scheduled.

A number of other procedural issues may be decided in hearings prior to the actual trial. Such motions as change of venue or request for suppression of evidence will be handled in this manner.

The trial itself is conducted along well-established lines, with the prosecutor presenting the government's case first, followed by the defense case. The trial may or may not have a jury. If it does, the jury size may vary from six to 12 persons, depending on the type of case and jurisdiction.

If the person is found guilty, the trial enters the sentencing phase. Normally, a presentence investigation is conducted. The judge accepts the investigation but may or may not adopt its recommendations. In some states the jury determines sentence while the judge fulfills this function in others.

Following the trial, the defense may wish to appeal the case to a higher court. Appeals may be based on either substantive or procedural issue. In some jurisdictions the government may also appeal, but on a limited number of issues.

The criticisms of the trial process in America are that it is cumbersome, slow, expensive, and inconsistent. Moreover, the obsession with process has led the court system to become focused totally on means without much consideration of ends.

DISCUSSION QUESTIONS

1. Compare indictments and informations. How is each obtained?

2. How does a grand jury differ from a petit jury?

3. Why is the outcome of a motion to suppress hearing critical to a case involving possession of illicit drugs?

4. Describe the jury selection process. What are the controversies surrounding jury selection?

5. Why is the American legal process slow?

6. Discuss the criticisms of the American court system. How could these shortcomings be rectified?

NOTES/REFERENCES

1. Henry Campbell Black, *Black's Law Dictionary* (St. Paul, Minn.: West Publishing Company, 1979), p. 1062.

2. Dean J. Champion, *Criminal Justice in the United States* (Columbus, Ohio: Merrill Publishing Company, 1990), p. 210.

3. George F. Cole, *The American System of Criminal Justice,* 5th ed. (Pacific Grove, Calif.: Brooks/Cole Publishing Co., 1989), p. 132.

4. Sue Titus Reid, *Criminal Justice,* 2nd ed. (New York: Macmillan Publishing Company, 1990), p. 359.

5. Walton Coates, "Grand Jury, the Prosecutor's Puppet: Wasteful Nonsense of Criminal Jurisdiction," *Pennsylvania Bar Quarterly,* Vol. 33, 1962, p. 11.

6. Reid, p. 359.

7. Cole, p. 441.

8. Sue Titus Reid, *Criminal Justice: Procedures and Issues* (St. Paul, Minn.: West Publishing Co., 1987), p. 322.

9. Apodaca v. Oregon, 406 U.S. 404 (1972).

10. Reid Hastie, Steven D. Penrod, and Nancy Pennington, *Inside the Jury* (Cambridge, Mass.: Harvard University Press, 1983), p. 17.

11. Howard Abadinsky, *Law and Justice* (Chicago: Nelson-Hall Publishers, 1988), p. 168.

12. Reid, 1990, p. 438.

13. Reid, 1990, p. 438.

14. Joan Petersilia, *Probation and Felony Offenders* (Washington, D.C.: U.S. Government Printing Office, National Institute of Justice, Mar. 1985).

15. Herbert Jacob, *Justice in America: Courts, Lawyers, and the Judicial Process,* 4th ed. (Boston: Little, Brown and Company, 1984), p. 6.

16. James V. Calvi and Susan Coleman, *American Law and Legal Systems* (Englewood Cliffs, N.J.: Prentice-Hall, Inc., 1989), p. 52.

17. Reid, p. 313.

Chapter 11

Police Deviance

Key Terms

Mooching
Chiseling
Favoritism
Prejudice
Shopping
Extortion
Bribery
Shakedown
Perjury

Premeditated theft
Code of secrecy
Pad
Score
Meat-eaters
Grass-eaters
Voyerism
Sexual harassment

Chapter Objectives

At the conclusion of this chapter, students should be able to:

1. Understand the various types of police misconduct.
2. Identify the forms of corruption found in policing.
3. Identify the forms of police sexual misconduct and explain the factors that contribute to such behavior.
4. Understand why the police use deception and identify the various kinds of lies that are pervasive in police work.
5. Identify the lesser forms of police misconduct and explain why such behavior is a problem for the organization and public.

INTRODUCTION

All organizations have deviant members; people who function within their own personal set of values and rules at the expense of others. Police deviance, however, offers society a unique set of problems. The vast power wielded by the law enforcement official makes it imperative that every effort be made to control the tendencies of officers to misuse their authority. When police officers are corrupt, innocent people get hurt and criminal activity flourishes. When police officers misuse their authority, the relationship between the police and public suffers. Sometimes the harm done can take generations to repair.

The amount and types of possible police deviance are much broader than among most other organizations. The police are involved in so many activities, many of these regulatory in nature, that misbehavior is limited only by one's imagination. For ease of discussion we focus on several broad categories of deviance: corruption, abuse, sexual misconduct, and deception. Similarly, we look only at deviance that is symptomatic of police work rather than people in general. It is accepted that police officers are drawn from a wide segment of society. They bring with them values and personal idiosyncrasies that make police officers as likely to engage in misbehavior as anyone else. Some officers abuse their spouses, children, and neighbors. Others become thieves, killers, and arsonists. There is no research that suggests that the police are any more prone to this type of conduct than the population in general. That type of behavior—individualized misconduct—will not be a subject of the following discussion.

CORRUPTION

According to Herman Goldstein, police corruption includes those forms of behavior designed to produce personal gains for the officer or for others.[1] Although there are other definitions of corruption, this will suffice for our purposes. Using this definition, we can say that officers engage in corrupt activities to gain something of value.

Ellwyn R. Stoddard has identified 10 activities that fit this definition. These are listed in order of least likely to invoke a legal sanction to most likely:

1. *Mooching:* receiving free coffee, cigarettes, meals, liquor, groceries, or other items either as a consequence of being in an underpaid, undercompensated profession, or for possible future acts that might be received by the donor.
2. *Chiseling:* activities involving demands for free admission to entertainment, whether connected to police duty or not, such as price discounts.
3. *Favoritism:* the practice of using license tabs, window stickers, or courtesy cards to gain immunity from traffic arrest or citation (sometimes extended to family members and friends).

4. *Prejudice:* situations in which minority groups receive less than impartial, neutral, objective treatment; especially those who have less influence at city hall and are less likely to cause the officer discomfort.

5. *Shopping:* the practice of picking up small items, such as candy, gum, or cigarettes, at a store where the door has been left accidentally unlocked after business hours.

6. *Extortion:* demands made for advertisements in police magazines or purchase of tickets to police functions or "street courts," where minor traffic citations can be avoided by the payment of cash bail to the arresting officer with no receipt required.

7. *Bribery:* payments of cash or "gifts" for past or future assistance to avoid prosecution; such reciprocity might be made in terms of being unable to make a positive identification of a criminal or being in the wrong place at a given time when a crime is to occur, both of which might be excused as carelessness but no proof as to deliberate miscarriage of justice.

8. *Shakedown:* the practice of expropriating expensive items for personal use and attributing it to criminal activity when investigating a break-in, burglary, or an unlocked door. Differs from shopping in the cost of the items and the ease by which former ownership of items can be determined if the officer is caught in the act of procurement.

9. *Perjury:* the sanction of the "code" which demands that officers lie to provide an alibi for fellow officers apprehended in unlawful activity covered by the "code."

10. *Premeditated theft:* planned burglary, involving the use of tools, keys, and so on, to gain forced entry or a prearranged plan of unlawful acquisition of property that cannot be explained as a "spur of the moment" theft.[2]

The problem confronting us is why officers become corrupt. Do people enter this occupation to misuse the position, or do good people become corrupt after they join the force? The latter is far more likely. Most police officers come from middle-class backgrounds, and if the research is accurate, most join for altruistic reasons. That being the case, what pressures turn the honest officer down the road to corruption? Perhaps that is the place to start our discussion.

Opportunity and Peer Support

Law enforcement offers a broad array of opportunities for corruption. The very nature of the job brings police officers into contact with individuals with a vested interest in corrupt officers. There is an old saying that is still appropriate: *People want police officers who cannot be bribed, but people want to bribe police officers.* Even the most honest of citizens sometimes wishes to give an officer a quick $5 or $10 bill to forget a traffic violation. This being the case with honest citizens, one can only imagine the lengths to which the dishonest person will go to remain free to continue the crime. In fact, some criminals view police payoffs as merely a business expense; a form of illegitimate business permit.

The nature of police work also provides the opportunity for corruption due to the amount of discretion inherent in the job. Each time an officer confronts a violator, a decision must be made. The choice to either issue a citation or make an arrest is the officer's and only the officer's. This discretion makes it easy to be corrupt, for every such decision also provides the opportunity for corruption. This problem is amplified because of the low level of supervision, which makes it likely that such activity will go unnoticed by higher-ranking officers.[3]

In addition to the opportunity for corruption, there is peer support for such activity. A number of organizational variables contribute to such behavior. Such things as the police subculture, with its code of secrecy, the subgroup restraints on supervisors, and the police image, all contribute to the peer support for corruption.[4]

First, the police subculture demands a *code of secrecy* that prevents officers from reported corrupt behavior among their colleagues. It is similar to the inmate code within a prison wherein no inmate snitches on another inmate. Similarly, no officer snitches on another. Since police misconduct is always more visible to other officers than to anyone else, we can honestly say that we have bad police officers because they are protected by good police officers.

Second, the police managers are also part of the police subculture. Management personnel come from the ranks of line officers; therefore, they are socialized in the same manner. Supervisors are as susceptible to the code of secrecy and bond of loyalty as are the regular officers. This makes it difficult, if not unlikely, for police supervisors to deal with police corruption. Indeed, in those agencies where there is pervasive corruption, management has either been a party to the corruption or ineffective in dealing with the problem. Moreover, one study found that a substantial amount of deviance and corruption is unofficially approved by the police at different levels of the organization.[5]

Finally, the police occupation is perceived as low status. The police are given power and responsibilities far beyond that of other occupations, but officers do not believe that they receive compensation adequate for the job they do. Despite recent gains in salary and benefits, many officers still feel unappreciated and not suitably compensated. This makes it easy to rationalize corrupt behavior. The officers tell themselves that they actually deserve the extra income. Also, they see criminals going free and cases unsolved. They can rationalize that since so many others are benefiting from criminal activities, there is no reason why they should not benefit as well.

Pervasive Corruption

The most detailed account of organized corruption available is the report of the Knapp Commission. This commission was created to investigate corruption within the New York City Police Department. Using inside information provided

Photograph 11–1   Frank Serpico

from police officers, such as Frank Serpico, as well as traditional investigative techniques, this extensive investigation and subsequent report uncovered a massive system of payoffs to officers in virtually every part of the organization.

Not the least of the information uncovered was the development and use of specific terminology that identified forms of corrupt behavior. Most notably were the terms *pad, score, meat-eaters, and grass-eaters.*[6]

The pad.   This term referred to weekly, biweekly, or monthly payments to the police. The payments were usually picked up by a police officer, known as the *bagman,* who then divided the money among fellow officers. People who made the payments and officers who received the payments were referred to as being "on the pad." The purpose of the pad was to maintain a steady payoff for police protection or at least for the police not to be around when the protected criminal activity was taking place.

The score.   This was a one-time payment that an officer might solicit from a person caught in an illegal situation. Such activities took place across a broad spectrum of incidents. A small score might be obtained from a motorist caught speeding or running a stop sign. A larger score would usually be obtained from a drug dealer, gambler, or pimp. This term was often used as a verb. An officer might say, for example, "I scored him for $2000."

Meat-eaters.   This term referred to individual officers who were "on the take." The meat-eaters were the most aggressive of the corrupt officers. This group also represented a minority of officers. These people spent a good portion of their working day actively seeking out situations they could exploit for financial gain.

Grass-eaters.   The vast majority of the officers involved in corruption were classified as grass-eaters. These officers did not actively seek out payoffs, but did not turn them down when offered. Many of these payoffs came from otherwise legitimate citizens who were caught in a legal predicament. Traffic offenses, for example, offered the best potential for payoffs to grass eaters. Sadly, the commission found that at least at the precinct level, the majority of officers were grass-eaters. Even officers not inclined to accept the money did so. To do otherwise was to make the officer an outcast within the department. Officers often accepted the money for no other reason than to gain acceptance from fellow officers.

ABUSE

Police abuse occurs when an officer, taking advantage of the authority of the badge, unjustly injures, kills, or humiliates an individual or group. There are three general types of abuse: unjustified brutality, deadly force, and verbal abuse.

Brutality

Police brutality is a somewhat vague term that covers a number of different kinds of actions. A. J. Reiss, Jr. has identified six activities that are usually found within the context of a citizen's accusation of police brutality. These are:

1. Profane and abusive language
2. Commands to move or get home
3. Field stops and searches
4. Threats
5. Prodding with a nightstick or approaching with a pistol
6. The actual use of physical force[7]

Clearly, some of these acts are not illegal most of the time, and all of them may be legitimate under the right circumstances. What distinguishes legitimate force from illegitimate force is nothing more than the circumstances in which the force is used. An officer has the authority to employ sufficient force to overcome an adversary. The line between sufficient force and abuse is a fine one. An officer crosses the line when he or she uses force, not for the purpose of subduing a suspect but to punish that person.

There are certain occasions where this occurs frequently. Some officers become emotionally involved in high-speed pursuits. It becomes a point of honor not to allow the person fleeing to escape. Upon capturing this suspect, the officer may feel duty-bound to administer a physical beating, to "teach him a lesson." In a sense the attempted escape becomes more than a "double or nothing" gamble for the person in flight. Capture not only means significantly more serious traffic charges, it also means being subjected to a physical assault at the hands of the arresting officer.

Cases in which people resist arrest also present opportunities for police abuse. The officer, receiving bruises and abrasions during the struggle, often feels compelled to play a little "catch-up." Once the person is subdued, the officer may inflict some additional pain to make up for that suffered.

Still other cases involve situations where the officer is pushed beyond emotional endurance rather than subjected to physical assault. While officers have no authority or right to attack someone physically who is abusing them verbally, most people, including police officers, do have limits beyond which they lose control of their temper. Some of the most blatant cases of police brutality have come when the victim "asked for it" by mounting a verbal barrage that ignited the officer's rage. This form of police abuse was much in evidence during the late 1960s and early 1970s when rioters deliberately attempted to provoke police officers. Unfortunately, this tactic was usually successful, much to the embarrassment of the police and to the detriment of the victim's health.

According to Thomas Barker, while all of the foregoing situations may lead to abuse, the largest percentage of brutality cases is the result of occupational socialization and peer group support.[8] That is, police officers use excessive force because other officers accept such use of force as a legitimate method of enforcing the law or demanding respect. Similarly, the police subculture considers it acceptable to use force to punish certain types of criminal. They believe that such persons might escape through the courts, but they will not evade punishment by the police themselves. Obviously, where excessive force is a major part of the police folklore and value system, there will be more brutality than in those agencies in which violence is not part of the value system.

Deadly Force

Every year statistics indicate that the police kill between 300 and 350 people in the line of duty.[9] Research, however, indicates that such actions may be badly underreported. In actuality there may be as many as 600 to 700 such killings per year; roughly two per day.[10] These figures become more meaningful when we realize that only about 30 percent of the people shot by police die as a result of those wounds.

Until recently, police officers were authorized to shoot in self-defense, defense of others, and to stop a fleeing felon. The fleeing felon rule produced the most controversy because it provided the officer with the most discretion. Under this rule, any felony, even one for which capital punishment could not be imposed, could lead to summary execution of the suspect.

The fleeing felon rule has now been stricken by the U.S. Supreme Court. Only situations involving an immediate threat to an officer or other person, or a situation involving the attempted escape of a dangerous felon or prisoner, can provide justification for the police use of deadly force.

Garner v. Tennessee
471 U.S. 1 (1985), 105 S.Ct. 1694, 85 L.Ed.2d 1 (1985)

At about 10:45 P.M. on October 3, 1974, Memphis police officers Elton Hymon and Leslie Wright were dispatched to answer a "prowler inside" call. Upon arriving at the scene, they saw a woman standing on her porch and gesturing toward the adjacent house. She told them she had heard glass breaking and that "they" or "someone" was breaking in next door. While Wright radioed the dispatcher to say that they were on the scene, Hymon went behind the house. He heard a door slam and saw someone run across the backyard. The fleeing suspect, who was Edward Garner, stopped at a 6-foot-high chain link fence at the edge of the yard. With the aid of a flashlight, Hymon was able to see Garner's face and hands. He saw no sign of a weapon, and, though not certain, was "reasonably sure" that Garner was unarmed. He thought Garner was 17 or 18 years old and about 5 feet 5 inches or 5 feet 7 inches tall. While Garner was crouched at the base of the fence, Hymon called out "police, halt" and took a few steps toward him. Garner then began to climb over the fence. Convinced that if Garner made it over the fence he would elude capture, Hymon shot him. The bullet hit Garner in the back of the head. Garner was taken by ambulance to a hospital, where he died on the operating table. Ten dollars and a purse taken from the house were found on his body.

In using deadly force to prevent the escape, Hymon was acting under the authority of a Tennessee statute and pursuant to police department policy. The incident was reviewed by the Memphis police firearm's review board and presented to a grand jury. Neither took action.

Garner's father then brought suit in federal district court, seeking damages under 42 U.S.C. § 1983 for asserted violations of Garner's constitutional rights. The federal district court ruled that the officer had relied on the Tennessee statute, thus acted in good faith, rendering him immune from a 1983 suit. The U.S. Circuit Court of Appeals reversed this decision, stating that the shooting was a seizure, thus subject to the constitutional requirement of reasonableness. The city of Memphis appealed that decision and the U.S. Supreme Court granted certiorari.

In upholding the decision of the circuit court of appeals, the Supreme Court removed the individual officers as defendants, leaving only the police department and city of Memphis for suit if Garner's father wished to refile the case. (The entire case, from the lower courts up, was constructed around the state law; the absence of any discussion of department policy left the Supreme Court unwilling to deal with that issue.) The crux of the Garner decision is that the Tennessee statute allowing police officers to employ deadly force against any felon was struck down. From this case forward, police were limited in the use of deadly force to those situations where the officer could reasonably assume that the force was necessary to prevent physical violence to the officer or another, or where the person fleeing the police had committed a crime of violence.

The issue of police deadly force is controversial for several reasons. First, a police killing is a non-court-ordered execution, an execution for which there is no appeal. When the officer is wrong, the mistake is irreversible. Obviously, any death also produces a natural emotional reaction from the friends and relatives of the person killed. When the killing involves some question of the legitimacy of the killing, public outrage can mount quickly. Also, due to the inordinate number of black people involved in the statistics, there is a lingering suspicion among minorities that the police are more likely to shoot them than to shoot whites.

There is strong agreement among researchers that blacks are the victims of police deadly force in numbers disproportionate to their representation in the general population. However, the agreement ends there. There is continuing debate over why blacks are overrepresented.[11] Some argue that a higher proportion of blacks are killed because of entrenched police racism.[12] Others believe that blacks are killed by police in numbers proportionate to their representation in violent crime. Thus since blacks commit a higher proportion of violent crime, they will be that much more likely to find themselves on the receiving end of police gunfire.[13]

Both points of view have some validity. The stronger argument appears, however, to be the second theory. Blacks are overrepresented not only in shootings but also in rates of incarceration and in criminal actions. The unanswered question is: Why are blacks more likely to be involved in crime. We know that a higher percentage of blacks are impoverished and live in high-crime areas. They seem to be hardest hit by economic conditions. If this is the reason, it is a social problem that is beyond the control of the police.

There are some officers who are more likely to use deadly force. Most research on which officers are more likely to shoot indicates a correlation between officer age and length of service. That is, younger officers with less experience are more likely to shoot than are older, more experienced officers.[14] This problem is aggravated by the tendency of some police agencies to deploy officers on the basis of seniority. This means that those officers most likely to use deadly force are placed on shifts at times where and when they are most likely to encounter situations in which deadly force is seen as an option.[15] Simple personnel assignment may therefore contribute to high rates of police shootings.

Another issue relevant to this controversy is the requirement by many departments that police officers carry off-duty weapons. The notion that police officers are never off-duty has been with us since early in the history of the American police. With this assumption has come the idea that police officers should carry both a weapon and an identification card or badge with them at all times. It is argued that off-duty officers should involve themselves in any criminal action they see. Moreover, some believe that officers are subject to vendettas and should be permanently armed for self-defense.

There is substantial research available presently to dispute those ideas and justifications. Occasionally, officers do make off-duty arrests. They also occasionally settle personal disputes and commit suicide with these weapons. Research has indicated that a significant proportion of all police shootings involve off-duty officers (15 to 20 percent), and many of these shootings are in violation of either department policy or law.[16] It is time that police administrators took a long hard look at off-duty weapons. These firearms may well be an idea whose time has past.

Verbal Abuse

Verbal abuse can be the result of several factors. The most obvious, and probably most pervasive, is the result of arrogance. Police officers become arrogant because of the power they possess. They represent an institution that gives them the power to take away a person's liberty and in some cases the person's life. Police officers also know that other members of the organization will protect them. The code of the police subcult assures the officers that no punishment will follow the improper use of language.

The citizen, on the other hand, is perceived as alone and powerless. The officer feels no compelling need to be polite to this person. As a result, rudeness can become standard operating procedure. Officers feel that they do not have to be nice to people who do not affect their position in the organization.

Arrogance is not just a police problem. All major institutions face similar problems with their employees. This is one reason why many telephone companies now require their operators to give their names to customers. Before, the nameless, faceless operator had no compelling reason to be nice to customers, who were dependent on the operator.

Verbal abuse is also a product of peer support. Many officers feel compelled to prove they are tough. Tough talk is sometimes seen as a means of appearing masculine. Young officers are told by their older counterparts that they must assert themselves in confrontational situations, to let the other person know "who is boss." The result is often verbal abuse, the use of harsh, often profane language.

Yet another reason for verbal abuse is fear. Many police officers resort to a tough facade when faced with a threatening situation. Unsure of what else to do, they become "macho" and stifle their sensitivity. Presenting a strong front takes precedence over calmly and quietly working through a situation.

SEXUAL MISCONDUCT

Sexual misconduct among police officers is so prevalent that it is almost a cliché. Several variables account for this problem. First, there are numerous opportunities for such behavior. Police officers represent power and authority. There are a certain number of women who are attracted to this image. Second, the police deal with people in trouble. Such people are vulnerable. The vulnerability may be manifested by an attraction to someone who appears stable and in control. Or the woman may be too frightened of the officer to reject his advances. Third, officers are sometimes affected by their own mystique. Their ego gets in the way of their common sense. Whatever the reasons, sexual misconduct is a topic that is beginning to cause quite a bit of concern among police administrators.

The types of sexual misconduct are varied. Some only show poor judgment, others represent behavior that violates the law. In this section we deal with several types: on-duty sex, voyeurism, sexual harassment, shakedowns, bribery, and rape.

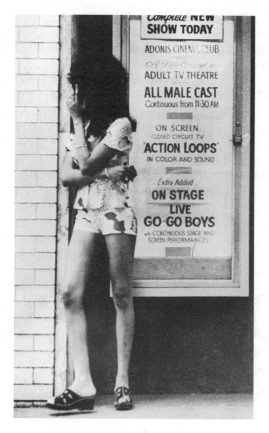

Photograph 11–2 Streetwalker

On-Duty Sex

The number of opportunities for officers to enter into intimacy with members of the opposite sex almost ensures that there will always be officers who engage in such activities while on duty. If one were to compile a list of places where officers have consummated such liaisons, it would take a book much larger than this one, and probably make more interesting reading. Needless to say, no department accepts this form of behavior as legitimate. The long, quiet nights, combined with imperfect supervision, however, means that this behavior will occur. For purposes of discussion, we will focus on those situations where both parties are not engaged in this activity with equal enthusiasm. We will keep in mind that even when both parties are consumed with unbridled passion, on-duty is the wrong time, regardless of the place.

Voyeurism

Voyeurism refers to officers who spend their time seeking opportunities to view unsuspecting women partially unclad or nude.[17] There are numerous opportunities for this type of behavior among the police. Even male officers who do not go out of their way to catch women unclothed will, over the course of their careers, encounter such situations. That is not the problem. The problem lies with those officers, predominantly male, who seek out such situations.

The officer who is a voyeur will spend an inordinate amount of time looking for nude women. The most likely form this will take is the routine harassment of young couples who seek solitude by parking their vehicles in out-of-the-way locations. Under the guise of investigating possible rapes or other illegal acts, the voyeuristic officer will challenge each car parked in such a manner. Some officers even go so far as to develop techniques for catching women in compromising positions. They will quietly approach the target vehicle with their lights off, then silently approach the parked car, shining their flashlight in the window at the last minute. The goal is to catch the couple in an intimate embrace, hopefully while undressed.

Still other variations of this behavior can be seen in officers who search the area for women who have left their curtains up. Using binoculars, the officer then attempts to watch the woman while she prepares for bed.

Another form of this behavior can be seen in the treatment sometimes afforded rape victims. Upon learning that a rape victim is in the station, some officers will attempt to get a look at her. They wish to judge the sexual taste of the rapist. This might be called imaginary voyeurism, since the victim is already clothed when seen by the officers. The officer wishes to view her so that his imagination can fill in the hidden areas.

This behavior is destructive for both the officer and the agency. At the very least it indicates an officer who is not functioning normally. The only real difference between this behavior and that of the "Peeping Tom" is the officer's authority to behave in such a manner. The authority allows it, but it is wrong. The agency suffers through two avenues. First, the potential for bad public relations is always inherent in this behavior. It does not take long for officers to develop reputations. The voyeuristic officer will develop this reputation, first among his peers, then among the public. The second problem lies in the loss of productivity. Officers on the prowl for women are not looking for anything else.

Sexual Harassment

There is a certain amount of pseudosexual conduct that occurs in all organizations. This is the banter that occurs between men and women in the workplace. Most frequently, this behavior takes the form of double entendres and off-color jokes told in mixed company.

This behavior is a form of testing. The man tells a dirty joke in front of a woman in order to gauge her reaction. He is watching to see how she reacts to the topic of sex. The same is true of double entendres. Double meanings are transmitted through the careful selections of words and stories. Once more the man (or woman) is asking the question, "are you interested?" Her (or his) response answers the question without either person having to run the risk of rejection.

This is normal game playing between men and women. At the workplace, however, if this type of behavior occurs frequently, productivity declines proportionately. Furthermore, where this is routine behavior, the atmosphere can quickly degenerate to one of harassment and resentment. People get tired of constant come-ons from their co-workers. At some point, they come to dread going to work.

Of course, the worst offenders never know when enough is enough; they continuously test their colleagues. Moreover, at some point subtlety gives way to brashness. The jokes get worse, the remarks become more graphic and brazen. Eventually, the organization suffers through a breakdown in morale. The end result is often one of two possibilities. The harassed person leaves the unit, either through resignation or transfer, or the situation ends up in a grievance proceeding or court.

In its most malignant form, *sexual harassment* takes place when a person of a higher rank attempts to coerce a member of the opposite sex, who is of lower rank, to become intimate; or when members of one sex always seem to be touching a member of the opposite sex. The touching need not be overtly sexual to be offensive. It is bad enough to be constantly "pawed" by a co-worker. These activities are illegal and incredibly counterproductive to morale in the organization.

Unfortunately, police organizations do not have a good track record in this arena. The situation is changing. As more women enter law enforcement, they are forcing changes that are badly needed. The problem may stem from the fact that historically, policing was a man's job. The macho image may contribute to the belief that women want this kind of attention from male officers. Whatever the reason, sexual harassment is a problem in many police organizations.

Shakedowns

The shakedown is sexual harassment of a different form. At least it occurs with different victims. This activity occurs when an officer coerces a citizen into an intimate situation. This can happen through one of several avenues.

The traffic stop offers an excellent opportunity for this kind of behavior. There have been, and still are, officers who use the threat of a traffic citation to coerce the victim into a "date." In its least offensive form, officers use the traffic stop merely to meet women. Although they do not use coercion—they attempt to be charming—they still fail to realize the trauma associated with being stopped by a police officer. The coercion is there whether the officer accepts that fact or not.

Other shakedowns occur between officers and women engaged in vice activities. The relationship between police officers and prostitutes has always been fraught with danger. The prostitute wishes to remain free to maintain a steady cash flow. The officer, having the discretion to arrest or release, is in a position to offer freedom for free samples. The same possibility exists for the male officer who catches any woman in a compromising situation.

Bribery

Sexual bribery is similar to shakedowns except that in this case it is the woman that initiates the opportunity. Rather than coerce the victim, the officer is the recipient of the woman's offer. The difference, from the point of view of the agency, is not a significant one. It still involves the officer engaging in an act of intimacy with a woman so that she may not be burdened with the cost and inconvenience of the justice system. Legally, however, there is a difference between accepting a bribe and extorting one. Such is the difference in these situations.

Rape

Rape is the ultimate sexual shakedown. This usually occurs when a woman is actually in custody. It may happen in the back of the police car before she is transported to the jail. Or the assault may take place in the jail cell where she is held. Clearly, this behavior is unlawful and unacceptable. It happens because the woman is at the mercy of her captors and because the officers involved believe that she either will not report the attack, or if she does, will not be believed.

A Prisoner's Odyssey

On August 5, 1986, Marilyn Cantrell was arrested by the Military Police at Edwards Air Force Base on the basis of a warrant issued in Camden County, Missouri, for bad checks. Not wishing to go through an extradition hearing she knew she would probably lose, the young woman waived extradition. She thought she would be flown to Missouri in the company of two police officers. Instead, Ms. Cantrell was turned over to a private extradition company, where she was loaded into a company van for a five-day trip she said was a terrifying ordeal.

According to Ms. Cantrell, in a lawsuit filed against Extradition Incorporated, the following events occurred during the trip:

Bakersfield, California: She was placed in the van, where the drivers immediately asked her if she "fooled around."

San Diego, California: She was referred to as a murderer by her guards in front of other people at a gas station.

Yuma, Arizona: Ms. Cantrell and the other passengers spent the night at the Yuma jail. When picked up in the morning, she is referred to as "my girlfriend" by one of the guards.

Nogales, Mexico: Her guards bribed border guards and tried unsuccessfully to sell her for sex.

Colorado: Ms. Cantrell is forced to make sexually suggestive comments over a CB radio.

Delta, Colorado: A guard watches Ms. Cantrell take a shower in a local jail.

McPherson, Kansas: The van picked up the last of eight male prisoners.

Salina, Kansas: The guards dropped off the last of the male passengers and took Cantrell, alone, to Missouri. Just outside Salina, she is raped by one of the guards.

Camdenton, Missouri: She arrives at Camden County Jail on August 21, where she stays for more than a month before being placed on probation.

Marilyn Cantrell is not alone in her complaint against this company. Barbara Pater has joined the law suit alleging that a guard raped her in a company van near Wartburg, Tennessee, while being transported from West Virginia to Van Nuys, California.[18]

In many way this behavior is the ultimate form of abuse of authority. The police officer has the authority to take a woman prisoner. Once a prisoner, she is held in a cell where she cannot escape and is ill prepared to defend herself. In the cases cited above, the guards accused of this behavior were not police officers. They were, however, authorized to act as law enforcement officials as far as their prisoners were concerned.

Fortunately, rapes by police officers do not occur often, but they do occur. Even one such attack is one too many. Where this behavior is uncovered, it is usually dealt with quickly and responsibly. Unfortunately, we have no way of knowing how many women fail to report such actions. We know that overall, the report rate for rape is low. We can only imagine what the effect of being raped by a police officer in a jail has on the willingness of the victim to go to the police. This is especially true in those cases where the woman is a prostitute or in an occupation that brings her into frequent adversarial contact with the police.

DECEPTION

It is quite likely that there are more forms of lying and more routine lying in law enforcement than in any other occupation. The reason for this is probably that police officers have more opportunities and reasons to lie than most other occupations. Also, there is peer group support for many of the forms of police deception.

Peter K. Manning has identified three aspects of law enforcement that are conducive to police lying. The first is the number of quasi-legal situations faced by the officers. Lacking the authority to resolve these issues, the police resort to nonlegal, sometimes illegal, means to control such situations. These means include lying, duplicity, and secrecy.

Second, a consistent theme in law enforcement is the centrality of controlling and concealing information. There are legitimate reasons for police secrets, but the police keep many more secrets than are necessary. Information is power and the police go to great lengths to control the flow of information.

Third, the police in large urban areas are in an adversarial relationship with large segments of their community. Their services are sometimes unwanted and the police perceive themselves to be unappreciated.[19]

For our discussion, we look at four forms of police deception: lying in reports, lying in court, lying to the press, and lying to the organization.

Lying in Reports

The police lie in reports for several reasons. First, supervisory practices sometimes mandate such behavior. As an example, consider the case where an officer makes an arrest as a result of a drug seizure. The officer, wanting to do the right thing, writes the report honestly. In so doing, it becomes clear to the sergeant that the search is illegal. The correct procedure should be to point out the error to the officer and release the suspect, since the arrest is illegal. Unfortunately, that is not what will happen in most agencies. Instead, the sergeant often orders the officer to rewrite the report to make the seizure legal. The officer is left little choice but to engage in some creative writing to make the arrest appear legal. The officer has little choice because the sergeant may also point out that if the report stands as is, not only will the suspect go free, but the officer may face disciplinary charges as well as a potential law suit.

Faced with the reality of the situation, the officer submits a false report. The rationalization for altering the report is that the suspect was caught "dirty"; therefore, an innocent is not suffering. The officer is merely applying the proper procedure to ensure that a guilty person does not go free.

With time, most police officers no longer need the supervisor's opinion to engage in this type of behavior. The officers know what information is necessary for a report to meet the procedural requirements of the court. This information is routinely put into the report. Moreover, the report may be fabricated unintentionally. Many of the incidents requiring fast action of the officer, such as when an officer stumbles into a drug deal or drug party, are situations in which the officer makes a lot of decisions and actions in a hurry. The report is written several hours later, at which time the officers involved must try to remember what happened and when it happened. The order of events in such cases is crucial to a successful prosecution. The officers may not remember exactly what happened when, but they know how it must have happened if it is to meet procedural requirements. Thus the incident is described as it should have happened rather than as it may have actually happened.

When the case eventually goes to trial, which may be a year or more later, the officer has only the report to go by. Other memories will have faded. The report therefore becomes the police record. It reports what officially happened. All further legal actions proceed from that document, which is assumed to be accurate.

Photograph 11-3   Police Officer in Court

Lying in Court

Officers lie in court for the same reasons they lie in reports. It is a case of ends justifying the means. The officers lie so that the truth is heard.[20] If this appears to be a paradox, that is because it is. Rules of evidence are such that the primary weapon of the defense attorney is the attempted exclusion of evidence. The defense tries to get the truth excluded. The officer lies about how the truth was obtained so that the truth will be admitted by the judge.

Judges are well aware that this happens. In fact, most judges are aware that a great amount of deception takes place in the courtroom. Courts have stopped being sensitive to the truth. Perhaps the procedures have become so rigid that many judges find it necessary only to require the image of truth, so that the process can go forward to an accurate conclusion. Whatever the reason, judges know that officers falsify reports and testimony, as do defendants. Such actions are commonplace and accepted.

Another reason for police lying in court is self-protection. Officers lie to cover improper behavior. An example of this is the officer who in a fit of rage physically assaults a suspect. Rather than face disciplinary action, the officer may decide to charge the suspect with assaulting a police officer. The officer therefore goes into court and swears that he was assaulted by the suspect and it was the efforts of the officer to defend himself that caused the suspect's injuries. In these cases the citizen is a double victim. He suffers physical abuse at the hands of the officer and faces possible incarceration and fines at the hands of the court.

Lying to the Press

According to Peter K. Manning, "enforcing the law requires preserving a degree of ignorance on the part of the public."[21] The police lie to the press because they do not trust the media and because they wish to maintain control of the situation, including information released. They believe, with some justification, that if they control the information available to the press, they limit the damage the press can do.

The majority of lying that occurs regarding the media is not lying by commission but by omission. The police fall into a state resembling a semitrance when responding to the press. They use a special quasi-legal jargon designed to sound official while releasing as few facts as humanly possible. The concern of the police is rarely related to tactical considerations, although such situations do occur. The police concern is self-image. They wish to be presented in a positive light. Many police administrators go to great lengths to keep controversial decisions and actions out of the public eye.

Good public relations translates to bigger budgets, more personnel, and general goodwill. Poor press frequently presages a change in police administration. At the very least it makes it difficult for the police administration to obtain more resources. Controlling the public's image of the police is therefore a major concern of the police. Controlling the media through information control is a primary instrument for maintaining the desired image.

Lying to the Organization

Lying takes this form for self-protection. Most police organizations employ negative discipline almost exclusively. Upon making a mistake, the officer is faced with the possibility of punishment. This may take the form of anything from a verbal reprimand to dismissal from the force. The alternative is to cover the mistake, which sometimes includes lying.

It should be noted that law enforcement agencies are mired in an extensive network of rules and procedures. It may be impossible in large organizations to get through a day without violating some rule or procedure. Moreover, "rule enforcement by supervisors seems to resemble a mock bureaucracy where ritualistic and punitive enforcement is applied after the fact."[22]

Officers learn to lie for the same reason that children learn to lie. Telling the truth brings on certain punishment; lying offers a 50–50 chance of escape.

OTHER DEVIANCE

Not all deviance is for the purpose of personal gain or self-protection. Some deviance is a by-product of laziness or a self-destructive tendency. Such problems are apparent in sleeping and drinking on duty.

Sleeping on Duty

Thomas Barker has referred to the police car as a "traveling bedroom" because of the amount of sleeping and sex that takes place in the car.[23] The late-night shift is especially suited to such behavior. It is quite likely that all occupations in which there are late-night shifts have some problem with sleeping on the job. Law enforcement, however, has refined this activity to the point of creating a special descriptive term. The "hole" refers to a location where the officer can hide and sleep with little fear of discovery.

The conditions that contribute to sleeping on duty are a lack of sufficient sleep during the day, boring, monotonous duties late at night, and lax supervision. The problem is more intense with officers who work or go to school during the day. Also, officers who are not happy with their job may spend as much time as possible sleeping. It not only makes the time pass faster, it also prevents them from becoming embroiled in situations requiring action on their part.

Drinking on Duty

A major violation of both rules and standards of police conduct is the consumption of alcoholic beverages while on duty. The officer is armed and in command of a multiton vehicle. Intoxicated officers pose a threat to everyone they contact. Research has demonstrated that a significant amount of on-duty drinking occurs.[24] The reasons for this appear to be twofold. First, there are numerous opportunities for officers to drink while on duty. They are in contact with bar owners, bartenders, and people who are themselves intoxicated and in possession of more intoxicants. A common method for dealing with juveniles who have illicit alcoholic beverages is to seize the contraband. The officer may pour it out or may keep it for personal use.

The other reason relates to dissatisfaction. Workers who are alienated often turn to alcohol. Police officers are no exception. In these cases alcoholism may be a symptom of occupational burnout.

SUMMARY

Police work, with its inherent power base, low-intensity supervision, and vast amounts of discretion, is ready-made for abuse. Police misconduct is a broad term that can denote many forms of improper behavior. Two of the most widely reported forms of police misconduct are corruption and brutality.

Corruption may be institutionalized, with the entire organization participating as a profit-making enterprise. When this happens, lower-ranked officers collect the money to be divided by everyone, including senior officers. Individual officers may be corrupt within either a corrupt department or a clean organization. These officers seek out ways of using their position and authority to extort payments from either citizens or criminals.

Brutality is often the result of immaturity, poor training, and poor supervision. The unnecessary use of force may also be the result of overreaction on the part of an officer who is not usually brutal. The often emotional atmosphere in which the police must function occasionally leads to physical abuse by the officers.

Less reported, but probably more common forms of misconduct are sexual misconduct and verbal abuse. The police find themselves in many situations where females can be sexually exploited. This form of misconduct can range from voyeuristic behavior all the way up to the extortion of sexual favors or rape. Moreover, it is often to the woman's advantage to offer sex to a male officer as a bribe. Even when there is nothing lost or gained by the sexual contact, the normal sexual attraction between men and women coupled with the late-night shift work of officers makes sexual liaisons a common occurrence in many departments. On-duty police officers have been responsible for more than a few divorces other than their own.

Verbal abuse is very common in law enforcement. This is due to the emotional nature of many police–citizen contacts and to a feeling among many officers that they are sufficiently powerful to treat people pretty much as they please.

Name calling and the use of profanity are all improper forms of communication, yet this form of abuse is and has been prevalent in policing.

Deception is also a problem of misconduct. Police officers lie to each other, to the courts, and to the media. There are different reasons for lying. Control of information is a means of self-defense. Officers often lie to keep misconduct from becoming known by supervisors or the public. They also lie on reports or in court in order to strengthen their case. The unfortunate aspect of this behavior is the acceptance of perjury as a normal part of the police reporting and testifying function.

Finally, there are other forms of misconduct that are routine. Sleeping on duty, for example, is widespread among the vast majority of police organizations. Less common, but still pervasive, is the consumption of alcoholic beverages on duty.

All in all, there are numerous forms of police misconduct. Some are illegal, others merely dysfunctional. The fact that so much misconduct occurs is evidence of the need for strong management and supervision within law enforcement organizations.

DISCUSSION QUESTIONS

1. Identify the various types of corruption found in law enforcement.
2. What is meant by the statement "there is peer support for corruption"?
3. Under what circumstances can a police officer legally use deadly force?
4. Identify the various types of police sexual misconduct. Why is this behavior destructive to both the agency and the officer?
5. Discuss the causes of police brutality.

NOTES/REFERENCES

1. Herman Goldstein, *Policing a Free Society* (Cambridge, Mass.: Ballinger Publishing Co., 1977), p. 190.
2. Ellwyn R. Stoddard, "Blue Coat Crime," in *Thinking about Police: Contemporary Readings,* Carl B. Klockars, Ed. (New York: McGraw-Hill Book Company, 1983), pp. 340–341.
3. Lawrence Sherman, *Police Corruption: A Sociological Perspective* (Garden City, N.Y.: Anchor Books, 1974), pp. 12–14.
4. Geoffrey P. Alpert and Roger G. Dunham, *Policing Urban America* (Prospect Heights, Ill.: Waveland Press, Inc., 1988), p. 95.
5. Thomas Barker, *Peer Group Support for Occupational Deviance in Police Organizations,* dissertation, Mississippi State University, 1976.

6. From "City of New York, Commission to Investigate Allegations of Police Corruption and the City's Anti-corruption Procedures," *Commission Report* (New York: George Braziller, Inc., 1973), pp. 61–69.

7. A. J. Reiss, Jr., "Police-Brutality: Answers to Key Questions," *Trans-Action,* Vol. 5, July–Aug. 1969, pp. 15–16.

8. Thomas Barker, "An Empirical Study of Police Deviance Other Than Corruption," in *Police Deviance,* Thomas Barker and David Carter, Eds. (Cincinnati, Ohio: Pilgrimage Press, 1986), p. 72.

9. Mark Blumberg, "Issues and Controversies with Respect to the Use of Deadly Force by Police," in *Police Deviance,* Thomas Barker and David Carter, Eds. (Cincinnati, Ohio: Pilgrimage Press, 1986), p. 232.

10. Lawrence W. Sherman and Robert H. Langworthy, "Measuring Homicide by Police Officers," *Journal of Criminal Law and Criminology*, Vol. 70, as cited in Blumberg, p. 232.

11. Blumberg, p. 237.

12. Paul Takagi, "A Garrison State in a Democratic Society," *Crime and Social Justice: A Journal of Radical Criminology,* Spring–Summer 1974.

13. James J. Fyfe, "Race and Extreme Police–Citizen Violence," in *Race, Crime and Criminal Justice,* R. L. McNeely and Carl E. Pope, Eds. (Beverly Hills, Calif.: Sage Publications, Inc., 1981).

14. Blumberg, p. 234.

15. Michael F. Brown, "Use of Deadly Force by Patrol Officers: Training Implications," *Journal of Police Science and Administration,* Vol. 12, 1984, pp. 133–140.

16. James J. Fyfe, "Always Prepared: Police Off-Duty Guns," *The Annals of the American Academy of Political and Social Science,* 1980, as cited in Blumberg, p. 230.

17. Allen D. Sapp, "Sexual Misconduct and Sexual Harassment by Police Officers," in *Police Deviance,* Thomas Barker and David Carter, Eds. (Cincinnati, Ohio: Pilgrimage Press, 1986), p.86.

18. James A. Fussell, "No Way to Treat a Lady," article in *The Kansas City Star,* June 18, 1989, p. 1-A.

19. Peter K. Manning, "Lying, Secrecy and Social Control," in *Police Deviance,* Thomas Barker and David Carter, Eds. (Cincinnati, Ohio: Pilgrimage Press, 1986), pp. 99–101.

20. Jerome H. Skolnick, "Deception by Police," in *Police Deviance,* Thomas Barker and David Carter, Eds. (Cincinnati, Ohio: Pilgrimage Press, 1986), p. 122.

21. Manning, p. 100.

22. Manning, p. 103

23. Barker, p. 73.

24. Barker, p. 74.

Chapter 12

Police and Higher Education

Allen D. Sapp and David L. Carter

Key Terms

The Wickersham Commission
President's Commission on Law
   Enforcement and Administration
   of Justice
Law Enforcement Education Program

National Advisory Commission on
   Criminal Justice Standards and Goals
Davis v. *Dallas*
PERF
BFOQ

Chapter Objectives

At the conclusion of this chapter, students should be able to:

1. Understand the rationale for requiring college education for police officers.
2. Describe the historical factors leading to the college requirement for police officers.
3. Understand how college education can be validated as a bona fide occupation qualification (BFOQ).
4. Identify those aspects of policing that research has shown are enhanced by college-educated officers.

INTRODUCTION

The question of college education for police officers has been a persistent issue in policing for many years. The question of whether police officers should have a college education has been debated for many years. The debates have focused on questions about the benefits of higher education, the effects of higher education on police performance, police educational needs, and the quality of educational programs. Several national commissions have included police higher education in their recommendations. In 1930, President Hoover established the National Advisory Commission on Law Observance and Enforcement (popularly known as the *Wickersham Commission*).[1] The Wickersham Commission laid the ground work for higher education in law enforcement by identifying the need for professional law enforcement officers who were highly trained and competent.

In 1967, the *President's Commission on Law Enforcement and Administration of Justice*[2] was established. The President's Commission made a number of detailed recommendations for police higher education. The President's Commission's work led to passage of the Omnibus Crime Control and Safe Streets Act of 1968, which in turn established the *Law Enforcement Education Program* (LEEP). LEEP provided college tuition, fees, and book costs for in-service and preservice police officers. In 1973, the *National Advisory Commission on Criminal Justice Standards and Goals*[3] (NAC) issued its report, which contained specific standards for police education.

The National Advisory Commission on Criminal Justice Standards and Goals recommendations for police higher education included:

- To ensure the selection of personnel with qualifications to perform police duties properly, every police agency should establish the following entry-level educational requirements:

    1. Every police agency should require immediately, as a condition of initial employment, the completion of at least one year of education (30 semester units) at an accredited college or university.

    2. Every police agency should, no later than 1975, require as a condition of initial employment the completion of at least two years of education (60 semester units) at an accredited college or university.

    3. Every police agency should, no later than 1978, require as a condition of initial employment the completion of at least three years education (90 semester units) at an accredited college or university.

    4. Every police agency should, no later than 1982, require as a condition of initial employment the completion of at least four years of education (120 semester units or a baccalaureate degree) at an accredited college or university.[4]

Unfortunately, the educational standards recommended by the NAC have not been achieved. However, significant progress has been made in raising the overall educational level of police officers, and much of the credit for that increased level of education should be attributed to the work of the national commissions. Rapid growth of law enforcement/criminal justice education programs followed the 1967 President's Commission, the passage of the Omnibus Crime Control and Safe Streets Act, and the general environment of social upheaval that occurred in the 1960s. Not only did undergraduate programs increase significantly but also the number of graduate programs.

A great deal of research has been directed to the issue of police educational needs. The entire issue is difficult to study because so much of what police officers do is not readily evaluated or measured. Because the problem is ambiguous and difficult to study, the results of research on the topic have been mixed, with some researchers identifying specific benefits of police education and others finding negative aspects of higher education for police officers. An aspect of the debate is the general difficulty the police have in deciding what is "good performance." Historically, good performance has been closely associated with high arrest rates in the most visible cases. As greater understanding about how crimes are solved and what police do with their time has developed, less emphasis has been placed on making arrest. However, as the police have made greater efforts to measure performance, the complexity of the measurement problem has become more evident. In most instances, education becomes one of the many variables that must be considered, but education defies isolation to the degree necessary to arrive at definitive conclusions about its effect.[5] Some of those benefits and negative aspects are discussed below.

BENEFITS OF HIGHER EDUCATION FOR THE POLICE

No discussion of the benefits of higher education is complete without a word of warning about the difficulties of defining what is or is not a "benefit." In one of the most comprehensive recent studies of police education, Carter, Sapp, and Stephens noted: "The 'benefits' of higher education for law enforcement are 'in the eye of the beholder.' That is, what one person might define as an attribute of the educated officer might be viewed by someone else as a detriment. Creativity and flexibility in the use of discretion, for example, are characteristics of college-educated officers that are viewed differently—positively or negatively—depending on one's perspective."[6]

Sterling summarized the benefits of higher education for police as:

- Greater knowledge of procedures, functions, and principles relevant to [the officers'] present and future assignments
- Better appreciation of their professional role and its importance in the criminal justice system as well as in society
- More desirable psychological makeup, which includes such qualities as alertness, empathy, flexibility, initiative, and intelligence

- Greater range of interpersonal skills centered in their ability to communicate, to be responsive to others, and to exercise benevolent leadership
- Greater ability to analyze situations, to exercise discretion independently, and to make judicious decisions
- Strong moral character which reflects a sense of conscience and the qualities of [honesty], reliability, and tolerance
- More desirable system of personal values consistent with the police function in a democratic society[7]

These factors suggest that college education helps to produce a more "professional" police officer. It should be noted that even the definition of what constitutes "professional" police officers is subject to debate.[8] However, a recent court decision has clarified that issue. *Davis* v. *Dallas,* a 1985 Fifth Circuit Court case, affirmed the Dallas, Texas, Police Department requirement of 45 semester credits with a minimum C average from an accredited college or university for entry employment. Throughout its opinion, the court recognized the professional nature of the police job. The court also noted the need to establish employment standards, including college education, that are in keeping with the professional responsibilities of the police.

Davis v. City of Dallas
777 F.2d 205 (5th Cir. 1985)

The Dallas Police Department required that applicants for positions on its police force, at the time of application, (1) must have completed 45 semester hours of college credit with at least a C average at an accredited college or university, (2) must not have had a history of "recent or excessive marihuana usage" as determined by the Department's marihuana usage chart, and (3) must not have been "convicted of" more than three "hazardous traffic violations" in the 12 months, nor convicted of more than six such violations in the 24 months, preceding the date of application. Once the applicant had been hired, he or she was required to successfully complete academy training, field training, and probation before attaining "permanent" status.

Brenda Davis and Cynthia Jane Durbin brought action against the city of Dallas. Davis alleged that she was denied employment because of her race (she was black). Durbin alleged that she was dismissed from the department because of her gender. The police department claimed that Davis was dismissed because she falsified her application; Durbin allegedly performed inadequately during the field training process. In July 1978, both cases were certified as class actions. Davis also applied for injunctive relief to prevent the city from using discriminatory selection criteria in future police officer hiring. Injunctive relief was denied.

The circuit court ruled that:

1. The city's requirement that applicants for positions on its police force must have completed 45 semester hours of college credit with at least a C average, at an accredited college or university, despite its statistically significant disparate impact on blacks was justified by business necessity where police officers combined aspects of both professionalism and significant public risk and responsibility.

2. Because of the professional nature of the job of the major city police officer, coupled with the risks and public responsibility inherent in that position, empirical evidence is not required to validate job relatedness of the requirement that applicants for the position of police officer must have completed 45 semester hours of college credit with at least a C average, at an accredited college or university.

3. The district court's finding that the city had shown sufficient job relatedness or business necessity of requirement for applicants for the position of police officer must have completed 45 semester hours of college credit with at least a C average, at an accredited college or university, was not clearly erroneous.

4. The district court's finding that the requirement that applicants for the position of police officer in a major city not have a history of recent or excessive marihuana use was job related, despite the contention that it had a disparate impact on black applicants, was not clearly erroneous.

5. The district court's finding that the city's requirement that applicants for the position of police officer not have more than three convictions for hazardous traffic violations in the preceding 12 months or six convictions in the preceding 24 months was job related, despite the contention that it had a disparate impact on blacks.

The plaintiffs appealed to the U.S. Supreme Court. Relying on expert testimony from police administrators and academicians, the Court noted that national commissions had consistently recommended college credit as a minimum requirement for police officers. The Court upheld the lower court decisions and rejected the arguments of Davis and Durbin.

Researchers have stressed the need for police officers to have effective communications skills. The skills obtained through college study can aid significantly in basic law enforcement tasks. Girand noted:

> [An] important skill required of the law enforcement officer is an ability to write. Every activity must be reported in a clear, complete, concise manner so that the reporting officer can testify from [his/her] report anywhere from a month to several years hence. The officer who cannot write has no future in law enforcement. . . . A [police] officer must

be able to read and interpret instructions related to the [completion] of a myriad of forms, briefing sheets, rules and regulations, police procedures, and not the least, the law describing the perimeters within which officers may exercise their authority.[9]

Police officers must also be able to communicate effectively with the citizens they serve. It is noteworthy that the general level of education of the American public is increasing. As Gambino noted: "We must provide our officers with the mental and psychological tools at least equivalent with, if not superior to, those of the general populace wherein [the police] must function."[10]

Included in the police educational issue is recognition of the need for police officers to be capable of recognizing and reacting to social change. Saunders noted: "Knowledge of changing social, economic, and political conditions; understanding of human behavior; and the ability to communicate; . . . are important in sustaining a commitment to public service."[11]

Lee P. Brown, while Chief of Police in Houston, Texas,[12] stated that

in order to function in a society characterized by massive socioeconomic problems . . . we need a *new police [officer]*—one who understands the complexities of human life—one who is able to understand the legacy of discrimination in this country and reflect positively upon the demands for freedom, justice, and equality; one who is able to understand the philosophy of dissent; one who understands that [he/she] has a

Photograph 12-1   Lee Brown (Photograph courtesy of the Houston, Texas Police Department.

legal and moral obligation to be responsive to the people—all the people and not merely the prevailing power structure in the [officer's] community.[13]

Research has found a positive relationship between higher education and fewer citizen complaints, fewer disciplinary actions against officers, and fewer allegations of excessive force.[14] Trojanowicz and Nicholson[15] found that college-educated officers tend to be more flexible, and Roberg[16] and Dalley[17] found college-educated officers to be both less dogmatic and less authoritarian. Barry[18] found that "college-educated persons in the criminal justice system . . . attribute better job performance to work taken in college." Thus the perception of police personnel, for the most part, is that college experience has a positive effect on the job performance of police officers.

Several studies have shown a positive correlation between education and "job performance."[19] Finnegan[20] found that college-educated officers consistently received higher ratings from supervisors. Sanderson[21] found college education to have a positive effect on academy performance and career advancement. Cohen and Chaiken,[22] as well as Sanderson,[23] found positive effects of education on attainment of promotions. Other studies indicated that college officers take fewer leave days, receive fewer injuries, have less injury time, use fewer sick days, are absent less often, and are involved in fewer traffic accidents than are noncollege officers.[24] College-educated officers also tend to be more innovative in performing their responsibilities[25] and have, overall, less rigid attitudes about policing.[26] College-educated officers tend to have better peer relationships[27] and are more likely to take a leadership role in the organization.[28] These attributes are significantly different from those of earlier police leaders. The increasing complexity of police responsibility has created a need for new types of police executives, and higher education is an important ingredient in shaping that new executive.[29]

Bell summarized many of the benefits resulting from college:

Photograph 12–2   Criminal Justice Classroom

The objective of liberal education is *not to teach the individual all they will ever need to know.* It is to provide individuals with habits, ideas, and techniques that will require them to continue to educate themselves. Education is the acquisition of the art of the utilization of knowledge and aims to develop the powers of understanding and judgment. In this respect it is impossible that too many individuals are educated since there cannot be too many individuals with capabilities to understand and make sound judgments [emphasis added].[30]

Finally, Fischer noted that "despite the controversy surrounding the value of higher education, it does appear that higher education's benefits outweigh the negative factors associated with it ."[31]

EGATIVE EFFECTS OF HIGHER EDUCATION ON THE POLICE

As indicated above, support for police higher education has not been unanimous. Some of the most common criticisms were summarized by O'Rourke[32] and have been echoed by other critics of higher education for police.[33] Those researchers who have questioned the value of higher education do so from the perspective of the effects of education on police performance. Some of the concerns reported by O'Rourke are paraphrased below:

- Many good officers do not have degrees.
- Many poor officers do have degrees.
- Degree requirements will negatively affect minority recruitment.
- Degreed officers will be bored with the job.
- Degreed officers will expect special treatment.
- College-educated officers cause animosity within the ranks.
- Officers without college can develop necessary people skills through in-service and on-the-job training.
- Police departments cannot competitively recruit college graduates.[34]

These perceived problems are discussed in detail below.

Good Cops and Bad Cops

All of the concerns noted by O'Rourke[35] are important, but the two that appear most frequently are that there are good officers without degrees and poor officers with them. Some will argue that officers with a college education lack "common sense." Aside from the difficulty of defining common sense and deciding whether one has it or not, the charge appears to be based on one or two implicit assumptions. First, officers with degrees have been sheltered from the real world and have not developed the common sense that the real world teaches. Second, the educational process somehow erases any common sense the person might have had in the beginning. These arguments are frequently accompanied by stories about some officer who had a college education who did something or behaved in such a way as to demonstrate a lack of common sense. Some point to good officers who do not have college education as an example.[36]

The argument ultimately reduces to defining good or poor police performance and one's individual perception of how officers perform. The evidence is clear that some college-educated officers perform poorly and some officers without college education perform admirably. Collectively, the evidence favors college-educated officers.[37]

Minority Recruitment

One of the hardest issues for the police to address in establishing educational standards is the effect on minorities. As a practical matter, most large, urban police agencies have not been able to increase the number of minority officers to a level representative of the communities they serve. In addition, an increasing number of departments are experiencing difficulties in filling vacancies with qualified applicants of any race or sex. Many believe that the addition of educational standards would reduce the pool of applicants even further while incurring the risk of the standards being viewed as a subtle way of excluding minorities from the police service. Resolution of these issues is not a simple matter. From a legal standpoint, it is necessary to establish that any educational standards are a valid business necessity. At the same time, specific programs must be designed to attract minority candidates who meet the standards and to assist those who do not achieve them. Despite the effects of educational standards on minorities, programs can be developed that will overcome the potential discriminatory influence.[38]

Boredom

After the first two or three years of patrol work, the potential for boredom and frustration exists for all police officers, not just those with college education.[39] Boredom and frustration are produced by a complex interaction of occupational expectations, occupational socialization, the nature of policing tasks, and management strategies employed by administrators.[40] Police executives are trying to deal with this problem through greater delegation of authority to officers, problem-oriented policing, community policing, career development programs, and other creative police management strategies.[41]

Prima Donnas

When college-educated officers were rare in the police ranks, there was some expectation of preference and/or accelerated advancement for them. As college-educated police personnel became more commonplace—even in agencies with no postsecondary educational requirement—the expectations of special considerations diminished. In most law enforcement agencies today, this concern is no longer an issue, with the exception of the need for more flexible scheduling practices to accommodate class schedules.[42]

Animosity in the Ranks

As the proportion of college-educated officers has increased, animosity between the haves and have-nots has declined. Nevertheless, there still appears to be some distance between college-educated subordinates and older, non-college-educated supervisors and managers. Such animosity is usually a transitory phenomenon that diminishes with each passing year.[43]

Experience Is Best

"Street knowledge" is an unquestionably important element in an officer's occupational socialization, but it is not the only qualification for police service. Indeed, the National Commission on the Causes and Prevention of Violence[44] was critical of officers with too much street knowledge because of their provincial (or subcultural) interpretation of events and behaviors. The Commission suggested that officers need broader empathy of social conditions affecting individual and group behaviors.[45] In other words, for effective law enforcement, street knowledge must be tempered with a more global perspective of issues and dynamics. Higher education is not meant to replace street knowledge or training. Rather, it is an additional tool that will facilitate the use of street knowledge in a lawful, civil, humane, and effective manner.[46]

Recruiting Is Impossible

Many police officials have said that they would like college graduates in the police ranks but that law enforcement cannot compete with private industry for candidates. An important point that is overlooked in this argument is that college criminal justice programs are brimming with students whose career goals are to work for a law enforcement agency. Langworthy and Latessa[47] (1988) found that criminal justice programs nationwide have roughly 175,000 students. Many of these students hope to be working in a patrol car following graduation. Police agencies additionally are able to recruit college graduates from other disciplines. The reason for this is threefold. First, some persons simply want to be police officers, regardless of their college major. Second, college graduates frequently find that they are unable to get a job in their major area, due to crowding in the job market; hence they seek a career in another profession. Finally, law enforcement salaries, despite popular belief to the contrary, are very competitive with those for other occupations.[48] "According to a new study released by the Census Bureau . . . law enforcement officers outearn other degree holders such as biologists, journalists, psychology majors, teachers and nurses.''[49]

THE QUALITY OF POLICE COLLEGE EDUCATION

Hoover[50] found that many educational programs for police officers included courses that were vocational/training rather than liberal arts courses. Hoover argued against vocational curricula because that approach failed to provide the intrinsics of the college education experience. Similarly, Goldstein stated:

> The factor that makes the whole movement toward college education for police personnel most vulnerable to attack is the emphasis which has been put upon the acquisition of college credentials without sufficient concern for what is to be learned. Given the multitude of colleges and the number of people who attend them, the degree itself reflects little about the values or relevance of the educational experience.[51]

Echoing this concern, Sherman directly confronted the issue of the quality and relevancy of police education:

> Whatever the potential of higher education for changing the police, police education is now falling short of that potential. The early vision of police reform through education assumed that police education would be intellectually rigorous, conceptually broad, and provided by a scholarly faculty. Yet, much police education today is intellectually shallow, conceptually narrow, and provided by faculty that are far from scholarly. Rather than helping to change the police, police education appears to support the status quo, *teaching what the police do now instead of inquiring what they could do differently* [emphasis added].[52]

The concerns expressed by Hoover, Goldstein, and Sherman appear to have diminished somewhat during the 1980s. Law enforcement/criminal justice has matured as a discipline, and curricula generally have taken on a more liberal arts orientation.[53]

PERF
Police Executive Research Forum
Darrel W. Stephens, Executive Director

The *Police Executive Research Forum* is a national membership organization of progressive police executives from the largest city, county, and state law enforcement agencies. *PERF* is dedicated to improving policing and advancing professionalism through research and involvement in public policy debate. PERF's primary source of operating revenues are government grants and contracts and partnerships with private foundations and other organizations.

The foundation for PERF was laid in 1975 when 10 police executives from some of the nation's largest cities met informally to discuss common police concerns. Driven by the successful exchange that took place at their meeting, the chiefs decided to meet on a regular basis to explore tough issues and develop a professional body of knowledge aimed at reducing crime and improving the quality of policing.

In 1977, PERF was incorporated to accomplish the following goals:

1. Improve the delivery of police services and crime control nationwide.
2. Encourage debate of police and criminal justice issues within the law enforcement community.
3. Implement and promote the use of law enforcement research.
4. Provide national leadership, technical assistance, and vital management services to police agencies.

Membership in PERF is limited to law enforcement executives who hold a four-year degree from an accredited institution and who head an agency of at least 100 full-time employees or a jurisdiction of at least 50,000 persons. Members must also be committed to the organization's principles and be willing to take on tough issues.

Since its inception, PERF has been involved in the development and implementation of police problem-solving models, new approaches for coping with repeat offenders, national accreditation standards for law enforcement, and the testing of criminal investigation models. Moreover, research has commenced regarding problems experienced by women and minority police officers, asset forfeiture, innovative ways to address community drug problems, effects of police videotaping of suspects under interrogation, and case studies of police command decision making.

In 1987, PERF established METAPOL, the nationwide electronic telecommunications network through which police executives and others concerned with law enforcement issues can communicate and receive immediate feedback. Through its Management Services Program, PERF offers technical assistance, training, and a wide array of services to member and nonmember police organizations of all sizes. Furthermore, PERF provides assistance in policymaking to law enforcement agencies through its Policy Center, which contains policy and procedures manuals collected from law enforcement agencies throughout the United States and Canada.[54]

PERF is located at 2300 M. Street, Suite 910, Washington, DC 20037.

THE STATE OF POLICE EDUCATION

In 1988, Carter, Sapp, and Stephens[55] completed a national study of police officer education for the Police Executive Research Forum (PERF). In that study they found that the average level of college education for officers in the 700 largest law enforcement agencies was 13.6, well into the sophomore year of college. In contrast, the President's Commission[56] in 1967 found an average educational level of only 12.4 years. Female law enforcement officers had an educational level of 14.6 years, a full year more of college education than their male counterparts. Female officers accounted for 12.1 percent of the sworn officers in the agencies included in the study.[57]

The PERF study also found that educational levels of minority law enforcement officers were comparable to the level of white officers. In addition, the researchers noted that the overall representation of minorities on the police force did not differ significantly from the population proportions of minorities.[58] Blacks averaged 13.6 years of education, Hispanics 13.3 years, and officers of other race/ethnic backgrounds averaged 13.8 years of schooling.[59] In graduate degrees, 8.6 percent of black officers, 5.2 percent of Hispanic officers, and 8.0 percent of other races had a graduate degree. In contrast, only 3.7 percent of white officers held a graduate degree.[60] This study suggests that college-educated minority and female officers can be, and more important are being, recruited and retained in law enforcement agencies across the country. An important part of the attraction and retention of officers is the provision of educational incentives and benefits. The most common educational support policies of law enforcement agencies are tuition assistance, educational incentive pay, permitting on-duty class attendance, and permitting schedules adjustments to accommodate college classes.[61]

The authors of the PERF study[62] note that the law enforcement agencies are increasingly employing college-educated officers and that formal education is increasingly being identified as an important criterion for promotion in policing. Higher education appears to provide officers with the knowledge, skills, and abil-

	More Than Two Years	Two Years or Less	No College
All sworn officers	55.1%	19.7%	25.2%
Nonsupervisory officers	56.5%	17.8%	25.7%
First-line supervisors	29.9%	27.6%	42.5%
Management/ command level	69.5%	23.2%	7.3%

Illustration 12–1   Education Level of Police Officers

	Blacks	Hispanics	Whites	Others
No college	28.2%	27.3%	34.1%	19.4%
One year	36.3%	49.6%	20.5%	36.1%
Two years	9.8%	6.5%	15.6%	13.6%
Three years	8.2%	4.7%	6.9%	13.3%
Four years	8.9%	6.7%	9.2%	9.6%
Grad degree	8.6%	5.2%	3.7%	8.0%

Illustration 12–2   Education level of police officers by race.

ities to be more effective in performing police tasks and to be more responsive to the community they serve.

Educational requirements, by themselves, do not appear to discriminate against minority applicants. The data in the PERF study indicate that there may not be a need to establish differential educational criteria for minority-group members to meet affirmative action goals. While the requirement of college education for entry into police work may be most disadvantageous to minority-group members, the requirement may withstand court challenges if the requirement is validated as a *bona fide occupational qualification (BFOQ).*[63] The BFOQ of college education for police officers can be validated using expert opinion rather than using traditional quantitative methods of validation.[64] Departments should develop policy papers outlining the need and rationale for requiring college preparation for entry into law enforcement. Law enforcement executives are becoming increasingly aware of the benefits of college education as a way to reduce police liability.[65]

The trend is clearly in the direction of requiring college education for entry and promotion into policing. The Police Executive Research Forum, an organization of executives from the larger law enforcement agencies in America, passed a resolution in 1989, by nearly unanimous vote, to urge all law enforcement agencies to implement a phased plan of requiring college education for police officers, with an ultimate goal of a four-year degree, from an accredited college, as a minimum entry requirement. The same resolution called for immediate implementation of requirements for college education for law enforcement officers promoted above the rank of patrol officer.[66] As the social problems in America become more complex, so will the law enforcement strategies and tactics for dealing with those problems. Better educated and better trained officers are required to better serve our society.

SUMMARY

Despite the fact that two major government commissions in this century have recommended college education for police officers, it has only been in the recent past that significant progress has been made toward this goal. Research has demonstrated conclusively that, overall, college-educated officers perform better than do their non-college-educated counterparts. Similarly, research has shown that most of the arguments against college-educated officers have no substance.

The most significant problem associated with a college requirement for the police relates to the necessity to hire minorities. It is argued that college requirements are discriminatory because fewer minorities go to college. Research conducted by the Police Executive Research Forum discovered, however, that innovative recruiting techniques have been used successfully by law enforcement agencies to overcome this problem. Additionally, college education as a requirement has been upheld as a bona fide occupational qualification in at least one court case. It would appear, therefore, that this one problem is insignificant. College-educated police officers are a necessity if law enforcement is to become truly professional.

DISCUSSION QUESTIONS

1. What were the reasons given for the Wickersham Commission's recommendation that police officers have some college credit?
2. What were the findings of the Task Force Reports regarding the police and higher education?
3. Identify the arguments against requiring police officers to be college graduates.
4. Identify the arguments for a college requirement for police officers.
5. Discuss the merits of college education as a BFOQ.

NOTES/REFERENCES

1. National Commission on Law Observance and Enforcement, *Report on Police* (Washington, D.C.: U.S. Government Printing Office, 1931).
2. President's Commission on Law Enforcement and Administration of Justice, *Task Force Report: Police* (Washington, D.C.: U.S. Government Printing Office, 1967).
3. National Advisory Commission on Criminal Justice Goals and Standards, *Police* (Washington, D.C.: U.S. Government Printing Office, 1973).
4. National Advisory Commission on Criminal Justice Goals and Standards.
5. D. L. Carter, A. D. Sapp, and D. L. Stephens, *The State of Police Education: Policy Directions for the 21st Century* (Washington, D.C.: Police Executive Research Forum, 1989).
6. Carter, Sapp, and Stephens, p. 10.
7. J. W. Sterling, "The College Entry Level Requirement," *The Police Chief,* Vol. 41, No. 8, 1974, p. 28.
8. cf: W. Geller, *Police Leadership in America* (Elmsford, N.Y.: Pergamon Press, Inc., 1986); L. Radelet, *Criminal Justice and the Community,* 4th ed. (New York: Macmillan

Publishing Company, 1986); A. Blumberg and E. Niederhoffer, Eds., *The Ambivalent Force,* 4th ed. (New York: Holt, Rinehart and Winston, 1985); A. D. Sapp, "Issues and Trends in Police Professionalism," *Criminal Justice Monographs* (Huntsville, Tex.: Sam Houston State University, 1978).

9. D. Girand, "What Is Right for Education in Law Enforcement?" *The Police Chief,* Vol. 44, No. 8, 1977, p. 30.

10. F. J. Gambino, "Higher Education for Police: Pros and Cons," *Law and Order,* Vol. 21, No. 2, 1973, p. 65.

11. C. B. Saunders, *Upgrading the American Police* (Washington, D.C.: The Brookings Institution, 1970), pp. 82–83.

12. Lee Brown is now Commissioner of Police for New York City.

13. L. P. Brown, "The Police and Higher Education: The Challenge of the Times," *Criminology,* Vol. 12, No. 3, 1974, pp. 116–117.

14. cf: W. F. Cascio, "Formal Education and Police Officer Performance," *Journal of Police Science and Administration,* Vol. 5, No. 1, 1977; B. Sanderson, "Police Officers: The Relationship of College Education to Job Performance," *The Police Chief,* Vol. 44, No. 8, 1977; B. Cohen and J. Chaiken, *Police Background Characteristics and Performance* (New York: Rand Institute, 1972).

15. R. C. Trojanowicz and T. Nicholson, "A Comparison of Behavioral Styles of College Graduates Police Officers v. Non-College-Going Police Officers," *The Police Chief,* Vol. 43, No. 8, 1976.

16. R. R. Roberg, "An Analysis of the Relationships among Higher Education, Belief Systems, and Job Performance of Patrol Officers," *Journal of Police Science and Administration,* Vol. 6, No. 3, 1978.

17. A. F. Dalley, "University and Non-University Graduated Policemen: A Study of Police Attitudes," *Journal of Police Science and Administration,* Vol. 3, No. 4, 1975.

18. D. M. Barry, "A Survey of Student and Agency Views on Higher Education in Criminal Justice," *Journal of Police Science and Administration,* Vol. 6, No. 3, 1978, p. 354.

19. cf: Barry; W. F. Cascio and L. J. Real, "Educational Standards for Police Officer Personnel," *The Police Chief,* Vol. 43, No. 8, 1976; J. C. Finnegan, "A Study of Relationships between College Education and Police Performance in Baltimore, Maryland," *The Police Chief,* Vol. 43, No. 8, 1976; Trojanowicz and Nicholson.

20. Finnegan.

21. Sanderson.

22. Cohen and Chaiken.

23. Sanderson.

24. Cascio; Sanderson; Cohn and Chaiken.

25. Trojanowicz and Nicholson.

26. Roberg; Dalley.

27. J. D. Madell and P.V. Washburn, "Which College Major Is Best for the Street Cop?" *The Police Chief,* Vol. 45, No. 8, 1978; C. L. Weirman, "Variance of Ability Measurement Scores Obtained by College and Non-College Educated Troopers," *The Police Chief,* Vol. 45, No. 8, 1978.

28. Weirman; Trojanowicz and Nicholson; Cohen and Chaiken.

29. D. Couper, "Quality Leadership: The First Step toward Quality Policing," *The Police Chief,* Vol. 55, No. 4, 1988.

30. D. J. Bell, "The Police Role and Higher Education," *Journal of Police Science and Administration,* Vol. 7, No. 4, 1979, p. 473.

31. R. J. Fischer, "Is Education Really an Alternative? The End of a Long Controversy," *Journal of Police Science and Administration,* Vol. 9, No. 3, 1981, p. 58.

32. W. J. O'Rourke, "Should All Policemen Be College Trained?" *The Police Chief,* Vol. 38, No. 12, 1971, p. 12.

33. J. Miller and L. Fry, "Reexamining Assumptions about Education and Professionalism in Law Enforcement," *Journal of Police Science and Administration,* Vol. 4, No. 2, 1976.

34. O'Rourke.

35. O'Rourke.

36. Carter, Sapp, and Stephens.

37. Carter, Sapp, and Stephens.

38. Carter, Sapp, and Stephens.

39. Blumberg and Niederhofer; R. M. Regoli, "The Effects of College Education on the Maintenance of Police Cynicism," *Journal of Police Science and Administration,* Vol. 4, No. 3, 1976.

40. R. J. Aldag and A. P. Brief, "Supervisory Style and Police Role Stress," *Journal of Police Science and Administration,* Vol. 6, No. 3, 1978; J. S. Hillgren, R. Bond, and S. Jones, 1976 "Primary Stressors in Police Administration and Law Enforcement," *Journal of Police Science and Administration,* Vol. 4, No. 4, 1976; M. D. Roberts, in *Job Stress and the Police Officer,* W. H. Kroes and J. J. Hurell, Jr., Eds., U.S. Department of Health, Education and Welfare, Public Health Services (Washington, D.C.: U.S. Government Printing Office, 1975); J. Q. Wilson, *Varieties of Police Behavior* (Cambridge, Mass.: Harvard University Press, 1963).

41. Carter, Sapp, and Stephens.

42. Carter, Sapp, and Stephens.

43. Carter, Sapp, and Stephens.

44. National Commission on the Causes and Prevention of Violence, *Law and Order Reconsidered* (Washington, D.C.: U.S. Government Printing Office, 1969).

45. National Commission on the Causes and Prevention of Violence.

46. Carter, Sapp, and Stephens.

47. R. Langworthy and E. Latessa, *Criminal Justice Education: A National Assessment,* paper presented at the Annual Meeting of the Midwestern Criminal Justice Association, Chicago, 1988.

48. Carter, Sapp, and Stephens.

49. B. Bucqueroux, "Law Enforcement Degree Can Pay Off," *Footprints Newsletter,* Fall–Winter, 1988.

50. L. T. Hoover, *Police Educational Characteristics and Curricula* (Washington, D.C.: National Institute of Law Enforcement and Criminal Justice, U.S. Government Printing Office, 1976).

51. H. Goldstein, *Policing a Free Society* (Cambridge, Mass.: Ballinger Press, 1977, p. 289.

52. L. W. Sherman and the National Advisory Commission on Higher Education of Police Officers, *The Quality of Police Education* (Washington, D.C.: Jossey-Bass, Inc., 1978, p. 19.

53. Carter, Sapp, and Stephens.

54. Darrel W. Stephens, *Fact Sheet* (Washington, D.C.: Police Executive Research Forum, 1990).

55. Carter, Sapp, and Stephens.

56. President's Commission on Law Enforcement and Administration of Justice.

57. Carter, Sapp, and Stephens, p. 43.

58. Carter, Sapp, and Stephens, pp. 40–42.

59. Carter, Sapp, and Stephens, p. 40.

60. Carter, Sapp, and Stephens, p. 43.

61. Carter, Sapp, and Stephens, pp. 60–62.

62. Carter, Sapp, and Stephens.

63. David L. Carter, Allen D. Sapp, and Darrel L. Stephens, "Higher Education as a Bona Fide Occupational Qualification (BFOQ) for Police: A Blueprint," *American Journal of Police,* Vol. 7, No. 2, 1988.

64. Davis v. Dallas [777 F.2d 205 (5th Cir, 1985)].

65. D. L. Carter and A. D. Sapp, "The Effect of Higher Education on Police Liability: Implications for Police Personnel Policy," *American Journal of Police,* Vol. 8, No. 1, 1989.

66. *Subject to Debate,* Vol. 3, No. 4, 1989.

Index